CAMBRIDGE STUDIES IN RUSSIAN LITERATURE

The Russian Revolutionary Novel

CAMBRIDGE STUDIES IN RUSSIAN LITERATURE

General editor HENRY GIFFORD

In the same series

Three Russian writers and the irrational: Zamyatin, Pil'nyak, and Bulgakov
T. R. N. EDWARDS

Novy Mir: a case study in the politics of literature 1952–1958
EDITH ROGOVIN FRANKEL

Word and music in Andrey Bely's novels
ADA STEINBERG

The enigma of Gogol: an examination of the writings of N. V. Gogol and their place in the Russian literary tradition
RICHARD PEACE

Forthcoming

Poets of Modern Russia
PETER FRANCE

The Russian Revolutionary Novel

TURGENEV TO PASTERNAK

RICHARD FREEBORN

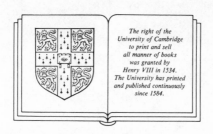

The right of the
University of Cambridge
to print and sell
all manner of books
was granted by
Henry VIII in 1534.
The University has printed
and published continuously
since 1584.

CAMBRIDGE UNIVERSITY PRESS

CAMBRIDGE

LONDON   NEW YORK   NEW ROCHELLE

MELBOURNE   SYDNEY

Published by the Press Syndicate of the University of Cambridge
The Pitt Building, Trumpington Street, Cambridge CB2 1RP
32 East 57th Street, New York, NY 10022, USA
10 Stamford Road, Oakleigh, Melbourne 3166, Australia

First published 1982
First paperback edition 1985

Printed in Great Britain at the University Press, Cambridge

Library of Congress catalogue card number: 82-4259

British Library cataloguing in publication data
Freeborn, Richard
The Russian revolutionary novel: Turgenev to Pasternak. – (Cambridge
studies in Russian literature)
1. Russian fiction – 20th century – History and criticism
2. Revolutionary literature, Russian
3. Russian fiction – 19th century – History and criticism
I. Title
891.73′09 PG3098.4
ISBN 0 521 24442 0 hard covers
ISBN 0 521 31737 1 paperback

Contents

Preface

In attempting to identify and define the revolutionary novel in Russian literature, the present study has striven to differentiate it from such phenomena as the anti-nihilist novel, the Populist novel, the intelligentsia novel, the post-revolutionary Soviet novel of reconstruction, the Five-Year-Plan novel and other types of novel in Soviet literature that are concerned to describe the creation of a socialist society. For this reason such famous novels with obvious political content as Dostoyevsky's *The Possessed*, Turgenev's *Virgin Soil*, Gladkov's *Cement* or Sholokhov's *Virgin Soil Upturned* have been omitted in favour of novels, equally political in content, that have attempted to explore more directly the revolutionary pressures in Russian society and the complexities of revolutionary experience in the wake of revolution and civil war. Simultaneously this study has hoped to show how the revolutionary novel as a genre revolutionised itself in response to revolutionary change while always asserting its literary independence. It has acquired as a result a freedom that has since made it the cornerstone of dissident literature in the Soviet Union.

Another important purpose of this study has been to demonstrate the richness of the novelistic heritage in Russian and Soviet literature. It has sought to draw attention to little-known novels or, in certain cases, novels that have received no attention in Western critical studies and little more than passing mention in Soviet works of literary criticism. It could, of course, have discussed many other examples – novels about revolution and civil war have become a boom industry in Soviet literature – but those chosen for discussion have been thought to be the most representative. Apart from the historical interest of such novels, their literary value has always been defined in terms of their degree of success in conveying experience, in being a witness to their time; it has not been defined in structuralist or other specifically technical, literary-critical terms. It has become my profound conviction that the novelists who contributed to the development of the Russian revolutionary novel were concerned to practise a literature of high moral purpose, intended to be truthful in its witness and edifying in its message. A student of their works should respect that aim at all times.

It is not the intention of this study to follow orthodox Soviet definitions of literature or periodisations. Though Socialist Realism is referred to, it is not a principal aim of this study to consider its role in influencing the course of literature; nor is this study concerned with the literary politics that led to the adoption of Socialist Realism as the sole doctrine in Soviet art. It is concerned to identify and define the evolution of a particular kind of novel in Russian and Soviet literature. The uniqueness of this phenomenon lends it importance, but its central role in determining the character of Russian realism and the revolutionary image of man in Russian and Soviet literature makes it an essential element in understanding the development of that literature from the middle of the nineteenth century to the middle of the twentieth.

Consistency in transliteration is a laudable aim but virtually un-attainable with the present abundance of transliteration systems. My aim has been to be consistent within reason. For example, unless in quotation from other sources, the soft sign has been omitted in commonly known names (e.g. Gorky). With a preceding soft/hard sign or a vowel, *e* has been rendered as *ye* (e.g. Bakhmet'yev, Chapayev), except in such cases as Veresaev or Maevskaya; in the case of forenames and surnames the initial *y* has been omitted, except in the case Yev. Zamyatin and fictional names; *ë* has been rendered as *yo* in all cases. Otherwise the transliteration conventions of *The Slavonic and East European Review* have been followed.

Page numbers have not been given for quotations from novels unless the source quoted is an English translation attributable to a reputable translator. Where no such English translation is acknow-ledged, the translations are my own, based usually on the earliest available published text, and all the faults are attributable to me. I have tried to achieve accuracy while respecting the literary quality of the Russian. To facilitate source identification, chapter and/or section numbers have been indicated after quotations where relevant. In the notes and bibliography the place and date of publication of a source have been given except where a publisher's name might provide easier identification. In this connection, M. = Moscow,

L. = Leningrad, Spb. = St Petersburg, O.U.P. = Oxford University Press, C.U.P. = Cambridge University Press. In quotation from American sources the spelling may have been altered to suit English usage.

Parts of this work have appeared elsewhere. The section devoted to Kolokolov's novel has earlier appeared in my article 'Nikolay Kolokolov', *The Slavonic and East European Review*, 56, 1 (1978), 13–31; and parts of the concluding chapter have been drawn from my recording for Exeter Tapes 1980 'The Russian Revolutionary Novel'.

No study of this kind would be possible without the helpful co-operation of library staff, and I take great pleasure in being able to express my thanks to the staff of the British Library, the Lenin Library, the library of the School of Slavonic and East European Studies and the library of the University of California at Los Angeles. I am very grateful for the help I have received, in many incidental ways, from Martin Dewhirst, Lydia Saharova and Henry Gifford; special thanks are reserved for Dr Jane Grayson, whose comments on chapters 3 and 4 of this study have been invaluable to me. I have incurred a warm debt of gratitude to Miss Jane Hodgart for her help in subediting my typescript so scrupulously, expertly and courteously. Finally I take great pleasure in thanking my wife, without whose expert typing ability and constant encouragement this study would not have been completed.

Introduction

Is there such a thing as a revolutionary novel? Can one write its history? It would be hard to answer such questions in the context of English literature. In the context of Russian literature the questions can be posed and answered for perfectly good historical reasons. Although the special case of Russian literature is this book's chief concern, the roots of the modern realistic novel as a literary form have their beginnings in English literature, and a reference back to such beginnings, though cursory, may explain the relationship between the novel as realistic literature and its principal purpose as an informative, improving and even revolutionary genre.

Henry Fielding, the most celebrated English claimant to the title of first realistic novelist, attached great importance to the novelist's knowledge of the world. In *Tom Jones* he insisted that a novelist should lawfully have learning – 'a competent knowledge of history and the belles lettres', on the one hand, and 'another sort of knowledge, beyond the power of learning to bestow, and this is to be had by conversation', by witnessing the acted word, by being conversant with people, the high and low life of society, by being, in short, a *historian*. This is the term Fielding constantly used to describe his principal function as a novelist. Such criteria were of course in need of an important qualification. A novelist may be a historian, but the most important quality for being a novelist was his genius:

'By genius I would understand that power or rather those powers of the mind, which are capable of penetrating into all things within our reach and knowledge, and of distinguishing their essential differences. These are no other than invention and judgment...by invention is really meant no more (and so the word signifies) than discovery, or finding out; or to explain it at large, a quick and sagacious penetration into the true essence of all the objects of our contemplation. This, I think, can rarely exist without the concomitancy of judgment; for how we can be said to have discovered the true essence of two things, without discerning their difference, seems to me hard to conceive' (*Tom Jones*, Book IX, ch. I).

'Invention' and 'judgment' in the context of the eighteenth-century
English novel were assets characteristic of an emergent bourgeoisie
and a vision of man as self-sufficient, single-minded, resourceful and
successful. The model example was Robinson Crusoe, whose image
has passed into the mythology of Russian literature as much as it
has passed into English. In the process it has undergone the sea-change
of political adaptation to socialist rather than bourgeois aims, so that
it is not very difficult to see in the enterprise of the shipwrecked
Crusoe a kind of catechism for Chernyshevsky's Rakhmetov and
subsequent purposefully socialist or Socialist-Realist heroes. As for
the form of the genre, the single hero–narrator or the epistolary
heroine busily divulging her supposed intimacies in public (*Clarissa*,
La Nouvelle Héloïse) gave obviously too limited a viewpoint for that
omniscience – Fielding's 'competent knowledge', in short – to which
the novelist–historian laid claim. When all else is considered, omniscience must be the ultimate prerogative of the single artificer, the
novelist–creator. And in his omniscience, which may pretend to be
God-like but must always be humanly particular in its selectivity and
emphasis, there must always be present the novelist's viewpoint as
the onlie begetter. If the viewpoint of Richardson is to be discerned
in the moral emphases that he gave to his heroines' attitudes and
fates, then the element of teaching, the didacticism of the early novels,
must also be accounted a supreme reason for their enormous success
and influence and a reason why, as a genre, the realistic novel quickly
acquired such pre-eminence.

For all his insistence on truth or what might be called objectivity,
Fielding was also quite conscious that the novelist had a further role:
he had to be *improving*. *Tom Jones* fits the description of an
'improving' work, full though it is of colourful and morally im-
provident incident. It showed how a young man may improve himself
and how the evils of society may be finally made to serve improving
ends. In creating such a novel, Fielding was both 'discovering' the
real life of his times and employing his 'judgment', in the sense that
he was using his genius to judge and criticise the society of his time.
This improving, or critical, role made the novelist both a historian
of his society and its judge. The twofold responsibility thus acquired
quickly brought to the novel and the novelist a unique status.
Fielding was aware of this, if only obscurely, and indicated that
among the priorities of a novelist's role was his need 'to pursue the
method of those writers, who profess to disclose the revolutions of
countries' (*ibid.*).

The role of the novelist when, a century after Fielding, it became acknowledged in mid-nineteenth-century Russia tended to follow Fielding's definition in an almost literal sense. By 1860, for instance, it had become literally true that the main purpose of Russian literature was to disclose the potential for revolution in Russian society. Readers, critics and novelists all assumed this, in private with candour and apprehension, in public obscurely but with enthusiasm. In that year, also, the English connection asserted itself in a peculiar and perhaps providential way, for it was in 1860 that the first Russian revolutionary hero was conceived in a small English seaside town. The connection between this fact and the publication of the first true Russian revolutionary novel is tenuous but nonetheless real, for it was in fact written in English and published in England some twenty years later. Similarly the novel that forms the keystone of the genre in this century, and a founding work of Socialist Realism, can arguably be considered a work of American and English literature. In other words, the tradition of writing in the novel that sprang into existence in Russian literature in the 1860s has international implications and connections, and it lays bare in a more literal way than Fielding could ever conceive how novelists need 'to pursue the method of these writers, who profess to disclose the revolutions of countries'. But for all its international implications this tradition of writing in the novel is specifically related to Russia, its history and its literary circumstances.

The object of this book is to demonstrate that Russian and Soviet literature is distinguished by a tradition of writing in the novel that can be called 'the revolutionary novel'. Such a tradition can be considered unique to Russian literature of all European literatures. It is also arguable that this tradition of writing in the novel is central to the history of the realistic novel in Russian literature and that without it the Russian novel would be profoundly impoverished.

1

Egoistic nihilism and revolutionary nihilism

In August 1860 Turgenev spent three weeks in Ventnor in the Isle of Wight. During that short period, and in characteristically wet and stormy English summer weather, he conceived the figure of his most significant literary hero, Bazarov, of his most famous novel, *Fathers and Children*, published two years later. The reasons for Turgenev's apparently sudden creation of such a positive hero, at such a moment in his life and in such an unlikely place, involve the much larger question of the 'revolutionary' situation that existed in Russia on the eve of the emancipation of the serfs in 1861.

The reforms upon which the Tsarist government had embarked after the defeat of Russia in the Crimean War were designed to modernise certain parts of the machinery of state while ensuring that the principle of autocratic rule remained unchanged. The linch-pin of the reforms was the emancipation of the serfs, but it was a linch-pin that, if allowed to slip, could easily precipitate the kind of peasant unrest that had assumed its most serious form in the revolt of Pugachyov, the Don Cossack, in 1773 and 1774. Worse still, perhaps, it could lead to civil war. Moreover, a change of such magnitude in a semi-feudal society would inevitably mean that the nobility, which depended so greatly upon serfdom for its economic as well as its social *raison d'être*, would be undermined as the leading class.

The Russian nobility had been both a privileged and a suspect class during the thirty years of Nicholas I's reign, from 1825 to 1855. It was privileged by virtue of its landowning and serf-owning rights (the *krepostnoye pravo*, as it was called), but the nobility had also – however over-simplified such a description of the relationship may seem – been 'suspected' by the Tsarist government throughout Nicholas's reign. He had come to the throne at the moment when leading members of the Russian nobility, specifically the officer class of the leading guards regiments, had demonstrated their disloyalty to the Crown during the so-called Decembrist Revolt of 14 December 1825 (O.S.). Although the revolt had involved no more than a few dozen officers, who had marched their regiments onto the Senate Square in St Petersburg on the morning of the day they were required to swear allegiance to Nicholas on his accession to the throne, their action in opposing the new Tsar and Nicholas's reprisals (the hanging of five ringleaders and the banishment of a hundred or so Decembrists to Siberia) were to cast a long shadow of martyrdom and dissent across the ensuing thirty years. What is more, the example of the Decembrists was to be an inspiring example to a younger generation of the nobility who could do little under the oppressive reign of Nicholas I save dream of future change in Russia. To the government of Nicholas even dreaming, whether in the form of student groups or, more seriously, dreaming aloud in the columns of journals or newspapers, smacked of treason and suffered persecution and censorship. The result was that the dreamers among the younger generation of the nobility began to seek their political ideals less in the realm of constitutional democracy or liberalism than in stormier, more exciting and radical visions of a utopian socialist or communist future for Russia.

The leading dreamers of the post-Decembrist generation were Alexander Herzen (1812–70) and his friend and collaborator Nikolay Ogaryov (1813–77). To Alexander Herzen especially the revolutionary example of the Decembrists became a lifelong inspiration. To him also belongs the honour of initiating both the first attempts to direct Russia towards socialism and, when he finally left Russia for self-imposed exile in the West in 1847, the first practical efforts to establish a free voice for Russia in the shape of the Free Russian Press, which he set up in London. Both Herzen and Ogaryov were of the generation of the so-called 'men of the forties', to which Turgenev also belonged. They were known by this title because it was during the 'wonderful decade'[1] of the 1840s that, by their efforts and the work of the leading literary critic of the period, Vissarion Belinsky (1811–48), Russia acquired both a socially conscious literature and an articulate public opinion. It simultaneously acquired what became known as the pre-revolutionary Russian intelligentsia. Put very briefly, the 'men of the forties' expressed a belief in the importance of the individual, the role of an educated – as distinct from a hereditary or privileged – élite in Russian society and the need for Russia to discover a separate, 'Russian' path of development.

Until the defeat of Imperial Russia in the Crimean War (1854–5) and the death of Nicholas, no political or social change in Russia occurred or seemed likely. Russia was an autocratically governed state controlled by a vast bureaucracy. Although Herzen deliberately chose exile in the West ('Demand of me anything but don't demand of me duplicity...respect the free man in me!' he urged of his friends left in Russia[2]), Ogaryov, already financially ruined, was forced into provincial exile and eventually succeeded in joining him in London in 1856; Turgenev was imprisoned for a month and then exiled to his country estate and Belinsky died in near-poverty in 1848. It was only in the changed circumstances of Russia after the Crimean War, with the new government under Alexander II prepared to contemplate reforms, that the possibility of future change became a reality. When, after 1858, the government permitted open discussion of the reforms in the press, it was soon apparent that an entirely new situation had developed, and it was a situation not entirely to the liking of the older generation of the intelligentsia, particularly Herzen and Turgenev.

In retrospect it may hardly seem very surprising that a new generation should suddenly spring into prominence after the defeat of Imperial Russia and the death of Nicholas. At the time the phenomenon undoubtedly had the power to shock. The new generation was not educated in principles of respect for the individual, for culture, for aesthetic, even if aristocratic or élitist, values, as had been Turgenev's generation. Cut off from direct experience of Western Europe by the exceptionally repressive measures of Nicholas I's government during the final period of his reign, 1848–55, the new generation had to discover its ideals for itself and looked not to Goethe and Hegel but to George Sand and Feuerbach for answers. The emancipation of women, like the emancipation from Idealism, was in essence a reflection of a deep-felt moral, political and social desire to repudiate the past in all its forms. This desire received its theoretical justification in the publicistic writings of the leading spokesman of the new generation, N. G. Chernyshevsky (1828–89), who first became prominent in 1855 with the publication of his thesis on aesthetics, *The Aesthetic Relations of Art to Reality*. Chernyshevsky repudiated the superiority of art to reality and declared that art was no more than a surrogate, at best only a replica of the real, and that a principal function of art was to be 'a textbook on life'. In a series of articles for the leading radical journal *The Contemporary* he advocated the priority of content over form in art, materialism (based largely on Feuerbach) as the only viable philosophy and an anthropology that rejected the spiritual side of man. But Chernyshevsky, although providing what could loosely be described as a programme for change, assisted the emancipation of the new generation in a more general sense – he called into question previous assumptions and teachings and he fostered a rationalist, questioning approach based on respect for the natural sciences.

If these features of the new generation's ideology tended to alarm, then in their social origins and attitudes, which necessarily had political undertones, they tended to shock and frighten. The generation that sprang into prominence after the Crimean War under the tutelage of Chernyshevsky's publicism became known as the 'men of the sixties' and they differed not only in terms of generation from the 'men of the forties' but also, generally speaking, in their social origin. They were the so-called *raznochintsy*. They belonged not to the privileged class of the landowning nobility but to an intermediate social layer between the nobility and peasantry, who 'derived from different ranks' of the Tsarist civil service or from the poorer squirearchy, the professional classes and the priesthood. In social origin they had little or no stake in the *status quo*; in their natural aspirations they sought change through education, but such change inevitably implied greater social and political power for themselves. They were an emergent technical meritocracy, indifferent to subtleties of culture or art, uncouth in their narrow scientific dogmatism but brutally clear-minded in their youthful denunciation of the past and the rather wishy-washy, if well-meaning, standards of the older generation.

In literature such a type had been a familiar but minor figure in several works of the 1850s. The young student Belyayev in Turgenev's only full-length play, *A Month in the Country* (1850), bears some of the hallmarks of the type. His freshness, spontaneity and Quixotic enthusiasm anticipate the future, whereas the world-weary cynicism and introspection of his older counterpart (a character named Rakitin, clearly modelled on Turgenev himself) are features of a Hamletism characteristic of the generation of the 'fathers'. The distinction between the generations is as yet only adumbrated. For Turgenev the problem of the difference between the generations was paramount and abiding, both for its relevance to the development of the Russian intelligentsia (of which, in literary terms, he was to be the chronicler) and for its inspirational effect on the development of his art as a novelist. It was also important to him for the universality of its meaning, since the potency of its myth helped to define the essential contrast at the source of revolutionary conflict.

Though we know little about it, he appears to have attempted to diagnose the problem in a large novel that was provisionally entitled *Two Generations*.[3] In 1855 he dropped this project in order to write what we now know as his first novel – *Rudin*. Its fame as a study of failure has tended to obscure its equally justifiable importance as a study in contrasts between dissimilar types, between, that is to say, the idealistic, though intellectualising, pedagogic, introspective type portrayed in Rudin and the heroine's youthful, strong-willed, essentially emotional character. For all that, Rudin's portrait has a depth and complexity that far surpass the other issues in the novel. It is the fullest portrayal that Turgenev ever offered of the weaknesses and strengths of his own generation. It poses as fully as any fictional portrayal before Bazarov the question of the intelligentsia's role in Russian society. Even though it is critical, and that criticism could hardly redound to the credit of his own generation, Turgenev succeeded in creating in the novel as first published (in 1856) a vivid and sympathetic portrait of an eloquent intellectual, a teacher of new ideas and a man capable of inspiring respect for freedom and truth in receptive members of the younger generation.

But Rudin could not *act* on his ideas, and what was demanded of literature by the younger generation was a hero who could act.[4] In this way literature was to become more than a barometer of social change; it was to be a pretext for violent disagreement between the two generations of the intelligentsia – a fact demonstrated by the effectiveness of Dobrolyubov's brilliant combination of literary criticism and publicism in his famous critique of Goncharov's *Oblomov* (1859). If Goncharov in his famous novel portrayed the spirit of lethargy that seemed to possess the older generations, then no figure of the period represented the spirit of the younger generation more ardently and poignantly than N. A. Dobrolyubov (1836–61). He joined the radical journal *The Contemporary* in 1857 after having been befriended by Chernyshevsky and soon became its leading literary critic. His review of Goncharov's novel was his first spectacular critical success. *Oblomov*, the classic study of sloth, had been temporarily overshadowed when it first appeared in 1859 by the publication of Turgenev's second novel *Home of the Gentry*. It was only after the young Dobrolyubov had demonstrated how Oblomov could be interpreted as the latest – and the last – in a line of noblemen–heroes who all manifested in varying degrees traits of social superfluity that the social relevance of Goncharov's masterpiece became widely appreciated. Simultaneously, Dobrolyubov was able to show that Oblomov's *malaise*, the social origin of his slothfulness, could be traced back to the kind of moral servitude that united the landowning nobility and the enserfed peasantry. Just as important, he was able to argue allegorically that the nobility could no longer be accounted the leading class in Russian society. By implication this meant that the leading representatives of the older generation, meaning chiefly Herzen and Turgenev, could not be regarded as having the right to exert a progressive influence upon the younger generation of the Russian intelligentsia.

In 1857, largely on Ogaryov's initiative but with the active support of Herzen, the Free Russian Press in London began to publish a regular journal, *The Bell*. It quickly became enormously influential as the older generation's principal mouthpiece, despite the fact that it had to be smuggled into Russia and could only circulate clandestinely. It was intended initially as a means of exposing injustices in the Tsarist administration and of disseminating in Russia information about European politics and ideas. Strictly speaking, it had no programme. Cut off as it was from direct contact with current feelings in Russia at a time when the feelings were beginning to run high, *The Bell* reacted to the sometimes anonymous or incompletely attributed articles in *The Contemporary* by assuming that criticism of the older generation, particularly criticism of the 'superfluous men', was a deliberate attempt by the reviewers of *The Contemporary* to curry favour with the Tsarist authorities. This was the gist of Herzen's reply to Dobrolyubov's attacks. What appeared to be hardly more than a fairly mild difference of critical attitude over a literary phenomenon became the cause of a serious quarrel and what eventually proved to be an ideological rift between the two generations, or wings, of the Russian intelligentsia.

Supposedly in order to seek a truce, if not actually to make peace in the feud that had developed, Chernyshevsky travelled to London in June 1859 and met Herzen. What they discussed is known only indirectly and at second hand. As personalities they were utterly opposed. Herzen was a patrician democrat, eloquent, ebullient, even haughty, with a caustic wit and an intellect as spectacular as a firework. Chernyshevsky was a deeply moral, somewhat withdrawn, even ascetic pedagogue, of lowlier origins and less pyrotechnical brilliance, at heart an activist who would have preferred to be a politician rather than a journalist. Whatever they discussed, they certainly did not get on well. One subject that may have been raised was the possibility of publishing *The Contemporary* in London if it were to be banned in Russia. In any case, there appears to have been a secret aspect to the meeting, which may have had conspiratorial connections, as we shall see.

In the desire to turn this obviously reformist period 'on the eve' of the emancipation of the serfs into a 'revolutionary' situation, Soviet commentators have tended to exaggerate the revolutionary planning of both the St Petersburg radicals and the London exiles. If there was any such planning, its scale was small. That there was a desire for revolution in the hearts and minds of leading sections of the younger generation is not in any doubt. The older generation was committed to change, but on gradualist principles. Revolution in their eyes, with peasant unrest on the scale of the Pugachyov uprising, was abhorrent. Thus, a fairly clear alignment of interests began to emerge. The left-wing younger intelligentsia were in favour of any change, even to the extent of violent, revolutionary overthrow of the autocracy; the more right-wing older generation were in favour of gradual changes of a liberal–democratic character, which would rid Russia of its most obviously backward anomalies and allow it to become more modern and Westernised. For literature, as for all those concerned with projecting the image of the age, it was a question of asking Who? and What? Who was to be the activist type best suited to achieve the necessary changes? And what form were these changes to take?

To Turgenev the question was principally one of types. He sought an answer in the fundamental contrast, as he saw it, between the dominant literary heroes of European culture – the types of Hamlet and Don Quixote. He developed the idea that Don Quixote represents selfless dedication to an ideal, in the pursuit of which he nevertheless must ultimately appear comic, while Hamlet represents the type of introspective egoist who is ultimately tragic in his lack of faith or ideal. The wholly integrated man should of course combine both these poles of human nature, just as the wholly integrated relationship between hero and heroine should combine the heart and head, the idealistically enthusiastic and the cynically realistic, the Quixotic and the Hamlet-like. If the contrast has universal meaning, then for Turgenev it had specific meaning as a way of identifying the aspiration towards change, liberation and revolution which could be discerned in the younger generation but which Turgenev himself did not share and which he could not as yet discern in Russian society at large.

He published his article 'Hamlet and Don Quixote' in *The Contemporary* early in 1860, almost simultaneously with the publication of his third novel *On the Eve* in *The Russian Messenger*, Katkov's liberal journal. Turgenev's refusal to let *The Contemporary* publish his novel was invitation enough for Dobrolyubov to attack him for making his hero, Insarov, a Bulgarian. 'What's the point of having a Bulgarian hero, why not a Russian?' he asked in a review with a suitably interrogative title, 'When will the Real Day Come?'[5] The question was obviously designed to elicit a revolutionary answer. Similarly, Chernyshevsky's answer to *On the Eve*, even though less immediate, was also to take the form of the question posed in the title of his famous novel *What is to be Done?* Inherent in the question was the idea that humanity should be fundamentally transformed, or that the Hamlets should become Don Quixotes. If Turgenev could see only Hamlets in the Russian males of this epoch, he could discern Quixotic impulses in such female types as his heroines of *Rudin* and *Home of the Gentry* and especially in Yelena Stakhova of *On the Eve*. Yelena's transformation into a young woman dedicated to her own moral liberation as well as that ideal of national liberation which she shared with Insarov is one that summarised the younger generation's appetite for revolutionary change more fully, if only by implication, than any portrayal to date.[6] The role of the Russian nineteenth-century novel as a chronicle and criticism of its time acquired at this point – on the eve of the emancipation of the serfs – a revolutionary dimension. Its revolutionary character hinged both on its publicistic function as a forum for opinion and on its specific literary power to project images of change. The image of womanhood emancipated from conventional constraints was one such revolutionary image, but more essentially novel, and relevant to the time, was the image of humanity liberated by scientific knowledge.

The combination of scientific knowledge and revolutionary idealism was destined to exert a mesmerising influence on generations of the Russian intelligentsia. The catalyst may well have been provided by the English historian H. T. Buckle, whose history of English civilisation became so popular among the Russian younger generation of the 1860s. Buckle laid particular stress on the idea that physical science had contributed significantly to the revolutionary process in France. If 'the hall of science is the temple of democracy', as Buckle claimed,[7] then the coupling of science with the French Revolution meant that social rebellion might somehow be summoned into being as assuredly as the physical, external world might be seen to be governed by scientific laws. Buckle did not put it quite as categorically, though what he implied amounted to the same thing:

The intimate connection between scientific progress and social rebellion, is evident from the fact, that both are suggested by the same yearning after improvement, the same dissatisfaction with what has been previously done, the same restless, prying, insubordinate and audacious spirit.[8]

Turgenev felt challenged by this spirit and was the first to give it a name. He recognised that the liberalism of his generation, together with his own reputation as a writer, formed the targets of this challenge. To meet it he had to formulate his own answer to the question: 'What is to be done?' It was with this in mind that he resolved to have a holiday in Ventnor in the Isle of Wight in August 1860.

Ventnor in the Isle of Wight had become a favourite holiday venue of the Russian émigré community. Turgenev was aware that a group of his compatriots, including Herzen (though he changed his mind and went to Bournemouth – or 'Bunmuss', as he called it),[9] would be gathering in Ventnor that summer. The aim of such a gathering was not only to enjoy the sea-bathing but perhaps also to discuss the state of Russia and consider certain plans for the future. On 8 August Turgenev arrived in London, apparently met Herzen, and then on 12 August, a Sunday, travelled to Ventnor, where he took rooms in Rock Cottage, Belgrave Road. In a letter to his friend, Countess Lambert, of 18 August he announced that he had 'begun to work a little: I've thought of the subject for a novel – will anything come of it?'[10] We also know from his Literary Reminiscences that it was in Ventnor that he conceived his most famous novel, Fathers and Children, and his most famous hero, Bazarov:

I was sea-bathing at Ventnor, a little town on the Isle of Wight – it was in August 1860 – when I had the first idea for Fathers and Children, that work thanks to which the kindly disposition towards me of the Russian younger generation has ceased – and has ceased apparently for ever. More than once I have heard and have read in critical articles that in my works I 'start from an idea' or 'accompany an idea'; some have praised me for this, others, on the contrary, have censured me; for my own part I must admit that I have never attempted to 'create an image' unless I have had as a starting point not an idea but a living person, to which suitable elements have gradually been added or applied.[11]

He goes on at this point to mention that his hero Bazarov was based on the personality of a young provincial doctor who had much impressed him (the man had apparently died in 1859). This living prototype of Bazarov has given rise to all kinds of speculation. No doubt, if he actually existed, he personified for Turgenev the 'nihilist' type. It is far less certain that he exemplified the revolutionary vocation, with its educative, transforming role, which became a primary characteristic of Bazarov and may have had its source in Turgenev's three-week stay at Ventnor, as we shall see later. In his *Reminiscences* he goes on to explain what the provincial doctor meant to him:

In this remarkable man were embodied – in my eyes – that scarcely conceived, still fermenting principle which later received the name of nihilism. The impression produced upon me by this person was very strong and at the same time not entirely clear; at the start I was unable to define him – and I listened to and studied intently everything around me, as if wishing to endorse the truthfulness of my own feelings. I was upset by the following fact: not in a single work of literature did I come across so much as a hint of what I sensed everywhere.[12]

Turgenev here stresses the novelty of the phenomenon of nihilism and his own intuitive awareness of it. When he wrote these words, in 1868 or 1869 (at least eight years after his Ventnor holiday), he may have wished to justify the rightness of his intuition and he perhaps over-stressed the novelty. Yet he always liked to stress the truthfulness and novelty of his perception of the type of Bazarov in his *Reminiscences* and, when he summarised the reasons for the critical reaction to his hero, it was precisely the truthfulness and novelty that he emphasised:

The entire cause of the misunderstandings, all – as one might say – the 'trouble' resided in the fact that the type of Bazarov as reproduced by me did not have the time to pass through the gradual phases through which literary types usually pass. It was not his lot, as it was Onegin's or Pechorin's lot, to undergo an epoch of idealization, of sympathy and acclaim. At the very moment when this *new* man, Bazarov, appeared, the author approached him critically... objectively.

And when he first mentioned his idea for Bazarov to one of the

Russians staying in Ventnor with him, he was astonished to hear him remark: 'But surely, it seems, you have already presented a similar type in Rudin.' On hearing this, Turgenev was at a loss for words. 'What was there to say? Rudin and Bazarov – one and the same type!'[13]

In spite of Turgenev's professed astonishment, the mention of Rudin may not have been altogether accidental at this particular moment, nor altogether inappropriate. Although he had written *Rudin* five years before, in June 1860, in an anonymous review appearing in *The Contemporary*, Rudin had been severely criticised.[14] Such criticism had been personally hurtful to Turgenev. He had construed it as an attack on his liberalism and the liberalism of his generation. One tantalising possibility now emerges. If, in the version originally published in 1856, Rudin had ended as 'a homeless wanderer', then at some point in 1860 Turgenev added what we now know as the final scene of the novel depicting the hero's death on the Paris barricades of 1848. It seems possible to assume that, either during his European travels before reaching the Isle of Wight or while he was at Ventnor, he took a decision to turn Rudin into a revolutionary. For those who died on the Paris barricades of 1848 were revolutionaries, there can be no doubt of that, and Turgenev was therefore deliberately 'revolutionising' his hero.

In doing this he was apparently doing two things. He was not only creating the first true revolutionary hero in Russian literature, he was also redeeming the reputation of his own older generation in the eyes of the younger generation. Simultaneously, it seems, he was conceiving the image and the story of his hero Bazarov 'critically...objectively'. The initial image of his Bazarov may have been tragic: that of a dying man.[15] But the ideological impulse behind the portrait must have been educative, concerned, that is to say, with the dissemination of new social attitudes and new ideas in a manner similar to his portrayal of such a type in the figure of Rudin. The reasons for this emphasis in Bazarov's portrayal may be traceable to two influences that could have affected him while he was staying in Ventnor.

The first influence was obviously revolutionary. Herzen may have had little stomach for the actual organisation of revolution; not so his friend Ogaryov. His role as one of the first – if not *the* first Russian of his generation – to engage actively in revolutionary organisation, perhaps on lines that may ultimately have influenced

Lenin, has only fairly recently received the attention due to it.[16] Ogaryov's planning seems to have been prompted by the visit of Chernyshevsky to London in 1859.[17] What he planned, under a heading of 'Ideals' (a clandestine document that he had presumably only shown to trusted sympathisers), was a society aimed at establishing in Russia a social structure based on the communal ownership of the land. The ensuing democratisation[18] of Russia would be effected by the creation of a centre in Russia permanently linked to a 'chief organ' (presumably *The Bell*) in London. The internal Russian organisation would be in the hands of politically conscious activists and organisers, known as 'apostles',[19] who would in turn have 'pupils', and the further such members of the society were from the centre the more 'unconscious' as agents of the society they would be. In Ogaryov's view, this secret society, as a thinking minority, had a paramount duty to forge vital links with the peasantry in order to ensure the twin revolutionary aims of confederation and the independence of the village.

A considerable part of this programme, in broad terms, was published by him in *The Bell* for 1 August 1860 in an article entitled 'Letters to a Compatriot'. It is unthinkable that Turgenev did not know of these 'Letters' either through having read them or through discussions among his fellow Russians gathered in Ventnor. Whether or not he knew the *secret* programme of Ogaryov's 'Ideals' is uncertain. It is certain that the idea of 'propagators of knowledge for the peasantry' must have been known to him, for at the end of his 'Letters' Ogaryov added, as a kind of after-thought:

Yes, I've still forgotten another question: popular education...It is necessary to prepare teachers, propagators of knowledge for the peasantry, for the people, itinerant teachers who could carry useful and practical knowledge from end to end of Russia.[20]

Ogaryov's mention of the importance of 'popular education' no doubt served to provide the second influence that Turgenev experienced during his Ventnor holiday – the question of education in Russia. It may be no coincidence that on 15 August 1860 there appeared in *The Times* a lengthy report and an editorial on a parliamentary debate devoted to the Ragged Schools. What the report of the debate and the editorial served to stress was that the Privy Council did not originate anything in the field of popular education in England but gave money to those who were willing to subscribe money for such a purpose. As *The Times* pointed out, the Education Committee of the Privy Council was less concerned with pecuniary aid than with 'making the education given as much as possible the base and beginning of a course of self-improvement and social utility'.

Whether or not Ogaryov's 'Letters to a Compatriot' or the report and editorial in *The Times* had a direct effect cannot be determined from any testimony by Turgenev, but it would be reasonable to suppose that they must have had some role to play, for the greater part of Turgenev's time at Ventnor was taken up with discussing and preparing a draft programme for 'A Society for the Propagation of Literacy and Primary Education' in Russia.[21] The aim was to establish a voluntary society in Russia with the object of persuading the government (perhaps in the same way as the Privy Council would be persuaded in England) that the cause of 'emancipation' would also be served by emancipating the Russian people from the slavery of ignorance. The society would concern itself with primary education and the organisation of schools that would be 'as simple, uncomplicated and inexpensive as possible'.[22] In other words, the aim was to provide limited elementary education of a quite practical kind.[23] Implicit in such an aim was the idea that the liberally-inclined sections of the Russian nobility should be seen to be actively engaged in supporting the government's reforms and should not be regarded as having any revolutionary or seditious intent.

We may reasonably assume that, confronted by the revolutionary aspirations of the younger generation of the Russian intelligentsia and revolutionary planning by such a leading spokesman of his own generation as Ogaryov, Turgenev answered the question 'What is to be done?' – at least during the three wet and windy weeks in Ventnor – by doing his own planning. What he planned took the form of a draft programme for educational change in Russia – a subject in which he had not previously shown interest and which he did not pursue actively beyond his Ventnor stay. At the same moment he was formulating his ideas for his new fictional hero, Bazarov. And at the heart of this newly conceived figure, living prototypes apart, was the 'idea' of nihilism, and it was an 'idea' that evidently had another significance. If he was apparently concerned to display his loyalty to the Russian government in his draft plan for popular education, then in his 'idea' for Bazarov there may have been more than just a 'critical' and 'objective' portrayal of nihilism. As he put it in the most explicit statement of his intentions, the letter that he wrote to the young poet K. K. Sluchevsky shortly after *Fathers and Children* appeared in 1862: if Bazarov 'is called a nihilist, then in place of that word one ought to read: revolutionary'.[24]

'Rudin and Bazarov – one and the same type!' The idea apparently astonished Turgenev, but the roles of teacher and revolutionary have something in common. Turgenev turned his most pedagogic hero, Rudin, into a revolutionary; he made his most revolutionary hero a teacher. At the opening of the novel, in chapters 5 and 6, when Bazarov first emerges as the hero-figure with a central role in the work, he is deliberately portrayed as a teacher who has a natural vocation for explaining to the peasant boys at Mar'ino why he catches frogs. In his absence from the breakfast table his most adept pupil in the novel, the young Arkady Kirsanov, offers his definition of Bazarov as a nihilist ('A man who does not acknowledge any authorities, who does not accept a single principle on faith, no matter how much that principle may be respected') and when Bazarov is confronted for the first time by the needling of the 'aristocratic' Pavel Petrovich Kirsanov and questioned by Nikolay Petrovich on the subject of soil fertilisation and Liebig's discoveries, his reply and Nikolay Petrovich's thought serve at once to underline the conjunction of teacher and nihilist:

'I am at your service, Nikolay Petrovich, but there's no need to bring in Liebig! You've got to learn your ABC first, only then can you start on a book, but we haven't even set eyes on the letter A yet.'
Well, I can see you really are a nihilist, thought Nikolay Petrovich (ch. 6).

The difference between Bazarov and all the other characters in the novel is beyond question. He is different, for instance, in the formal role allotted to him, as a stranger to the place of the fiction whose significance is revealed stage by stage as the scene moves from Mar'ino to the local township, then to Odintsova's estate and finally to the humble home of Bazarov's parents.[25] Different in formal terms, he is also different in social pedigree, different in his supposed commitment to science and different chiefly in his nihilistic concern for negation and denial. When taxed by Pavel Petrovich, the proponent of aristocratism and individuality, to explain his views, Bazarov simply asserts that 'we act on the strength of what we consider useful...At the present time denial is of more use than anything else, so we deny' (ch. 10). He commits himself to a spirit of denial not only through a cast of mind or temper that, in its youthfulness, makes him an opponent of the older man, but also because he repudiates all attempts to idealise the peasantry or to redress the situation by talk of art, parliamentary institutions or a new legal system:

'When it's all a matter of one's daily bread, when the crudest superstition holds sway among us, when all our joint stock companies go bust through lack of honest people, when even the freedom about which the government is making such a fuss won't be much good to us, because the peasant'll be only too glad to steal from himself in order to drink himself into a stupor down the local tavern.'

Revolutions are bred, it seems, as much in the minds of establishments as in the hearts of revolutionaries. Pavel Petrovich may seem an inadequate opponent for the hard-headed Bazarov, but he reveals in his own way how prone are establishments to erect barriers of 'principles', 'rules', 'habits' and '-isms' to fend off the ostensibly unprincipled, emotional assaults of the revolutionary young. By contrast the revolutionary young, in this fairly simplist form of confrontation, must just as inevitably repudiate rational argument as they repudiate all authority accepted on faith. To Pavel Petrovich such nihilism is to be equated with abuse; it is no more than talk. But if it is to become action it will inevitably be mindless and destructive. It is here that Pavel Petrovich enunciates more than just a rationalisation of the *status quo*. When he deplores the use of force and extols the value of civilisation, he speaks with greater passion than his character would seem to justify. He speaks with the passion of Turgenev himself, who perceived more acutely than any of his contemporaries (with the exception of Botkin and Dostoyevsky)[26] the uncivilising negatives of the nihilistic pose.

He declared in his *Literary Reminiscences* that he shared practically all Bazarov's convictions, with the exception of his views on art.[27] It is, though, an exception of the utmost significance. Bazarov may dismiss Raphael in his apostolic pursuit of a utilitarian materialism, but the dismissal is an acknowledgement of his own sensuous impoverishment and the essentially unaesthetic bravado of his Quixotic nihilism. The reversal process upon which his fictional existence depends, for this is precisely what the stages in his characterisation are designed to achieve, demands that he should discover through love, through the 'romanticism' that he so abhors, the aesthetic sense in his own nature. That this does not romanticise him or unbalance his portrayal is one measure of Turgenev's success. Bazarov's greatness as a piece of characterisation is attributable to the absence of the sort of over-intellectualising of emotion that we find in Rudin. He exhibits precisely the opposite of all artiness in his healthy rejection of nature-worship, art-worship and peasant-worship. In contrast to the artificiality of the Kirsanovs, the amiable exhibitionism of other members of the younger generation (Sitnikov, Kukshina), the pretensions of Odintsova and her grandiose Nikol'skoye, Bazarov himself and his parental background are deliberately portrayed as natural, honest, kindly at heart. Or as Turgenev put it in explaining that his novel was directed against the nobility as the leading class in Russian society:

All the true *iconoclasts* (*otritsateli*) I have known (Belinsky, Bakunin, Herzen, Dobrolyubov, Speshnev *et al.*) have without exception come from relatively kindly and honourable parents. And this enshrines something of great significance: it removes from the *activists*, the iconoclasts, any taint of *personal* dissatisfaction, personal grudge-bearing. They follow their chosen path simply because they are more sensitive to the needs of the life of the people.[28]

This points up very concisely the positive virtue of Bazarov as one who follows his own path out of sensitivity to the needs of the peasantry, though they may in the end reject him in much the same way that he rejects the nobility. Although an apostle of new ideas, echoing distantly the words of a Chernyshevsky or a Dobrolyubov, Bazarov acts upon his convictions not in a revolutionary way but rather in the manner of a practical reformer. He is seen to serve the needs of the peasantry as a teacher who enlightens, as a doctor who heals. His vocation may be 'bitter, harsh and lonely', as he tells Arkady (ch. 26), and after its fashion it may seem revolutionary to the older generation, but it gives no impression of having the utterly dedicated, annihilating impulse of the political nihilist (of Kojukhov, say, in *The Career of a Nihilist*). He negates, but in order to prepare the way for the elementary practical tasks of the future.

Yet at the very centre of his appeal as a character is the egoism inseparable from his nihilism. Altruistic though he may appear to be in his Quixotic denial of self, he is ultimately as preoccupied with his own ego as any Hamlet. As he puts it to his 'pupil' Arkady: 'It's not for the gods to bake the pots!' (ch. 19). For such an apostle of nihilism the only thing that will make him alter his high opinion of himself is an encounter with someone who shows no deference towards him. No bully, not really uncouth, Bazarov is distinguished in his egoism by a form of social inferiority complex that compensates with displays of assumed hatred and aggression. He declares himself ready to fight, and if he tilts at many illusory windmills to prove his knightly valour in the manner of a Quixote, then he just as readily allows his sense of purpose to be 'sicklied o'er with the pale cast of thought' that emphasises the metaphysical despair at ever achieving any form of real change in life, whether among the peasants for whom he will sacrifice himself or the nobility to whom he is opposed.

Pascal's vision of man seems to be at the source of his despair.[29] It is also at the source of his rage against the dying of the light. In conception a tragic figure, as Turgenev insisted more than once, Bazarov has in the end only one destiny in life – to die decently. To this extent he is more poignantly real to us as a humanly comprehensible character of fiction than any revolutionary hero could be, but it is precisely in his increasing awareness of the purposelessness of his life that he loses socio-political meaning as a character. In rejecting the nobility, in devoting himself to the peasantry, he becomes socially outcast, perhaps finally as much superfluous after his fashion as Rudin. He is represented as a man who, having failed in his attempt to achieve happiness through love, is given no choice save to fill his time with some form of activity until death fishes him from the waters of life.

Bazarov's legacy has taken many forms, but the most durable and profound has probably been his importance as the apotheosis of scientific respect for truth.[30] That we know very little about the scientific research that he undertakes in the novel is scarcely relevant. What we do know is that he denies all authorities save those which can be justified by reference to the natural sciences. He stands for denial of God, social institutions based on custom and all principles accepted on faith. He stands for what is honest, straightforward, useful and necessary in life, but above all he exemplifies an image of man as self-sufficient and independent.[31] His questioning of assumptions, like his denial of authorities, is the most potent of his legacies, for it is in this respect that he embodies not just a commitment to science but also that essential challenge to parental authority, the essential revolt of the children against the fathers, which justifies his nihilistic independence. His is an independence, moreover, as much moral or ethical as it is anti-establishment; it questions the place of God in the material universe as much as it queries the right of the past to legislate for the present. It is the same kind of independence that a Raskolnikov or an Ivan Karamazov will claim to assert in the name of free will. That it in turn seeks to arrogate to itself the sole right to enunciate the truth is the basis of Bazarov's revolt, just as it is what foredooms him in Turgenev's eyes.

For Bazarov the decent death is not made simple by the expedient of an adversary's bullet. He survives the ludicrous duel with Pavel Petrovich, an event that serves only to highlight his innate nobility and superiority. Not for him, as for Rudin, anything as simple and theatrical as the waving of a red flag and a blunt sword on a revolutionary barricade. No bullet passes through his heart and ends it all. His finale was to be more grandiose and terrible, for as Turgenev puts it:

I dreamed of a sombre, wild, huge figure, half-grown from the earth. Powerful, wicked and honest – and yet doomed to perish – because it still stands on the threshold of the future – I dreamed of some strange pendant to the Pugachyovs and so on...[32]

He dreamed of the doomed revolutionary as well as the hero-figure, no matter how great, who faces in the last resort only the single elemental fact of death. Darkness covers over Bazarov's life at the end, as his last word emphasises. He was not needed by Russia, any more than his vision of himself as engaged on a gigantic task was needful to life. However apparently accidental, his death resembles a martyrdom in the name of some incomplete but magnificent vision of human perfection. This is what lends the figure of Bazarov such enduring appeal.

Turgenev did not answer the question 'What is to be done?' but he did suggest, if only by the power of his art, that literature had a role to play in anticipating future change as well as in defining the latest phenomena in Russian society. Chernyshevsky's *What is to be Done?* (1863) obviously relates directly to Turgenev's novel in the sense that it is an answer to it and an extension of it. Where Turgenev had always supposed that literature involved creation – the creating, for example, of a new type such as Hamlet, whom Shakespeare discovered, as it were, and made accessible to all men – Chernyshevsky did not suppose at the time he wrote his novel that

art could ever be more than a surrogate of reality and life.[33] The
fundamental purpose of his own novel was as utilitarian as its title.
It may have owed nothing to Turgenev's masterpiece in terms of
literary example, but it nevertheless owed something in terms of
impulse, even though diametrically opposed. Whereas Turgenev
deliberately portrayed his hero as one who denied all authority save
that of the natural sciences, Chernyshevsky concerned himself with
establishing a utilitarian code of conduct for the 'new men' of the
sixties, which would essentially be authoritative, didactic and
affirmative.

What is to be Done? springs directly out of a revolutionary
situation that was a personal tragedy for Chernyshevsky. The
emancipation of the serfs, promulgated in February 1861, had been
denounced by many, including Chernyshevsky, as scarcely more than
emancipation in name. By the spring of 1862, and almost at the same
time as the publication of Turgenev's *Fathers and Children*, large-scale
public disturbances were occurring in St Petersburg. They were
directly connected with the younger generation's dissatisfaction over
the reformative measures of the government. Proclamations had
begun to appear, some perhaps the work of Chernyshevsky himself,
but by far the most inflammatory was the proclamation entitled
'Young Russia' calling for bloody revolution. Then, towards the end
of May 1862, widespread arson occurred in St Petersburg, the work
supposedly of nihilists and revolutionaries. One consequence was the
banning of *The Contemporary*. Chernyshevsky was already under
suspicion for his publicistic activities and his days of freedom were
already numbered, but the pretext for his arrest was the discovery
of his name in a letter from Herzen intercepted on the Russian
border. Herzen had stated in this intercepted letter that the London
émigrés were ready to publish the recently banned *Contemporary* in
London or Geneva – a proposal that may have had something to do
with Ogaryov's suggestion in his 'Ideals' for a 'chief organ' situated
abroad but permanently linked to a revolutionary organisation in
Russia. However, Chernyshevsky was arrested on 7 July and incar-
cerated in the Peter and Paul fortress. His novel was written at great
speed while he was under judicial investigation between December
1862 and April 1863, in between hunger-strikes and various other
literary enterprises. It may seem surprising that the authorities
permitted him to write; it is far more surprising that the manuscript
of his novel was permitted to leave the fortress for onward trans-

mission to his cousin, A. N. Pypin, who in turn passed it to Nekrasov, editor of *The Contemporary*. *En route* to the printer's, Nekrasov apparently lost it. By the oddest of ironies he then arranged for the loss of the manuscript of this 'revolutionary' work to be advertised in the St Petersburg Police Gazette, offering a reward of 50 silver roubles for its recovery. The manuscript was found by a minor official and returned. To cap the astonishing saga, the novel was in fact published in *The Contemporary* in 1863[34] through a mix-up between the commission investigating Chernyshevsky's revolutionary connection and the censor appointed to vet it for publication. Needless to say, as soon as the subversive character of the novel became known it was banned for the rest of the century.

By any standards *What is to be Done?* can hardly be considered a dangerously subversive work, although its effect, largely due to the proscribing of it, was to prove revolutionary in several important ways. The novel can be easily sniped at and mocked. Its story is implausible, its manner portentously earnest and some of the writing displays only too clearly the speed with which it was written. It opens with the contrived suicide of Vera Pavlovna's husband, shows us by lengthy flashbacks her background, the reasons for her marriage to Lopukhov and then gradually her disenchantment with him and her growing interest in his friend Kirsanov. The supposed suicide of Lopukhov is the 'secret' of the novel, its appeal as a mystery story and the falsehood at the very centre of its oft-proclaimed truthfulness. By means of this providential suicide Vera Pavlovna is enabled to marry Kirsanov and thus fulfil her real desires. It is giving nothing away to reveal that towards the novel's close a certain C. Beaumont arrives in St Petersburg from America, marries a girl called Katya and the Beaumonts and the Kirsanovs live happily ever after *à quatre*.

Throughout his novel Chernyshevsky likes to insist that it is drawn straight from life without recourse to either artifice or art. Despite this, for all his professed repudiation of artifice, it is ironic that at the centre of his true-to-life novel he should have been obliged to maintain the fiction of concealing the truth. But the collision between ostensible truth to life and the need for fictional interest never amounts to much, for the simple reason that *What is to be Done?*, as its title implies, aspires to be a textbook on life and unlike any novel before it. Designed to capture the novelty of the ideas of the time 'borne on the air like the aroma of the fields when the flowers are in bloom', the novel, it is assumed, will act upon the reader in a revolutionary way, much as the ideas that she encounters act upon the heroine and change her way of life.

No one was perhaps more changed by this novel than V. I. Lenin. Describing the impact of the novel on him, he is reputed to have said:

> Chernyshevsky's novel is too complicated, too full of ideas, to understand and evaluate at an early age. I myself tried to read it when I was about fourteen. That was an utterly pointless, superficial reading. But after the execution of my brother, knowing that Chernyshevsky's novel was one of his favourite books, I set about reading it properly and sat over it not just a few days but whole weeks. It was only then I understood its depth. It's a thing that can fire one's energies for a lifetime.[35]

Lenin is also reputed to have claimed that hundreds of people became revolutionaries after reading Chernyshevsky's novel. We are dealing therefore with a novel of which the ideas constituted a blueprint for revolutionary change. That change is demonstrated in the novel by the revolutionary effect of new ideas on the heroine.

She is influenced by them initially to achieve a domestic revolution of the first magnitude – to become independent of her mother by marrying Lopukhov, that is – and she also succeeds in escaping from the role of sexual chattel that the society of the time had prescribed for her. Given the stuffy proprieties of the time, Chernyshevsky is remarkably candid in his treatment of sexual relationships. The neutral room between Vera Pavlovna and her husband may seem absurdly prim, but the idea is clear enough: Lopukhov's relationship to Vera Pavlovna is that of teacher rather than lover. It is he who introduces her to the theory of rational egoism. Through him she learns to distinguish between her 'real desires' and those that are simply the product of fantasy.[36] Under his influence, she experiences her first dream of freedom, in which she must escape from her 'underground'.[37] She is the youth of her generation attacked by a disabling paralysis, just as she is the image of all women seeking emancipation and independence. If she emancipates herself by marriage, she achieves a form of socio-economic independence in real terms by organising a co-operative for seamstresses on socialist lines.

None of these ideas can of course become effective without the ingredient of work. This, as we learn from her second dream, is the principal element in reality.[38] Though it has to be supposed that Vera Pavlovna 'works' in organising and expanding her co-operatives, in a conventional sense she actually seems to *do* very little. She never cooks a meal, does no dusting or even light domestic work; she has no children to look after, it seems, although a baby Mitya is found in her arms (Part IV, ch. 12); she is emancipated from all the customary burdens of womanhood. Like her, her husbands are inoculated from most of the hardships common to the non-professional classes.[39] In material terms, the basis of the new life as envisaged in her second dream (and in her final, fourth, dream) would seem to be hydraulic: field irrigation, drainage, the maintenance of humidity. Work as heavy labour is no part of her dream of the future. All her activities are to be ordered by a doctrine of rational egoism, which presupposes self-interest as the guiding impulse, the pursuit of 'real desires' as the object of life and the source of true happiness. Her working relationships with others are to be governed by principles of equality, mutual respect and co-operation, whether in her successful co-operatives for seamstresses or in her relations with her two husbands.

On the face of them all these ideas appeal to reason and practical commonsense. They are to serve as a rational basis for a new life-style. In their lack of sophistication they invite the mocking cynicism of Dostoyevsky's 'underground man' and the crude hostility of so much anti-nihilist literature of the 1860s. Of course, the chief object of such hostility was Chernyshevsky's much fuller demonstration of these rational precepts in the figure of his revolutionary hero, Rakhmetov, who is ancillary to the main relationships in the fiction but undoubtedly illustrative of its main issues.

Rakhmetov is 'ploughed up' by the compulsion to self-improvement more fundamentally than Vera Pavlovna. His repudiation of his gentry background, his total, humourless dedication to becoming a 'rigorist', involving him in a severe course of physical and intellectual self-discipline, his suppression of all personal feelings, including the rejection of love, his concern to know only the essential data and the essential people, his preposterous self-mortification by sleeping on a bed of nails, notwithstanding his failure to give up smoking cigars – all these features make him, in Chernyshevsky's famous words, 'the flower of the best people, the movers of the movers, the salt of the salt of the earth'. The implication of his role as one of 'the movers of the movers' is that by subjecting himself to such revolutionary rigorism he will help to cause revolutionary change in the society around him.

The casual reader, not to mention Chernyshevsky's own ineptly funny 'perspicacious reader', can hardly fail to notice the artificiality of such types as Rakhmetov or Vera Pavlovna and her two husbands. Flying, as it were, in the face of reason, but evidently in order to make a self-fulfilling prophecy, Chernyshevsky insists on their typicality: 'I wanted to depict ordinary decent people of the new generation, people of whom I've met hundreds...I wanted to show people behaving like all ordinary people of their type, and I hope I've succeeded.'[40]

Their behaviour, with its obvious challenge to the hypocritical standards of the time, presupposes a new morality in which the guiding criterion is the pursuit of universal happiness. The central contrivance of the fiction is just as utilitarian. So that Vera Pavlovna should fulfil her real desires – sexually, one supposes, as well as in other respects – and should not be held to have violated her marriage vows, Lopukhov contrives his suicide, Rakhmetov connives at the deception and Vera Pavlovna is left free to pursue the course of true happiness with Kirsanov. At this stage in the novel the appeal to reason resolves itself into a far more emotional, impassioned and genuine summons to make the pursuit of happiness the true aim of life:

Climb out of your slums, my friends, climb out, it's not all that bad, come out into the free light of day, life's splendid here, and the way is easy and attractive, try it, try making yourselves more developed...Desire only to be happy – that's all you need desire. For this you'll enjoy taking trouble over your development: this is happiness (Part III, ch. 31).

This plea for what Chernyshevsky calls 'development' (*razvitiye*) as the clue to universal happiness is not rationally argued but emotionally proclaimed. For in the end Chernyshevsky respected the heart as much as the head. Kirsanov who is to bring Vera Pavlovna the ultimate happiness has the knack of loving, it seems. This seems to be what chiefly differentiates him from Lopukhov. Although the story of his love for a consumptive girl can be dismissed as sentimental, it illustrates a very important feature of Chernyshevsky's ideal future society. The need for love as the lasting cement in human relations is emphasised by him at the crucial point in the novel when Vera Pavlovna, acknowledging how Kirsanov's love has made her independent, dreams her fourth dream about the gradual emancipation of women throughout history and the creation of that all-aluminium, electrically-lit Crystal Palace of the utopian future. The social revolution that will emancipate women must be accompanied by a revolutionary changing of nature and man's relation to it. The creation of this revolutionary state of things is 'what has to be done' in answer to the novel's title:

Tell everyone: this is what it will be like, a future bright and beautiful. Love it, strive for it, work for it, bring about as much of it as you can: your life will be bright and full of goodness, rich in joy and happiness, only to the extent that you can bring to it something from the future (Part IV, ch. 16: 11).

For all its sententiously propagandising manner and sketchiness of both characterisation and form, the novel aims above all to express this deeply cherished *credo*. As a novel it aspired to break with tradition in literary terms quite as much as it aimed to project a utopian vision of the future. The final artifice of pretending that he is writing about 1865 when the date at the end of his text is 4 April 1863 serves to emphasise Chernyshevsky's indifference to realistic conventions in literature. As a novelist he sought to free himself from formal literary constraints by proclaiming 'truth' as the substance of his fiction, just as his heroine sought to emancipate herself from her servile role in society by proclaiming socialism as her life-style. The over-simplifications involved in such claims should not detract from their potency as hallmarks of the revolutionary novel in Russian literature. The teleology of the revolutionary ideal as of the literary phenomenon was paramount. Chernyshevsky, writing as a prisoner confined in the Peter and Paul fortress, could hardly do otherwise than assume that human relations should achieve through the example of his utopian novel that dignity and freedom which were denied to him personally. What mattered, therefore, was the future, for only the future could bring revolutionary change.

By contrast, the novel's final image may seem contradictory and pessimistic. It is the image of the 'woman all in black' considered by many commentators as a portrait of Chernyshevsky's grieving wife, to whom the novel is dedicated. For all its connotations of bereavement and sorrow, this figure appears to be less that of a widow or a woman waiting her beloved (her final song suggests as much) than that of a mother who sings to entertain her children. Such a final image of motherhood is symbolically appropriate. It underlines the fact that revolution involves giving birth to a new life. In the Russian novel it is an image signalling change, renewal and revolutionary transformation. *What is to be Done?*, with its emphasis on an emancipated, revolutionary womanhood and its final image of motherhood, signals from mid nineteenth-century Russia that ideal of the revolutionary mother which is to be given literary coherence for the first time by Maxim Gorky.

The Russian novel became the midwife to the revolutionary impulse in Russian society. In turn, it drew inspiration and creative life from that impulse.[41] All the great novels of the 1860s and 1870s can be said to be reflections of the impulse toward change that swept through Russian society in the form of anarchism or nihilism, the 'thinking realists' of Pisarev, the 'critically thinking individuals' of Lavrov, the subjective sociology of Mikhailovsky, the anti-capitalist idealism of Populism, the political activism and, finally, the terrorism of 'Land and Freedom' and 'The People's Will'. From Turgenev's *Fathers and Children* to Dostoyevsky's *The Brothers Karamazov* the Russian novel consciously echoed and recreated not only the conflicts between generations but also those between East and West, radicalism and conservatism, atheistic socialism and Christian belief, metropolitan bureaucracy and rural communalism, ever-increasing industrialisation and decaying agrarian ideals. These conflicts were endemic to Russian social growth during the Epoch of Great Reforms and the Epoch of Great Endeavours, during the 1860s and 1870s, that is to say. Though none of the great novelists could be regarded as wholly sympathetic to Chernyshevsky's utopian vision of the future, his novel challenged all who followed in his wake to create a literature that would be relevant to Russian purposes, visionary as well as realistic, purposive as well as objective. Tolstoy's *Anna Karenina*, for all that it records the tragedy of its heroine's destruction by a vicious and hypocritical society, presupposes the moral regeneration of the hero in Levin's discovery of faith at the end, just as we may suppose that Solomin's activity at the end of Turgenev's *Virgin Soil* promises the unforeseen but implied technocratic utopia that excited so many apprehensions in Turgenev himself.[42] Similarly, Dostoyevsky's vision of the new Christ with his boy-disciples promising a new heaven on earth at the close of *The Brothers Karamazov* suggests that Russia should aim to realise the precepts of Zosima rather than to cultivate the sour-tasting manna of the Grand Inquisitor.

In such novels as these literature is not only the conscience of a nation, not only its 'living memory', as Solzhenitsyn has called it,[43] but also a textbook on life in a revolutionary sense. It is a literature, in other words, that aims to change men's minds about the way they should live. But in the revolutionary novel, more than in any other version of the genre, the essentially solipsistic character of literature stands more nakedly apparent than the illusionism of a realistic literature usually allows. For if literature is in any allowable sense the creation of new life, then the revolutionary novel purports to show how that new life can be created. *What is to be Done?* leaves the reader in no doubt that life must be changed; it may seem too naive a blueprint for the infinitely complex and wilful human spirit to find appealing, yet, for all its silliness, it challenges literature to be true to its power to create and infect and influence, and in doing that it raises the need, to which Russian writers felt a keener response than other European writers of the nineteenth and twentieth centuries, for literature to revolutionise itself in the name of revolutionary change.

Neither *Fathers and Children* nor *What is to be Done?* spawned immediate successors in the genre, and of the two works the Turgenevan masterpiece was clearly the more influential in purely literary terms. Russian literature had to wait almost until the end of the nineteenth century for the first true revolutionary novel to appear in Russian, although such a novel had appeared in English in 1889. In the quarter of a century or so that intervened the anti-nihilist novel flourished in a number of bizarre examples during the 1860s[44] and achieved its greatest expression in one of the finest novels of the century, Dostoyevsky's *The Possessed* (1871-2). Among the very few novels that can claim to reflect the radicalism of the period only two deserve any attention at all and neither of them has any right to serious consideration as a work of literature.

A. V. Sleptsov's *Hard Times* (*Trudnoye vremya*) was published in *The Contemporary* in 1865.[45] It concerns the visit of a certain Ryazanov, a man with supposed radical views, to an estate-owner, Shchetinin, a former university friend of his. The object of the novel is to show up the inadequacy of Shchetinin's professed liberalism, the squalor of the 'difficult time' that faced both landowner and peasant after the emancipation of the serfs and the pusillanimous hypocrisy of establishment liberalism by contrast with the ostensible intellectual and moral strengths of radicalism. The touchstone is Shchetinin's wife, who begins to question her husband's aims in life under the influence of Ryazanov, though it is far from clear why she didn't do this much earlier. Ryazanov is so strong and silent as to be quite incredible as a character and makes in the end the poorest of successors to the impressive Bazarov.

I. V. Omulevsky's *Step by Step* (*Shag za Shagom*) appeared in 1870.[46] Obviously autobiographical in sections dealing with the hero's boyhood in Kamchatka – the freshest and most vivid passages in the novel – it tells of Svetlov's return to his parental home after some ten years away at university. Priggishly progressive in his views, he delivers sententious diatribes to all and sundry, including his parents, but apparently succeeds in converting many to his views, including a married woman, Lizaveta Prozorova, whose children he is engaged to teach. At the end of the novel she leaves with him for abroad. In the meantime, he has participated in a revolt among the peasant workers at a local factory, has been arraigned before the Governor and has suffered imprisonment for his views. These views, as the title indicates, are concerned with the 'step by step' approach to revolutionary change in Russian society. He enunciates his aims as follows:

To go step by step doesn't mean, in my view, that you've got to drag your feet; on the contrary, it means you've got to go firmly and unwaveringly towards your object, without any jumps – at least, that's the sense in which I use the term. The essential thing is not the speed of the steps you take, but their firmness and good sense, it seems to me.

Despite the Siberian setting and the introduction of political exiles into the story, the hero's character and aims are insufficiently interesting to hold the reader's attention and the succession of dialogue scenes makes for tedious, unenlightening reading. The very boredom of the work's characters and manner successfully defuses its revolutionary effect.

The English connection with the Russian revolutionary novel is most clearly apparent in S. M. Stepniak-Kravchinsky's *The Career of a Nihilist*, first published in English in 1889 and not translated into Russian until 1898. Similarly, the connection with Turgenev is also strongest here, for Stepniak greatly admired the author of *Fathers and Children*, wrote prefaces to Constance Garnett's translations and was intending to write a scholarly monograph on the writer before he was tragically run over by a train at a level crossing near his home in Bedford Park.[47] The debt to Turgenev is obvious in many parts of his novel and most particularly in the treatment given to the love story.

Stepniak wrote his novel in English between 1886 and 1889 with the twofold aim of increasing English interest in the cause of Russian freedom[48] and of explaining, as fully as he was able, the kinds of self-sacrifice and dedication that had inspired the revolutionaries of the 1870s, to whom Stepniak had himself belonged. He stated his aim in the preface:

Having been witness of and participator in a movement, which struck even its enemies by its spirit of boundless self-sacrifice, I wanted to show in the full light of fiction the inmost heart and soul of those humanitarian enthusiasts, with whom devotion to a cause has attained to the fervour of a religion, without being a religion.

In reviewing the novel *The Star* immediately seized on the novelty of psychology and type to be encountered in it:

The Career of a Nihilist is almost a new study in psychology. The 'illegal' people, as they are called, are an entirely fresh type. We all know the conventional Nihilist – many of us, too, know Tourgenieff's Nihilist, who is simply a double of the gentle, interesting, but *manqué* character, full of charm but invariably weak – which possesses such a peculiar attraction for the Russian novelist. Stepniak's heroes and heroines are an entirely different order of beings.[49]

In essence this is true. *The Career of a Nihilist* is the first Russian revolutionary novel, the first work of literature to attempt to explore the experience of being a revolutionary in Russian society and the first to show how nihilism had transformed itself from negation in the name of reform to terrorism in the name of revolution. Or as Evgeniya Taratuta has put it:

In *Andrey Kozhukhov* Stepniak-Kravchinsky, like a genuine creative artist, introduced *a new hero* to Russian and world literature.

The images of revolutionaries in all preceding Russian literature cannot compare with Stepniak's heroes. Due to censorship conditions the image of the Russian revolutionary could not appear in its full stature in legally permitted works of literature.

The revolutionary heroes of the novels of Chernyshevsky, Turgenev and Sleptsov are only approximate silhouettes.[50]

In fairness to the novel, it should not be compared with the great works of Russian or world literature. The 'new hero' that it arguably introduces is new only in relation to a literature that had previously not been permitted to dwell on such facts of Russian life. He is 'new' not in being a development of Bazarov or Rakhmetov, though he owes something to their prior example, but in being portrayed as a dedicated revolutionary. To English sensibilities, the first to respond to the novel, the newness of the psychology impressed rather less than the tragic 'waste of endeavour, this desolating loss of genius and character', as the reviewer in *The Star* called it, that was so symptomatic of the 'frightful crusade' for freedom in Russia.[51] As a work in English on so specifically Russian a subject the work is also a curiosity. It elicited a kind of wonder at the competence of its English that might be expected, though perhaps rather less from the English readership already used to Stepniak's other, non-fictional works, than from Stepniak's own compatriots.[52] But Stepniak was no Conrad and the novel was not the success that he had hoped it would be.[53]

It tells the story of Andrey Kojukhov (the English spelling), a young Russian exile in Geneva, who learns from a coded letter that one of his revolutionary comrades has been arrested by the Tsarist authorities. Consequently he decides to return to Russia. After clandestinely crossing the frontier, he arrives in St Petersburg and meets up with his close friend George, who in turn introduces him to an attractive girl, Tatiana or Tania Repina. Andrey devotes himself to propaganda among the workers and engages in attempts to release revolutionary colleagues from prison. When some of his closest friends are arrested and sentenced to death, he vows to dedicate himself to the final martyrdom of attempting to assassinate the Tsar. Tania, who has become his wife, tries to prevent him, but he is set in his resolve and would no doubt have succeeded had he not foolishly used an unfamiliar gun in making the attempt.

The novel gives a very plausible picture of the harassment that young revolutionaries can expect from the police, the constant fear of the nocturnal tap on the door and the need for continuous vigilance. It also represents the revolutionaries themselves as people fully satisfied with their vocation, generally happy in each other's company, models of right conduct, honesty and sincerity. They appear convinced of their social necessity and the rightness of their cause. 'Their propaganda', we are told, 'its small extent notwithstanding, was very fruitful. They not merely imparted to their men certain doctrines, they educated them in the same high feelings that animated themselves.' Through such very general statements about their revolutionary aims, we are given only the vaguest of descriptions about the precise political attitudes of the youthful revolutionaries.

In part such vagueness must be attributable to the author's desire to cater to the tastes of an English reading public. There is mention of 'revolutionary socialism', the Jewish problem, Gambetta and Bismarck, differences between liberalism and revolutionary nihilism, but the essential and central purpose of the fiction is to illustrate the sacrificial heroism that inspires the revolutionaries, as Andrey himself expresses it in a conversation with his liberal father-in-law:

'...we have shown an example of manly rebellion, which is never lost upon an enslaved country. With your permission, I will say that we have brought back to Russians their self-respect, and have saved the honour of the Russian name, which is no longer synonymous with that of slave.'[54]

Even their most personal relationships are governed by this heroic aim. When Andrey and Tania get married, their love is described in the following *exalté* terms:

The dangers which surrounded their path were the torchbearers of their love. What they valued and loved in each other most, was precisely this unlimited devotion to their country, this readiness to give up for its sake everything and at any moment. If they were able to love each other without doubt, division, or restraint, with all the powers of their young enthusiasm, this was because they each found in the other the embodiment of that lofty ideal of heroism after which each of them aspired.

Similarly, when Andrey decides to avenge the public execution of his revolutionary comrades, he describes his intentions to Tania in an exclamatory manner that hardly surprisingly makes her keen to dissuade him:

'If we have to suffer – so much the better! Our sufferings will be a new weapon for us. Let them hang us, let them shoot us, let them kill us in their underground cells! The more fiercely we are dealt with, the greater will be our following. I wish I could make them tear my body to pieces, or burn me alive on a slow fire in the market place,' he concluded in a low fierce whisper, his face burning as he looked at her with fixed glowing eyes.

Such shoddy melodramatic rhetoric naturally undermines the veracity of Andrey as a character, and since there are no other revolutionaries portrayed as fully in the novel the overall effect is one of an impoverished, uninspired flatness in the characterisation, despite attempts to poeticise or even glamorise relationships and occasions.[55] The quality of the writing may not be able to sustain the heroic impulse in the characterisation, yet the novel suggests well enough both the first causes of the heroism and the processes whereby conversions to revolutionary nihilism are made. At the opening of the novel, before his return to Russia to rejoin the revolutionary struggle, Andrey is represented in a particularly Wagnerian passage as undergoing a 'tumult of emotion'.

> Out of this tumult of emotion – like the cry of an eagle soaring in the eternal calm of the skies, far above the regions of cloud and tempest – there rose in his breast the triumphant, the intoxicating consciousness of the titanic strength of the man, whom no danger, no suffering, nothing on earth, can compel to deviate one hair's-breadth from his path. He knew that he would make a good and faithful soldier of the legion which fought for the cause of their country. Because this is what gives one man power over another's heart; this is what imparts the spell of contagion to his zeal; this is what infuses into a word – a mere vibration of the air – the force to overturn and remould the human soul.

No other passage in any Russian revolutionary novel captures the exultation of revolutionary commitment as powerfully as this. It is, of course, theatrical as well as Nietzschean, Bible-thumping as well as politically propagandist, and the highflown, blowsy rhetoric probably encapsulates as perfectly as one could wish the frankly adolescent, grandly operatic view of the revolutionary that appealed to so many young Russians of Stepniak's own generation. But this vision of the revolutionary as one of titanic strength, undeviating in his commitment, and of the revolutionary word as having 'the force to overturn and remould the human soul' is the key to Andrey Kojukhov's meaning as the first true revolutionary hero in Russian literature. The devotion to 'the cause of their country' may be ill-defined in its detailed aims, and the activity in support of the cause ultimately ineffectual, but the heroism of being a revolutionary is what the fictional hero demonstrates, and it is this that comprises the unique distinction of *The Career of a Nihilist* in both English and Russian literature.

The principal heroine, Tania, also undergoes a moment of change in her life. After hearing the story of a revolutionary colleague's self-sacrifice in surrendering himself to the authorities in place of another revolutionary, we are told that:

> ...she felt her heart swelling with a piercing, overwhelming pity. It was as if she had outgrown in an instant her girlhood and womanhood, her motherly instincts reaching their maturity within her maiden breast...A flush rose to her brow, a rapid something which she had not time to analyse, but which she felt with some surprise was neither hatred nor revenge, sent

a flash of light into her eyes, and all was over. The great deed was done. Here, in this out-of-the-way corner of the town, in this poor room, the echo of a noble act had riveted for ever a new heart to the same great cause.

The dreadfulness of the writing can be shrugged off, for although the sexual suggestiveness of 'a rapid something which she had not time to analyse' can only invite sniggers, this is the description not of a seduction but of a conversion. Stepniak's insistence that he sought to describe the devotion to a cause which 'has attained to the fervour of a religion, without being a religion' is exemplified many times in his novel. When Andrey sees Zina being transported to public execution along with other condemned revolutionary comrades, he experiences what is virtually a form of religious revelation, an epiphany more divine than political:

Neither then nor afterwards could Andrey understand how it came to pass, but in that moment everything was changed in him...Anxieties and fears, nay, even indignation, regrets, revenge – all were forgotten, submerged by something thrilling, vehement, undescribable. It was more than enthusiasm, more than readiness to bear everything. It was a positive thirst for martyrdom – a feeling he always deprecated in others, and never suspected himself to possess – which burst forth within him now...Forgetting the place, the crowd, the dangers, everything, – conscious only of an irresistible impulse, – he made a step forward stretching both his hands towards her. He did not cry aloud words which would have ruined him irrevocably, only because his voice forsook him; or perhaps his words were lost in the noise of the drums, as his movement was in the rush of the crowd which closed in on both sides, swelling the enormous following of the advancing procession.

From this moment Andrey Kojukhov dedicates himself to the martyrdom of attempting to assassinate the Tsar. The author's efforts at suggesting poignancy in the farewell scene between Andrey and Tania have echoes of Turgenev in them but the total effect is verbose and mawkish. In the same way, the unduly verbose preoccupation of Andrey with his own martyr's fate rather than the Tsar's death eliminates tension in the final stages. When the assassination attempt is finally made, the effect is dream-like, containing pre-echoes of Kafka and Nabokov:

The next moment he rushed onward, his brow knitted, his face pale, firing shot after shot. The Tsar, pale likewise, the flaps of his long overcoat gathered up in his hands, ran from him as quickly as he could. But he did not lose his presence of mind; instead of running straight, he ran in zigzags,

thus offering a very difficult aim to the man running behind him. That saved
him.

And so the story of Andrey Kojukhov ends. He suffers the usual
fate of those who attempt to assassinate Tsars, 'but the work for
which he died did not perish', we are told. 'It goes forward from
defeat to defeat towards the final victory, which in this sad world of
ours cannot be obtained save by the sufferings and the sacrifice of
the chosen few.'

A reader can hardly fail to be entertained by the image of the Tsar
running in zigzags from the assassin's bullet.[56] As a final bizarre touch
it points up the ridiculous element in what is a supposedly sublime
purpose. Hardly intentional, perhaps; certainly out of keeping with
the unduly serious tone of the preceding narrative. What mattered,
though, to many of Stepniak's acquaintances was that his novel
should end with regicide as the final martyrdom of a nihilist's career.
To Vera Zasulich, the most famous name among the women
terrorists of the 'Land and Freedom' movement,[57] a revolutionary
struggle conducted not arm-in-arm with revolutionary comrades but
in the form of single-handed murder could never attract forces to its
cause, no matter how popular it might be; it was 'too sombre a form
of struggle'.[58] In fact, it celebrated a policy of terrorism that had
already been largely discredited by the time the novel appeared in
English (1889) and must have seemed politically anachronistic to a
Marxist-inclined intelligentsia of 1898 when the novel eventually
appeared in Russian.

Stepniak's belief in 'the chosen few', an élite of revolutionaries,
that is to say, dedicated to changing Russian society by means of
terrorism, had its historical justification in the terroristic activity of
the élite of 'The People's Will', but the ideal of a single revolutionary
acting in isolation is one that seems to belong as much to literature
as to fact. There is no doubt that the influence of Turgenev is partly
responsible for this. To George Bernard Shaw, in a lengthy but
little-known obituary notice, Stepniak

was very definitely conscious of the two opposing strains in the Russian
character, the fatalist oriental side, and the energetic, creative, critical
occidental one, both typified for us by Tolstoy on the one hand and
Turgénieff on the other. Stepniak belonged emphatically to Turgénieff's
party. He was a man of life, action, change, as against resignation,
contemplation, passive beauty of character. He would, I believe, have
willingly exchanged a good deal of the charm of his countrymen for some

of the less pleasant virtues of the English, a feeling with which I, as an Irishman, was peculiarly qualified to sympathise.[59]

Although such a contrast between Tolstoy and Turgenev has a good deal of Shavian impishness in it, there is a satisfying shrewdness about Shaw's estimate of his friend. Stepniak undoubtedly kept himself aloof from the principal revolutionary organisations of his compatriots and gave the impression that he identified closely with the Turgenevan vision of the isolated, influential *intelligent* who could change Russia by his words and his example.[60] Writing of Rudin in his introduction to Constance Garnett's translation of the novel in 1894, he described such a Turgenevan intelligentsia as 'the brain of the nation':

Although small numerically, the section of Russian society which Turgenev represents is enormously interesting, because it is the brain of the nation, the living ferment which alone can leaven the huge unformed masses. It is upon them that depend the destinies of their country.[61]

Such a 'brain of the nation', if unlike Rudin's in being able to implement its ideas through various acts of heroic immolation, had a literariness to it in Stepniak's case that attributed to literature as mighty a role in causing revolution as the heroic act itself. In a brochure of 1892 he stressed quite explicitly, in speaking of the way foreign attitudes toward Russia had changed, the role of literature in achieving this change, and in doing so he must have had his own novel in mind to some extent:

This change of feeling has come about gradually during the last fifteen or twenty years. The way was prepared by a number of serious investigations which acquainted the scientific and literary world with the Russian people and with Russian culture. But the principal forces at work in the accomplishment of this decided transformation were undoubtedly the Russian novel on the one hand and the Russian revolutionary movement on the other: the poetry of form and the poetry of action; the fascination of the genius of creation and of the genius of self-sacrifice.[62]

The 'poetry of form' in his novel *The Career of a Nihilist* expresses itself chiefly in rhetorical monologues or highflown descriptions of emotional states, but there are one or two exciting episodes and moments when an image can strike a spark of interest. During his night-time ramble along the banks of the Arve in Switzerland, before returning to Russia, Andrey Kojukhov finds his attention attracted by the sight of a cornfield: 'It was a mere patch, a few score yards

square, so that on the vast green turf it looked like a lady's
pocket-handkerchief on the carpet of a drawing room.' The image
is neat and exact. Or later, after his return to Russia, Andrey is
directed to call on two sisters (whose surname – Dudorov – echoes
forward, perhaps by a generation or more, to Nicky Dudorov in
Pasternak's *Doctor Zhivago*) and after some difficulty found 'their
grim unplastered hungry-looking red brick house', an image that for
the moment summons up the urban terraces of London that Stepniak
himself knew in the 1880s. But always dominating the literary
purpose of his fiction was that 'poetry of action' which presumed
that revolution could be caused by some individual heroic act and
celebrated that heroic ideal.

At the International Socialist Congress in Paris in 1889, within
months of the appearance of Stepniak's novel, G. V. Plekhanov
declared:

The task of our revolutionary intellectuals...amounts, in the opinion of the
Russian Social Democrats, to the following: they must master the views of
modern scientific socialism, spread them among the workers and, with the
help of the workers, take by assault the citadel of autocracy. The revolutionary movement in Russia can triumph only as the revolutionary movement
of the workers. There is not, and cannot be, any other way out for us.[63]

This declaration sets in relief the absence of any commitment to
'modern scientific socialism', i.e. Marxism, in Stepniak's novel or,
for that matter, in his political philosophy. Some of the most telling
criticism of the political inadequacy of the work emphasised the lack
of contact between the revolutionaries and the people. No figures of
working people have any prominence, nor is there any depiction of
revolutionary workers. Stepniak's revolutionaries are middle-class
and intended for what would no doubt prove to be a predominantly
middle-class readership, even though when published in Russian the
novel appears to have attracted readers from many layers of society.
In its basic emphasis on solitary revolutionary endeavour or, at best,
the idea of a 'chosen few', Stepniak's novel proclaimed a concept
of revolutionary and revolution that was already beginning to yield
before the scientific socialism of Marx and Engels and the notion that
the working class would have a vanguard role in the struggle against
the autocracy.

2

Proletarian heroism and intelligentsia militancy

The two novels that illustrate the literary response to the so-called 'first' Russian revolution of 1905 more clearly than any others are both concerned to show how capitalist society, whether in its economic or its political forms, dominates and reifies human life. Human beings are represented as at one remove from natural surroundings, divorced from a natural, uninhibited relationship with their environment and themselves by the institutions of economic and political life that dominate them. Throughout the major prose fiction of the decade following the failure of the 1905 revolution there was a tendency to depict human behaviour as partly motiveless – the most obvious example of such an approach was the work of Leonid Andreyev,[1] but it can also be seen in the work of Kuprin, Bunin, Serafimovich, Sologub and others – and in a quasi-impressionistic, symbolic manner that substituted behavioural representation for the psychological motivation so essential to nineteenth-century Russian realism. Arguably a smaller literature with smaller talents and smaller concerns than the literature of Dostoyevsky, Tolstoy and Chekhov, it could still lay claim to one writer of acknowledged genius and international repute in Maxim Gorky, and it was to throw up probably the most original of literary talents on the European literary scene in the pre-First World War period, Andrey Bely. The depictions of environment in their respective 'revolutionary' novels illustrate the evolution of manner and style that occurred in a literature that was naturally responding to the socio-economic and political forces of the time:

Every day the factory whistle bellowed forth its shrill, roaring, trembling noises into the smoke-begrimed and greasy atmosphere of the working men's suburb; and obedient to the summons of the power of steam, people poured out of little grey houses into the street. With sombre faces they hastened forward like frightened roaches, their muscles stiff from insufficient sleep. In the chill morning twilight they walked through the narrow, unpaved street to the tall stone cage that waited for them with cold assurance, illumining their muddy road with scores of greasy, yellow, square eyes. The mud plashed under their feet as if in mocking commiseration. Hoarse exclamations of sleepy voices were heard; irritated, peevish, abusive language rent the air with malice; and, to welcome the people, deafening sounds floated about – the heavy whir of machinery, the dissatisfied snort of steam. Stern and sombre the black chimneys stretched their huge, thick sticks high above the village.

In the evening, when the sun was setting, and red rays languidly glimmered upon the windows of the houses, the factory ejected its people like burned-out ashes, and again they walked through the streets, with black, smoke-covered faces, radiating the sticky odour of machine oil, and showing the gleam of hungry teeth.[2]

Zola-esque, resonant with the ponderously over-stated, unsubtle didacticism of a semi-documentary realistic manner, this opening passage to Gorky's famous novel *Mother* (1906–7) demonstrates its chief effect purposefully enough: the workers, dominated by the machine of the factory, which summons them in the morning and ejects them at night like burned-out ashes, are zoomorphised into cockroaches and appear to lead reified lives that have less reality than the machinery and steam of the factory itself. The purpose of the description shines through the manifestly lurid writing without difficulty. Ten years after the first appearance of *Mother* Andrey Bely published the first separate edition of his most famous novel, *Petersburg* (1916), and the first description of the St Petersburg environment at the time of the revolution is concerned with achieving a quite different kind of effect:

The carriage was flying towards Nevsky Prospect.

Apollon Apollonovich Ableukhov was gently rocking on the satin seat cushions. He was cut off from the scum of the streets by four perpendicular walls. Thus he was isolated from people and from the red covers of the damp trashy rags on sale right there at this intersection.

Proportionality and symmetry soothed the senator's nerves, which had been irritated both by the irregularity of his domestic life and by the futile rotation of our wheel of state.

His tastes were distinguished by their harmonious simplicity.

Most of all he loved the rectilineal prospect; this prospect reminded him of the flow of time between the two points of life.

There the houses merged cubelike into a regular, five-story row. This row differed from the line of life: for many a wearer of diamond-studded decorations, as for so many other dignitaries, the middle of life's road had proven to be the termination of life's journey.

Inspiration took possession of the senator's soul whenever the lacquered cube cut along the line of the Nevsky: there the numeration of the houses was visible. And the circulation went on. There, from there, on clear days, from far, far away, came the blinding blaze of the gold needle, the clouds, the crimson ray of the sunset. There, from there, on foggy days – nothing, no one.

And what was there were lines: the Neva and the islands...

Apollon Apollonovich did not like the islands...

Apollon Apollonovich did not wish to think further. The islands must be crushed! Riveted with the iron of the enormous bridge, skewered by the arrows of the prospects...[3]

A metropolitan landscape, unpeopled, because the symmetry-dominated mind of the senator cannot allow for their existence, not only does this impressionistic or symbolical picture of St Petersburg suggest the way in which that 'fantastic' city created by Peter the Great can impose a kind of political symmetry on its inhabitants, or indeed materially symbolises the logic of state power, but it also deliberately creates an effect of fragmentation, instantaneous glimpses, scattered impressions, a moment-by-moment interaction of visual item and mental image, which allows no room for the didactic purposefulness of Gorky's manner (though in several ways *Petersburg* is as didactic a novel as *Mother*). The 'sophistication' of Andrey Bely's prose also distinguishes it from Gorky's, in the sense that the meanings are inferred rather than explicitly stated. The political significance of 'the scum of the streets' is indicated no more explicitly than by the almost casual-seeming reference to 'red covers'; the images of straightness, which contribute to the symbolic meaning of Ableukhov as a representative of imperial power, are curtailed by opposed concepts in the form of 'intersection', 'irregularity', 'futile rotation' and that breakdown of straightness which culminates in 'the islands' where revolution is hatched. In the one case the realistic manner argues a case for revolution; in the other, the very literary means at the disposal of the writer seem to be enacting their own revolution against what is literally real.

No Russian writer sought more keenly than Maxim Gorky to make his writing serve the cause of revolution. His stories of the 1890s offer many brilliant portrayals of types of outsider – gipsies, thieves, *déclassés*, *bosyaki* and mischief-makers (*ozorniki*) – who exist on the fringes of capitalist society or are its victims. By their very existence they reproach that society, but Gorky often made them into spokes-men of such reproach through giving them fables to tell ('Makar Chudra') or biographies ('Starukha Izergil'') or, in a more realistic

way, by illustrating the tragic implications of their protest ('Chel-
kash', 'Konovalov', 'Ozornik'). His romantic treatment of such
types necessarily had the effect of making them seem exceptional.
Towards the end of the decade, especially when he abandoned the
short story for the novel and drama, he turned to examination of the
likely revolutionary potential of types of bourgeois liberalism. The
tragedy of his Foma Gordeyev illustrates the ultimate ineffectiveness
of the type of bourgeois dissident, just as the liberalism of the
younger generation of the Bessemyonov family in his first play,
Meshchane (1901), proves ineffectual against the older generation's
immovable conservatism. Of the characters in that play only the
adopted son, Nil, an engineer, exemplifies the notion of heroic
proletarian protest against the *status quo*. Recognised as the first
representation of such a type in Gorky's work, Nil is a somewhat
sketchy and unconvincing piece of characterisation, and in any case
in his second – and most famous – play, *The Lower Depths* (1902),
Gorky turned to the idea of the Comforter (*uteshitel'*) in the figure
of the false prophet Luka to illustrate his own doubts about the
possibility of changing those whom society had abandoned in the
'lower depths'. His play offered a rhetorical and frankly romantic
vision of Man as a free agent, not in need of the false comfort of
a Luka.

In 1902 Gorky heard of the heroic action of a young worker and
political activist, Pyotr Andreyevich Zalomov (1877–1955), who
while participating in the May Day demonstration in Sormovo, a
suburb of Gorky's native Nizhny Novgorod, had refused to abandon
the banner he was carrying and was consequently arrested along with
several others. When he was brought to trial in late October 1902
Gorky is believed to have helped him compose his speech. After being
sentenced to exile, Zalomov was given financial help by Gorky to the
tune of 15 roubles a month and was eventually enabled to escape
from exile in 1905 with the help of a further 300 roubles from Gorky.[4]
The activity of Pyotr Zalomov did not pass unnoticed by Lenin.
Writing of Zalomov's speech along with those of the other defendants
at his trial, Lenin had the following to say in his newspaper *The Spark*
on 1 December 1902:

What is remarkable in these speeches is the simple, authentically precise
description of how the most everyday facts, occurring in *scores and hundreds of
millions*, of the 'misery, oppression, slavery, degradation, exploitation' of the
workers in present-day society lead to the awakening of their consciousness,

to their growing 'revolt', to a revolutionary expression of this revolt
(I have put in quotation marks the words I *had* to use in describing the
speeches of the Nizhni-Novgorod workers, for they are the famous words
which Marx uses in the last pages of the first volume of *Capital*, and which
evoked such clamorous and unsuccessful attempts on the part of the 'critics',
opportunists, revisionists, etc., to refute the Social-Democrats and accuse
them of not telling the truth).[5]

Lenin's insistence on the changeover from 'spontaneity' (*stikhiy-
nost'*) in the workers' protest movement to political awareness and
from such awareness (*soznaniye*) to revolutionary demonstration of
their dissatisfaction is a paradigm that Gorky himself was the first
to illustrate in a literary form in his novel *Mother*, but only after he
had been brought into close contact with proletarian agitation
through his acquaintance with the Zalomovs, mother and son.
Gorky's own experience during his years of wandering across
southern Russia had brought him into contact with many people;
yet he had had no direct experience of factory work and he remained
all his life unsure of the realities of proletarian experience. Hence his
own insistence that he drew on vast quantities of factual material
supplied by such people as the Zalomovs or his friend Savva
Morozov when he planned his novel, even though he appears not to
have had access to this material during the actual writing of it. There
is no doubt that the central episode of his novel is based on the May
Day demonstration in Sormovo on 1 May 1902 and that the hero
of his novel is based largely on Pyotr Zalomov. The figure of
Nilovna, the 'mother' of the novel, is similarly based on Zalomov's
mother, Anna Kirillovna Zalomova (1849–1938). A distant relative
of the Kashirins, in whose house in Nizhny Novgorod Gorky passed
his childhood, she used to visit them and was evidently known to
Gorky as a boy. Her husband had been a worker at the Kurbatov
factory. A drunkard, he died prematurely, leaving her seven children
to look after. When her son Pyotr also went to the Kurbatov factory
and began to organise a group of workers, she was apparently
persuaded to join him in his political activity and continued to do
so after he had been exiled for his part in the Sormovo demonstration.
In other words, by drawing on the experience of the Zalomovs and
other materials, Gorky was to base his novel on 'the most everyday
facts, occurring in *scores and hundreds of millions*, of the "misery,
oppression, slavery, degradation, exploitation" of the workers in
present-day society' and to have, as it were, the sanction of both

Marx and Lenin for demonstrating how those facts must inevitably lead to the workers' political awareness and their expression of dissatisfaction by revolutionary means.

For his own part, Gorky knew at first hand what opposition to Tsarism could mean. He had suffered arrest and imprisonment for his advocacy of his views. At the beginning of the 1905 revolution he had spent a month in the Peter and Paul Fortress in St Petersburg after the Bloody Sunday demonstration of 9 January 1905 (although he had not taken part). Widespread protests by leading intellectuals and writers in the West secured his release from prison. In December 1905 he was forced to flee to Finland and from there to Western Europe and America. In April 1906 he embarked in New York on a much-publicised campaign to raise funds for the Russian opposition parties, especially the Bolsheviks. His initial success quickly turned into a quite remarkable rejection of him by a large section of hypocritically prudish American society when it was learned through information carefully leaked by the Russian embassy that the woman with whom he was travelling was not his legal wife. He found himself literally turned out onto the street overnight. His response was a vitriolic attack on America (*The City of the Yellow Devil*). He was then befriended by an American couple, the Martins, who offered him lodging in their home on Staten Island and their vacation home in the Adirondacks. Here, between June and October 1906, he wrote the first part of *Mother*, immediately after completing his play *Enemies* on a roughly similar theme. The second part of *Mother* was written on Capri in Italy between October and mid-December. It is not hard to see that the novel sprang directly out of Gorky's personal involvement in the 1905 revolution and was no doubt given a certain edge and urgency by the treatment that he received in America. He wrote the first draft of it in great haste, without the necessary materials to hand, but with a feeling that it had to be written. Lenin was among the first to recognise its 'timeliness', having read the novel in typescript. In May 1907 he pronounced it 'a much-needed book; many workers participated in the revolutionary movement unconsciously, instinctively (*stikhiyno*) and now they'll read *Mother* with great benefit to themselves. A very timely book.'

The 'timeliness' of it may now be obscured by the fact that it is related to a period far removed from the present day; it is also less apparent because the present-day version of the novel derives from Gorky's final reworking of the text for the edition of 1923.[6] By an

agreement that he made in New York Gorky was obliged to submit
each new work of his in English and in Russian. The English text
would be considered the original, the Russian text the translation.
Having made this agreement, Gorky then entered into negotiations
with D. Appleton and Co. and by an agreement of 4/17 September
1906 the first part of *Mother* was to be lodged with the publisher at
once already translated into English.[7] And the second part was to
be sent to the publisher not later than 15/18 December. Accordingly,
Mother began to appear in *Appleton's Magazine* in December 1906
and in April 1907 the first separate edition appeared in New York,
followed by a London edition entitled *Comrades*.[8] The New York
and London editions of 1907 have to be regarded as effectively the
first versions of Gorky's *Mother* and related as much to American
and English literature as to Russian literature. They are considerably
longer than the final textual reworking and they contain elements
that, if on the whole minor, can be said to illuminate emphases in
Gorky's work which the first published Russian text (Ladyzhnikov)
did not contain and which became increasingly less pronounced in
the subsequent reworkings.

The publication of the novel in New York and London met with
no hindrance of any kind, unlike its publication in Russia, and even
if it caused no lasting ripples in American and English literature it
is not without irony that this work, generally regarded as the
keystone of Socialist Realism, should have found its first readers in
an English-speaking environment and should have taken its first
most 'timely' form in English versions that were inaccessible to a
Russian readership. Apart from their greater size, these versions
differ from later editions particularly in their treatment of the trial
scene, which does not conform in certain respects to what was then
established court procedure in Russia, and in certain of the episodes
(the murder of the spy Isay, committed by Andrey Nakhodka in the
English version; the May Day demonstration; the arrest of Rybin
and of Nilovna) and in some lengthy digressions on the theme of
music. No doubt Gorky scrapped some of these features of his first
version in order to shorten and tighten his work. But in the process
emphases undoubtedly changed and it is these emphases that reveal
a subtle, yet important change in the portrayal of the novel's central
figure.

Despite the changes, Gorky's final version is very like the original
version of *Mother*. Although the success of the novel has been

fostered to some extent by official Soviet approval of it, the importance of this work is due also to the fact that it quite properly has
priority over all other examples of the proletarian revolutionary
novel in Russian literature. Moreover, no writer of the genius and
stature of Maxim Gorky had previously committed himself so fully
to the cause of proletarian revolution. In *Mother* Gorky went as far
as he ever went in writing specifically about the proletariat. All his
later work, even if connected with revolutionary themes (one thinks
of *The Artamonov Business, The Life of Klim Samgin* or his final
plays), is concerned with the merchant class or the intelligentsia,
which Gorky himself knew far more intimately than he knew the
factory worker. It is significant that, though he made plans to write
a continuation of his novel to be called *Son*, he never did this. The
powerful autobiographical element in Gorky's genius always kept his
subject-matter tightly reined to his own experience. In *Mother* he
moved as nearly towards pure fictional invention as in any work of
his and the true extent of his fictional creativeness is to be gauged
primarily by the central invention of his fiction, the portrait of the
mother herself.

Briefly, this is the story of the mother, Pelageya Nilovna Vlasova,
a woman of forty, married to a drunken worker. He dies and she
suspects that her son Pavel may also fall prey to the dissolute, brutish
ways of the factory settlement. But Pavel surprises her by his
seriousness. He begins to bring friends of his home and the mother
soon realises that these young people, with their idealism and their
self-sacrificial dedication, have a message for her, and for the whole
world of the factory, which is likely to bring religious as well as
political and social renewal to all men. Her life is transformed. When
Pavel is arrested during the May Day demonstration that concludes
the first part of the novel, the mother moves in with a teacher and
intellectual of Populist inclinations, Nikolay Ivanovich. She respects
this man and his sister almost as much as her own son,[9] but she
becomes increasingly devoted to working for her son's cause by
acting as courier and helping to distribute pamphlets in the factory.
After the trial, which is the culminating episode of the novel's second
part, she is herself arrested at a railway station while distributing
copies of her son's speech.

The novel contains, as do so many of Gorky's plays, characters
who can be said to be little more than spokesmen for points of view.
Such are Andrey Nakhodka, the Ukrainian, who expresses the idea

of socialist internationalism (a character much reduced in status during Gorky's reworkings), and the anarchist peasant agitator Rybin. Although involved in episodes that are designed to illustrate their opposition to authority, they are chiefly eloquent mouthpieces. Pavel Vlasov himself also fits this description in the sense that his principal role is that of spokesman for revolutionary socialism during the trial. By describing the characters in this way one may be in danger of seeming to represent them as caricatures, which would be unfair: they possess an inherent vibrancy in their characterisation due to the very reverberations of their eloquence, though as types they are necessarily without psychological depth or emotional distinctiveness. What endows them with a measure of sympathetic interest, and is in turn a measure of Gorky's success in giving them a living resonance as characters, is the fact that they are projected to us almost invariably through the mother's apprehension of them, whether through direct response or stage-managed comment. Consequently, the mother herself immediately assumes both a central role and an organising function in the novel's structure. Her portrayal is organic to the novel's form, just as her presence is a prerequisite of characterisation and description throughout the narrative.

If life for the proletariat is hard, this life is not depicted for us explicitly in the narrative, for we are never admitted into the working of the factory, but we are admitted into the working of the mother's heart and her response to factory life. When Pavel declares that his aim is 'to learn and then to teach others' because the workers have to learn to understand why life is so hard for them (Part I, ch. 4), the learning and the understanding are illustrated initially through the mother's response to her son's friends and their ideas. A primitive rhetoricism in the eloquence of the 'socialists' and a cloying over-simplification of response to their socialist utterances are essential to the projecting of the mother as the single, universal agent for apprehending, appreciating and loving them – for being their mother, in fact. The characters themselves are necessarily idealised to some extent through the mother's understanding and compassion, for they tend to become attributes of her own characterisation and hence less distinct as individual characterisations. Since they must be attributes of her own fondness for her son they tend to be alike in their virtuousness, as distinct from the representatives of Tsarist society who are alike in their odiousness because they are necessarily hateful to the mother in their hostility to her son and his friends. The

issues emerge distinctively, if simplistically, by this means. Gorky's
reworkings tended to reinforce the simplifying and humanising role
of the mother in the fiction. If she unifies structurally, she is also
ideologically a means of demonstrating the way in which the cause
of socialism can unite the generations and put an end to the
generation conflict that had been so dominant a theme in Russian
literature since *Fathers and Children*.

The fundamental message of the novel, when uttered by Pavel in
his speech at the trial, is couched in explicitly propagandist terms.
By this point in the novel the message can hardly fail to have a
forceful emotional ring to it. It summarises all that the mother has
learned, as it were, and all that her son had sought to teach. Though
less patently rhetorical than Satin's speech on Man in *The Lower
Depths*, it is after its fashion a successful blend of political sloganising
and high-key oratory:

'We are Socialists! That means we are enemies to private property, which
separates people, arms them against one another, and brings forth an
irreconcilable hostility of interests; brings forth lies that endeavour to cover
up, or to justify this conflict of interests, and corrupt all with falsehood,
hypocrisy and malice. We maintain that a society that regards man only as
a tool for its enrichment is anti-human; it is hostile to us; we cannot be
reconciled to its morality, its double-faced and lying cynicism. Its cruel
relation to individuals is repugnant to us. We want to fight, and will fight,
every form of the physical and moral enslavement of men by such a society;
we will fight every measure calculated to disintegrate society for the
gratification of the interests of gain. We are workers – men by whose labour
everything is created, from gigantic machines to childish toys. We are people
devoid of the right to fight for our human dignity...Our watchword [A:
slogan] is simple: "All the power for the people; all the means of production
for the people; work obligatory on all. Down with private property!"'[10]

Though this message is principally political, throughout the novel
the message of socialism had been perceived by the mother chiefly
in a religious form and had been expressed by her and others in
semi-religious terms. In the first – English – versions this aspect of
the message had been given considerable prominence.

The transformation that occurs in the mother is best gauged by
her changing attitude towards religion. Fairly early in the novel,
during a discussion between Pavel Vlasov and Rybin, at which of
course the mother is also present, the question of God is raised and
the mother's feelings towards Rybin are immediately coloured by his
attack on *her* God and *her* church. Though she protests that they

must not take her own God from her, she is clearly influenced by the fierce discussion of the issue which occurs between Rybin and her son and, one presumes, by Rybin's final assertion that 'God is in the heart and in the mind, but not in the church. The church is the grave of God' (Part I, ch. 11). On more than one occasion she equates the socialism of her son and his friends with a faith akin to a religion and, while admiring the selflessness of the revolutionaries, wonders whether their faith can be sufficient to transform the world. With the coming of spring and the approach of the May Day demonstration (Part I, ch. 23), the unifying and transforming aspects of socialism are stressed both in the emphasis that is now given to the mother as the mother of all revolutionaries and in the importance attributed to the unity of the socialist movement as Andrey Nakhodka expresses it in his slogan: 'People of all countries, unite in one family!'[11] It is Andrey Nakhodka who more than once engages in turgid rhetoric about freedom and love of truth as essential ingredients of socialism or proclaims that they are crusading for a new God (Part I, chs. 24 and 27). For the mother, less grandiosely, the path to socialism involves a gradual changeover from belief in an Orthodox God to faith in a new Christ, which she expresses most eloquently after the arrest of her 'children' during the May Day demonstration. Recalling a new idea born in her own heart, we are told, she declares: 'There would have been no Lord Jesus Christ unless people had not died for his greater glory' (Part I, ch. 28).[12]

In the second part of the novel, through learning of the revolutionary activity of Nikolay Ivanovich's sister Sofya, for example, and through discovering at first hand the perils and sacrifice of a revolutionary vocation, the mother becomes consciously committed to political activism in the name of revolution. Simultaneously she comes to a deeper appreciation of the significance of Christ:

Christ now became closer to her and was different – higher and nobler, more joyous and luminous in appearance, as if he had been literally resurrected to life, washed and given life by the warm blood shed so generously in his name by those who wisely did not proclaim the name of the unfortunate friend of humanity (Part II, ch. 8).

The association of Christ and resurrection and revolution assumes fuller meaning in the thoughts expressed by Sasha on the death of Yegor Ivanovich when she claims to believe in the immortality of honourable men, in the immortality of those who had given her the

happiness of living the fine life that is presumably hers as a result
of her work for the cause. The idea of Christian discipleship is less
important here (though it is certainly present) than the idea that there
are certain men who confer immortality – an idea that is to pervade
and enrich the portrayal of Yury Zhivago in Pasternak's novel. It
is a concept that helps to define the revolutionary novel in Russian
literature and must be regarded as a distinguishing part of the
teleology of the whole genre.

Towards the close of the novel (in its final version) this concept
becomes closely associated with the role of the mother herself. In the
penultimate chapter, the mother declares exultantly: 'It's just as if
a new God had been born for mankind!...In truth you are all
comrades, all related to one another, all children of one mother, who
is truth!' (Part II, ch. 28). In the English-language versions the mother
was given even more explicit statements to make. Shortly before her
arrest she was made to address the people in the railway station in
the following biblical language:

'In order to change this life, in order to free all the people, to raise them
from the dead, as I have been raised, some persons have already come who
have in secret seen [A: secretly seen] the truth in life; in secret, because, you
know, no one can speak the truth aloud. They hunt you down, they stifle
you; they make you rot in prison, they mutilate you. Wealth is a force, not
a friend to truth. Thus far truth is the sworn enemy to the power of the rich,
an irreconcilable enemy for ever! Our children are carrying the truth into
the world...Along the route of their hearts it will enter into our hard life;
it will warm us, enliven us, emancipate us from the oppression of the rich
and from all who have sold their souls.' [A: Believe this.]

Obviously socialism, as the truth, is equated here with a new gospel,
persecuted by the Tsarist authorities, but intended to save the soul
of mankind. In the same way, the mother herself and her children
are represented as disciples of this new gospel who, in the manner
of the early Christians, will carry its message of salvation to all
working people. The form of the message, resembling that of a prayer
or ministration, becomes apparent in the English-language version's
amplification of her cry that 'The word of my son is the honest word
of a working man, of an unsold soul. You will recognise its
incorruptibility by its boldness!'

'It is fearless, and if necessary it goes even against itself to meet the truth.
It goes to you, working people, incorruptible, wise, fearless. Receive it with
an open heart, feed on it; it will give you the power to understand everything,

to fight against everything for the truth, for the freedom of mankind. Receive it, believe it, go with it toward the happiness of all people, to a new life with great joy!...'

Undoubtedly the excision of such passages from later versions simplified the characterisation of the mother and she appears less of a zealot or religious martyr in consequence. On the other hand, along with the excisions have also gone several significant ideological aspects of the mother's role: her Madonna-like function coupled with her eloquent advocacy of the religiously transforming, proselytising character of the socialist message, aspects that are reduced to slogans for the most part in the final version. What seems chiefly to be missing from the final version is the emphasis on the way in which the mother finds herself resurrected in spirit by the truth of socialism and thereby enabled to preach the gospel of socialism to all working people as if it were in some way a message of spiritual resurrection for all mankind.

About the literary value of Gorky's novel there are legitimate grounds for doubt. Gorky himself expressed them as well as any hostile critic when, in reply to one of the first of those to pass an opinion on it, he admitted that it was 'an unsuccessful thing, not only in its external appearance, because it is long, boring and carelessly written, but chiefly because it's insufficiently democratic'.[13] The correspondent in question was the critic and friend L'vov-Rogachevsky, who knew that Gorky had tended to substitute for his own natural mother his maternal grandmother, the *babushka* whom he was so brilliantly and lovingly to evoke in his *Childhood*. This must explain L'vov-Rogachevsky's initial reaction:

I was delighted in your book, as if it were 'a real mother'. It has in it signs of much emotion and something very moving; one can only write about a mother like that if one is far from home and only if one has never known a mother's love in one's childhood.

Now everyone's talking not about Turgenev's 'Fathers and Children' but about Gorky's 'Mothers and Children' and the grandiose fusion of the universally maternal and the universally human. You are the first to have projected the figure of the *new* mother, unjustly done to death and resurrected, and to have placed her as high as she deserves.[14]

These observations underline both the very personal meaning of the novel for Gorky, who can be said to have idealised his fictional mother because he felt the keen lack of a real mother in his own life, and the larger literary and ideological meaning of the concept of

motherhood in relation to revolution. If Turgenev's novel initiated
the tradition of the revolutionary novel in Russian literature, Gorky's
novel established the tradition as an integral part of Russian
literature and by stressing the importance of the role of the mother
suggested the very close identification of the twin ideas of motherhood
and revolution. It may be said to have superseded Turgenev's
essentially contrasting concept of 'children against fathers' by posing
an essentially unifying notion of the mother as the spirit of revolutionary socialism engaged in ensuring a future of truth and amity for
the children. In its simplistic treatment of political issues, Gorky's
novel is intellectually callow; in its creation of a myth – the identification, that is, of the mother and revolution – it is a remarkably
potent and prescient work. From it is to grow the opposing myth
of the motherless children who are the victims of revolutionary
change. In some ways they tend to dominate the picture of revolutionary experience as we find it in the Russian revolutionary novel.

It is obvious that in Gorky's *Mother* the opposite applies. For all
the callowness and thinness of his characterisation, Pavel Vlasov, the
son, has the role of positive revolutionary hero. As image and
mouthpiece he may appear to be idealised to the point of unreality,
but as the mother's son he is given a degree of veracity, however
remote-seeming, through the mother's own perfectly understandable
love and concern. The heroism of a proletariat in its struggle against
Tsarism is articulated as a struggle not only for freedom or socialism
but also for the humane, compassionate dignity of motherhood, the
maternal love of children, the solicitude for the future as for a united
family.

Gorky's *Mother* was rejected by broad sections of the Russian
intelligentsia. For one thing, it professed allegiance to the left wing
of Russian Social Democracy, although not explicitly to Marxism,
in a propagandist manner that entirely repudiated the nihilistic
revolutionism celebrated by Stepniak. Of the many consequences of
the revolution of 1905 the most serious for the Russian intelligentsia
was the apparent failure of the dream of revolutionism as an
honourable vocation. In the ensuing reaction against the revolution
during the third Duma, 1907–12, the intelligentsia was forced to
reappraise its aims and purposes and the most serious of the acts of
self-appraisal was the symposium *Signposts* (*Vekhi*) of 1909.[15]

To the first of the contributors, N. A. Berdyayev,[16] the Russian intelligentsia had tended always to adopt social utilitarianism and worship of 'the people', whether peasant or proletarian, as a moral dogma. But inherent in such worship was a tragic contradiction:

The intelligentsia, in its finest examples, was always fanatically prepared for self-sacrifice and no less fanatically professed a materialism which denied any form of self-sacrifice; the atheistic philosophy by which the revolutionary intelligentsia was always attracted could not sanction anything as holy, while the intelligentsia endowed that very philosophy with the character of something sacred and treasured its materialism and atheism fanatically, almost in a Roman Catholic spirit.[17]

To the second of the contributors, S. N. Bulgakov, the revolution of 1905 was an 'intelligentsia' revolution and the failure of the revolution was attributable to the inherent contradictions in the intelligentsia's beliefs and aims. Conditioned by Tsarist repression and isolated from life by such repression, the Russian intelligentsia had always been anti-bourgeois in the name of its eschatological dream of the City of God and the approaching kingdom of truth. By its striving to save humanity, if not from sin, then from suffering, the Russian intelligentsia became distinguished by that very same puritanism, moral rigorism and asceticism that it so deplored in the teachings and traditions of the Orthodox Church. It exhibited a form of religious guilt and repentance before the people while maintaining an atheism that involved both extreme dogmatism and astonishing ignorance of religious questions. The dogmatism involved the embracing of a religion of Godmanhood, which inspired in the intelligentsia the idea that it was called on to play the role of Providence in relation to its country and its people. From this grew the 'heroism' of the Russian intelligentsia.

The heroic member of the intelligentsia had to dream of saving mankind or, at least, the Russian people. Political maximalism became his guiding principle. Such a hero was to a certain extent a kind of superman adopting the arrogant and suggestive pose of a saviour. For all its professed democratic tendencies the intelligentsia was just another kind of aristocracy, which haughtily opposed itself to the 'man in the street' or the bourgeoisie. At the source of such an attitude was a form of adolescent arrogance that Bulgakov branded as 'spiritual pedocracy', the greatest evil in Russian society, in his view, as well as being the symptom of so-called intelligentsia heroism, for it presupposed that the intelligentsia hero could do without a personal moral code. In a succeeding article (A. S. Izgoyev,

'On Intelligentsia Youth') it was precisely to lack of family influence that the immorality, ideological shakiness and ineffectual character of the intelligentsia were ascribed.[18]

In general, the contributors to the symposium exempted Russian literature from the taint of being an 'intelligentsia' literature. To S. N. Bulgakov it was only Dostoyevsky who had really understood the intelligentsia and P. B. Struve claimed that 'the great writers Pushkin, Lermontov, Gogol, Turgenev, Dostoyevsky and Chekhov do not have an intelligentsia look'. By contrast, Russian literature enshrined truths, ultimately having a religious meaning, that were rightly proclaimed as sacred and inviolable, whereas the intelligentsia, since it was an irreligious splinter group cut off from the state as a whole, had tended to show moral frivolity and political impracticality (so Struve insisted) or out of a form of moral nihilism had always tended to be anti-cultural (so claimed S. L. Frank). Furthermore, the classical type of Russian *intelligent* was 'a militant monk professing the nihilistic religion of earthly well-being' whose principal article of faith was hatred of wealth. Such hatred prompted the 'revolutionism' inherent in the nihilist religion of the intelligentsia. It is to S. L. Frank that we owe a terrifyingly prophetic interpretation of what this 'revolutionism' was to mean for Russia within a decade of the publication of *Signposts*:

'Die Lust der Zerstoerung ist auch eine schaffende Lust,' said Bakunin; but the limiting 'auch' has long since disappeared from this aphorism, and destruction has been recognised not only as *one* of the instruments of creation, but has been generally equated with creativity or, to be more accurate, has entirely taken its place. Here we have an echo of that Rousseau-ism which implanted in Robespierre the certainty that the kingdom of reason could be established by the single expedient of mercilessly ridding the fatherland of its enemies. Revolutionary socialism is shot through with the same faith. In order to establish an ideal order of things it is necessary to 'expropriate the expropriators', and for that one had to achieve 'a dictatorship of the proletariat', and for that one had to destroy this, that and the other political – and generally speaking external – obstacles. Thus, revolutionism is no more than the reflection of a metaphysical absolutisation of the elemental importance of destruction. All the political and social radicalism of the Russian intelligentsia, its proneness to see in political struggle and in its most extreme aspects – conspiracy, rebellion, terror and so on – the most direct and important way to achieve the people's welfare, derives exclusively from the belief that struggle, the annihilation of the enemy, the forcible and mechanised destruction of the old social forms can of themselves ensure the realisation of the intelligentsia's social ideal.[19]

The lesson of this prophetic interpretation is spelt out slowly, word by word, in the pages of the many novels that were eventually to depict the February and October revolutions and the civil war. In the end, as the novels were to show, the very 'revolutionism' of the intelligentsia was to bring about its own destruction.

A short novel – very popular in its time – which depicted the dilemma of the intelligentsia revolutionary was V. Ropshin's *The White Horse* (*Kon' blednyy*) (1909).[20] It is the story of George O'Brien, alias Malinovsky, etc., a terrorist who eventually succeeds in causing the death of the Governor-General of Moscow. His relations with his fellow terrorists involve inconsequential, pseudo-Dostoyevskian exchanges about Christianity and the revolutionary ethos. The terrorist Vanya, who eventually succeeds in throwing the fatal bomb, is a Christian believer; George is not. He is a personality devoid of any depth, as colourless and sketchy as the shorthand, impressionistic glimpses of townscape and park that intermittently decorate the text (the action covers a period from 6 March to 5 October, presented in the form of ostensible dated diary entries). George is preoccupied, though hardly very deeply, by his passionate relationship with a young married woman, Yelena, whose husband he murders. The woman Evna, who loved him devotedly, he finally rejects. The study is one of a revolutionary without dedication or aim. Towards the story's close George is brought to an acknowledgement that all his life is no more than a marionette theatre in which he will participate with no greater effect or entertainment than Pierrot or the three musketeers. Heroic deaths such as the sailors' deaths at Tsushima[21] are no part of his experience. He concludes by confessing a death-wish in which the only source of meaning in his life, the love of his mother, is obliterated:

I used to look at the sun when I was a child. It blinded me, burnt me with its radiance. In childhood I used to know love – the tender love of my mother. I loved people innocently, loved life with joy. Now I love no one. I do not wish and I do not know how to love. In the space of an hour the world has become accursed and barren for me: all is falsehood and all is vanity.

The Pale Horse (of Revelation 6: 8) whose name is Death has trampled on the green grass and the grass has withered.

A further novel by the same author *What Never Happened* (*To, chego ne bylo*) (1912) gives an even more pessimistic view of the

terrorist's fate. It depicts the bankruptcy of intelligentsia revolutionism in the post-1905 period by describing how the Bolotov family
virtually destroys itself through its dedication to the revolutionary
cause. Of the three Bolotov brothers who, for no very clear reason,
sacrifice themselves to the cause, the most active and articulate is
Andrey, who is eventually captured after the failure of an assassination attempt. In the early stages of the novel he is involved in
constructing barricades in Moscow in late 1905 and the realisation
comes to him that revolution is not created by individual revolutionaries but by some spontaneous elemental and grandiose movement of the masses:

Through a Moscow empty and denuded of inhabitants, through streets piled
high with a night's snow-storm, through the boarded-up windows,
warehouses and shops locked and bolted, the absence of police and Cossack
patrols, and through this barricade being built at Chistiye Prudy, he saw with
his own eyes that something grandiose was being accomplished in Moscow,
something that did not depend on him or any single individual will. He saw
that it wasn't the power of the Party that had roused up teeming, wealthy,
mercantile and peaceful Moscow, and all the Party meetings in St Petersburg
seemed to him pitiful and ludicrous. He tried to understand, and couldn't,
precisely what hidden force it was that had impelled people in Lefortovo,
in Kozhevniki, in Miusy and the Arbat all of a sudden to build barricades,
simultaneously to kill and be killed. And now, standing in the radiance of
a frosty sun, in snow unusually white for urban snow and among happy,
healthy armed men vigorously engaged in doing something unfamiliar and
dangerous, he experienced a joyous and uplifting feeling. It seemed that
Moscow had risen as one man, in all its centuries-long Russian might, and
he was shaken by an awareness of a new and heavy responsibility, a
responsibility not to the Party and its leaders but to Russia itself in the throes
of revolution.

Although Andrey, as a member of the revolutionary intelligentsia,
may hope to lead this spontaneous revolutionary upsurge, the
important feature of this passage and of the novel is the recognition
that revolutionary feeling tends to manifest itself on a mass scale by
instinct and not by choice. Andrey's conscience becomes dominated
by this awareness. The killing of the political or class enemy, though
it invites crises of conscience, is something that he and his fellow
terrorists may have to experience, but as he points out in a revealing
passage of self-questioning it is either a matter of having an unlimited
right to kill or of observing the law that 'Thou shalt not kill.' Where
is the law laid down? he asks.

'In the Party programme? In Marx? In Engels? In Kant? That's a lot of nonsense,' he whispered excitedly, 'because neither Marx, nor Engels, nor Kant ever murdered anyone...Do you hear that? They never murdered anyone...That means they haven't any idea, they simply can't know what I know...No matter what they may have written, they remain entirely in the dark as to whether one should kill or one shouldn't. That is something known only to us, only to those who have actually killed...'

And on the eve of being hanged Andrey remains as puzzled by this dilemma as on all previous occasions. He concludes by assuming, in a callow self-justifying way, that 'I killed and I'll be killed...All are right and all are guilty...There are no just men and no guilty men...There are two mortal enemies, enemies for thousands of years, and no one on earth can be their judge.' And he declares that he will die with a prayer on his lips to freedom and the Russian people – in a manner consistent with the intelligentsia militancy so scrupulously diagnosed and exposed by the contributors to *Signposts*.

The reaction of Russian literature to the challenge of the 1905 revolution is best seen, at least in the evolution of novel-form, in Andrey Bely's *Petersburg*.[22] It may be said to celebrate the West, whereas his earlier work *The Silver Dove* (1909) celebrated the East, but nowhere in Bely's work is there an exact polarity of interests. All tends to flux, to intimation of an essentially interfusing relation between phenomenal and noumenal, rational and irrational, East and West in patterns of opposites that suggest a fascination with the balance of algebraic or geometric constructions. *Petersburg*, as the Prologue intimates, is about the symbol of imperial Russian state power, the symbolic capital city that exerted such a strong, even mesmerising, influence on Pushkin and Gogol. It is also about the mind of Russia, as it is about Bely's own mind, and the necessary pressure to break out from, or explode, the mental abstraction into the phenomenally real. *Petersburg* is about the revolutionary process that is essential to all literary creation: the taking of images from nature which symbolise truth, and in so doing reveal the latent meaning in all things, but which may only be demonstrated by the explosion that occurs in the meeting of two opposed elements. These two opposed elements are, as Ropshin had his hero proclaim, 'two mortal enemies, enemies for thousands of years', symbolised in this case by the opposition of father and son, of the established system and the revolutionary impulse, of the geometric city and the anarchic

islands, of the twin forces of 'revolutionary terror' and 'ice';[23] and
there are other patterns of opposition discernible in this elaborately
ornamental work. By offering symbolic renderings of the fissionable
elements that caused revolution, the novel points to the explosion
imminent in Russian life.

The work's primary appeal is its display of literary virtuosity. The
verbal brilliance is sustained throughout, though it is a brilliance seen
to greatest effect in the descriptive passages rather than the
characterisation. A quite conscious use of lyrically alliterative clusters
in the nomenclature – *Appoll*on *Appoll*onovich *Abl*eukhov ('*pll-
pll-bl*'), or Ni*ko*lay *Apoll*onovich *Abl*eukhov ('*kl-pll-bl*'), or the use
of such combinations as 'lak, losk i blesk' – suggests both an
iteratively mechanising effect in the characterising of the main
figures, as mechanical as the clockwork of the bomb in the sardine
tin timed to explode in the novel's finale, and a motif effect designed
to emphasise the luxury of upperclass St Petersburg life.[24] Such
literary affectation in the name of symbolism may invite Plekhanov's
charge that a literature

resorts to symbols when it is not able (to use Hegel's happy expression) to
utter those magic words which bring to life a picture of the future...And
when the art of a given society shows signs of moving towards symbolism,
then it is a sure sign that the thought of that society – or the thought of the
social class which leaves its impress on art – does not know how to penetrate
to the meaning of the social development occurring before its very eyes.[25]

Bely's literary virtuosity depends on the 'symbolical' affectation
of alliterative clusters, on reifying imagery and a conscious ornamentalism that may well seem to be a substitute for that 'penetration
to the meaning of the social development occurring before its very
eyes' of which Plekhanov speaks. Yet his achievement as an orna-
mentalist in words was revolutionising for the language and shape
of the Russian novel. He was to have many conscious imitators of
his virtuosity among early Soviet novelists. They copied the rhythmical, ornamental prose and the deliberate fragmentation of sentence-
shape and narrative pattern, the rather arch alliterations and verbal
sleights of hand. The panmongolism, classical and Dantean imagery,
the surreal mixing of the fantastic and ostensibly factual were not
copied, though since they formed an integral part of Bely's examination of revolution they tended to sanction an equivalent daring
freedom of ideas in works that aspired to Bely's symbolical sophis-

tication. In essence, however, Bely's sophistication is seen to greatest effect in finely orchestrated impressionistic passages describing the 'fantastic' city of St Petersburg, where word-pictures and sound-pattern coalesce, where facet after facet, in a kind of verbal pointillism, contributes to a layered patina, frequently brilliant, sometimes lush to the point of tastelessness. Plekhanov's remarks have proper relevance to Bely's achievement precisely in respect of the way he lavishes such gloss on an essentially superficial world – a world that has more surface brilliance to it than substance – and devotes less attention to characterisation than to chiaroscuro.

It is the world of the Ableukhov family, father and son, and, contingently, of the St Petersburg environs of the 'others', the revolutionaries. Apollon Apollonovich Ableukhov symbolises official, government St Petersburg and he never surmounts as a piece of characterisation the symbolic mould in which he is conceived. For him the dominant symbol is the straight line – the lines of the streets of the capital city, the squares and straight lines of his thoughts born from his head like gods and goddesses from the head of Zeus. Whatever has not come out of his head is not *his* St Petersburg, meaning the Vasilevsky Island and the low wooden houses on the other side of the Neva, which he would wish to stamp on and destroy. They, in their turn, are the source of the revolutionary activity that is ready to destroy him. His mouselike, scuttling steps, his insulation from life through his work, his travels by carriage, his secluded domestic environment, are the composite elements that contribute to the impression of an almost non-human, partly mechanical, clockwork artefact of the city. His son, Nikolay Apollonovich Ableukhov, is an *intelligent* and exhibitionist who likes to affect a domino mask, has a bust of Kant in his room but no knowledge of Kant in his head and passes his time in a tawdry relationship with the wife of an officer, Sofya Petrovna Likhutina, who lives in an ambience of Japanese pictures, chrysanthemums, dolls and black silk dresses. Nikolay Apollonovich's nihilism disposes him to revolution: he becomes involved with a revolutionary party and is given a bomb in a sardine tin to look after, but is only indirectly responsible for the ultimate explosion. His relationship with his father is similarly oblique. This is a novel in which there is no direct contact between human beings. Isolated within the geometric patterns of St Petersburg, each character moves on separate lines and in routines that are timed to the ticking of the bomb. At the first intimation of contact between father and son there is an explosion of feelings that highlights several significant features of the novel's manner.

Apollon Apollonovich dropped a pencil (by the staircase). From ingrained habit, Nikolai Apollonovich rushed to pick it up. Apollon Apollonovich rushed to forestall him, but he stumbled and fell, his hands touching the bottom steps. His head fell forward and down and unexpectedly landed under the fingers of his son's hand. Nikolai Apollonovich caught sight of his father's neck (an artery was throbbing on one side). The neck's warm pulsation frightened him. He snatched his hand away, but he snatched it too late: at the touch of the cold hand the senator's head convulsed in a spasm. His ears twitched slightly. Like a jumpy Japanese ju-jitsu teacher, he threw himself to the side and straightened up on cracking knees. All this lasted but a moment. Nikolai Apollonovich handed his father the tiny little pencil.
'Here!'
A trifle had knocked them one against the other, and had produced in both an explosion of thoughts and feelings. Apollon Apollonovich got completely flustered by the fear he felt in response to politeness (this male in red was the flesh of his flesh, and to be frightened by one's own flesh was disgraceful). He had been sitting *under* his son, on his haunches. Apollon Apollonovich felt annoyance as well. He assumed a dignified manner, bowed from the waist, and compressed his lips primly:
'Thank you. I wish you pleasant dreams.'[26]

This snatch of text illustrates the 'nowness' of the narrative manner. To emphasise the symbolic ultimate meaning of the novel everything in *Petersburg* is presented as a concatenation of instants composed from dialogue or passages of impersonal, impressionistic description. There is no assumed viewpoint of narrator towards narration. The symbol, once intimated, has no inherent dynamism. Its strength is its secret potential, but once that 'secret' is divulged it is just another component in a series of component parts. This is a novel made up of components that almost deliberately do not cohere; or, put another way and more accurately, the components of the symbolic, in the act of being described, appear separate and therefore literally *incoherent*. The instant, the moment, is always frozen, for the component must be still, statuesque, in its revealed meaning. The 'moment' described in the above passage sets in relief the symbol of the sitting or squatting man, which is bizarre and potent in all the axial moments of the novel. The symbolic figure of Peter the Great sitting on his horse in the Falconet statue is depicted as one of grotesque and nightmarish power. Here Apollon Apollonovich is represented as sitting under his son and transfixed by the same kind of look that the eyes of the symbolic Peter directed at all who stood in the way of his imperial destiny. Dudkin, the revolutionary who eventually murders the terrorist leader Lippanchenko, is depicted at the end as squatting on his victim. Ugliness, whether the ugliness of servility or of an act of violence, degrades and is represented by Bely as part of a process of reification. The masses of the St Petersburg world *outside* the Ableukhov world are represented as a mass of human machines engaged in the manufacture of revolution. Such obviously symbolic components in the novel as the Bronze Horseman,[27] which accompanies each discussion of Russia's future, or the bridges across the Neva, which have a crucially important role in deciding the destiny of Nikolay Apollonovich, reinforce the tendency to reify personality in Bely's creation of character. A section called 'The Last Judgement' ('Strashnyy sud') illustrates the way in which the Ableukhovs themselves assume towards each other symbolic roles. Nikolay Apollonovich, with his head resting on the sardine tin containing the mechanism designed to kill his father, imagines his father in the symbolic form of a Mongol forebear, Ab-lei, entering his room and his life like Chronos, the god of time. He is reminded that he has the atavistic Turanian blood within him that will explode him into Nirvana as surely as the mechanism in the sardine tin. But all ends with nothing more terrible than the nightmare image of the exploding Pepp Peppovich Pepp, the bouncing ball of his childhood that has been transmogrified into the ticking bomb of his maturity.

An image of the spherical, whether ball- or bomb-shaped, is pervasive in the novel. It 'widens and brings about disintegration and death',[28] as Maguire and Malmstadt have noted; it also encloses and confines. The rectilinear world of official Petersburg peters out into the fragments of the revolutionary islands, but the spherical world of Nikolay Apollonovich's bouncing ball and bomb suggests an implosion of meaning, interconnected and interdependent in its destructiveness, which encloses the entire novel in its spherical form ('we realise eventually that the structure of the novel as a whole is circular'[29]). The 'nowness' of reality in the novel demands a virtual stasis as a result. Though 'the novel as a whole unfolds between September 30 and October 9, 1905',[30] a presumption of timelessness dwells over the work, as if it referred symbolically to all Russian revolutionary periods or to the whole history of Petersburg Russia, from its beginnings with Peter the Great to its imminent end.

Similarly, the conflict between father and son can be understood on several planes simultaneously. But the political ideas, few though they are, have the look of some features associated with Nietzscheanism and a puerile fascism. For example, Dudkin, the revolutionary, who received his revolutionary ideas in Helsinki, where he had encountered a Persian citizen with a Russianised surname Shishnarfne (reversed, of course, it spells 'enfranchise'), recalls that he then cultivated a paradoxical theory about the necessity of destroying culture. As a replacement of the outworn humanism of the previous culture there was to be a period of healthy animality breaking through from the dark depths of the people in the form of hooliganism and apache fury. Art was to revolt against established forms; there was to be a love for primitive culture and a fondness for the exotic among the rich, while among the bourgeoisie the revolt was to take the form of eastern fashions in women's clothes and Negro dances like the cakewalk.[31] Nikolay Apollonovich's 'revolt' against his father has no real ideological basis therefore, though it is obviously nihilism against authoritarianism, the intelligentsia against the establishment or, more simply, the exhibitionist son with a penchant for dressing up in a red costume who succeeds by his antics in disgracing his father and bringing his senatorial career to an end. In this sense, the novel may be interpreted as Bely's judgement not only on generational conflict but also on the pointlessness of revolution as a means of transforming humanity. His father and son, for all their antagonism, seem to exhibit a complementary apprehensiveness in face of the danger ticking away in their lives.

In another, and deeper, sense, the father and son are linked by the fact of procreation and this fact is only comprehensible if there is a wife and mother. In its final stages the novel becomes the story of the return of the prodigal wife or the rediscovery of the errant mother, but it is significant that the long-awaited encounter between husband and wife, son and mother, is depicted as more cerebral than emotional. The theme of motherhood appears ultimately to fuse with that of ticking creation, the real symbol of revolution, which Nikolay Apollonovich sets loose in the life of the Ableukhov family. Even so, he is only the oblique agent of the final explosive act. It is Apollon Apollonovich himself who, having kept a key-hole watch on his son, carries the lethal sardine tin from his son's room into his own study where it explodes, causing a fire but no injury.

Both father and son are represented as isolated from life. Revolution threatens them as a phenomenon that will abolish their way of life in the case of the senator and cast them into a solitary isolation, as in the case of his son at the end of the novel – a fate symbolic of that which awaited the bourgeois intelligentsia. The novel can be regarded, in its portrayal of the Ableukhov family, as apocalyptic; it may even be considered as 'revolutionary' in its exposure of the revolutionary tensions at work in history, or as a Soviet critic has put it *Petersburg* is 'a world catastrophe' and 'the novel is of its kind a tragedy which tells of the violation of every form of equilibrium in the world – individual–psychological, public–political, social, national, etc.'[32] But it is clearly not a political novel as such; it bears closer resemblance to a deliberately stage-managed anti-political act.

In many of its literary effects *Petersburg* consciously rejects the conventions of the bourgeois novel. Although it can be described as a symbolist work that incorporates certain revolutionary features, the true 'revolutionism' of the novel is in its exploding of the objective illusionism of realism. In doing so, it is often very successful in fusing different planes of reality, the phenomenal and noumenal, the historical and symbolic, but the ideological issues reflect, however darkly, Bely's own class-based fear of revolution as well as his interest in anthroposophy and are on the whole subordinated to stylistic means. As Mochulsky interprets these issues:

Both old Russia and her new reaction and revolution are in the dark power of Mongolian-Turkish forces. The only salvation is 'secret knowledge' – anthroposophy. The 'spiritual incarnation' of Christ will save Russia, and in her a new human race will be born.[33]

The concept of revolution for Bely was fundamentally a revolution, or transformation, in the human consciousness, and the novel as the literary vehicle of this revolutionary transformation acquired therefore its own supra-political and supra-personalist role as an autonomous means of projecting the revolutionary experience that was to come. His *Petersburg*, in company with Gorky's *Mother*, established a pattern of opposites in the Russian revolutionary novel. If his hero is motherless, revolution is equally portrayed as sterile, and the intelligentsia aims of Nikolay Apollonovich lead only to isolation and the tragedy of world catastrophe. Gorky's revolutionary image of motherhood presupposes the birth of a new political era, the salvation of the working class and a resurrecting force of life. These opposites are accompanied by revolutionising processes in the fictional form. Gorky's novel has achieved a reputation and influence as a founding work of Socialist Realism in which the explicitly political purposes can be seen to be welded into the portrayal of Nilovna, the central figure. Propaganda and portraiture, naturally combining in the need to create purposeful central figures, exerted a guiding influence in the early Soviet novels about revolution, but more dominant initially was the deliberate incoherence of Bely's experimentalism, his fragmentation of reality and his challenge to the supposed veracity of realism. Bely's truth, in the end, like that of all the greatest Russian writers, becomes coherent only as the vision of a humanity transformed in conformity with a spiritual ideal.

3

The revolutionary novel

Introduction

In its depiction of the revolution of 1917 and the ensuing civil war
the Russian revolutionary novel of the Soviet period celebrates events
that had epoch-making significance for the Russian people. Whatever
the political colouring given to these events by historical
interpretations then and since, the revolution of 1917 and the civil
war were concerned with confrontation between Whites and Reds,
between capitalism and socialism, between the pre-revolutionary
possessor class and the industrial proletariat in alliance with the
poorer peasantry. In the end, the industrial proletariat and the poorer
peasantry were the victors. The significance of this victory still
reverberates in innumerable ways in all parts of the world.

The Russian revolutionary novel, in its depiction of revolutionary
events, offers not so much a record as a multi-faceted re-animation
of the human dimensions of events that may all too easily seem to
lose their vital meaning in the pages of history books or even in the
flickering, unstable images of the silent cinema. The smell and colour
of those years of revolution and civil war, the human dimensions of
the horror, outrage, terror and blood-letting, the sheer complexity
of the experiences involved, the paradoxes of choice and allegiance
that changing political and military situations forced upon so many
and the problems of daily survival in the face of unbelievable
shortages, plagues and catastrophes – these are what the literature
of the period reflects. But a literature is by its very nature a survivor
of events. The horror can be recounted, but the living word of the
novelist has its own faith in its survival. It outlives. And in outliving
it proclaims, perhaps only obliquely, the triumph of the surviving
viewpoints over others, the living truth over the dead. Though
literary works may undergo reworkings, they tell a truth about
human experience that is not an easily manipulable truth. It demands
that a reader should accept it because it is partly empathy, partly

65

infection, partly mythology, partly legend, because it is the raw truth of experience enlivened and vivified by art. Furthermore, it is a truth that the novelist himself, no matter how great or flexible his talent, could never hope to encompass completely. The events of the revolution and civil war were physically of such scale and consequence that no single individual experience could be expected to know more than a relatively small part of an infinitesimally small part of the total. The traumatic impact of the events, in which so many shared, made the assimilation of the events in literary terms both infinitely challenging and in some degree or another part of a common national experience.

To this the novelist with his two or three hundred pages of letterpress could bring very little not already known. Yet the grandeur of the event challenged the novelist to surmount his own limitations and the limitations of his genre. It dignified the novel not only as a recording genre that could have as much presumed objectivity as a chronicle but also as the one literary genre with sufficient inherent versatility and power to transcend authorial subjectivity. The process of authorial self-effacement that had become so marked a feature of certain brands of realism in the novel in the decades before the revolution acquired further technical endorsement and validity in the 'cinematic' mannerisms of some early revolutionary novels. At the same time, the almost compulsory renunciation of the conventions of the bourgeois novel opened the way for innumerable experiments in the novel-form, which naturally enough sanctioned various kinds and degrees of authorial exhibitionism. Fragmentation, ornamentalism, exuberant metaphoricism, allegory, *skaz*, an iconoclastic modernism deriving from and elaborating on pre-revolutionary experimental writing, all designed to suggest the kaleidoscopic variety and disjointedness of revolutionary experience, were the most obvious indices of the literary revolution in the novel. Novelty became the novel's 'revolution'. But it was also a novelty that stressed factuality and was validated by the sheer novelty of the times. It represented simultaneously an abandonment of the supposed boundary between fact and fiction and a compulsive, not to say heroic, assault on all the assumptions and devices associated with realistic representation in literature.

The main outlines of the revolution and civil war as reflected in the Russian revolutionary novel involve the following facts. The revolution of 1917 was two revolutions, the so-called bourgeois revolution of February 1917 and the so-called socialist revolution of October. The February revolution brought about the downfall of the Romanov dynasty and the establishment of a provisional government. The only major figure to emerge from this period was Kerensky, who was first War Minister and then Premier. Of greater significance in the longer term than the provisional government were the Soviets (or Councils) of Workers' and Soldiers' Deputies that sprang up in the capital Petrograd (the Russified form of St Petersburg, so renamed in 1914 as a patriotic anti-German gesture) and in the major cities. Though the provisional government attempted to exercise some authority in the political vacuum left by the downfall of Tsarism, real power lay with the Soviets and in the course of the summer of 1917 the Soviets became increasingly dominated by left-wing elements, particularly the Bolshevik wing of the Social Democratic Party.

Vladimir Ilyich Lenin, the leader of the Bolsheviks, had returned to Russia from his Swiss exile in April. He argued that it was the duty of all who believed in a socialist revolution to oppose the provisional government and work for its overthrow. Though the influence and power of his words and his party amounted to little at the beginning of the revolution, as the provisional government began to lose credibility and became subject to intensifying hostility from several quarters Lenin gradually broadened the base of his power. The most serious challenge to the power of the provisional government occurred in the late summer of 1917, when Kornilov, a general of monarchist sympathies, despatched Cossack cavalry against Petrograd. The so-called Kornilov revolt came to nothing, but it precipitated a widespread increase in pro-Bolshevik feeling in the Soviets and convinced Lenin that the time was ripe for armed insurrection. Under the leadership of Leon Trotsky preparations were made for such an insurrection, Red Guard units were placed in a state of readiness and in late October, with the active assistance of sailors from the Baltic fleet, the Winter Palace was stormed and the provisional government overthrown.

The triumph of Bolshevik power in Petrograd was no more than a preliminary to what was to become a time of troubles throughout the greater part of the former Russian Empire. The violent confrontations between Bolshevik-led Reds and the anti-Bolshevik Whites were merely a feature of what was a haphazardly lawless period in which the former enemy, the Germans, became partial allies and the former allies, principally the British and French, took on the role of villains. National as well as class enmities, racial as well as political hatreds, minority as well as majority aspirations, all had a part to play in the ensuing upheavals.

By the time of the treaty of Brest-Litovsk, in early March 1918, which ensured peace between Germany and the new Soviet government, civil war had already broken out in the Don area. Ukrainian and Cossack nationalism began to play a conspicuous part in fomenting mistrust of the new régime. Moreover, under Generals Kornilov and Alekseyev a Volunteer Army of former Tsarist officers and White sympathisers had been formed and this force gradually became the nucleus of large-scale military opposition to the Red Army. Some of the richest agricultural areas in southern Russia soon passed largely out of Soviet control with the upsurge of counter-revolutionary forces, and the link with Siberia and the Far East was either impaired or severed by the fact that in May 1918 a Czech army corps seized control of some of the major stations on the Trans-Siberian railway. The Soviet government, virtually ignored by Russia's former allies, had become isolated and embattled in its new capital of Moscow, to which the centre of government had removed when Petrograd proved too vulnerable.

By the end of 1918 the White armies in the south, under the command of Denikin, had made significant gains and Admiral Kolchak had been declared Supreme Commander of the Whites in Omsk. With the approach of the German defeat in the West, their puppet in the Ukraine, Skoropadsky, was ousted by the socialist Petlyura. In the meantime the issue was complicated by the allied intervention. It was ostensibly undertaken with the object of protecting military property but in fact it contributed to an aggravation of the conflict by tending to aid the anti-Soviet effort in the civil war. Troops, chiefly British, landed in Murmansk and at Baku. United States and Japanese troops landed at Vladivostok. At the beginning of 1919, therefore, the anti-Soviet counter-revolutionary movement had acquired an international complexion. Victory for the Soviet cause became equated with the ideal of proletarian socialism triumphing over capitalist imperialism, but in immediate practical terms it meant the mobilisation of armies of workers to meet the challenge posed by the largely peasant armies recruited in the White cause.

During 1919 a threefold threat to Soviet power developed. The first threat came from Kolchak's armies advancing on Moscow from the east. Soviet forces under Frunze were able to inflict serious reverses on Kolchak's troops and by the summer the threat from that quarter had virtually evaporated. Far more serious was the second threat posed by Denikin in the south. Throughout the summer his armies had successes and by mid-October had come within 250 miles (400 km) of Moscow. Simultaneously a third threat developed with the attack of Yudenich on Petrograd. Soviet counter-attacks eventually succeeded in disposing of Yudenich's threat and driving Denikin back to his last base of Novorossisk on the Black Sea. He handed over command to another White General, Wrangel, who established his military base in the Crimea.

In 1920 the civil-war situation became temporarily more complex with the Polish invasion of the Ukraine and the capture of Kiev. Budyonny's Red Cavalry achieved rapid fame with the panache of its encircling movement against the Poles and contributed to the hasty retreat of the Polish forces towards Warsaw. Wrangel now broke out of the Crimea and threatened the Soviet rear. But the Red advance against Poland was stemmed in August and then reversed, a situation that led to an armistice in October. This permitted the Red Army to devote all its efforts to the defeat of the last White stronghold in the Crimea. In November 1920 a bloody but heroic assault by Red Army troops on the White defences in the Isthmus of Perekop brought about final victory and drove Wrangel from Russian soil. So ended the major military engagements of the civil war.

All major political revolutions create their own mythology and invite renewed scrutiny of their allegorical effectiveness. This is not to deny that revolutions are part of history. The French Revolution created historical tremors that spread, ever widening and dissipating, throughout the nineteenth century, but its mythology has acquired an effectiveness extending beyond purely historical limits. To treat it as did Thomas Carlyle as though it were the enactment of anarchic forces, as the irruption of the fanatical and irrational into an age of conventionalities, is to pump the historical fact so full of windy rhetoric as to render it practically incredible. But Carlyle appreciated the mythological appeal of the French Revolution. He identified as the mythological source what he called the '"destructive wrath" of Sansculottism'.

Surely a great Phenomenon: nay it is a *transcendental* one, overstepping all rules and experience; the crowning Phenomenon of our Modern Time. For here again, most unexpectedly, comes antique Fanaticism in new and newest vesture; miraculous, as all Fanaticism is.[1]

Sansculottism was to purge the world of falsehood and to provide the miraculous beginning for a new truth. Revolutionary fanaticism has always been assumed to have this grandiose function – to sweep away the former hierarchies and conventions, abolish the rotten privileges of the past, burn away the tawdry trappings and allow a new truth to blossom from the ashes of the old. Or, to put it in the grandiloquent phraseology of a Carlyle, revolutionary fanaticism was to be the miraculous World-Phoenix: 'Behold the World-Phoenix, in fire-consummation and fire-creation...skyward lashes the funeral flame, enveloping all things: it is the Death–Birth of a World!'[2]

The idea of simultaneous death–birth is one that illuminates the literary response to the Russian Revolution and civil war. It identifies the phoenix spirit that is elementally involved in the vitality of a literature, that makes literature the survivor of events as well as their consummation, their chronicler and their recreator. The metaphor of revolution as a birth trauma is no doubt hackneyed, but viewed against the fiery backdrop of death and destruction that colours all experience in the Russian revolutionary novel the idea of birth and motherhood is frequently the only symbolic means of expressing renewal and vitality. It is the miraculous event that sustains, though in its outward appearance it may resemble the obscenity of death. As Lenin described it:

Human childbirth is an act which transforms the woman into an almost lifeless, bloodstained heap of flesh, tortured, tormented and driven frantic by pain. But can the 'individual' that sees *only* this in love and its sequel, in the transformation of the woman into a mother, be regarded as a human being? Who would renounce love and procreation for *this* reason?

...Marx and Engels, the founders of scientific socialism, always said that the transition from capitalism to socialism would be inevitably accompanied by *prolonged birthpangs*.[3]

In the end, as the Russian revolutionary novel demonstrates, what endured beyond revolution and civil strife was precisely the love that transcended the birth trauma, the love at the conception and the parental love towards the new-born child. But the odour of sexuality and blood is what dominates the initial literary response; the instincts, not reasoned appraisal, assert their power over human conduct in the first revolutionary novels.

In any literature about revolution it is valuable to remind ourselves of the pressures that language itself has to sustain in meeting the challenge of the myth. It is impossible, of course, to separate the myth from the human image or to make a sharp distinction between the revolutionary ideal and the language used to give expression to it. Raymond Williams provides the useful reminder that:

Almost all our revolutionary language in fact comes from the Romantics, and this has been a real hindrance as well as an incidental embarrassment. Romanticism is the most important expression in modern literature of the first impulse of revolution: a new and absolute image of man. Characteristically, it relates this transcendence to an ideal world and an ideal human society; it is in Romantic literature that man is first seen as making himself.[4]

The idea of man making, or remaking, himself is one that we find at the very beginnings of the Russian revolutionary novel, and it proved to be central to the heroic ideal that early Soviet literature had to create for the revolution of October. In his foreword to *Literature and Revolution*, Trotsky, writing in 1923, insisted that the literature of the immediate future would inevitably have the revolution as its theme and object:

The art of this epoch will be entirely under the sign of revolution. It demands a new awareness. It is incompatible, first of all, with mysticism, whether overt or disguised as romanticism, because revolution proceeds from the central idea that only collective man should be lord and master and the limits of his power are to be defined only by his knowledge of the forces of nature and his ability to use them. It is incompatible with pessimism, scepticism and all other forms of spiritual exhaustion. It is realistic, active, full of a spirit of active collectivism and limitless creative faith in the future.[5]

All the overblown rhetoric of revolutionary romanticism is there in Trotsky's words, just as the image of man remade in the likeness of a collective hero is offered as the ideal to be emulated by revolutionary art. The actual forms of that art may have had all the bold, sloganising simplicity of Mayakovsky's *okna ROSTA*, the angularity of Lissitzky, the tautness of Tatlin, but so far as literature was concerned such a supposedly non-tragic, non-individualistic, overtly optimistic literature could be expected only to promote official policies and to serve as little more than propaganda. Trotsky

himself was not an advocate of such a debased literature; he
acknowledged to some degree the autonomy of art,[6] but there is no
denying that his view of literature tended to give it a subservient role.
The validity of its place in responding to the revolutionary changes
occurring in society was to be judged by its ability to create an image
of collective man who would know how to use the forces of nature
and be able to demonstrate 'a spirit of active collectivism and
limitless creative faith in the future.' The denial of pessimism and
scepticism would of course relieve literature of its most important
prerogative: the right to depict human experience as tragic. At the
end of the revolutionary novel, seen in this light, the rest would never
be silence and Hamlet himself would never be accorded the last rites
of a tragic hero. For the tragic hero would be abolished and tragedy
itself as a condition incompatible with the optimistic, collectivist
spirit of the new society would become outmoded. Could any
literature worthy of the name flourish in such an arid, sterile soil?
Could the long tradition of the Russian realistic novel, so profoundly
and honestly committed to exploring all conditions of humanity, be
expected to survive into a revolutionary age that denied it the right
to depict man as doomed? These are questions which, if unspoken,
always lurked in the background of critical thinking. To acknowledge
them was to admit to a tragic aspect of revolution that contradicted
to some degree the notion of revolution as materially and spiritually
liberating for all men. Perhaps the very idea of 'the tragedy of
revolution' is an impossibility, much as the idea that for Christian
believers heaven is tragic must seem impossible. But we know in our
hearts that, so long as human actions can produce tragic results,
revolutions will be tragic, and a literature born of revolutionary
experience will have the right to expose such tragedy. Raymond
Williams, writing of 'the tragedy of revolution', has done a further
service to criticism by pointing out that the idea of 'the total
redemption of humanity' so essential to revolution is not incompatible with a tragic view of life:

This idea of 'the total redemption of humanity' has the ultimate cast of
resolution and order, but in the real world its perspective is inescapably
tragic. It is born in pity and terror: in the perception of a radical disorder
in which the humanity of some men is denied and by that fact the idea of
humanity itself is denied. It is born in the actual suffering of real men thus
exposed, and in all the consequences of this suffering: degeneration,
brutalisation, fear, hatred, envy. It is born in an experience of evil made the

more intolerable by the conviction that it is not inevitable, but is the result of particular actions and choices.

And if it is thus tragic in its origins – in the existence of a disorder that cannot but move and involve – it is equally tragic in its action, in that it is not against gods or inanimate things that its impulse struggles, nor against mere institutions and social forms, but against other men. This, throughout, has been the area of silence, in the development of the idea. What is properly called utopianism, or revolutionary romanticism, is the suppression or dilution of this quite inevitable fact.[7]

The Russian revolutionary novel, as a particular kind of novel responding to particular needs, can be said to bear out the problem identified here. Although what might be called utopianism or revolutionary romanticism can easily be discerned in some of the novels, the 'inevitable fact' of the tragedy that springs from a denial of the idea of humanity itself, from the consequences of suffering, from an experience of evil resulting from particular actions and choices, is the chief theme, the living heart of the finest revolutionary novels and the one significant feature that unites them to the long tradition of the realistic novel in Russian literature.

Yet it is hard to speak of continuity in this context, not because the 'inevitable fact' fades or vanishes, but because the form of the genre itself undergoes such profound changes. As a leading historian of the Russian Revolution has put it: 'Every great revolution affords a concrete illustration of Schiller's phrase: "Die Weltgeschichte ist das Weltgericht." ("The history of the world is the judgement of the world.")'[8]

If the Russian Revolution was the judgement on Russian history, it may not be too extravagant to argue that the Russian revolutionary novel can be considered as the judgement on the Russian novel. A novelistic tradition that can survive the shock of a revolution against its own tradition must demonstrate the inherent vitality of the genre. That there is sufficient continuity to enable us to speak of it as a tradition in Russian literature is a contention of this study. In brief, then, the Russian revolutionary novel sprang out of a revolutionary situation that developed in Russia after the Crimean War. It had several sources, but it was above all a central element in the evolution of a realistic literature responding to the aspirations of a radical intelligentsia. Though the greatest novels of Turgenev, Dostoyevsky and Tolstoy cannot be said to have a revolutionary purpose, they could not help reflecting, as any truly realistic literature must, the revolutionary ideas and desires that were part of the intelligentsia's political ambitions for Russian society. More than this, the great Russian novels of the 1860s and the 1870s had a role to play in an on-going polemic. They were manifestly contentious and publicistic in the name of a better life, a better society and a better future. None of the greatest novelists was, strictly speaking, a novelist of the intelligentsia. Dostoyevsky and Tolstoy were openly opposed to most of the revolutionary aims of the intelligentsia and urged instead the adoption of religious ideals that the intelligentsia was only prepared to contemplate seriously in the decade immediately preceding the revolution of 1917 (as *Signposts* was to prove). Their novels were, however, motivated by a desire for change that was expressed at its keenest and most obvious in the revolutionary novel.

With the destruction of the pre-revolutionary intelligentsia Russian literature lost a central and traditional *motif*. It also lost a role and a readership. In the context of the novel, this tended to mean that, as the socio-economic and political circumstances changed, so the novel as a 'bourgeois' form ceased to have a role. Equally, its independently polemical role as a critical mirror of social life, seen at its finest in *Anna Karenina* or *The Brothers Karamazov*, acquired a more overtly political bias with Gorky's *Mother* or tended to distance the political reality by universalising it in the symbol of Bely's *Petersburg*. Arguably such changes in the pre-revolutionary novel might be taken to indicate that realism itself as a literary method was being challenged and that, as a consequence, the novel of character, the ideological novel, the novel as chronicle and criticism of its times was already showing signs of fragmentation. But more certainly the very contentiousness of the 'serious' novel, which owed so much to the question-asking traditions of the Russian intelligentsia, simply ceased to have relevance. Revolutionary events overtook its revolutionism. The grand and human tradition to which it belonged became channelled into what can be called the revolutionary novel but in a form that displayed in its most elementary nakedness the formlessness of the novel as a literary genre, its aptitude for novelty in the simplest sense.

If one poses the question: what kind of novel is to be found in early Soviet literature? there is no easy answer. Categories, like literary forms, liquefied. Russia, as the critic Voronsky observed in 1922, was 'in a post-earthquake state'.[9] Or as Trotsky put it, referring in particular to Pilnyak but making a point of general validity for the literature of the period:

Revolution is a bivouac life. Private life, institutions, methods, thoughts and feelings – it's all out of the ordinary, temporary, transitional, aware of its temporary nature and almost always expressing itself even in the very name given to it. Hence the difficulty of the artistic approach. The bivouac life and episodic experience have an element of the accidental in them, and this accidental element has the mark of insignificance on it. Revolution, taken episode by episode, seems suddenly insignificant. Where is the revolution? That's the difficulty. The difficulty will only be overcome by the man who understands and plumbs to its very depths the meaning of this episodic experience and reveals behind it the historical axis of its crystallisation.[10]

The novel, which as a literary form had been nourished by its relevance to society, reacted to the fundamental unsureness of the revolution by stressing precisely the episodic and accidental character of the experience. In short, it became episodic, fragmented, fluid. Part of the consequent literary revolution involved a revolt against definitions, so that to describe some works as 'novels' (Pilnyak's *The Naked Year*, Malyshkin's *Fall of Dair*, Furmanov's *Revolt*) is to say very little in terms of defining them. The fluidity of the form also reflected the abundance of works and writers that appeared in the wake of the revolutionary events.[11] Any examination of the subject has to confront the question: Is this a novel or isn't it?[12] In the case of this study the choice has been based on criteria of relevance – how close a reflection of revolutionary experience the work is – and of adequacy and profundity (in Trotsky's sense in the final sentence of the above quotation). All questions of 'adequacy' and 'profundity' in judging the effectiveness of literary response in a genre such as the novel ultimately depend on a writer's ability to create character or to reflect the human scale of an event. Of course, a literature that has given birth to a new style, as one critic has put it, 'of hard surfaces that reflected brilliantly and refracted feebly',[13] cannot – or perhaps should not – be judged in terms more appropriate to its nineteenth-century predecessors. Its relevance to revolutionary experience makes it seem a bivouac literature – and the initial, avowedly experimental examples of the revolutionary novel in early Soviet literature are proof of this. But no critical assessment is going to claim that such examples can be considered adequate, let alone profound. The ability of a writer and his work to reflect the human scale of an event is the criterion used in all the principal Soviet assessments, so that it is not surprising to find the search for the revolutionary hero becoming the principal concern of both novelists and critics as soon as the first experimental wave of revolutionary novels had passed.

Any anticipation of adequate, even profound, instances of revolutionary characterisation may perhaps be nipped in the bud by recalling Ralph Fox's outspoken criticism that 'the least credible figures in the novels written about revolution are the revolutionaries'.[14] It is a harsh judgement, but one worthy of respect if only because Ralph Fox was the only English critic with communist sympathies to confront the issue of literature and revolution. More significantly, though, it underlines the problem of all writers, and especially all novelists, who can so easily be seduced by 'the fatal lure of action'[15] into attempting to create reality as well as fiction, to be the part in life as well as the active, revolutionary character in their novels. So that the revolutionary novelist can easily find himself consumed by a crisis of identity and in the process lose sight of the need for credibility in what he creates.

For Henry Fielding, as was mentioned in the Introduction, the genius required by the novelist must involve what he called 'invention' and 'judgment'. The 'discovery' of revolution (to use Fielding's explanatory term) naturally became the first aim of all those writers who offered the initial literary response to the revolution of 1917 and the ensuing civil war. 'Judgment' as such was suspended at the beginning. But for a novelist to be a novelist at all, he must employ 'judgment' in his attempt to discover the true essence of things, and when a clear distinction has to be made between two things, as must inevitably be the case in the novel concerned with violent revolutionary change, the 'judgment' displayed by the novelist is the true measure of that novelist's genius. In the same way, one measure perhaps of the awfulness of such catastrophes as revolution and civil war is that they numb the judgement so essential to profound literary understanding. But all else is numbed as well, and the reaction of a literature to such an event, like any human reaction to shock, is one of gradual recovery of poise in which the element of 'invention' is slowly nourished by an increasing awareness of the need for 'judgment'.

The absence of this element in the first revolutionary novels of the Soviet period produced a concomitant emphasis on the importance of instinct as the basic human response to revolution. It tended to be equated with a natural phenomenon over which human beings had no control. Only later, about half a dozen years after the end of the civil war, did this view yield to an emphasis on the ideals and ideologies that collided during the revolutionary period. At this point

both the elements in Fielding's definition of a novelist's genius began
to assert their rightful priority in depicting revolutionary conflict and
in creation of character. By this time, also, the revolutionary novel
of the Soviet period began to acquire a stable form, which in turn
gave rise to an enlargement of that form into works of epic
proportion.

I *Revolution and instinct*

Introduction

For Andrey Bely revolution 'reminds one of nature: thunder, floods,
waterfalls: everything about it "spills over"', everything is extreme',[16]
but in literary terms it was 'the act of conception for creative forms
which had been gestating for decades'.[17] His own gestation as a writer
had achieved its act of conception in *Petersburg*, and his post-
revolutionary novels, though claiming to be full of 'historical
thunder', were really filled with 'philological thunderings' and had
nothing important to add to his own brand of revolutionary novel.[18]
An imagery of wind, thunder and natural calamity, however, became
a hallmark of literature about revolution. But the most obvious sign
of excess, the release of instinctive forces due to revolution, is to be
seen in the emphasis on sexual licence. As a commentator remarked:
'The revolution is permeated through and through by sexuality,
becomes inseparable from it and ultimately dissolves in it. The
philosophy of history is very nearly replaced by the problem of sex.'[19]
This is not only a gestating of the decadent pornographic trends
observable in Artsybashev's *Sanin*, Kuzmin's *Wings* and Sologub's
The Petty Demon in the pre-revolutionary novel, but an emphasis
deriving chiefly from Pilnyak's *The Naked Year*, a work that in so
many respects set the tone for the literary response to revolution in
the immediate post-revolutionary period.

It became almost a literary convention for the effect of revolution
on a stagnant Russian provincial life to be expressed in terms of
violent sexual release. Nikitin's *Fort Vomit* (1922) illustrates the
torpid, lecherous indolence of provincial life in the limited ambience
of a small fort during the civil war. Lust wearies all the inhabitants
of the place, including the flies, but it is not so much the explicit
sexuality of the relationships as the sensuous stylistic atmospherics
that give the work its distinction. Staccato short sentences, scraps of
dialogue, shorthand cursory details and a repetitious imagery are the
most conspicuous components of the prose–poetic manner. The

compression inevitable in this manner of writing must always court sketchiness and Nikitin's manner tends to look sketchy by comparison with Pilnyak's or Vsevolod Ivanov's.

A more successful work on a similar theme is Sergey Budantsev's *Revolt* (1923).[20] Soviet power in a provincial town is overthrown by a revolt of officers. The revolt is fairly quickly suppressed by pro-Bolshevik troops. A staccato, disjointed manner, giving brief glimpses of events and scraps of conversation, deliberately avoids consecutive narrative. The references to the sun are almost the only sure indicator of the changing fortunes from White to Red, as it were: sick imagery, invoking addiction and deadness, accompanies the White revolt, whereas an imagery suggesting brightness, colour and light marks the Bolshevik resurgence. For example, 'the sun expanded like the eye of a cocaine addict, and the hands of the clock moved convulsively towards TEN' and 'The day stretched out at unbelievable length...the day was restless as an aching tooth; just like a tooth it fell out of the gaping mouth of regular time. But out of the clock-faces wide as the sun hours nevertheless occasionally dropped' are instances of the imagery associated with the White revolt, while the dawning of the day of the pro-Bolshevik resurgence is signalled by the following elaborate, domestic, Gogolian arabesque:

As if it were golden overripened grapes, as if it were blindingly clean and warm, like a bronze door handle rubbed with stone powder by a zealous housewife's green-stained cloths, the day freed itself from the first green light and dawned.

As the army commander Kalabukhov described it, 'Time seems to me sweet and condensed, like American canned milk', and it is precisely the condensed, almost impacted, manner of writing that, in startling imagery and the use of documents, newspaper reports, statements obtained during interrogation and apparently deliberate misusages,[21] effectively creates an atmosphere of inconsequence and fragmentation. The clockwork-governed portrayal of the human dimension of events in the novel is characteristic of a cynicism most evident in Kalabukhov's admission to his sister, who has accused him of having killed their father, that the revolution has long since exhausted his capacity for love:

'I've long ago forgotten how to love you or father or Yelena...I can love only moving surfaces, protuberances, geometric forms – towns and algebraic signs that are called populations, humanity, classes...'[22]

Knowing how unconvincing this may sound, he goes on:

'...to love these bloody and living abstractions means to make every single step one takes dangerous and fatal...Have pity on me that wherever I go I imperil you and everyone...Everyone can shed tears. But I, who have seen rivers of blood, can be touched and moved to tears only by oceans of it...'

For him the human heart can accommodate only one love; to attempt to force other loves into it would only make it explode. Budantsev's novel strictly speaking accommodates no love at all. Its human components are heartlessness and mindlessness, and even the most cultured, such as the former members of the Russian intelligentsia, Kalabukhov and his assistant Severov, have obliterated their feelings with cynicism or morphine addiction. Although Soviet power triumphs at the end, what the novel appears most to emphasise is human impotence in the face of revolutionary events.

The instinctive and spontaneous response to revolution is celebrated most powerfully and vividly in the work of Artyom Vesyoly. His *Russia Washed in Blood* (1925–32) is a 'fragment' – a subtitle that acknowledges an important truth about all novels on revolutionary themes: their inability to convey more than a fragmentary part of the total experience. Vesyoly's was an exciting but untamed talent; erratic, undisciplined, volatile, he wrote 'with a flourish', as his most important Soviet critic described it

...with sharp, colour-rich strokes. He does not draw out the details of setting or the subtleties of experience, as if in a desperate hurry to say what he had to say, but the most important thing he could say at that moment, to fix on paper one feature, but by far the most expressive. And the picture he creates is impressive and unforgettable.[23]

It is certainly true that no novelist expressed the sheer rapture of the first anarchic days of the revolutionary freedom more brilliantly. The opening sections of his novel have an impetuous freshness, hard to sustain at best and inevitably yielding to a fragmentary, more pedestrian manner towards the end, but in many of his exuberant codas he matches – and tends frankly to imitate – the stepped grandiloquence of Mayakovsky's *150,000,000* and other poems. Describing, for example, the epoch of soldiers' meetings in the summer of 1917, when the troops were 'voting with their feet', in Lenin's phrase, and leaving the front lines in droves:

Locomotives bellowed, the soldiers started to disperse without waiting for the long resolution about supporting the Bolsheviks to be finished, shouting:

'That's right! That's right! Down with war!' Trains unwound away into the distance.

Ropes with bells were stretched from the engines through all the rolling-stock. They slept with one eye open. The moment there was cause for alarm the bells began ringing, guns were fired, hooters sounded. They'd beat off attacks and roll on further.

Wheels chattered
          scattering
               stations
                    faces
                       days
                         nights...

The troops had a wild look, everywhere the people shouted like drunks.

The picture of the anarchic movement of the troops from the front is kaleidoscopic. Disorder, drunkenness, meetings, fragmentary glimpses of characters and snatches of dialogue, all are caught up in the continually rhythmic movement of the prose, supported by an unpretentious ornamentalism. The central figure in the opening sections is the lively peasant soldier Maxim Kuzhel' who is elected to the soldiers' committee after the February revolution. His growing awareness of the new power that he and the mass of peasant soldiers have acquired with the collapse of traditional authority is the only true measure of psychological and political change in the novel, but his later experiences in Novorossisk and in the steppes during the civil war hardly develop his characterisation at all. Sections devoted to the Cossack family of Chernoyarov, especially the youngest son, Ivan, who becomes the leader of a nomadic brigand band, anticipate or imitate Sholokhov, just as a section devoted to the capture of Yekaterinodar reads like a watered-down episode from Aleksey Tolstoy's *The Road to Calvary*. Vesyoly may have had little gift for 'invention', in Fielding's sense, little *understanding*, in a practical political sense. As M. Charny puts it:

Sometimes it seems that Artyom Vesyoly is bewitched by the storms of emotions, commotion of characters, instincts fiercely uncoiling like springs, the competing emotions of bravery and debauchery, as if the author were frightened that the contact of ideas would spoil the impression of immediacy to be obtained from the powerful beauty of the unfolding picture.[24]

In other words, he emphasised the instinctive elements at work in the revolution and civil war and gave no emphasis to the guidance provided by political ideas. The warmest tribute that could be paid to his talent has stressed that 'in the entire history of Soviet literature it would be hard to find a writer whose democratic feeling was as powerful, elemental and impassioned as Artyom Vesyoly's'.[25] His evolution as a writer was 'complex', as Soviet commentators put it euphemistically, meaning that it was unorthodox and tragic.[26]

Vesyoly's achievement and fate invite comparison with Izaak Babel's. Of the writers persecuted under Stalin none has acquired the same degree of posthumous fame as he; none has left us a smaller body of work with which to sustain that fame.[27] He composed the thirty-four quite brief sketches that comprise his *Red Cavalry* (1926) with masterly exactitude and exemplary slowness. So slowly did he write that by the time of the first Congress of Soviet Writers in 1934 there was a recognisable element of truth, as well as an acid irony, in his own self-deprecating claim that he had become 'the master of the genre of silence'. He spoke of the right to write badly, which must be the prerogative of all who aspire to write at all, and in a totalitarian atmosphere that kind of talk can easily be made to have a seditious ring to it.

His *Red Cavalry* cannot be regarded as a novel, despite the extreme fluidity of the form of the genre in the 1920s. Yet it has as much formal cohesion as many works of the period that have a right to be described as novels. It can claim our attention in an 'introduction' to the revolutionary novel of the Soviet period because it summarises the principal effects of violent revolutionary experience on a cultured individual better than any other literary work. By any standards it is a masterpiece. It enters a reader's blood with an enduring intensity. Like all great tragic works of art, it has the power to haunt – chiefly through the sharp contrast drawn between the meekness of war's victims and the baroque machismo of the Cossack martial ethos. The intensity with which this contrast is made through the medium of Babel's intricate and richly imagistic style highlights it as a unique study of the incongruous. Babel proves himself the unexampled master of that rapid juxtaposition of opposed or inappropriate facets which is at the source of all bizarre human experience.

An integral part of the incongruity is the pervasive contrast between an apparently mindless Cossack soldiery, the fugitive beauties of the natural scene and the Jewish–Polish–Catholic culture that the narrator finds as great a culture-shock as he does the Russo-Polish war.[28] The portraits of the Cossacks have pseudo-heroic

and heraldic proportions in equal measure. Some degree of irony and
parodistic exaggeration is discernible in the picture of Savitsky,
commander of the Sixth Division, whose 'long legs were like girls
sheathed to the neck in shining riding-boots' ('My First Goose');
or in the life story of Matvey Rodionich Pavlichenko, the Red
General, who wreaks a terrible vengeance on his former master, the
merry Nikitinsky, whom he trampled on for an hour or maybe more:

'And in that time I got to know life through and through...With shooting
you'll never get at the soul, to where it is in a fellow and how it shows itself.
But I don't spare myself, and I've more than once trampled an enemy for
over an hour...'[29]

The Cossacks, depicted as uncaring, unworried and two-
dimensionally heroic, are garishly projected as the instruments of
violent revolutionary change. The author–narrator coexists with
them, but he is never part of them.

In general, the author–narrator is neutral in his sympathies,
although there is no doubt that he feels himself drawn into a love–hate
relationship with the Jewish culture of Eastern Poland and the
aesthetic appeal of the Catholic Polish culture. The figures of Pan
Apolek, the painter, and Gedali, the antiquarian, are the most
carefully drawn of all the figures in the book. They epitomise the
virtues of artistic flair, artistic vividness, linked somewhat incongruously with the humility of the intellectual hanger-on (or *obyvatel'*),
the non-participant observer of life, which are the twin principal
facets of Babel himself as the work's creator. Pan Apolek, the
illustrator of local life, employs a religious and hagiographic manner,
just as Babel the narrator clothes his own subjects in a vivid and
ornate prose–poetry that has echoes of a psalmic, quasi-biblical style.
By the same token, Pan Apolek's art bears a similarity to Babel's in
its refusal to suggest censure or approval, judgement or compassion;
it proclaims no more than humanity's conceit, pride, self-possession
or humility, weakness and passivity. If Babel himself cannot bring
himself to kill, or implores fate to grant him 'the simplest of
proficiencies – the ability to kill my fellow-men', then in the humility
of Gedali he portrays the source of all human goodness. For it is
Gedali, and only he, among the many portrayals, who expresses a
sense of the pure futility of revolution, in the name of which the
slaughter and suffering are taking place. Gedali's is in essence the
same vision of how the world should be as is the narrator's. He insists

that the revolution should mean joy, an International of good people. So also does the narrator who, like the mad squadron commander Khlebnikov, looked on the world as a meadow in May – a meadow traversed by women and horses ('The Story of a Horse'). For this reason as much as from intellectual cowardice or conscience he cannot kill the terribly wounded Dolgushov and rides into battle without cartridges. In the guise of his narrator, K. Lyutov, Babel offers the memory that is the source of the ultimate incongruity in time of revolution and war: the ideal of peace.

On Sabbath days I am oppressed by the dense melancholy of memories. In bygone days on these occasions my grandfather would stroke the volumes of Ibn Ezra with his yellow beard. His old woman in her lace cap would trace fortunes with knotty fingers over the Sabbath candles, and sob softly to herself. On those evenings my child's heart was rocked like a little ship upon enchanted waves. O the rotted Talmuds of my childhood! O the dense melancholy of memories.

At the crossroads of the violent winds of the century all that can arouse compassion is the memory of one's mother. So said the wise antiquarian Gedali. It can serve as an epitaph to Babel's incongruously beautiful picture of the death–birth of a world.[30]

Nowhere does Babel explain the political purposes of the war, save by the oblique, whimsical comments of a Gedali. Revolution is expressed at its most eloquent in the instinctive machismo of the Cossacks. The unprotesting and poeticising attitude of the narrator towards the brutality that he witnesses is the most eloquent testimony to its barbarism, but it is simultaneously an abandonment of narrator's judgement. Such an attitude can be compared with Vsevolod Ivanov's celebrated study of revolutionary sacrifice in the short work *Armoured Train No 14,69* (1922). It is the story of the halting of a White armoured train on its way to assist in suppressing a Bolshevik uprising in Vladivostok. A Chinaman, who has joined the local peasant partisans, volunteers to lie down on the rails in the train's path. This act of heroism obviously has its purpose, but the White officers on the train are represented as crude and degenerate, the partisan leader Vershinin is hardly more than a cut-out and the Chinaman himself, Sin-Bin-U, is a chopsuey of mispronounced Russian words. In short, the story and the characters are banal. All that gives strength and sinew to the work are the forceful descriptions of the bleakly inhospitable seaboard terrain that forms the story's setting. Equally, though by its all-too-obvious propaganda for the

Bolshevik cause it can be said to demonstrate a political purpose, it exhibits the lack of depth in characterisation and in understanding that are symptomatic of the short story and less common in the novel (though, as we shall see, Vsevolod Ivanov's novels are not without this blemish). Babel's collection of brilliant stories contains the very essence of the novel: a deep humanistic conviction that life is non-episodic in form, non-schematic in intent. Vsevolod Ivanov's story is fundamentally one episode, and all the characters are tailored to suit the story's schematic purpose.

A novel that enjoyed very great success was A. Neverov's *Tashkent, City of Bread* (1923). It has the proportions and depth of a novel, in the sense that it explores a protracted and ramifying experience, even though it is basically a work of children's literature. It is the story of Mishka Dodonov, a twelve-year-old peasant boy, who, in the famine year of 1922, in the immediate aftermath of the civil war, makes a 1500-mile journey from his starving village to find the food that rumour claims is still abundant in Tashkent, city of bread. The picture that emerges is one of a mass peasant movement that sucks Mishka into it, but the real portraiture of the novel is achieved in the portrayal of Mishka himself, his stoicism, ebullience, enterprise and guts. He leaves behind him a fatherless family, with a mother who is dying and two starving brothers. His journey begins in the company of another boy, Seryozha, who dies of typhus. After many adventures, rejected by other peasants who are travelling on the precarious trains to the south, befriended by Bolshevik officials, he succeeds in reaching Tashkent and manages to earn enough to buy the seed-corn with which he finally returns to his native village.

Two further works deserve mention. They can be loosely classed as novels, though neither has the conventional appearance of a novel like Neverov's. Both are the work of Soviet women writers and are concerned with the reaction of women to revolutionary events.[31]

Lydia Seyfullina's *Virineya* (1924) tells of a peasant woman, Virineya or Virka, who had learned to read before the revolution and had even received some encouragement to 'improve herself' while she had been working in the city. She rejects the temptation and prefers to return to her village where she contracts an unhappy marriage. Her life reads conventionally enough: she falls in love with a stranger, a visiting engineer; the relationship brings shame on her; she begins to drink, leads an immoral life and is eventually widowed when her husband dies in prison after having been falsely suspected of murdering her lover. Left to her own devices, Virineya forms associations among the local soldiers, especially one of them, Pavel Suslov, who had been wounded in the Tsar's war and had recovered after treatment in a Moscow hospital. Pavel draws Virineya into working for the Bolshevik cause. During the civil war he actively organises the defence against the Cossacks, but in the meantime Virineya, realising she is pregnant, has to remain behind, and the work ends with the birth of her child and her own death after being seized by the Cossacks.

The telling is brisk and unornamented. There are chunks of naturalistic dialogue that may help to characterise but make tedious reading. The heroine's portrait is recognisably that of a simple but intelligent woman who is not really sparked into life until the revolution has set light to the world around her. She is to this extent a creature of circumstance and instinct, though Seyfullina successfully implies depths of misery and resentment in her heroine that make her characterisation appealing and explain the passion with which she finally devotes herself to the revolution.[32]

A much more sophisticated study of female reaction to revolution is to be found in the work of Marietta Shaginyan, especially her novel *The Change* (1924). It is evidently autobiographical in its description of the adventures of two girls, Lilya and Kusya, and their widowed mother in the Don region during the revolution and civil war. The story line is tenuous and the characterisation is thin, but there is liveliness, colour, acute observation, candour and a deftly ironic objectivity in the writing.

Such works as those mentioned in this 'introduction' to the theme of 'revolution and instinct' as it emerges in the earliest revolutionary novels of the Soviet period illustrate the range and variety of novella, novel-type or extended short story and other hybrid forms that are to be encountered. They show the striking mixture of modernism and traditionalism embraced in the prose fiction of the period. They also show not only that the revolution elicited many types of reactions from writers but also that literature itself acquired an instinct for change. It is a literature seemingly written by the events, seemingly authorless in its multi-faceted, multi-voiced response to the task of representing how one world died and another was born.

Conflicts of instincts: *Two Worlds*, *The Naked Year*, *One Week*
Vladimir Zazubrin's *Two Worlds* (1921) is generally regarded as the

first Soviet novel. Lenin said of it: 'Of course, it's not a novel', an accolade sufficient to give it a place of honour in Soviet literary histories.[33] Lenin added that it was 'a very frightening, horrifying book' and in this he was entirely correct. Although it has the formal shapelessness of a raw, semi-documentary work in which episode follows episode, its principal strength lies in its unflinching depiction of the savagery of the civil war in Siberia. The ideology emerges as unsubtle propaganda and the characterisation is never more than superficial. Paradoxically there is more about the White participation in the civil war than the Red, but this is partly dictated by the propaganda purposes of the novel.

The 'two worlds' of the title are of course those of the Whites and the Reds. As one of the Red characters expressed it: 'Two worlds, comrades, have met in mortal combat. There is no doubt that the new world will win. That is – we, we, comrades!' A White officer, comparing the civil war with the war against the central powers, expresses the bewilderment of a regular officer in circumstances of civil strife by saying that 'in this war it isn't the armaments that count but something else, certain obscure forces that are incomprehensible to me. All our victories in this war are based on something internal, something imperceptible.' The inability of the White officer to understand what is at stake in the civil war can be supposed to highlight the instinctive viciousness of the conflict. As a document the novel is memorable chiefly for the dispassionate and lurid detail with which it recounts the atrocities committed by the Whites under Admiral Kolchak. But it also attempts to show how revolutionary ideas may change a member of the officer class into a supporter of the proletarian cause. The officer is a certain Baranovsky, a very resourceful and dependable cadet, who has shown no political inclinations as an officer whether in the war against the central powers or in the civil war, but begins nevertheless to realise that the Red side may be superior.

Being a sensible man and a sensitive one, he had been undergoing recently a severe spiritual trauma. After the public statement by the captive brigade commander, on the basis of stories told by local inhabitants, on the basis of literature left by the Reds in the villages, he had formed a very good opinion of Soviet Russia...It was not so much in his mind, clearly, that is, and definitely, so much as in his soul, vaguely, that he had begun to feel truth was on the side of the Reds.

With such blatantly unsubtle psychological description Zazubrin conveys the beginnings of Baranovsky's change of heart. The end of the novel shows him and Commissar Molov, both recovering from typhus, engaged in arguing over the future. The unstated but clear implication is that Baranovsky, far from finding himself superfluous in Soviet Russia, will be able to participate actively in the creation of a new workers' republic.

The stridency and simplistic propaganda impact of *Two Worlds* were to be familiar features of dozens of Soviet novels on related themes. If the revolutionary novel of the Soviet period were to be limited to such works, then it would be a subject of purely historical and local interest. The inimitable, unique and enduring literary value of the Russian revolutionary novel rests on the heretical personalities of those writers who deliberately repudiated propaganda as a function of their literary role, though they necessarily became involved in the disabling and disenchanting conflict over commitment that so preoccupied writers during the first post-revolutionary decade. Of these heretics the first to achieve fame and influence was Boris Pilnyak with his most striking novel, *The Naked Year* (1922).

'Words are to me like money to a numismatist', Pilnyak wrote[34] and he treated them with the care, curiosity and enthusiasm of a fanatic. Zazubrin showed negligible verbal artistry in his own brand of revolutionary novel, but Boris Pilnyak could not help himself. He was an artist in words, unrivalled by any post-revolutionary writer with the possible exception of Babel and Olesha. He had the fondness of a collector for the antiquated and tarnished; his words have a worn, much-handled feel or perhaps a touch of verdigris from long neglect. They are always present in abundance in his work, suggesting the influence of such previous wordsmiths as Gogol and Bely and yet also possessing their own Pilnyakian richness of atmosphere and bizarre, jumbled variety. In no writer's work do words have as pungent a *smell* as in Pilnyak's. The much-quoted claim from his story 'Ivan and Maria' (1922) that 'the Revolution smells of sexual organs'[35] was to haunt Pilnyak throughout the Soviet period and no doubt contributed to his final tragedy. As a definition of revolution what it lacks in political tact it makes up for in biological candour.

Pilnyak was no intellectual, strictly speaking. He was certainly not a profound thinker. But he had a profound sense, evident from the earliest of his stories, of the biological essence of life and in his novel *The Naked Year* he gave very particular emphasis to the biological meaning of revolution as it expressed itself in Russian provincial life.

Superficially this might be taken to mean no more than a smell of sexual organs, sexual licence, drunken release, an assertion of the instinctive over the intellectual – for these are sensational features of revolution as Pilnyak depicted it in his novel. Yet his perception of revolution was much deeper and more complex. He insisted, for instance, that revolution in fact meant the exact opposite of the intelligentsia's vision of it. It meant an expression of purely physical, sensual licence, not the ascetic, puritanical denial of selfhood that the intelligentsia's monastic devotion to revolution proclaimed. It meant procreation in a bestial, instinctive sense, not the social engineering so dear to the intelligentsia's vision of the future. Pilnyak also insisted that it did not mean a revolution of the industrial proletariat but, rather, a backlash by populist, agrarian forces against the machine, against the city. In this process the 'leather jackets', Pilnyak's metaphor for the Bolsheviks, would be the midwives rather than the actual progenitors. With equal force Pilnyak insisted that revolution is elemental in nature and expresses itself instinctively in man. 'The Revolution came', as one character expresses it, 'like white blizzards and May storms' (p. 62). It came as a wind. The work is pervaded by the *noise* of wind, as is Blok's famous *The Twelve*. Here it is:

> And today's song in the snowstorm:
> – Snowstorm. Pines. Clearings. Terrors. –
> – Shooyaya, sho-yaya, shoooyayaya…
> – Gviuu, gaaauuu, gviiiiuuuu, gviiiiuuuu.
> And:-
> – Gla-vboomm!
> – Gla-vboomm!!
> – Goo-vooz! Goo-oo-voo-ooz!…
> – Shooya, gviiiuu, gaauuu…
> – Gla-vboommm!!
> And – (p. 31)

To the most articulate of the characters in this work, Boris Ordinin, the revolution represents both an element dominating human life and, by contrast, nothing more essentially effectual in terms of change than a boomerang. At the centre of the concentric circles that compose the novel is the Ordinins' world – a world of cathedral bells ('like a stone thrown into a creek with water lilies' (p. 80)), cloudy mirrors, unwholesome smells, syphilis and addiction. Here, in 1919, the brothers Boris and Gleb, grotesque latterday

martyrs of their beleaguered Orthodox world, discuss the issues that
beset the decaying Ordinin family, undermined by social collapse and
inherited disease. Boris describes what the revolution meant to him:

'One time in spring I was standing on Eagle Mountain looking at the water
meadows on the other side of the Vologa. It was spring, the Vologa had burst
its banks, the sky was blue – life was seething – both around me and within
me. And then, I remember, I wanted to embrace the world! I thought then
that I was the centre from which all radii spread out, that I was everything.
Later I realized that in life there are no radii or centres, that it is generally
revolution and that all things are just pawns in the paws of life' (p. 60).

The generality of revolution is something that the decaying
Ordinin household finds hard to accept. Doomed and morally
corrupted though the princely Ordinins may be, they seek in a
fragmentary, semi-articulate way to define their own problem and
the meaning of the revolution. Gleb, for instance, rehearses such
arguments as the indigenous piety of Russia, the Russian peasants'
worship of the figure of the Mother of God and the idea of revolution
as a return to pre-Petrine religiosity and religious sectarianism. He
asserts that the Russian intelligentsia cannot accept the October
Revolution:

'...The Russian intelligentsia did not follow October. And it couldn't. Since
Peter, Europe hovered over Russia, but below, under the rearing horse, lived
our people, like a thousand years ago, but the intelligentsia are the true
children of Peter...Every member of the intelligentsia repents, every one
grieves for the people, and every one knows nothing of the people. But
revolutions were unnecessary for popular rebellion – alien. Popular rebellion
is the seizing of power and creation of their own genuine Russian truth – by
genuine Russians. And this is a blessing!...The whole history of peasant
Russia is the history of sectarianism. Who will win this struggle – mechanized
Europe or sectarian, orthodox, spiritual Russia?...' (pp. 72–3).

But the principal object of attack in *The Naked Year* is the very
notion of statehood and all the apparatus of state control that the
concept implies. The revolution is to be a release above all from this.
Even though Pilnyak shows how the Bolsheviks inherit the Ordinin
house, they are represented simply as 'leather jackets' and appear
to have less overt political meaning in the context of his work than
do the anarchists. The anarchist commune, which flickers out its life
briefly during the summer of the naked revolutionary year, seems to
be the only political consequence of which Pilnyak approves, and
such approval is muted, perhaps neutralised, by his portrayal of the

leading anarchists as foreign to Russia, alien to Russia's spirit and, in the case of Comrade Laitis, unable to speak Russian correctly.

Revolution, so the confused argument of Pilnyak's work suggests, is deeper than beliefs. It is related organically to the fundamental processes of living and is thus akin to procreation and parturition. Its principal symbolic correlates are blood and birth. When Gleb Ordinin is speaking to the grey little priest, the following conversation makes the point clearly:

[The priest is speaking] 'You know, if you replace some of the words in your speech with the words – class, bourgeoisie, social inequality – you get Bolshevism!...But I want purity, truth – God, faith, universal justice...why blood?...'

'But, but, without blood? – everyone is born out of blood, red! And the flag is red! Everything's all mixed up, confused, you'll never understand it!...Do you hear the revolution howling – like a witch in a blizzard! Listen: Gviuu, gviiuu! Glav-buuum!...And the witches wiggling their rears and boobs...' (p. 75)

Gleb's saucy picture of revolution as Walpurgisnacht merely elaborates in comic folksy form the basic idea that it is born out of blood and enacts in a historical and social context the trauma of birth. In a conversation that follows shortly between Gleb and his sister Natalya, who has joined the Bolsheviks and is planning to leave home, she speaks as if she were equating Bolshevism and the revolution with her own personal, but loveless, yearning for a child. Such idealism is attended by a universal scepticism in Pilnyak's picture of the revolution. It is a revolution, for one thing, that has occurred in a semi-Asiatic, unrecognisably European country, as far removed culturally from European standards as the Middle Ages are from the twentieth century. To Comrade Yuzik, commenting philosophically to Andrei Ordinin on the human predicament *sub specie aeternitatis*, the revolution appears to have no significance beneath the light of the stars, but even such an earnest and poetic comment acquires a humorously sceptical tone through his speech impediment:

'What a quiet Spring here!' said Yuzik. 'And what quiet stars you have – they look so sad. Were you never attwacted by astwonomy? When you think about the stars, you begin to feel that we are totally insignificant. The earth is a worldly pwison; what are we, humans? What do our wevolution and injustice mean?' (p. 89)

In a spirit of profound irreverence that combines a keen awareness of the absurd with a sense of life's inherent value, Pilnyak created his own earthquake in the conventional, representational forms of the realistic novel. Reviewing Zazubrin's *Two Worlds*, he wrote:

The revolution is creating a new literary competence...The revolution has forced the plot-element (*fabula*) to be broken up into separate stories and has forced writers into writing according to a principle of displacement. The revolution has made the story operate with the masses – the masses of the people as an element have organically become the 'I' of the narrative.[36]

He might indeed have been writing about his own 'novel', which is less coherent in a formal sense than Zazubrin's and lacks even a chronology of civil-war events to give it narrative impulse. To speak of his work having 'heroes' in a formal sense would be impossible. The 'principle of displacement' means that apart from a loosely defined central section entitled 'Exposition' ('Izlozheniye') Pilnyak's novel is composed, as one commentator has put it, 'on a principle of concentric circles which encompass within their orbit separate parts of life that have been shaken to their foundations by the revolution'.[37] A panopticon effect results. There is no fixed viewpoint; all is displaced, whether by deliberately offering supposedly separate viewpoints ('Through Andrei's Eyes', 'Through Natalya's Eyes', etc.) or fragmentary separate stories (of Donat, old Arkhipov, etc.) or interruptions of dialogue passages with luscious, rhythmic descriptions of nature. In such a shaken kaleidoscope of fragmented impressions the pictures of revolutionary experience quickly separate into extremes of absurd degradation and absurd activity.

The absurd degradation is a vision of hell as Train No. 57 crawls across the black steppe. Crammed into it is the human detritus of civil war afflicted with lice and disease. Rapine, hunger and death amid stench and sickness are the brutalising and dehumanising accompaniments of the train's aimless journey. The glimpse of inexpressibly awful suffering is unrivalled for its expressionist harshness in any revolutionary novel of the early 1920s. The absurd activity, similarly distanced and therefore appearing aimless in its apparent irrelevance, describes the work of the 'leather jackets' at Mine No. 3 of the Taezhevsky factory, drilling and loading blast-holes. The Bolsheviks had chiefly to be seen to 'fuction energetically' (*energichno fuktsirovat'*) as their semi-literate spokesman somewhat ambiguously expresses it. All such fragmented impressions are dominated by Pilnyak's concern to make his 'story operate with the masses', as it were, to demonstrate the revolution as a mass experience. This becomes a pronounced feature of several early examples of the revolutionary novel of the Soviet period.

In Pilnyak's *The Naked Year* the masses, whether the anonymous peasantry, the inhabitants of Moscow's Chinatown, the wretched humanity of Train No. 57, are projected to the reader as part of the stylistic mosaic of the work as a whole. They are equated with, often permeated by, the forces of nature – storm, wind, oppressive summer, bitter frost – that represent the organic motives for change in life. The masses appear to have no separate identity, nor are they separable into individual identities (except in the loose sense that they are 'voiced') in Pilnyak's depiction of them. Their myriad presence is suggested darkly, through the chiaroscuro of the novel's fragmentariness. Despite the recondite literary mannerisms of the work, it does aim to suggest an *inhabited* world, not simply a literary construct (which must be one impression that a reader takes away from Bely's *Petersburg*), and a world moreover swarming with an instinctive, abundant human vitality. Perversely, perhaps, Pilnyak ascribes as much appeal to the decaying and dying, the old and antiquated, as he does to the naturally burgeoning or the Bolshevik creators of the new Russia, but in every fibre of his novel he demonstrates his power as a coiner of new images, a verbal alchemist creating mint-new pieces of gold from old literary currency.

At the source of the work's appeal as a picture, however ramshackle and strident, of the effect of revolution in the limited world of the Russian provinces there is Pilnyak's assumption that the 'freedom' offered by the revolution is not ideological but purely instinctive. He exploited the literary freedom that the times offered him as fully as any writer of the period. But he tended to see this 'freedom' as an instinctive flight from all restraints and to identify it with a sexual freedom conceived as the only permissible ideal, finer than Marxism or humanism. The sensuousness of this ideal is articulated by Irina, the sister who is the direct antithesis of the Bolshevik Natalya:

'I know – it will be evening. In the evening in my room I douse myself with water and weave my plaits. Through the windows comes the moonlight, I have a narrow white bed, and the walls of my room are white – in the moonlight everything seems greenish. My body has its own life, I am lying down, and it begins to appear as if my body is endlessly extending, very, very narrow, and my fingers are like snakes. Or on the other hand; my body is becoming flatter, my head is going into my shoulders. And sometimes my body appears huge, it keeps on growing surprisingly, I am a giant, and there's no possibility of moving my arm, as long as a kilometre. Or I seem to myself to be a small ball, light as down. There are no thoughts – a languishing feeling invades my body as if my whole body is becoming numb, as if someone is stroking me with a soft little brush, and it seems that all objects are covered with soft chamois: the bed, and the sheet, and the walls – all wrapped in chamois.

'Then I think. I know – modern times, like never before, bring only one thing: the struggle for life, to the death, that's why there is so much death. To the devil with fairy tales about some sort of humanism! I get no chill when I think about this: let only the strong survive. And the woman will always remain on a beautiful pedestal, there will always be chivalry. To the devil with humanism and ethics – I want to experience everything which freedom, intelligence and instinct have given me – instinct because surely modern times are the struggle of instinct?!' (p. 109)

The nakedness of the times is here literally revealed in its instinct for survival and its glorification of the sensuous. Pilnyak denied any organising focus to life as he denied any organising centre to his fiction. In doing this, he probably came closer to suggesting the haphazardness and displacement, both physical and ethical, that characterised the revolutionary period. But in stripping naked, as it were, he stripped away all the clothing of ideas and cultured habit that contribute to civilisation and provoked both a relatively short-lived new dynamism in Soviet literature and the beginnings of a reaction against his own innovatory manner. The *clothing* of literature in 'bourgeois forms' (i.e. conventional novelistic forms) became a long-term objective of Soviet writing in reaction against the naked experimentalism of 'revolutionary' literature. But Pilnyak's *The Naked Year* retains its *alla prima* freshness and formlessness, and both these characteristics are highlighted when it is compared with the work that was written to challenge it, Yury Libedinsky's *One Week* (1922).

One Week (*Nedelya*)[38] is a short novel that aims to show what revolutionary change means, in contrast to Pilnyak's sceptical picture of revolution as nothing more than an anarchic release of instinctive passions. Its style may seem derivative and 'quite out of keeping with the subject matter',[39] but it possesses a crisp, economical sharpness and an effective imagery that distinguish it from so many turgid treatments of the same subject. It tells of communists in a small town during a frosty week of the civil war. Discontent among the local peasantry is fomented by Whites into an anti-Bolshevik uprising. The revolt is finally suppressed, but only after the majority of the communists have been killed. Characterisation is sure, if not very deep. The work is important in the history of the revolutionary novel for its attempt to use a social situation, that of communists engaged in trying to create a socialist base in the township, as a means of revealing their characters. They are shown in their working relationships and through their feelings, both their personal feelings towards their roles as communists and their love and affection for each other. These are not the 'leather jackets' of Pilnyak, and yet, though given individual identities, the communist figures in Libedinsky's novel have only minimal appeal as personalities.

Though the novel underwent a reworking that substantially altered it, the most significant and original feature of its portrayal of communists – the dilemma of conscience, or the annihilating effect of communist allegiance upon one of them, Martynov – remained central to the revised version. This was the first such psychological study of character among communists to appear in the Soviet novel. Martynov's isolation from his fellow communists due to his bourgeois background is examined sentimentally, through frequent emphasis on his recollection of the past and particularly through his love for Nadya, a girl from one of the bourgeois families of the town whom he had known before the revolution. He is equally given (at least in the first version) to daydreaming about the future communist society:

Taking in his room at a glance, Martynov caught sight of the portrait of Lenin looking at him with intelligent and strongly mocking eyes.

And he imagined to himself the entire life of this man and felt ashamed. He threw on his overcoat and went out into the street, on which the light of a spring evening was casting its varicoloured cloth.

Now he walked and dreamed.

He dreamed of the sunny cities of the future suspended in the air like snowflakes in water, of palaces of jasper and streets of glass, of people living happy and – for us – unpleasantly beautiful lives.

And Martynov felt himself to be a builder of their life, in which they would work joyfully and with inspiration to create enchanting smokeless factories looking like palaces, but far more beautiful and delightful...

And, bursting out of his daydreaming, Martynov gazed with astonishment at the little houses and the unsightly and lopsided signboards above the shops.

This kind of romantic *intelligent*, who was formerly of the bourgeois intelligentsia but has embraced communism in the revolution, is a type familiar from other novels. Martynov's dilemma is not elaborated, nor given any depth. The romanticism of his attitudes not only cuts him off from those colleagues of his whose backgrounds were more humble, it also prevents him from assessing his own past correctly, an aspect brought out rather conventionally through the agency of a former expert employee of his father's tannery. As the quotation above suggests, he has difficulty in distinguishing reality from fantasy and is eventually shown as 'superfluous' in the community of communists to which he aspires to belong. For the essential message of Libedinsky's novel as an answer to Pilnyak's is contained in its picture of the consolidating, organising activity of the communists, their isolated existence as the new masters in a hostile environment and the profound personal convictions that unite them in the task of laying the groundwork for a new society.

If it were only this, *One Week* would be a simplist propaganda work. It would hardly have merited the deliberate neglect and enforced reworking that became its fate. The novel, at least in its first version, has a fresh and ungainly truthfulness. Its honesty is to be seen in the portrayal of the time-serving communist, Matusenko – the first such portrait in Soviet literature, as Libedinsky himself asserted[40] – who would doubtless be the most likely type to survive the ensuing decades of Stalinist bureaucracy. It also shows the genuine depth of feeling at the basis of the communists' personal relations.[41] But in two respects its honesty is outstanding. First, the novel represents communism as embattled and outnumbered, opposed by the vicious, blind instincts of the peasant masses, who rise up and kill practically all the communists with the exception of the time-serving Matusenko. The unleashing of so much vengeful and mindless violence is suggested with hair-raising vividness. Secondly, a more personal, yet far more anguishing, degree of violence is conveyed by the intense honesty of a letter received by the leading communist, Klimin, from a younger colleague who has been killed in the service of the Cheka.[42] He reminds Klimin how they had both participated in the shooting of five White counter-revolutionaries in a monastery forest in the depths of winter. Klimin had ordered the Whites to strip naked before being shot.

They sat down on tree-stumps, took off their boots and trousers, stripped off their underwear. The bodies of those in the translucent shade of the trees seemed greeny-yellow, as they would have looked through translucent lake water. The bodies of those in the moonlight were pale blue...Oh, how noiseless and incomprehensible it all was, as in some terrible, unrepeatable dream, in some icy nightmare!

I'd often been to these places in summer. The old divided fir tree by which we stood was well-known to me. I knew every branch of it. I recognised the large axe-cuts made on its lower trunk.

I loved that fir, but it seemed to me then strangely alien and hostile. Just as strangely alien and hostile as your mother seems in those awful moments when you see her in a nightmare, alien, pitiless, indifferent to you and your hands outstretched to her and your cries for help. The sight of these people stripping naked in the frost called to my mind a picture of bathing on the banks of a lake on a hot sunny day. The association was crazy, but I felt my thoughts were all mixed up and it was a good thing the loud noise of the volley got rid of all enchantments at a stroke.

Do you remember what I was like before this shooting? I was keen on my Cheka work and proud of it! I gladly signed the reports of investigations and implemented the death sentences without the slightest qualm. And all because I knew for sure, and still know, that it's a bloody way, but it's the only way out of that horror which is called capitalism. I took pity on people and underwent their sufferings with them, but I knew that the only way to Communism was through the deaths of enemies of the revolution. That's why I was so merciless. I transformed my great pity into a great hatred. And I think every Communist does the same.

A time will come, and I hope it'll come soon, when this great human compassion will make life on this earth beautiful. Then the sufferings of one's neighbour will genuinely pain one. People will take the greatest care of another's organism, of this beautiful human body which is just like yours and mine, which can be tormented and made to suffer in the same way. It will be like that! But now one must turn this pity into hatred. And before this shooting I could do that.

But in this case the blood of those naked Whites literally spurted into my soul! I can still remember them stripping in the moonlight, their trembling naked bodies, the thunder of the shots and their groans...Those dreadful groans, as if resounding in some quarry! Groans of bodies leaving go of life, dying! You'll call it softheartedness perhaps, but you ought to know that when they were undressing I quite suddenly imagined to myself, as clear as anything, that I was undressing, that the frost was striking my naked body, that the bullets were puncturing my muscles and bones and that I was giving terrible earsplitting howls.

I lost the knack of signing death warrants...You conduct investigations, you yourself look into living eyes, at their hands, you follow the play of wrinkles on a face and you never forget for a moment that they are your enemies, and yet you still ask yourself: Is it my hand that will send this organism to its death?

For me the limits of hatred have been crossed...

Though the young author of this letter admits that he will remain true to his vocation as a Chekist and communist, his revulsion at his work is instinctive, non-ideological. His testimony is as terrible a personal acknowledgement of what revolution can mean as any that can be found in the literature of the period.

For all its honesty, *One Week* is uneasily poised between the documentary and fictional genres. In terms of literary appeal, it lacks that heretical idiosyncrasy which is present in every sentence and nuance of Pilnyak's *The Naked Year* and gives that work its unique place in the revolutionary novel of the Soviet period.

Elementalism and the hero-mass: *Coloured Winds, Sky-Blue Sands, Fall of Dair, Wind, The Iron Flood*

Elementalism, or a rage, that is to say, to celebrate the romantic, elemental power of the revolution, became a feature of some of the early revolutionary novels. Violent imagery, a stridency of manner that owed something to folk poetry and such classics of medieval Russian literature as 'The Lay of Igor's Raid', brilliant verbal coloration and the subordination of individual characterisation to a heroism of the masses or a placard style of figure drawing were the principal aspects of several works of literature that appeared in the first half of the 1920s. None can be regarded as masterpieces, despite high claims made for them. They have interest primarily as examples of a literature attempting to give heroic expression to revolutionary events that were just beginning to acquire the dimensions of legend or myth. They have the singularity – and curiosity – of novels that either comprise their authors' sole attempts to confront the problem of mythologising the revolution or represent the freshest, most exuberant response of their authors to the inspiration of revolutionary events. If no 'hero' can be said to emerge from them, then each aspires to encompass the problem of creating a revolutionary hero in a particular, sometimes original, way, but in no case is such heroism projected in other than a generalised and romantic form.

Vsevolod Ivanov early acquired a reputation as a leading writer of the post-revolutionary period.[43] His fame rested less on his capacity to register the political character of revolutionary change than on his sheer exoticism. One may wonder how he became so famous, for – with the prominent exception of his notorious *Armoured Train No. 14,69* (1922), which became as famous for its dramatised version as for its original prose version – he emphasised the elementalism of the revolutionary process, not its political effects, and resorted to an over-worked ornamentalism in his writing when the thematic impulse of the revolutionary narrative began to wear thin. His two novels directly concerned with revolutionary themes – *Coloured Winds* (*Tsvetnyye vetra*) (1922) and *Sky-Blue Sands* (*Golubyye peski*) (1923) – are short, formless works about primitive people responding primitively to revolution in remote, primitive parts of Russia.

The Siberian setting of *Coloured Winds* contributes extravagantly to the pseudo-folkloristic archness of some of the rhythmical passages. For example, a thin narrative line formed of short staccato sentences can be interrupted by such lyricising as:

O, that there should be no scraping of iron on the road, no wolf howling beyond the piles of snow – my heart, like a snow cloud, fills the sky, fills the earth!

The larches beat about in the wind. They try to brush the snow off their shoulders. But the snow on them is pale green, while on the fir branches it is bronze.

And the blue-gold wind is stuck in their branches, scrapes off its beard in them.

Ah, my pellucid snows, eye clear as morning, clear as a deer's eye – wait for me (ch. 10, xxxix).

That it has by its very compression in the Russian a sense of folk-tale plaint and lyrical power is undeniable, but that it also has the tendency to sound spurious in its blatant rhetoricism must be quite obvious. The work's title has no particular meaning: it echoes such 'ornamental' images as 'The red-bronze wind in the sky laughs and hisses and whistles' or 'The crimson wind answers from the sky and hisses hissingly over the dove-grey snow' or 'Ah, wind, wind, purple-bronze and taut' and so on. Deliberate use of dialect terms, onomatopeic forms and a shorthand, inexplicit manner of narration combine with the ornamentalism to suggest that revolution is basically elemental in its effect, age-old as nature and altering only by slow, implacable gestation. Or as Shklovsky defined the human dimension in Ivanov's work: 'In the books of Ivanov the soul of man was resonant, in its changing state, but it still remained an old soul with habits that had been formed over many centuries.'[44]

This is illustrated in *Coloured Winds* by the description of Siberia during the civil war, with Admiral Kolchak (referred to as Tolchak, i.e. 'The Crusher') and the *bolshaki* (Bolsheviks) having little more than a peripheral role in the life of the semi-articulate peasantry. Led by a Bolshevik, the peasants begin to offer organised resistance to the Whites under Kolchak, particularly when they are joined by an influential local peasant, Kalistrat Yefimych. His love for a peasant woman, Nastasya Maksimovna, is a touching, if sketchy, episode and anticipates in miniature the love story between Grigory and Aksinya in Sholokhov's masterpiece. But the nub of the revolutionary theme in the short novel concerns Kalistrat's own change of heart when one of his sons is caught and tried for the crime of killing a Red Army soldier for bounty: he gives paternal permission for the execution of the death-sentence on his son. The novel ends in prose-poetic passages that tell briefly of the defeat of the White officers and triumph of the peasantry. From it all Kalistrat emerges with a new-born child by Nastasya, a new faith and a renewed sense of commitment to the task of rehabilitating the land and the people.

More impressive and important is the second of Ivanov's novels, *Sky-Blue Sands*. In this work, it has been authoritatively claimed, Vsevolod Ivanov 'was the first to create an epic narrative about the revolutionary epoch, based in terms of subject on the well-coordinated story of one man's destiny'.[45] A study of *Sky-Blue Sands* bears this out only in part. It is basically a formless tale of the life and loves of a Bolshevik commissar, Vasily Zapus, sent to organise Bolshevik agitation in the Kirgiz steppelands from a base in Pavlodar. His words, we are told, were 'rose-tinted, strong as tarred rope and warm-hearted'. He was impetuous, passionate, undisciplined, courageous and strong, and chiefly he was a great womaniser. Hardly, then, a conventional portrait of a commissar, and not surprisingly he is on one occasion brought before a revolutionary tribunal by colleagues of lesser calibre and temporarily drummed out of the Party. His strengths as a character are declared rather than suggested by illustration in the text and his portrait lacks the final dimension of full-blooded vitality. By contrast, the setting of Pavlodar and the surrounding desert regions have a multi-faceted depth and variety to them that illustrate the true power of Ivanov's literary talent.

The dusty, futile world of the small-town bourgeoisie of Pavlodar has its unique smells[46] and sounds, just as the arid steppelands have their peculiar static decrepitude. Here neither telegraph poles nor a Red Army detachment on the way to suppress an uprising have any effect:

The grey wormwood was kissing the road. On the sawn telegraph poles sat huge dark-beaked eagles. Meadowsweet grew on the sand hillocks. The shadows were meagre as voices in the steppe.

The long carts went on their creaking way. Machine-guns were mounted up front.

The horses plunged their sweating mouths through the dry heat. The smell of water came from the Irtysh and then the horses neighed.

And everywhere, high as the sky, grew the wormwood. Clouds like bitter and dry wormwood.

Pebbles in the ravines shone orange, blue and pale yellow.

Laughter from the carts was short and sharp like the creaking of the wheels.

The eagle on the telegraph pole is slow and sullen. He knows it all. An eagle lives three hundred years and maybe more...

Laconic and artfully over-simplified as this style of writing may be, it owes a good deal to the intense selectivity and economy of Tolstoyan writing, and necessarily, as an integral accompaniment of such a Tolstoyan manner, there is a suggestion of 'making strange', of *ostraneniye*, of describing an object or a scene in such a way that it appears strange because the component parts or items are magnified at the expense of the familiar total effect. But the laconic, recitative effect of Ivanov's prose has its own stateliness, even poetry, and achieves a suggestion of distancing and mythologising by its deliberately non-sequential, decorational looseness.

In the narrative passages the consequences of such a laconic manner are seen particularly clearly in the descriptions of moments of obvious outrage – the cold-blooded killing of the prisoners on board the Bolshevik-controlled boat after Pavlodar has fallen to an anti-Bolshevik revolt, or the slaughter of Red Army guards. At such moments the impartiality objectifies and reinforces the lancinating horror. But Ivanov obtrudes into his narrative from time to time; he is no cold-blooded reporter. The warmth and empathy of his manner become apparent when he mingles his evident fondness for the Siberian landscape with a solicitous concern for his characters – chiefly, of course, Zapus, his mistress Olimpiada and the Bolsheviks. As he writes, in a brief aside:

My joy is Zapus with the golden topknot. Dark-cheeked Olimpiada, from the mill, from the settlements of the newcomers and the Cossacks. The steppes and the gullies, whether covered in grass or snow, of them I will say what I know because they have meted out evil and happiness to each and everyone in due measure, and my love in due measure is for them!

The importance of his love for landscape and character becomes paramount towards the end of the novel. 'Why', Ivanov asks in another aside, 'is it impossible for us to write nakedly about love and life, but possible to write about death? There's little joy in us.' The question, and the scepticism of the answer, lend a tone of bitterness to the novel's final stages. The hero Zapus, after his expulsion from the Party, is summoned back into harness when Pavlodar is again attacked, this time by Cossacks. He is seriously wounded in the fighting and the only person who comes to his aid is the woman who loves him, Olimpiada. By exploiting his reputation as a commissar and her own connections, she is able to ensure that, though seriously wounded in the shoulder, he is conveyed across the steppes to safety. But the moral of this, the virtual conclusion of the story of Zapus, is that man is destined rather for love than for heroism on this earth. In fact, Ivanov allows his hero to become superfluous to the revolutionary events and finally to vanish into the background.

The novel concludes with the defeat of the Whites and the trial of the principal ringleaders of the revolt. They are sentenced to concentration camp and will no doubt eventually be shot. But after Zapus has gone off to Petrograd to complete his political education, Olimpiada is one day accosted by one of the ringleaders, Chokan, who is out on a working party. Chokan tells her a legend about one of the Mongol hordes that wandered into the desert of Uba. The soil of the desert was sky-blue and it made the people think they were living in the sky. Among the tall cliffs of the mountains surrounding the desert there was said to be a golden path, no wider than a man's hand, up which one had to climb to find everlasting happiness. Few tried to climb. When some young men made the attempt, they fell headlong from the narrow path and the sky-blue sands were speckled with blood. One young man insisted, however, that he would climb the narrow path and bring them back happiness. He started the climb and disappeared from view, but he never came back. The horde waited for him, and finally all of them, including his girl-friend, gave up and left the sky-blue sands and returned to their former dwellings.

This concluding *skaz*[47] leaves a question-mark over the revolutionary intent of the whole novel. What are we to make of a work that compromises the revolutionary romanticism of its central portrait with such a deliberately deflating legend about the ideal of everlasting happiness? The novel's title, for all its suggestion of the folkloristic and exotic, seems in the end to imply that there is some degree of futility in the human aspiration towards happiness, that it is so much pie in the sky and that revolutionary change, though real enough, cannot alter the fundamental imponderability of man's nature. Vsevolod Ivanov never wrote another novel on a specifically revolutionary theme and his ambiguity in this case reflects both his own unsureness in adapting his racy fictional manner to serve obvious political ends and, to some extent, the unsureness of literature as a whole about the best means of expressing the magnitude of revolutionary events.

One example of mythologising that has received much praise from Soviet critics is Aleksandr Malyshkin's *Fall of Dair* (1923). It cannot be considered a novel but it exhibits in embryo several features that were to contribute to the 'monumentalism' of later Soviet novels on revolutionary themes, especially the revolutionary epic. It assumes, for example, a unification of historical record and artistic purpose. In earlier works the assumption that literature, for all its artistry, was 'fictional' had not been seriously challenged. Pilnyak's, Libedinsky's and Ivanov's novels had not presumed to celebrate historical events. Aleksandr Malyshkin's short work, by contrast, was designed to celebrate the victory of the Red Army storming the Isthmus of Perekop, the event that brought to an end both White resistance and the civil war. It resorted to a deliberate monumentalism of manner in its celebration of the event, but in making use of so many of the devices of pre-revolutionary literature Malyshkin consciously set out to achieve an artistry in his own work that differentiated it from the propagandist character of Zazubrin's novel, for instance, without abandoning any of the political purpose necessary to revolutionary art.

Scarcely thirty pages in length, with an 'epic' manner that recalls in part the style of the Chronicles and 'The Lay of Igor's Raid', it simultaneously endows the fall of Dair, meaning the Crimean stronghold of the Whites, with the monumentalism of a biblical subject. It succeeds chiefly as an evocation of the mass surge of the multitudes of the Red Army and of those, the greater, distant multitudes of the proletariat, engaged both in destroying the last stronghold of the Whites and in ending an epoch. The sunset world of Dair itself, well evoked in several passages of fragrant but unsubtle prose, is contrasted with the dawning world of a victorious Red Army. The manner of the work suggests on more than one occasion the poeticised rendering of an official communiqué. The paradox of this juxtaposition of the poetic and official styles reveals the work's weaknesses and its strengths. If it has a literary monumentalism, reinforced by colour and auditory imagery that produces hard, bold effects, the historicism that demands that facts be respected is a paradoxically weaker constituent and appears to falsify and trivialise the poetic impulse.

It is not hard to discern in Malyshkin's description of the doomed world of Dair his personal love–hate fascination for its allure, a fascination that he made into a significant, and disillusioning, motive in the portrayal of Shelekhov in his first novel.[48] The most satisfying verdict on the literary quality of *Fall of Dair* has been given by a Soviet critic who, in acknowledging its role as a forerunner of much Soviet literature, described it as 'a lava flow that has grown cold', composed of 'layers of alien influences, of alien artistic styles – of "modernism", decadence, Leonid-Andreyevism...'[49] Such a mixture of styles and manners cannot detract from Malyshkin's central achievement in demonstrating how historical record and artistic purpose can combine, awkwardly but powerfully, to mythologise the elementalism of the Red Army's victory in the civil war.

Such elementalism is better expressed in literary terms in a short novel by Boris Lavrenyov, *The Wind* (*Veter*) (1924).[50] It is the story of Vasily Gulyavin, a sailor from the Baltic Fleet. He becomes a Bolshevik deputy during the initial days of the revolution. After October 1917 he is despatched to the south to fight against the insurgent Whites. The novella describes his education as well as his evolution. He is 'educated' not only by books he reads when in hospital before the revolution but also by a close relationship with a young lieutenant of the officer class, Stroyev, who is the first commander of his detachment in the struggles against the Whites. A passionate, volatile man, given to instinctive likes and dislikes, Gulyavin falls prey to the wiles of a seductive female gang-leader who is shortly afterwards responsible for the death of the young Stroyev. He learns a bitter lesson from this episode. Forced into semi-retirement after this and other ordeals, Gulyavin frets. He eventually returns to the front line, only to be involved in a final, bizarre act of heroism. He acts the role of a White officer, insinuates himself into the White H.Q. and then dramatically kills himself after wreaking a bloody vengeance on the Whites with a revolver and hand grenade.

In terms of its story this novella may seem melodramatic to the point of absurdity, but its telling is a skilful mixture of briskly narrated episodes, interpolated but not obtrusive passages of poetic prose and, chiefly, a gradual accretion of information about Gulyavin that serves to develop and enlarge his character. In the history of the Russian revolutionary novel it is the first sustained attempt to describe the evolution of a working-class hero from a state of anarchic revolt to one of purposeful revolutionary consciousness. The final state of Gulyavin is blurred by the over-dramatising of the denouement, but the personality of Gulyavin himself is portrayed with sufficient sympathy and insight to make him credible and even poignant. He of course represents the wind of the title. Lavrenyov admitted that 'there was no Gulyavin as such. He is a collective personality. He contains many of the individual features of the sailor-soldiers whom I met during the Civil War. I chose the most characteristic features of the type during that period.'[51] This does not mean that Gulyavin emerges as a symbolic figure, despite the absence of specific information about his background. He is presented as a simple, instinctive man caught up in the wind of revolutionary change and unable to remain unaffected by it when it summons him to action. When given a desk job, he is described in the compressed, romantic manner of the novella as 'awaiting execution':

Towards evening his head was fit to burst and he went into the park to get some fresh air – and there was no peace there from the blasted trilling of the nightingale, the sighs, the whispering and the dizzy, irritating fragrance of the lilac.

Gulyavin hadn't joined the Bolsheviks in order to rummage about among papers like a rat.

To each his own.

Some love fire, others water.

Gulyavin loves the wind.

The impetuous, blazing wind which casts into wide-open spaces the thousand-fold masses inflamed by hatred and revolt and hurls skyward the shouts of hunted locomotives and the reddish manes of smoking conflagrations.

Not for Gulyavin the writing of revolution with a pen on paper, but with blood that is hot and sticky on open fields.

He is a romantic, strongly-drawn personality, but vivified by his instinctual weakness of lust and impetuosity. The writing captures the spirit of the character at almost every turn. 'The energetic, stormy development of the plot', as a critic has written, 'the precise, dynamic dialogue, the almost total absence of landscape-painting and descriptive elements in general help to convey the impetuosity and the unusualness of the epoch and the "explosiveness" of the character of the hero.'[52] Much may be over-written and couched in terms of such hyperbole that it seems close to parody, but the vigour of the hero's portrait and the *élan* of the narrative have freshness and distinction.

Lavrenyov's work had no 'explosive' effect on Soviet literature. His novella may have contributed significantly to that search for a heroic image of revolution which was becoming the battle-cry of Soviet criticism, but it proclaimed in essence the instinctive rather than the ideological commitment of the hero and the elemental force of the revolution itself. The 'explosion' occurred when the romanticising, dynamic manner so common in the early revolutionary novels became not only historicised, or devoted to the illustration of a particular historical event, but also concerned to depict the hero-mass brought to unified revolutionary consciousness through heroic leadership. Such was the significance of the first acknowledged 'classic' novel of Soviet literature, Aleksandr Serafimovich's *The Iron Flood* (*Zheleznyy potok*) (1924).

Based on history though it may be, it is in all essentials a piece of fictional recreation drawn not from the author's first-hand experience but from his creative imagination. Aleksandr Serafimovich[53] took no part in the epic event that he describes and he endowed it with the characteristics of an 'epic' in much the same way that Tolstoy created a literary epic out of the Napoleonic invasion of Russia. Serafimovich's is an unusual case of topography having as great an inspirational effect on him as history. His imagination was seized by the exotic magnificence of the Caucasian scenery long before he found a subject of sufficient grandeur to match that magnificence. He visited the Caucasus in 1913 and for five years at least he found no way of responding to the experience, though he had clearly been inspired by it. He recalled vividly how, after the October revolution, he used to walk through the Moscow streets:

Whether I am trudging through shabby streets, stumbling without a word into snowdrifts beneath drooping tramwires or sitting at some meeting amid an impenetrable haze of tobacco, my sight and hearing are continually assailed by the blueness of mountains, the whiteness of snowy peaks and unceasingly, limitlessly translucent green rollers plunge upon the shores, blindingly uncoiling their dazzling foam.[54]

The imagery of the majestic Caucasian scenery haunted the writer's imagination, but he did not in fact learn of the events that he describes in his novel until two years after they had occurred. As he explained later, his aim was 'to present realistic truth, not, of course, photographic truth, but synthetic, crystallized truth'.[55] His experience as a war reporter and a writer of documentary fiction helped him to research the background material to his novel with scrupulous care. He interviewed participants and derived much information from the hero of the historical event, Epifany Kovtyukh.[56] Even so, Serafimovich omitted certain aspects of the event – the horde's entry into Novorossisk by train, for instance, or the opposition to the occupying German and Turkish forces organised by Soviet elements within the town – that might be construed as conflicting with the primitive, elemental image of the 'iron flood' that he was at great pains to project in his novel.[57]

In the summer of 1918, the so-called Taman' army was encircled by insurgent Cossacks and others from the counter-revolutionary settlements in the area, cut off from the main Red Army and in danger of being slaughtered. To save itself and the mass of peasantry threatened by the Whites in the area, it was obliged to retreat along the eastern seaboard of the Black Sea through Novorossisk to Tuapse and then inland, through the Caucasian mountains, to join up with the Red Army in the Kuban' on the North-Caucasus front. The enormous trek by tens of thousands of starving peasants, supported by cavalry, sailors and some Bolsheviks, lasted thirty-three days. Serafimovich chose to write about this remarkable event not only because the Kuban' adjoined his own native Don area but also because it represented 'the revolutionary transformation' of an anarchic, petit-bourgeois peasantry into a 'hero-mass'. When later criticised for his failure to show the proletarian leadership of the event, Serafimovich rather lamely appealed to the facts in the case – 'I allowed this error to happen because I slavishly followed the concrete events, and the workers played only a small role in them'[58] – and then went on to an abject admission of his own wrongdoing. Nevertheless, he showed the importance of leadership in the figure of the iron-jawed 'common man' Kozhukh, based on the historical Kovtyukh though, as Serafimovich insisted, by no means identical.

Kozhukh is the first portrayal of a revolutionary leader in the Russian revolutionary novel. Too easily dismissable as a marionette figure, the portrait has subtlety and a degree of depth. Kozhukh is given a biographical background of a kind that at least explains his own commitment to the cause of the poverty-stricken and hungry peasant masses. No matter how insistently Serafimovich himself represents Kozhukh as 'one bone and one flesh' with the 'iron flood', there are character traits in this 'leader' that suggest his individuality and his aloofness as well as resemblance to an epic or biblical hero. But his primary characteristic is sheer iron toughness. He is a harsh disciplinarian, administering justice with a merciless brutality to his enemies and with a strictness tempered by compassion towards those over whom he has command. He is quite without humour. With his total absence of human failings, he appears too often to behave like a clockwork mannikin designed to illustrate the ideal revolutionary leader. The effect, though entirely un-Tolstoyan in its lack of 'rounded' characterisation, was a consequence of Serafimovich's desire to emphasise only the most striking aspects of each character.[59] Thus, in the case of Kozhukh, the iron jaws, gimlet eyes and other attributes emphasise his iron determination as a leader, contrasted as he is with other, more volatile, aspirants to such leadership like Smolokurov or the sailors; similarly, in the case of the old crone, Gorpina, the author was concerned that she should have the role of a 'collective type', the concentrated representation of the rebirth of the impoverished peasantry under the influence of revolution.[60] In the area of characterisation, then, the propagandist element is obvious and, on the whole, too unsubtle to merit serious critical attention.

The iconic form of the work, its concentration on visual effects and its self-imposed conventions are most obviously evident in the opening and closing scenes, which are presented as formal meetings, the first to decide on a leader, the final one to allow the revolutionary moral to be pointed. These two meetings, typical of the era of meetings that characterised the early stages of the revolutionary process, enclose the body of the work describing the awesome march of the motley horde of illiterate Ukrainian peasants from Taman' to the Kuban'. Serafimovich admitted that he wrote the work in fits and starts, with no rigid plan, and something of this higgledy-piggledy effect remains in the final text. Its vitality as a kaleidoscopic picture of such an event is no doubt partly due to this manner of writing. The rapid succession of small scenes, the multitude of characters, the touches of horror mingled with humour and the very formlessness of the horde's own composition and of its purposes, leading to factional struggles and rivalries, suggest that it is little better than a rabble. Pursued by Cossacks, bombarded by German naval vessels, their way blocked by Georgian Mensheviks, ambushed by Whites, the horde's chief enemy remains the natural torment of extreme heat and thirst. But even such forging does not create from them the revolutionary 'iron flood'. One particularly memorable episode, apparently fictitious, helps to suggest such unified feeling. The marchers find a gramophone in a looted house, take it on the march with them and discover among the records one of laughter, which soon causes volleys of hysterical laughter to pass down the ranks of the crazed masses. Kozhukh, humourlessly, puts a stop to such levity. He orders the marchers to make a detour to witness five corpses strung up on telegraph poles, victims of White atrocities. This episode leads finally to the forging of the 'iron flood':

From these five exuded silence and a sickly sweet smell of putrefaction. Kozhukh removed his battered floppy hat. All who had caps removed them. Those who didn't took off the straw, the grass, the small branches perched on their heads.
    The scorching sun burned down on them.
    And the sickly sweet smell filled the air.
    'Comrade, give it me.'
    An adjutant tore the white piece of paper from the pole near one of the corpses and handed it over. Kozhukh clenched his jaw and the spoken words emerged through his teeth.
    'Comrades,' and he flourished the paper which flashed in the sunlight with a blinding whiteness, 'this is from the White general to you. General Pokrovsky writes: "All who are known to have had the slightest association with the Bolsheviks will be executed as ruthlessly as these five scoundrels from the Maikop works."' And he clenched his jaws, biting off the words – there was nothing to say.
    Thousands of shining eyes watched unblinkingly. There was a beating of a single, inhumanly enormous heart.
    Out of the eyeholes of the corpses dripped black droplets. The sickly sweet stench floated on the air.
    In the ensuing stillness the resonance of the torrid air and the delicate humming of the swarms of flies ceased. There were only a graveyard silence and the intensely sweet stench. The droplets dripped down.
    'Atten-shun!...For-ward march!'
    The thunder of heavy footsteps at once broke the silence, even and regular it enveloped the torrid heat, as if it were the footsteps of a single man of superhuman height and superhuman weight, with the beating of a single, inhumanly enormous heart.

After this fashion the motley horde is transformed into an iron flood united in the beating of 'a single, inhumanly enormous heart'.

It endures further confrontations but eventually catches up with the Red Army in the Kuban'. At the meeting that concludes the novel, the horde achieves its apotheosis. It has triumphed over death. It has endured its Calvary. Simultaneously, but trusting so devotedly to its leader, it can hardly fail to create out of Kozhukh a cult figure. He, in turn, surveying the ragged emaciated multitudes, cannot fail to think of them as his creation, saved by him from death in a manner suggestive of biblical example:

And Kozhukh looked out of his blue eyes upon them while in his heart the thought was like fire:
   'I have no father, no mother, no wife. I have only these whom I have led from death. I, I myself have led them...And there are millions of such people, with a noose round their neck, and I shall fight for them. These are my father, my home, my mother, my wife, my children...I, I, I have saved these thousands, these tens of thousands of people...'

The notion of some Christ-like role of saviour is fairly clearly implied by these thoughts. Kozhukh, as the revolutionary leader created by the revolutionary masses, is epitomised as one so totally identified with their cause that he is both their creation and their godhead. As a parable on the way in which the masses seek, in their very deliverance from tyranny, to summon new gods to rule over them, *The Iron Flood* unintentionally reveals in all their nakedness the processes that lead to 'a cult of personality'.

Wickedly but effectively *The Iron Flood* received its most perceptive criticism as literature from Zamyatin, author of the anti-Utopian novel *We (My)*. He suggested that if a piece of this 'iron' were sent to a factory laboratory for analysis it would turn out that it has 'long been rusting in the cellars of *Znaniye*'. He complained that 'The thickest overlay of tinsel is reserved for the ending – the apotheosis of the hero, whose figure is assembled in strict conformity to all the known operatic rules.'[61]

It is true that, stylistically, the novel owes something to the exaggerated and exotic ornamental writing of much pre-revolutionary writing as well as to the realism of Gorky's *Znaniye* school. But at its best *The Iron Flood* transcends all stylistic mannerisms and seems to be composed of words that have been newly minted like coins (Serafimovich's own expression).[62] 'Everything about the novel looked extremely big', runs the accepted Soviet view, 'as if seen through a magnifying glass, intensifying the brightness, boldness and tautness of the picture.'[63] In this 'bigness' of theme and treatment, tinselly, for sure, in some of its grandly operatic effects, but also having epic strength in some of its episodes, *The Iron Flood* lays claim to be Serafimovich's supreme achievement and a classic example of the revolutionary novel.

It is consciously 'novel' in its employment of techniques, such as montage, close-up and tracking, that derive from cinematography. Although we may assume that it has a single hero in the figure of Kozhukh,[64] it creates the dense, manifold character of the iron flood as a single heroic mass by providing many 'voices' (a technique of *mnogogolosiye*), which, through snippets of uttered sentences, suggest the multi-faceted experience of the march. The denseness of the multi-voiced illustrations is compounded by the use of a Ukrainian dialect that suggests excessive primitiveness in the peasant characters. Technically, of course, it is no more modern than Tolstoy's use of similar conversational snippets to illustrate rank-and-file reaction to war in *War and Peace*. But the contrast between a laconically shorthand manner in presenting dialogue exchanges and a strongly lyrical, even hyperbolic, manner in the descriptive passages tends to efface the human components in the narrative.

The splendours of the work are practically all a consequence of Serafimovich's visual manner. The glowing scenery of the Caucasus is conveyed in a series of excellent word-pictures, which match in their representation of natural grandeur the majesty and travail of the epic human achievement in the foreground. Even so, the work tends to lose momentum and impact at precisely those points where human characterisation is given more than superficial emphasis. In chapter 25 the exploration of the thoughts of a Georgian sentry before the Red assault dissolves into melodrama, just as the characterisation of Prince Mikheladze (chs. 24/26) is one-sided and stilted. Though obviously more sympathetic, the treatment of the talkative old crone, Granny Gorpina, is a tiresome mixture of homely diatribe and a blatant chorus element.

High claims for the originality of *The Iron Flood* have had to be modified in the half-century or so since its appearance.[65] Its effect was explosive and it continues to exert fascination as a novel depicting the making of a minor piece of revolutionary history. If its explosion now seems no more than the recollection of a long-dead thunder, it remains a reverential, iconic portrayal of an instinctive mass flood of the people that has become fixed in the iron mould of a Bolshevik theodicy.

Mythmaking and factography: *The Badgers, Chapayev, Revolt*

No younger Soviet writers of the 1920s seem to stand in more marked contrast with each other than Leonov and Furmanov. This opposition appears most obvious when their literary manners are compared – Leonov's conscious literariness with echoes of Gogol and Leskov, his Dostoyevskian preoccupation with human complexity and the introspective, divided personality, Furmanov's deliberately factographic concern for literature as a branch of reportage and political propaganda. Such a contrast, easy enough to make in superficial terms, becomes less marked and important when their novels on civil-war themes are closely scrutinised. Yet the contrast is rewarding. Each writer was, broadly speaking, concerned with a similar task: the anatomy of the heroic myth. In Leonov's case the anatomy of the myth supplied the literary motivation for his first novel and highlighted the causes and gestation of revolutionary feelings in one individual's experience. In Furmanov's case the myth was already there, as it were: he 'reported' the myth of the famous partisan leader in his first novel, while in his second novel he offered a moment-by-moment account of a revolt's gestation and collapse. The differing approaches to approximately similar issues reveal – or at least help to clarify – the way in which the revolutionary novel of the Soviet period had begun to acquire maturity as well as range, literary strength as well as novelty.

Leonid Leonov has become an outstanding novelist of the first half-century of Soviet literature, whose reputation is equalled only by Sholokhov's. His first novel *The Badgers* (*Barsuki*) (1924), the only novel of his to deal with a civil-war theme (although this is not strictly correct, because the events of the novel supposedly occur shortly after the end of the civil war), established him as a novelist who could deal with some of the most fundamental and complex problems in Soviet society but so angled or presented that those problems appeared at once in sharp relief and seemed as age-old and profoundly human as they were obviously contemporary and politically acute. The most fundamental of the problems was the conflict between the urban and the rural, the city-bred and peasant mentalities. Related to this problem was a theme that was to have enduring meaning in Leonov's work: the issue of the preservation of the past and of links with earlier traditions. This issue had literary meaning, in the sense that Leonov chose to write out of the richest traditions of nineteenth-century Russian literature, in conscious indebtedness to Gogol, Dostoyevsky, Leskov and such immediate predecessors as Remizov and Zamyatin.

It had social and political significance as well, in the sense that it tended to run counter to the emphasis on 'progress', especially technological progress, that had so many advocates in Soviet literature. Leonov was more modern than the modernists in his early advocacy of the preservation of the environment, chiefly the Russian forests; he was perhaps less modern in his fondness for those who attempted, never of course with any success, to turn their backs on progress. Misguided though they might be, they appeared to have a fascination for Leonov by reason of their very eccentricity, the very 'madness of the brave', which Gorky portrayed so sympathetically in his 'Song of the Falcon' or his 'Konovalov'. For Leonov it is in part such fascination that made 'the badgers' so prominent in his first novel, though they are not necessarily to be regarded as the principal interest. Finally, he addressed himself in his novel to the problem of mythmaking. What makes myths, especially myths of heroes? Never concerned to provide boldly emphatic answers like Tolstoy, Leonov played with the question in all his novels, but in *The Badgers* he provided as neat an anatomy of the problem as anywhere in this work.

The novel is the story of the two brothers, Semyon and Pavel, who are transported from a peasant, rural background into the commercial district of Moscow, where they are to be trained as tradesmen. In their respective ways, both reject the world of commerce. Pavel leaves to find work in a factory and is absent as a character for the greater part of the novel. Semyon, though attracted to a tradesman's daughter, Nastya, is a prey to conflicting loyalties and eventually finds himself drawn back to the rural world from which he sprang. But it is a rural world torn by accidents of history and geography into two opposing factions – the pro-Soviet village of the Ganders (*Gusaki*) and the richer, anti-Soviet village of the Thieves (*Vory*). The cause of such enmity and conflict lies in the absurd passion of a nineteenth-century landowner for fighting geese and his decision to sell a neighbour a hundred or so serfs for one particularly successful fighting gander. The serfs were settled on poor land adjoining the rich Zina meadow, but after the Emancipation of 1861 they were denied the right to use the Zina meadow and consequently became impoverished. After 1917, with Soviet support, they reacquired their right to the land, while their opponents, the richer peasants, in an effort to resist the enforced requisitioning of foodstuffs, came out in open revolt against Soviet authority and took to the local forests, where they turned themselves into 'badgers'. As their leader they chose Semyon. This revolt against Soviet authority is finally suppressed by troops under the command of one named Anton, who is in fact Semyon's brother Pavel.

The schematic form of the story suggested by this very short digest is scarcely very obvious upon first acquaintance with the novel. It is obscured by the tripartite shape, in which the first part serves very much as an introduction to the central issue of the succeeding two parts, the revolt of 'the badgers', and by the close texture of the writing. The *skaz* manner is used brilliantly to distance the author's relationship to his story. No novel of the 1920s, Pilnyak's work included, has the pungency and raciness of Leonov's. The portrayal of character tends to be engulfed by the teeming style, so that, though the novel is copiously 'peopled', there are always obtrusive stylistic elements that convey vigour without ever endowing the human portraits with outstanding vitality. The effect is one of cramping, and if one is to single out an image that summarises the total sense of the novel it is that very cramped, congested, cosy image of the badger-hole indicated by the title. The badger-holes of the novel's second part repeat the congested conditions that poverty has caused in the commercial area of Moscow and emphasise a similar desire for insulation from progress. So many of the characters are depicted as 'holed up' in helplessly constricted lives, whether the setting be urban or rural. Images of smallness, just as diminutive forms, crowd the pages and leave an impression of lives filled with concerns as small and pointless as dust. Even stronger, repeatedly occurring groups of images suggest wetness and dampness in association with stoniness and imperviousness, but always with an accent on the minuscule proportions of things and experience, just as the thematic oppositions of town and country, of Soviet power and an atavistic peasant attempt to remain in badger-like apartness, are somehow reduced, for all their inherent importance, to issues shorn of grandeur, diminished in the everlasting scale of things.

At the centre of this teeming, unusual, self-consciously literary novel is the figure of the leader of 'the badgers', Semyon. He it is who becomes the myth, who acquires fortuitously a second *persona*, that of 'Simon the Badger' about whom songs were made that were 'sung at fairs and drunken orgies, wherever blind men recount their threadbare prolix tales'. But the Semyon of legend is a threadbare popular myth by comparison with the detailed portrayal of his early life given in the novel and the intimations of contradictory and complex emotions that illuminate his private *persona*. His attitude to the city is governed by an instinctive revulsion against the humiliating beating administered to his father for taking part in the peasant unrest of 1905, the responsibility for which, in the young Semyon's simplistic view, can be attributed to those from an urban world who came to impose a city-made law and order on the rebellious peasantry. Part of his zeal on behalf of 'the badgers' is due to a deeply cherished private wish to avenge himself on the city for his father's humiliation. Yet he also knows that 'the badgers' are little better than animals, mindless in their atavistic rejection of change and dependent for such civilising influences as reach them on the city and its industry. The heroic myth of 'Simon the Badger' is anatomised and shown to have no real basis. On the other hand, Semyon's brother Pavel, despite his revolutionary soubriquet and leading role in suppressing the revolt, is hardly the portrait of a revolutionary leader. Shadowy, more philosophical than political in his opinions, Pavel does little more than intimate in a sardonic, incoherent fashion the kind of urban 'progress' that will supposedly emancipate 'the badgers' from their backwardness.

Pavel's motto – 'One's got to think out things in the open air' – contains a notion that appeals to Semyon and yet contradicts the imagery of smallness and secretiveness that had surrounded him in his city boyhood and his badger-like revolt. Strikingly, the setting for the confrontation between the two brothers at the close of the novel is a juniper copse. The trees are deliberately made to signify a durability and wisdom that set in relief the diminutive concerns of those, like 'the badgers', who do not 'think out things in the open air':

All that Semyon understood was the last thing his brother said: 'One's got to think out things in the open air.'

Both now thought about different things. The junipers surrounding them embodied in them, it seemed, the essence of their silence. The juniper is a secretive tree, prickly, forbidding, cramped, severe towards life, the wisest of our trees; it lays down its blue and rosy clumps meanly and unhurriedly and in each clump there is the fragrance of peace and silence and knowledge. In juniper copses, in their deep shade, there was hardly any grass. Undisturbed by man, the juniper grew tall and thick, full of translucent shadows. At the bottom of deep rivers there is the same silent blueness.

The immemorial unchangeability of the secretive juniper provides a setting for the brothers' silent contemplation of their separate and opposed lives, just as it also tacitly presupposes a frame of reference for the idea of progress that is implicit, like some unseen climatic change, in Semyon's evolution and in the novel as a whole. The challenge to superficial ideas of progress, or to the idea of revolution as something that occurs principally in the sphere of technology, is expressed most clearly in the novel in the famous Legend of Kalafat. This is really a folksy poking of fun at the heroic myth, but of course from a point of view sympathetic to 'the badgers' and their eccentric apartness. It is a *skaz*-type interpolated narrative about the son of a king who names himself Kalafat, that is to say 'one who can attain anything', and studies what is called 'eometry in order to name and number every blade of grass and every bird of the air. He determines to justify himself to the world by constructing an enormous tower. A Tolstoyan figure warns him against such folly, but he persists. After twenty or so years the tower is as complete as it will ever be, in view of the scoundrels who have flourished in the course of its construction. It takes Kalafat five years to ascend his tower, in order to climb right up to heaven. But all his 'eometry, all his technical skill, proves of no avail. As he has ascended his tower it has slowly sunk beneath his weight, so that by the time he reached the top it was no higher than ground level: 'And all about the forests rustled and forests were full of foxes. The fields were in bloom and fragrant, and in the fields were many birds. Nature had cast off Kalafat's documentation.'[66]

The Badgers is too verbose, too consciously folksy in its literary manner, to be a wholly satisfactory novel. The mannerisms, in their dependence on diminutives and a colloquial repetitiousness, prove tiresome. Leonov was to write more complex and sophisticated novels.[67] But he was never to probe the issue of the conflict between town and country more discerningly than in his anatomy of the division within Semyon and in the challenge posed to urban, technological influence by the instinctive revolt of 'the badgers' and the instinctive revolt of nature against the legendary Kalafat who attempted to impose on it his own 'eometry.

The factography of D. A. Furmanov (1891–1926) in his two novels, *Chapayev* (1923) and *Revolt* (*Myatezh*) (1925), dispenses with the literary embroidery of Leonov but, for all its insistence on factual reportage, has much about it that can be perfectly justifiably described as 'literary'. A kind of mythology has tended to spring up round the person of Furmanov himself, largely due to his early death and quite sincere commitment to the communist cause. The blurb, which reads:

Dimitry Furmanov. A peasant's son. A commissar of the Red Army. A prominent writer. Such was the life's journey of Dimitry Furmanov[68]

should be amended at once to read:

Dmitry Furmanov, son of Russified German parents, student of Moscow University, male nurse in 1914 War, actively co-operated with Social Revolutionaries, anarchists and maximalists in 1917 and did not join the Bolshevik Party until July 1918. Appointed by Frunze early in 1919 to accompany Ivanovo-Voznesensk weavers in Red Army struggle against Kolchak, became political commissar to Chapayev; later transferred to Party work in Central Asia and Caucasus, associated with Kovtyukh (Kozhukh of *The Iron Flood*). Returned to Moscow after civil war and died of over-work.

In other words, the biography of Furmanov, like the man himself, was far more complex than over-simplified commentaries tend to suggest.

The factography of Furmanov had its source in the assiduous, rather Germanic, methodicalness of Furmanov the diarist. He kept diaries as a student at Moscow University and continued the practice when he took part in the civil war. The difference between the student diaries and the later 'factographic' diaries is striking. In January 1914, when he was already twenty-three, he noted in his diary: 'I somehow have few points of contact with real life. I want to know and understand it – and yet at the same time I shield myself from it behind the thick spines of books. This is a drama of a kind.'

He may have yearned for some drama in his life, but he appears to have had the common-sense not to seek it out needlessly. The tenor of his diary entries as a student suggests one who was concerned principally with private matters, sensitive and immature. An entry of August 1914 attempts a summary of his character:

I'm exactly the same Mitya as I was many years ago; that's how I'll remain; with the same character, the same softness and the same constant, unsuccessful yearning to be as severe as Bazarov.

There are external changes, quite unimportant, but what's most dear to me remains constant; though it becomes much wider and wider.

In a curious way, Furmanov presents a dilemma in his life and evolution that calls to mind Turgenev's Bazarov. Furmanov was a scholar of scrupulous habits, a man of amiable, accommodating character and yet he was plunged into the turmoil of the civil war, into acting the role of political activist and commissar, in a way that would have tested even the strong will of a Bazarov to the limit. He acquired the severity of a Bazarov through the tempering processes of his civil-war experience, but behind the severely factual, apparently objective reportage of Furmanov's Bazarovism was the softness and romanticism of the private human being. One can easily discern the astonishment with which he viewed his earlier self in the following comments, written in 1921:

I was a student then. And I knew nothing, absolutely nothing: nothing about the newspapers, the public disturbances or the political parties. A student and an adult person, I had no idea at all about the so-called 'liquidators', the 're-callers' and so on, and I'd heard of the Social Democrats three or four times – the name I'd heard, but I'd had no idea what it meant. And I simply wasn't interested in the least...It's horrifying to recall that a sea of troubles was raging around me, the waves were rising, a storm was on the way and yet I didn't see a thing, a single thing...The veil fell from my eyes only during the days of the revolution, but until that time I'd been as innocent as a child.[69]

The truthfulness of Furmanov about himself and his accuracy as a witness are the factors that lend distinction and quality to a factographic manner that is on the whole rather pedestrian. He had very real powers as a descriptive writer (the scenic descriptions of the journey from Tashkent to Verny, now Alma-Ata, in his second novel bear this out) and he could convey speech forms with characterising exactitude. But this very rawness of the diary material on which he based his finished work and the haste with which he had to write inevitably left roughnesses, longueurs and a certain sketchiness – features, in fact, associated with mediocrity in a writer, and there is no disguising it in some of Furmanov's work. There is also no disguising the passionate sense of engagement with which he wrote, and this just as inevitably redeems.[70]

His documentary novel *Chapayev* tells the story of his association with the proletarian army of Ivanovo-Voznesensk workers, who were recruited to defend the beleaguered Soviet state against the armies of Kolchak advancing from Siberia. Chapayev, a legendary hero of the civil war, was appointed to command the army group to which the workers' regiment was attached. Fyodor Klichkov (the pseudonym that Furmanov gave himself in his novel) was posted to that army group to organise political work. Klichkov was entirely

inexperienced in battle and not all that experienced in politics. He
struck up a friendship with Chapayev based on mutual respect and
accompanied the military leader during the six months' campaign
that took the Red Army from the battles round Alexandrov-Gai to
the capture of Ufa and Uralsk. Throughout the telling of the story
a twofold characterising process is at work. We learn as much about
Klichkov as we do about Chapayev, despite the assumed obliteration
of authorial personality that might be thought so important in
factographic writing. Though we learn increasingly more about the
remarkable personality of Chapayev as the novel progresses, in the
case of Klichkov we discern part of that essential evolution of
character which changed the student Furmanov into Furmanov the
hardened Red Army commissar. As a study in the making of
revolutionaries, *Chapayev* is unique among early revolutionary
novels of the Soviet period in its attempt to diagnose the causes of
the revolutionising process, though it ends by simply reasserting the
potency of the heroic myth.

The portrait of Chapayev himself is a *tour-de-force*. Furmanov
succeeded brilliantly in delineating the human traits of Chapayev and
disentangling the man from the legend. Out of such a factographic
process there emerged the picture of a wiry, shrewd peasant commander of predominantly peasant troops, a man who had first
learned to read about the age of thirty, volatile, easily influenced, a
prey to adulation and the wildest of rumours, basically apolitical,
even anarchic, in his views, gifted above all with an astonishing
memory, a capacity to do without sleep and a charismatic power of
command over his men, especially his personal retinue. There is never
at any point in Furmanov–Klichkov's approach to Chapayev the
faintest shade of condescension or even the reverse of it, the kind of
sycophancy to which Chapayev himself was apparently accustomed.
But the portrayal, despite its objectivity, is permeated by a feeling
of respect for its subject that borders on love. A sense of the warmth
that developed practically spontaneously between the two utterly
dissimilar men is apparent throughout the novel. Simultaneously a
diagnostic process is at work that endeavours to illuminate the social
and psychological causes of Chapayev's magnetism.

For this purpose Furmanov provides biographical evidence taken
ostensibly from Chapayev's own recital of his background. Whether
or not his mother was actually the daughter of the governor of Kazan
and his father a gypsy actor matters less than the colourfulness of

the recital itself and the aptness of such unusual parentage for a man
of Chapayev's flair and *panache*. Yet a more important determining
factor in his early life was his abhorrence of the merchants among
whom he was forced to work: '...if I've got it in for merchants now,
it's all because I see right through the devils – on that point I'd make
a better Socialist than Lenin...' (p. 124).

This is really the only ideological motive, if it can be called that,
to which Chapayev's biography makes reference. His class
antagonisms were governed by instinctive dislikes, just as his brilliance
as a military commander was a product, it seems, of his instinctive
daring, staunchness and endurance. When Furmanov–Klichkov
attempts a diagnosis, the argument has a declarative ring to it that
rehearses the obvious. It becomes an essential part of the argument
that Chapayev should be represented as a product of his times and
his instinctive class allegiance. The forces over which he had command
were trustworthy:

It required only the ability to command them, and Chapayev possessed this
ability to the highest degree – the ability to command *such* a body of men,
in the *state* it was in, and at the *moment* in question. This human mass was
heroic but it was raw. The moment was a dramatic one, and in the heat of
the fighting, much was overlooked or pardoned in view of the exclusiveness
of the situation...

And there were Chapayevs only in those days – at other times there have
been no Chapayevs and there can be none. Chapayev was born of *that* human
mass, at *that* moment when it was in *that* state (p. 192).

He possessed, as Furmanov–Klichkov insists, the qualities of the
raw, heroic mass that were most valued by it: bravery, daring,
courage and resolution. Others were braver and more clever, but he
knew 'how to present his exploits, and he was greatly assisted in this
by his close friends' so that 'his deeds were invariably surrounded
by an aura of the heroic and the miraculous'. Chiefly, though,
Chapayev was 'the child of his environment' (p. 198) – a diagnosis
that says very little in real terms about the social or psychological
uniqueness of the man. It illuminates the myth without explaining
it.

For the myth of Chapayev the hero is the essence of the portrait.
Furmanov succeeded in surrounding his subject with 'an aura of the
heroic' despite all his use of documents, despite all his factography,
for the propagandist character of the portrayal justly reflected the
mythmaking quality of Chapayev himself and his times. He showed

both the timeliness of Chapayev, the way this hero-commander so adept at the sharp cut and thrust of civil-war engagements could exploit military situations to his advantage, and the ephemeral or fleeting character of Chapayev's achievement. Had not Chapayev been killed, drowned beneath the waters of the Ural river, the shortlived heroic substance to the myth would not have been there, as it were, for Furmanov to exploit.

The portrait of Fyodor Klichkov, or Furmanov's self-portrait, is as enriching for an understanding of the central impulse of the novel as is Chapayev's. Here, one feels, the factual truthfulness of this 'documentary' novel is most strongly evident. Klichkov is sensitive, intelligent and observant. His show of cowardice when first under fire has the sort of appealing frankness that immediately captures the reader's sympathy. When, after having described his initial approach to Chapayev, he gradually reaches the conclusion that Chapayev, 'that stern man of iron and guerilla hero, could be taken in hand like a child, that he could be moulded like wax' (p. 135), there can be very little doubt that the reader readily accepts the justice of this conclusion. He moulds Chapayev by influencing his ideas, or so he claims, though the extent of this influence is never demonstrated very clearly. He represents, loosely speaking, the influence of an industrial, politically conscious mentality, but this is little more than an aspect of the novel's tendentiousness as a whole, its propagandising intent as reportage. Furmanov's self-portrait shows not so much his influence on others as the influence of Chapayev and the times on him and his attempt to respond creatively to these stimuli. But 'influence' is always the central impulse: the beneficial mutual influence existing between Chapayev and Fyodor Klichkov and that later, more substantial, influence, which can be called propaganda, but which has so decisive a role in a civil war. On more than one occasion we are told how propaganda from the Red side decisively influenced the morale and intentions of the enemy. Such 'influence' was Furmanov–Klichkov's business and his novel documents it; this is its tendentiousness. In subtle, inexplicit but inevitable ways the effect is seen to greatest extent in the self-portrayal process. By the end, after Chapayev's death, he is able to say of himself:

Looking back to what he had been six months before, Klichkov could not recognise himself, so greatly had he developed, so much stronger had he become spiritually, and so tempered had he been by the ordeals he had undergone. Now he proceeded simply and confidently to solve the most diverse problems, which before his experience at the front would have seemed infinitely difficult. It was only now that he felt the mighty effect that the experience of fighting had had upon him, the great educational experience of life at the front (p. 229).

Throughout the novel, in minor ways, imagery breaks through the diarist's factographic manner and catches an instant out of the maelstrom of events. The crowd at the railway station in Ivanovo-Voznesensk 'looked like a solid faceless mass – shifting, rumbling, restless, like an enormous, shaggy, bear-like animal with a thousand paws and a thousand eyes'. Or, more graphically, the description of railway stations in the path of Kolchak's advance 'like bottles filled with ants'. Or the scream of the shell overhead that 'pierced the brain, curdled in the ears, rushed through the blood, the nerves and the muscles like a hurricane, setting them shivering'. At such points factography has an exactitude and power that resemble Tolstoyan art at its best. At other points the facts in their unillumined bareness seem as devoid of vitality as any pedestrian reportage.

Factography is seen more clearly in Furmanov's second and last novel *Revolt*. Serafimovich described it as 'a piece of the revolutionary struggle, a genuine piece with flesh and blood, narrated simply, sincerely, honestly and truthfully and in many places extraordinarily artistically'.[71] The artistic parts occur chiefly in the first part describing the author–narrator's journey from Tashkent to Verny, the capital of the 'region of seven rivers' (Semirech'ye). A central section describes the political circumstances in Verny on the eve of a revolt and a long third section gives a detailed account of the revolt supported by extracts from communiqués and other documents.

The time is 1920. Local opposition to enforced collection of foodstuffs, allied to political opportunism on the part of certain local chieftains and the town garrison's resentment of the arming of a Kirgiz brigade, led to the disaffection of some 5,000 troops from the Bolshevik cause. On the Soviet side there remained only between 15 and 20 Party members supported by a very modest administrative staff.

The insurgents clearly did not realise the extent of their own power and the weakness of their adversaries. They agreed to enter into negotiations with Furmanov and other loyal Party representatives. The blow-by-blow account of these negotiations is frankly tedious, but it sheds interesting light on the unconstitutionalism and arbitrariness of much Soviet behaviour during the revolutionary period. The insurgents' main demands are for an end to the searches and shootings undertaken by the Special Section and abolition of the Revolutionary Tribunal, both major instruments of Soviet power. The negotiations prove to be protracted. They are used by Furmanov as a means of stalling further moves by the insurgents until help can be obtained from Tashkent, but after a temporary accommodation has been reached Furmanov receives a secret report that he and the other Party officials are to be arrested and shot. His instantaneous response is to take the threat seriously and he at once contacts a Red Army cavalry regiment situated nearby. The next day the cavalry regiment marches on Verny and within a few hours the insurgents are in total disarray. The revolt had lasted from approximately 12 to 20 June 1920.

Thumbnail sketches of the insurgent leaders and his own colleagues demonstrate Furmanov's mastery of realistic reportage. What is lacking is the powerful central interest of an outstanding personality such as Chapayev. The revolt itself seems little more than a storm in a teacup and scarcely sustains interest. The central role of Furmanov as author–narrator serves merely to highlight the main attributes of the writer: his keen observation and intelligence, linked to an unremarkable literary ability. There is, in short, no mythmaking in this work, for the subject does not embody a myth that can be summoned forth as Chapayev's was. *Revolt* illustrates the mutual need uniting fact and fiction in the novel; where there are not the arts of fiction the facts appear orphaned in their isolation. Similarly, Furmanov himself, for all his honesty, was born like Chapayev, of the revolutionary situation – 'of *that* human mass, at *that* moment when it was in *that* state'. He was never more than that.

He epitomised a moment in the evolution of Soviet literature and the Soviet revolutionary novel when the tensions between mythology and factography produced 'novelty' in the genre, leaving it still fluid and indeterminate as a form but strong enough to create its own myth within a framework of fact. He epitomised that moment but could not transcend it. To have transcended it would have required an ideological breadth of which he was apparently incapable.

II   *Revolution and ideas*

Introduction

Ask point blank: What is revolution?

Some people will answer, paraphrasing Louis XIV: We are the revolution. Others will answer by the calendar, naming the month and the day. Still others will give you an ABC answer. But if we are to go on from the ABC to syllables, the answer will be this:

Two dead, dark stars collide with an inaudible, deafening crash and light a new star: this is revolution...

Revolution is everywhere, in everything. It is infinite. There is no final revolution, no final number. The social revolution is only one of an infinite number of numbers; the law of revolution is not a social law, but an immeasurably greater one.[72]

The question: what is revolution? is posed by all the novels that have so far been examined in this study of the revolutionary novels of the Soviet period. But in posing the question the novels have simultaneously tended to provide the answer that revolution had an instinctive source and manifested itself as an instinctive rebellion against the past. Such blanket categorisation may seem too drastic, for within the category of novels dealing with revolution as a manifestation of instinct there are different approaches and manners, which may make it seem that ideas as well as instinct had a significant motivating role to play. There is no doubt, though, that the posing of the question: what is revolution? has not elicited in any of the novels treated so far an answer involving the multiplicity of choices that are inseparable from intellectual consideration of an issue, that contribute to ideological awareness of the revolutionary character of events and attempt to confront, in an articulate way, the *pro* and *contra* of opposed ideological viewpoints and ideals.

Zamyatin was probably the only writer in the immediate post-revolutionary period who troubled to examine the question in depth. His answer clearly contained an anathema of a kind that no monist-based doctrine of revolution could countenance and certainly did not square with a Marxist–Leninist view of the October revolution. His insistence that revolution can embrace many things, that 'It is infinite', that it is not a social law, 'but an immeasurably greater one' could not fail to make him a heretic among orthodox Soviet writers. When, in furtherance of his heresy, he argued that 'heretics are necessary to health; if there are no heretics, they should be invented',[73] he was asserting the explosive, revolutionary function of those writers who challenge dogmatic ideologies and are the only means of countering the entropy of human thought. They may produce harmful literature:

But harmful literature is more useful than useful literature, for it is antientropic, it is a means of combating calcification, sclerosis, crust, moss, quiescence. It is utopian, absurd – like Babeuf in 1797. It is right 150 years later.[74]

His own contribution to anti-entropic literature was his novel *We* (*My*).[75] It cannot form part of the canon of the revolutionary novel, for it is not about the Russian revolutionary process, but it clearly has an introductory role in any study of the way in which revolutionary novels of the Soviet period attempted to deal with revolutionary idealism. It can be described as an 'anti-utopia', which has the partly satirical intent of ridiculing the idea that there can ever be a final revolution. It is also a piece of science fiction that claims our attention for its technically brilliant elliptical style, its poetry and the subtleties of its impressionist manner. In a fundamental sense it is a *tour-de-force* of literary illusionism. By this is meant that as a work of literature it presupposes the attempt of a highly specialised, numerate mind to articulate in a literary way feelings that it can hardly imagine.

The author of the work is a number, D-503, an important member of the Single State, who has been charged with the building of a kind of space ship called the *Integral*. The Single State is a mathematical utopia housed in a city made of glass and protected from the untamed, barbarian 'ancient' world by a Green Wall. All aspects of life are carefully regulated. Rest periods, sexual encounters between the 'numbers' and meals created from petroleum food are all subject to regulation. The novel achieves its interest as a work of fiction through the way in which the author, D-503, gradually discovers in himself the existence of what is quaintly called 'a soul' or 'a fantasy'. He is inspired in this discovery by his love for a female number, I-330, who turns out to be the leader of a revolutionary cult. Eventually the 'ancient' world breaks through the wall surrounding the Single State. It is not clear whether the revolution has triumphed, because the concluding statement by D-503 announces that he has undergone the 'happiness operation' for the removal of his 'soul' or 'fantasy' and he has become devoutly convinced that 'reason must conquer'. But he is also made aware at the very close of the novel that the Single

State has begun to wreak its vengeance on all who are opposed to it.

The nub of the satirical intent is the constantly reiterated depiction of humanity as a uniform mass, a uniform WE that enjoys a regulated, mindless happiness. Even the increasingly inquisitive D-503 assumes that humanity is differentiated chiefly by certain externally recognisable attributes, such as rosiness or negroid lips or the flapping sound that accompanies the act of walking. Personality differences have little significance. In fact, they are not easily discernible through the neutral, poetically photographic eye of D-503. His own personality is similarly a vague conglomerate of striking observations, *faux-naïf* judgements on the relationship between past and present or the mores of the Single State, and introspective, often fragmented, reflections on his changing emotional and mental condition. When he observes and participates in the mass hysteria that possesses the inhabitants of the Single State as they march in their orderly ranks, he serves to emphasise the satirical picture of a humanity that has ultimately succumbed to complete identification with the machine:

We march, a single million-headed body, and in each of us is that passive contentment which probably makes up the lives of molecules, atoms and phagocytes. In the ancient world the Christians, our only (though very imperfect) forerunners, understood this: for them passivity was a virtue, pride was a vice, and they understood that *We* belonged to God, *I* to the devil. (Entry No. 22)

If the picture of the uniformity of the *We* in Zamyatin's novel has a satirical complexion, the picture of the *I*, the single and unique experience of humanity, is saddening and tragic. D-503 discovers his 'I' only to become apprehensive of it and eventually to reject it. What he rejects of that 'I' is the subconscious part – the atavistic past that dwells beyond the Green Wall, glimpsed by him both when he makes visits to the ancient house for assignations with I-330, his mistress, and when his space ship, the *Integral*, finally takes off on its maiden flight. Strictly speaking no revolutionary himself, D-503 is continually surprised – and rather appalled – to discover how profoundly the ethos of the Single State has been undermined by the devilish, Mephistophelian proclivities of the revolution. It is not he who has such proclivities but his closest friends – I-330, for instance, and the poet with the negroid lips, R-13. They enunciate the blasphemy that the Single State has for long attempted to suppress in its citizens. The first of such blasphemies is the idea that the number of revolutions is infinite. The second is the idea (far more insidious and therefore dangerous) that perhaps man should not choose happiness as his ultimate ideal. This latter issue of choice is central to Zamyatin's argument in his novel and it obviously owes its provenance to the argument of Dostoyevsky's Underground Man. The poet, R-13, puts it in the following way:

'Those two in paradise were given a choice: either happiness without freedom, or freedom without happiness; there was no third choice. They, the fools, chose freedom and then, understandably, centuries were spent by humanity yearning after fetters for their freedom. The Weltschmerz of the centuries, you understand, was about those fetters. Century after century! And only we have once again discovered how to bring happiness back...No, no, you must go on listening to what I've got to say! The God of the ancients and we are now side by side, at the same table. Yes, indeed! We have helped God finally to overcome the devil – for it's devil that prompted men to break the law and taste of the obnoxious freedom, he was the cunning snake. But we flattened his head with our heel – cr-r-rack! And so we have paradise again. And again we're simple and innocent like Adam and Eve. No more of this confusing talk about good and evil. Everything is now very simple, paradisially, childishly simple...' (Entry No. 11)

By contrast, I-330 argues that all citizens of this new paradise of the Single State must return in their primeval nakedness to the primeval forests surrounding them. They must learn from the trees and wild animals and birds and flowers and sun. Those who did escape naked into those forests grew hairy skins but beneath their hairiness they preserved their fiery red blood, their true revolutionary selves. Speaking to D-503, she insists:

'It's far worse for you, you've grown numbers all over you, numbers crawl all over you like lice. You should be stripped of everything and driven into the forests. Then mankind may learn to shiver with fear and joy and furious anger and cold, then they may pray to the Gods of fire. And we, the Mephi, we want...'
'Wait a moment – the Mephi? What are the Mephi?'
'The Mephi? It's a name from the past, it's the one who...You remember the young man we saw carved on the stone...No, I'd better explain it in your language, so you'll understand it quicker. There are two forces in the world – entropy and energy. One leads to a heaven-sent peace of mind, to a joyous sense of balance, the other leads to the destruction of equilibrium, to tormenting and endless motion. To entropy our – or rather your – forebears, the Christians, bowed down as to God. But we, anti-Christians, we...' (Entry No. 28)

Though it is precisely the atavistic energy of blood-lust and the subconscious that D-503 seems in the end to reject, the atavism is still deeply enough rooted in his brainwashed numerate self for him to recognise the pressures within him that incline him to reject the Single State's uniform happiness in favour of freedom of choice. Ironically the one freedom that he does eventually have to sacrifice is, in its very essence, the source and purpose of all satire, especially political satire: the freedom to laugh. Intending to commit murder towards the close of the novel, D-503 is suddenly confronted by the fact that his victim has misconstrued his aggressive pose as a desire for love. The incongruity so appals him that he bursts into uncontrollable laughter: 'At that moment I saw from my own experience that laughter is the most terrible of all weapons: with laughter you can put an end to everything – even murder. (Entry No. 35).' And the most comic of all paradoxes occurs when, after realising that the greatest and most rational civilisation is being destroyed by the revolutionaries, he takes refuge in an underground public lavatory and his costive neighbour explains to him excitedly that he thinks he has finally proved there is no such thing as eternity. Such apocalyptic lunacy, like the ultimate constipation of human thought, is the note on which D-503 brings his account to an end.

The political implication of the satire is too obvious for comment. The banning of the novel in the Soviet Union testifies to its effectiveness. Equally important testimony is the acknowledged influence of the novel on George Orwell in the writing of his own *Nineteen Eighty-Four*.[76] Zamyatin's prophecy of political tyranny came to pass even as he was writing it. But the detail of his science-fiction prophecy has an endearing Wellsian antiquity to it. His space ship, the *Integral*, has a motive power of rococo Edwardian complexity, and, even though there may be 'aeros' that convey D-503 and his beloved on pleasant trips through the air, the need for tickets for love-making converts Zamyatin's Single State into an earth-bound bureaucracy all too reminiscent of the bureaucracy-embalmed world of War Communism. On the other hand, the most terrifyingly prophetic aspect of Zamyatin's novel is the accuracy of the prediction that a monolithic body such as the Single State of the Soviet Union must continually hark back to its revolutionary beginnings and must always celebrate the finality of that revolution. The idea that eternity should be finite consequently acquires the force of a historical law and is more terrible in its self-justifying complacency than any atavism.

Prophecy apart, Zamyatin's *We* articulates the central issue of all novels that strive to present the opposition of ideological viewpoints and are therefore concerned with revolution and ideas. It poses a central issue of choice. D-503 has to choose between the entropy of his cold rationalism and the revolutionary energy of his fiery emotions. The dilemma of choice is complex and tragic. If he accepts the mindless entropy of uniform happiness, he is denying himself the 'soul' and 'fantasy' that alone can make him aware of the revolutionary potential of human achievement, but if he chooses such 'freedom' he is also predestining himself to the tragic dilemma of choice between good and evil that has caused such agony to humanity over the centuries. The intellectual response to the meaning of revolution is what the novel, as a literary form, is splendidly suited to reflect. The Russian tradition of the ideological novel in the nineteenth century points the way. Zamyatin's novel, in its obvious reference to Dostoyevsky's thinking on the nature of freedom and Chernyshevsky's utopian *What is to be Done?*, belongs to the nineteenth-century tradition, while intimating how the intellect of the twentieth century can respond to the issue of ideological choice posed by the October revolution.

We is especially important as a remarkable experiment in the 'revolutionising' of literature. Zamyatin has consciously adjusted his literary manner to the purposes of illustrating the presumed emotional 'revolution' in his hero, D-503. As he falls in love with his 'revolutionary' mistress, I-330, he begins to record the revolutionary change in himself in a consciously poetic manner, or as Robert Russell has expressed it: 'the development, or rather revelation, of a soul in D-503 coincides with the creative use of language and with the onset of a revolutionary mentality'.[77] The sheer virtuosity of Zamyatin's manner is matched only by Babel, Pilnyak and Olesha, and of these only the last is strictly comparable. The absence of his novel from Soviet surveys of the revolutionary novel in the early Soviet period may leave the erroneous impression that early examples of such novels were without intellectual interest, though full of any amount of daring verbal experimentation and ornamental writing. It was only towards the end of the 1920s that novels dealing with ideological reactions to the October revolution began to appear in reasonable numbers (chiefly after 1924 and especially in 1927). None compares with Zamyatin's in prophetic or 'science fantasy' daring. But of the very few novels dealing with such ideological reactions, on a fairly superficial level, admittedly, the most outstanding is a short novel by A. S. Yakovlev.[78]

October (*Oktyabr'*) (written 1918; published 1923) describes with remarkable candour the ideological confusion that leads the worker Ivan Petryayev to forsake his working-class origins and join the Whites during the ten days or so of armed conflict between Whites and Reds in Moscow in October 1917. The story also involves briefly his brother Vasily, who is little more than an appalled onlooker, and the young Akim, who joins the Bolsheviks and is killed. Ivan realises that he may have been guilty of this killing and in final atonement shoots himself on Akim's grave.

The picture of the street fighting, seen largely from the White side, appears to be based on first-hand experience. It has a chilling and remorseless candour. As an illustration of the way in which revolution became civil war in the twinkling of an eye this novel has documentary as well as literary value. But its true merit as literature lies in its coldly objective portrayal of the blood-lust and inhumanity that came immediately to the surface in the October events. Written in an unornamented manner, the novel occasionally offers a striking image that graphically records an instant in the fighting. The glimpse, for instance, of a truck filled with armed men:

Round the corner of the Okhotny came a heavy truck, in which, sitting and standing, were armed men in blue and grey uniforms. Rifles stuck out in all directions. A creeping vase of rifles, heads, arms and grey and blue uniforms looking just like flowers. It crept to the next corner and tried to hide.[79]

On the whole, the interaction of revolution and ideological attitudes, including those dictated by class allegiance or background, is explored most fully in those novels which deal with the intelligentsia's reaction to revolutionary events. A great many novels, of very uneven quality, deal with this subject and practically all of them are now quite justifiably forgotten. However, there are some that aroused interest in their first appearance and deserve to be noticed briefly.

One of them is Bakhmet'yev's *Martin's Crime* (*Prestupleniye Martyna*) (1928) about a young communist, Martin Baymakov, whose divided inheritance at birth – his father was a Volga fisherman, his mother from a rich landowning family – makes him too individualistic and, at a crucial moment, too concerned to save his own skin at the expense of defenceless women and children who are in his charge. His 'crime' can be said to have a social motivation, though the novel does not illustrate this particularly well, and his personal problem, one of glory-seeking and a bad conscience, seems to be better interpreted as another variant of the intelligentsia's inability to act decisively and unequivocally in the furtherance of a socio-political ideal. In the end he vindicates himself, it seems, by sacrificing his life to save the lives of others, but even this act of personal bravado receives only lukewarm commendation from the novel's 'positive' character, a man called Chernogolovy who had been Martin's long-standing friend and counsellor. He jots down in his notebook the following sententious epitaph:

Martin thought that the problem of conscience could be resolved by his own fear. He didn't even suspect that it's useless to embark on a singlehanded struggle with human nature. And he had nothing to say for himself, neither by his life, nor by his death, because what is the bravado of a hero if it is only the class as a whole that can display bravery: one may have fallen, there will be another to take his place.

The algebraic, sententiously rigid standards of Chernogolovy may be correct in a declaratively orthodox Marxist sense, but tend to deny his character depth or emotional resonance. The only successfully realised and sympathetic piece of characterisation in this very dated novel is Martin's girl-friend Zina.

A psychologically more interesting study of the kind of conflict of conscience posed by revolutionary change is to be found in D. I. Krutikov's *The Black Half* (*Chyornaya polovina*) (1928). It tells of Tikhon, a young medical student, who returns to his native village of Chalmyshnya where the only member of his family still living is his father, formerly the village priest. The return to the village is accompanied by lengthy reminiscences involving his brother Yakov, who had been killed in the civil war, and the young widow whom he left behind. The reminiscences also involve him in a reconsideration of questions of faith, which had been so burdensome to his brother and himself in their boyhood. Despite the superficial changes that have occurred both in himself and in his surroundings, Tikhon is confronted by the fact that his father and his native village remain essentially divided into two halves, the one seemingly civilised, the other locked in its black superstition and changelessness. He falls in love with his brother's widow and hopes that he can eventually marry her, though his life as a medical student and hers in the near-medieval world of Chalmyshnya create a divide between them that neither their mutual passion nor his promise to his dying brother can properly bridge. He becomes convinced that 'those who were once serfs have still not yet been freed completely from the shackles of serfdom and, unless we seize our soldering-iron firmly, we may have to be busy with it for a long time yet'. The implication is that the 'white' and the 'black' halves of the Russian countryside have finally to be welded together. The dialogue is unusually lively and Tikhon's problem, mirroring as it does the larger problem of change that revolution can bring to the countryside, is treated with psychological subtlety and depth.

Another little-known novel dealing with a similar theme, though more vigorously written, is P. Shiryayev's *Revelry* (*Gul'ba*) (1929). The effects of civil war on provincial life are seen here principally from the point of view of a type of 'superfluous man', *intelligent* Telepnev and his friend Chibrikov. The latter is a spry, cheeky, resourceful man, the local town know-all, who lodges with Telepnev's aunt. The 'revelry' of the first period of the civil war soon gives way to a more serious phase when banditry and mayhem take over. Telepnev and his friend decide to set off for Moscow after the aunt's death. Chibrikov has secreted in a drum all the aunt's gold and jewellery, which Telepnev had decided to renounce, and so the strange pair embark on their journey, only to be attacked by bandits on the way. Telepnev is in fact shot in the legs and shoulder and is nursed by the wife of one of the bandits, but when news comes of an approaching punitive detachment the husband kills him. The relationship between Telepnev and the wife, for all the apparent dissimilarity between the *intelligent* and the simple peasant woman, is the only poignant episode in the novel.

Apart from highlighting the fatuous character of intelligentsia attitudes in the post-revolutionary period, the novel also pokes fun at the heavy-handed treatment of the peasantry by the Germanic army commander of the Bolshevik punitive detachments. A wry, parodistic sense of humour informs many of the scenes. But what the novel points up particularly well is the distance between the intelligentsia, whether pre-revolutionary or Soviet, and the peasantry. It is a distance expressed most wittily in Chibrikov's remark:

Ninety million peasants are crawling along with the slowness of a louse, and their entire life crawls at the same speed, while above their heads are roaring the propellers of socialism going at two hundred miles an hour! You can appreciate from this the difference in speed between the two worlds, the two types of feeling and sensation, the two types of culture!

Essentially what such novels define – and this is no doubt the reason why so many of them have disappeared into the oblivion of forgotten literature – is the extent to which the revolution has failed to achieve its ideological ideals. It may have failed to bridge that gap between the peasantry and the intelligentsia which so excited Slavophil or Populist or Socialist Revolutionary sentiments in pre-revolutionary Russia. It may have shown up the failure of intelligentsia attitudes when confronted by the need to act. It may have failed because it was based on the false assumption that there can only be one revolution. Whatever their degree of success in diagnosing the doctrinal or ideological problems posed by revolution, all such novels have in common what Fielding called 'invention' and 'judgment' – the capacity, that is, for 'finding out; or...a quick and sagacious penetration into the true essence of all the objects of our contemplation' and the ability to discern 'the true essence of two things'. In a word, realism; but a realism that has more in common with the nineteenth-century tradition of Critical Realism than the more doctrinaire forms of Socialist Realism. The element of 'judgment' in all such novels that present revolutionary issues in ideological terms and therefore in terms of choice must involve a critical approach or at least a sense of appraisal that will not preclude criticism. Only by this means can a novelist hope to discover that 'true essence' which Fielding felt was so important – and which must, after all, be the object of any investigation of history, of human motivation and human behaviour.

Necessarily a part of this process of discovery, for it is concerned with discovering the true essence of the *human* reaction to revolutionary events, is the creation of character. One major difference between the majority of revolutionary novels discussed so far and under the heading of 'Revolution and ideas' those still to be discussed is that the earlier novels are not character-centred, are deficient in psychological understanding of character and are very little concerned with exploring the ideological motivation of character. In the later novels that confront the issue of ideological motivation the principal and central concern is that of character-creation. On the whole, their success and failure as novels can be judged primarily in terms of their success or failure in creating character, but there are other important ideological considerations that, if secondary, contribute vitally to their impact as revolutionary novels. There is also, of course, the fact that 'invention', not in

Fielding's sense but in the normal sense of innovation and resource, has its role to play in determining the originality of the novels as literature.

Briefly, the evolution of the revolutionary novel of the Soviet period follows a course from camera-like or cinematic depiction of revolutionary events, the death–birth of a world, through elementalist, mass-orientated portrayal of revolutionary heroism, to myth-making and then, gradually, towards more sober or 'realistic' attempts to examine the ideological issues at work in the revolution. Such attempts are merely a further stage in the evolution of a literary response to revolution than can only truly match the grandeur of the events by creating an equally grandiose literary form: that of the revolutionary epic. The Russian revolutionary novel, with its roots so firmly fixed in the central domestic issue of Russian nineteenth-century politics – the emancipation of the serfs – becomes also the central issue of Soviet literature in the twentieth century, the occasion of its only epic works and, paradoxically, the one sure yardstick by which the value of Soviet literature as a representation of 'true essence' can be judged.

Doubts and ideals: *Cities and Years, The Deadlock, The White Guard*

With unusual critical unanimity, Konstantin Fedin's first novel *Cities and Years* (*Goroda i gody*) (1924) has generally received high praise as one of the few early novels in Soviet literature to have the quality and range of the nineteenth-century Russian novel.[80] It has such distinction because, as the author of the only major study of Fedin in English has put it, 'Fedin was the first Soviet author to probe the psychological problems of the Revolution' and *Cities and Years* 'is the first big epic-like Soviet novel, and continues the nineteenth-century tradition of the lengthy, realistic, psychological, social novel'.[81] The novel certainly has psychological interest of a kind unmatched by any Soviet novel before it and it ranges further in terms of its fictional geography.

This is not a study of the impact of revolutionary events on provincial life seen through intellectual eyes, though that may be part of the story. It is not a picture of bourgeois metropolitan culture undermined by revolution, though that is true in part. It is a novel that, in its *range* of locales and characters, eludes easy categorisation, but it remains essentially a study of one individual's experience of the 'cities and years' that comprise his knowledge of war and revolution. In this sense it embraces places and issues in the manner of an epic work; yet the relationship of hero to setting or social milieu is never deeply rooted as it is in Lev Tolstoy or Sholokhov; the two principles of set-building and character-creation do not interact, so that the places and the issues seem in the end larger and more elaborate than the hero's real but small-scale humanity.

In 1946, on being shown the illustration on the cover of the Spanish translation of his novel, Fedin remarked:

It showed a man lying face downwards on the ground with an enormous hour-glass pressing down on him. That was all. And I thought this very faithfully conveyed the basic theme – of a man who was a victim of the epoch, a victim of the time.

We often seek a graphic means of expressing our ideas. How could I express this idea outwardly, in terms of the novel's composition? How could the composition help to reflect this idea in the best possible way? I decided that the theme of predetermination should be expressed by a circle or ring. A man who cannot find a way out because he is surrounded by a solid chain, a solid ring. From the image of the ring I drew the conclusion that I had to create a circular composition, that I had to show that Andrey would never break out of this solid ring. I constructed such a ring.[82]

Cities and Years is so constructed. In its initial form it may have been more orthodox.[83] As it is, it contains material published earlier in other forms (the story 'Uncle Kisel'', for instance, published in *Syzransky kommunar* (22 November 1919)) and it was written over a period of about two years, between May 1922 and September 1924. Fedin's claims for his work, made more than twenty years after its first publication, suggest a resoluteness of purpose the history of the novel's composition does not fully justify.

The novel opens at the point where the 'story' of Andrey Startsov ends, in his execution by his former friend, the German artist and Bolshevik, Kurt Wahn. His death is decreed because he has helped to save the life of an enemy of the Soviet state. Kurt Wahn, therefore, 'did for Andrey all that a comrade, friend and artist should do'.

After his fashion Andrey Startsov is a familiar type of *intelligent* – weak-willed, emotionally unstable, self-centred, unable to comprehend the purpose of the changes occurring around him and therefore increasingly 'superfluous' in the post-revolutionary world. His story clearly reflects in its central episode a most important experience in his creator's life. Fedin had gone to Germany as a student to perfect his German. At the outbreak of the First World War he had been seized in Dresden while attempting to return to Russia and was interned in a small provincial town (Zittau). The central episode in *Cities and Years* describes Andrey's experiences in Germany during his internment. The picture of wartime Germany, with its description of the gradual breakdown of the imperialist ethos, is impressive though ponderous and sometimes tedious. Bischofsberg, as the town is called in the novel, resembles small-town Germany in its jingoism, priggishness, hypocrisy and bourgeois respectability. It illustrates that fundamental weakness of Germany under the Kaiser which helps to explain the willingness of Germans to follow such leaders, despite the apparent strength of German Social Democracy. Fedin himself explains his meaning as follows:

'The hunger to obey orders' characteristic of the bourgeoisie made out of Europe's largest and, at one time, most respected Social Democracy, that of Germany, pretty good soldiers in the hands of the military...The Kaiser's socialists were essentially obedient.[84]

Andrey Startsov looks at Germany as a stranger and he looks at the revolution with the eyes of an outsider. For this reason his view of Bischofsberg perceives only the scantiest intimations of the deeper meanings in German life. Yet it is precisely in this viewing of the world from the angle of an outsider that the novel as a whole acquires interest and distinction. There are many instances, often subtle ones, of outside views that reveal truths about national attitudes and human relationships. Such novelty of viewpoint is well adapted to the 'making strange' effect that the reversal of chronology is designed to achieve. It is a novel about a fragmented epoch and the consequent fragmentation of experience presented as events viewed incoherently, almost sightlessly. The empty, sightless eyes, whether those of the murderer Karl Ebersochs, whose head is preserved in the local museum, or the sightless eyes of the gassed Italian prisoners of war who come between Andrey and his girl-friend at their meeting in the park of the seven ponds – such eyes, like the image of the silent witness, are important recurrent motifs, which emphasise Andrey's dilemma as the witness of an epoch who cannot understand it. The only 'seeing' in a visionary sense is supposedly done by his German friend, the young and talented artist Kurt Wahn, whose vocation as artist in Germany gives way to that of dedicated political activist in revolutionary Russia. The image of empty eyes receives by contrast

its fullest meaning when Andrey returns to Russia and encounters
in the small provincial town of Semidol the empty eyes of German
prisoners of war:

Each has his own eyes, and above the eyes sit the faded, bullet-holed peakless
caps. The eyes are suspicious, exhausted and empty. What was hidden behind
such emptiness? The cold murk of dug-outs and the sweetish stench of
hospitals, white bones twisted out of limp flesh, blood dripping from barbed
wire and the mouldy, stagnant dampness of the trenches. How could one
hope to astonish eyes like that? They have seen everything, they know
everything, they need nothing, they're vacant, endlessly vacant in this world.
The world of dug-outs, trenches and hospitals has not yet invented words
that could fill the vacancy of such eyes, and nothing in this world can remove
the look of immobility from faces fretted by a blood-stained wind.

Andrey Startsov's attempt to inspire such empty eyes by his rhetoric
ironically emphasises both his own superfluity and the incompre-
hension with which he views the revolution in Russia.

While in Germany Andrey meets and falls in love with a girl from
a wealthy German family, Marie Urbach. A rivalry for her affections
develops between Andrey and the local aristocrat, Markgraf von zur
Muehlen-Schoenau. In attempts to escape from his internment
Andrey is captured, held prisoner for a while in the Markgraf's
Schloss and then released. This act of gentlemanly charity is to prove
a debt of honour that Andrey can only discharge at risk to his own
life. After returning to Russia, Andrey is sent to an area of the Volga
where, in the company of Kurt Wahn and other Bolsheviks, he helps
to organise the infant forms of Soviet power. The only peasant figure
in the novel is a certain Lependin, a sketchy figure on the whole,
whose principal role in Andrey's story is that he falls victim to a
bloodthirsty uprising among the Mordov people, which has been
organised – improbably, to say the least – by the very same Markgraf
von zur Muehlen-Schoenau who had been Andrey's rival. But the
Mordov rising is put down and, in desperation, the Markgraf seeks
out Andrey and enlists his help in attempting to flee back to
Germany. Andrey, still deeply in love with Marie Urbach, despite
his relationship with a Russian girl who becomes pregnant by him,
is so keen to get in touch with Marie that he agrees to help the
Markgraf, both to discharge his debt of honour and because the
German is prepared to take Andrey's letter to Marie back to
Germany with him. Andrey steals documents relating to a German
prisoner of war called Conrad Stein and under this alias the

Markgraf is able to escape to Germany. Here of course he resumes his aristocratic place in German society and his bloodthirsty deeds in Russia are put behind him. For Andrey the past cannot be so easily erased: his crime is uncovered, he is condemned as one who has aided a class enemy and he is shot by his erstwhile friend.

The story is full of contrivances. The characterisation of the villains, meaning the Markgraf himself and incidental representatives of the bourgeois world, both Russian and German, is stilted and superficial. Marie Urbach herself is scarcely more than a phantom figure who only occasionally shows signs of acquiring the lineaments of a flesh-and-blood character. One may well agree with the judgement of Ernest J. Simmons: 'Basically *Cities and Years* is not a novel of characters; the men and women in it seem rather like illustrations of varying points of view in a deliberately wrought pattern of ideological struggle.'[85]

But the *atmosphere* of the German world, composed from so many isolated observations of small-town life, has richness and vitality. Similarly, the pictures of Russian life during the civil war, whether drawn from the experiences of Petrograd when faced by Yudenich or from the activities of young Bolsheviks in the Volga area, have moments of poignancy and intense veracity. There are some of the most sympathetic portraits of Bolsheviks to be found in Soviet literature in this novel – the brash and punctilious young Golosov, for instance, or the Finn, Pokkisen, who is another victim of the violent times. There is an attractive, if brief, portrait in miniature of an elderly professor, known as the 'trench professor', who accompanies Andrey on an enforced trench-digging exercise in beleagured Petrograd. No doubt declaratively, but also with a sincerity that rings true, this elderly professor proclaims the greatness of the times through which the cities are living, whereas to Andrey Startsov the revolution only seems to mean destruction and a vision of humanity doomed to mutual annihilation. The civilised tone of the novel's style seems to be of a piece with Andrey's sensibility, but the multi-faceted horrors and idiosyncrasies thrown up by the 'years' of the novel's setting contrive to make the style seem strange, alienated, almost on occasion an embroidering on the subject-matter. Consequently, the vision of doomed humanity that manifests itself in such moments of violence as the death of Lependin or Andrey's own violent end has a meretricious air and weakens the impact of the novel. There is a tentativeness about its claims on the reader's attention that makes the depiction of revolutionary violence seem a trifle unreal and creates in the novel an air of doubt about the moral worth of such violence.

This is represented most clearly, of course, in the dilemma of Andrey Startsov himself. It is a cautious, incomplete portrait composed of pacifist tendencies, a vague humanitarianism, some attributes of Tolstoyanism and an abstract, individualistic morality that, in Soviet eyes at least, inhibits total commitment to the revolution. His dilemma is as much psychological as moral. His trust in the humanitarian ideals of the pre-revolutionary intelligentsia is undermined by the cruelty of revolutionary reality, just as his passion for Marie Urbach, so psychologically damaging to him in that it actually makes him commit treason for his enemy's sake, proves in the end to be literally unbalancing when he discovers that Marie has abandoned him. As a Czech critic has pointed out:

War and love are just as sharply polarised concepts as war and humanism. Startsov suffers as much from the contrast between war and love as he does from the contrast between war and humanism...

Andrey Startsov is a tragic hero. There is none of the joy and fullness in him of simple human life...Startsov is a member of the Russian intelligentsia with a European education, the core of which was idealistic philosophy. The basic principles of abstract German morality had penetrated deeply into Andrey's soul and reinforced in him the 'superfluous men' traits.[86]

His tragedy, in an ideological sense, may certainly be equated with the tragedy of the pre-revolutionary intelligentsia, whose moral idealism drove them to seek revolutionary change while profoundly doubting the immoral means used to achieve revolutionary ends. But his tragedy is also psychological, or personal, in the sense that it is his own weakness of character or sheer lack of will that leads eventually to his isolation and superfluity. There is, equally, a confusing tentativeness about Fedin's approach to his hero's dilemma that deters the drawing of any final conclusion. The reader is asked, it seems, to pity rather than to understand. If, on the one hand, his hero was a victim of 'the lost generation', as Fedin described him, unable to discern the differences between war as such and the civil war that was being fought on behalf of the workers and peasants against the former exploiters, then, on the other hand:

he was unable to subordinate his personal life to the austere, but also the great, tasks of the period, and the period took its revenge on him. Weakness led him to crime. The way he perished was the judgement on him. This distinguishes him from 'the lost generation': it was not the tragedy of war that defined his fate, but he doomed himself to a just vengeance of his own accord. His fate was an exception, fairly widespread, true, in that section of the intelligentsia to which he belonged.[87]

In saying this, Fedin seems to be wanting to have it both ways: that Andrey's fate was exceptional, but widespread even though exceptional, and yet he also insists, in a kind of afterword to his hero's story, that:

We are ending our tale of a man who had waited with longing for life to accept him. We look back on the road which he followed in the wake of cruelty and love, on a road strewn with blood and flowers. He traversed it without having a speck of blood on him and without trampling a single flower.

O, if only he'd had just one speck of blood on him and trampled just one little flower! Perhaps then our pity for him would have grown into love, and we would not have left him to perish so miserably and insignificantly.

But to the very last moment he did nothing, just waited for the wind to carry him to the haven he was seeking.

The chief redeeming characteristic of Andrey Startsov is that he doubted. He may not have acted, or if he did act he may have acted wrongly, but in doubting the moral worth of the revolution he exhibited precisely that nonconformity and disobedience to the 'years' through which the cities were living that differentiated him from the leather-jacketed type of Kurt Wahn. If Andrey was 'superfluous', then Kurt Wahn was essential to Soviet power and Bolshevism. In creating such a monolithic figure Fedin was guilty of exaggeration to the point where the portrait lost all human semblance. 'Kurt is just one who executes orders', Fedin wrote.[88] He resembles all too closely one of those essentially obedient German Socialists to whom Fedin referred scathingly in his preface to the novel. In fact, Kurt's only role in the novel is to do obediently for Andrey 'all that a comrade, friend and artist should do'. That he should be represented as an artist, let alone a friend of Andrey, endows him with so bizarre a combination of attributes that there must inevitably be a false and contrived air about his portrayal.

Fedin reworked his novel for the editions of 1932 and 1959. For many years under Stalin the novel was not republished. Its stylistic sophistication, like its oblique and ambiguous treatment of the hero, made it suspect. If it remains, despite the subsequent growth in

Fedin's reputation, a work of which the political meaning leaves room for unorthodox interpretations, it still has a prominent place in the forefront of Soviet writing of the 1920s as an accomplished, highly literate novel and an outstanding example of the revolutionary novel of the period.

V. V. Veresaev's *The Deadlock* (*V tupike*) (1924) is one of the few conventional novels by established writers to deal with the experience of the intelligentsia during the civil war. It is a conventional novel in the sense that it makes use of the methods of descriptive writing, dialogue and narrative that are commonly to be found in realistic novels. There is no playing with chronology, no ornamentalism, no attempt to dehumanise the portraiture. But it has an authenticity and truthfulness that make it one of the most valuable studies of the dilemma of choice and conscience that troubled sensitive, morally upright members of the intelligentsia during such a period of changing fortunes.

The novel is dated '1920–1923' but is set in 1918–19, as Veresaev himself admitted in his autobiography:

In September 1918 I went to the Crimea for three months and stayed there for three years – near Feodosiya, in the settlement of Koktebel', where I had a small dacha. During that time the Crimea changed hands several times and much suffering had to be endured.[89]

He returned to Moscow in the autumn of 1921 and was able to complete his novel by early 1923. It is therefore a fresh record in novel form of events and personalities known personally to the author. The novel offers a multi-faceted picture of intellectual exiles living a dacha existence in the Crimea, engaged in the daily struggle for survival and in innumerable embittered, occasionally sardonic, discussions of their plight and the chaos facing Russia as a whole. Veresaev very successfully evokes a small community of talkative, bitchy, clever, sometimes humorous people at the mercy of exterior forces, whether they be the dreadful fluctuations in prices, the persistent rumours, the total breakdown of law and order or the arbitrary terror employed by both Whites and Reds.

At the centre of the novel is the Sartanov family. Dr Sartanov is an epitome of the old *intelligent* who believed in the sacred duty of the intelligentsia to preserve life at all costs. His own opposition to the death-penalty has led to his imprisonment in the past and causes his imprisonment under the Bolsheviks. A man of principle, he cannot accept the sententious justifications of bloodshed offered by the apologists of Bolshevik terror. In an exchange with Leonid Sedoy, a nephew who was to become an active supporter of Bolshevism, he protests when the latter declares that revolutions cannot be made with clean hands. He points out how Leonid had campaigned against the death-penalty under Kerensky and argued that the conscience of the proletariat would never countenance the death-penalty:

Leonid shrugged his shoulders in astonishment.

'Wonderful! We're speaking completely different languages... Well, in those days it was a question of the execution of soldiers courageously refusing to participate in a criminal imperialist war, whereas now we're talking about traitors who are stabbing the revolution in the back.'

'But surely you said the proletariat would never countenance the death-penalty on principle?'

'Okay, uncle, perhaps I did. So what? In those days it was a useful agitational point to make.'

Katya shuddered in disgust. Ivan Ilyich seized himself by the chest, pressed his hands to his heart and, biting his lip, stumbled around the kitchen.

'You've betrayed the revolution!' he cried in anguish. 'You've betrayed it hopelessly and irredeemably!'

Leonid's eyes lit up with ironic malice.

'Can't you understand, uncle, that revolution isn't almond cake, that it's always like that? Haven't you ever read about the French Revolution or heard of its giants – Marat, Robespierre, Saint-Juste, or even your petit-bourgeois Danton? They weren't just engaged in making almond cakes and yet you don't say they betrayed the revolution... Well, so we've betrayed it. But you, its loyal standard bearers, where are you now? There are masses of us, elemental forces are on our side, but you – how many of you are there?'[90]

This is the essence of the issue. Andrey Startsov's dilemma is brought into focus here just as is Ivan Ilyich Sartanov's and the crisis of conscience that faced the Russian intelligentsia in the civil war. Alexander Herzen had already diagnosed the real character of revolution in his *From the Other Shore*, and Sartanov's daughter Katya reads Herzen's words a short while later. She discovers his assertion that the coming revolution will not preside over history like a court of justice or even be concerned to right wrongs, but will be a cataclysm, an overturning of all things, an incursion of barbarians that will sweep away the civilisation of the past. Naturally the intelligentsia will form part of that civilisation. It is to be Katya's, not Dr Sartanov's, destiny to outlive the holocaust. Sartanov's destiny is to protest against the excesses, but his and the intelligentsia's guiding role is shown to be hopelessly redundant. Indeed, the role of 'thinking' people is shown to be no more than that of protesting onlookers at the revolution's cataclysmic degeneration into blood-lust and chaos.

Katya is the central figure. If her sister is shot, her mother murdered by drunken soldiers, her father arrested, she is the survivor, but she survives more through good fortune than by any evasion of her responsibilities. At the opening of the novel, she exhibits the characteristic dissatisfactions of her youth and the intelligentsia attitudes to which she is heir. After listening to songs being sung that had 'a stupefying, erotically seductive beauty', she and her friend Dmitry, on leave from the White army, go out into the open air and the wind:

Katya hungrily gulped in the sea breeze and the haunting beauty of the drowsy music was washed from her heart. Her shoulders gave a shudder and she started repeating:
   'What filth! What filth!'
   Dmitry asked in astonishment: 'What's so filthy?'
   'Everything, everything! How can such rottenness seem so beautiful and fragrant? As if you're in a Parfumerie in which all the expensive perfumes have been smashed and spilt and it's all gone to your head and you don't want to leave, when suddenly there's the sun, the wind, the open air...Oh, how marvellous!'

Katya's feelings epitomise some features of the dilemma facing the Russian intelligentsia. The pre-revolutionary past, although rotten in their eyes, had so many attractive fragrances, but was remote from the 'natural' truths of life as the intelligentsia understood them, and sun, wind and space are the bracing natural phenomena that revolution should have as its climate. The novel is about Katya's discovery that revolution is not one thing but many confusing and humiliating things.

Superficially the revolution for the intelligentsia may have seemed a 'dead end'; it was not, for sure, a revolution in which they could believe. *The Deadlock* explores the pathetic, self-righteous, yet honourable attempts of conscience-stricken men and women to adjust to the conscienceless fluctuations of civil war, but the reader is left in little doubt that the failure to adjust is due as much to an inflexible objectivism, a refusal to make total commitment, as to any superior highmindedness. Dr Sartanov can lament over the way in which the Bolsheviks have exterminated the conscience of the

Russian people and torn out its soul, but there are no examples of 'the beautiful Russian people' in this novel. On the whole, the peasantry and tradesmen are represented as greedily awaiting their chance to pillage and denounce, and when the Bolsheviks finally arrive they are shown as recruiting to their cause the most unsavoury riffraff. Though Katya protests, she gradually becomes disheartened by the oppressive atmosphere of dissemblance and falsehood surrounding her. The jokes, of which there are several good instances in this novel, become progressively more cynical and bitter.[91] But there is no joking about Katya's eventual horror at the realisation that the intelligentsia whose honour she had defended so fiercely is being systematically betrayed by its own kind. In a scene towards the end of the novel she encounters a member of the intelligentsia who turns out to be a notorious Chekist, Voronko. His justification of terror seems not only inhumane, but redoubled in its awfulness by the supposed logicality that animates it. To this Katya has no reply. When the Bolsheviks are driven out by the Whites, the former terror is replaced by another. The vicious circle continues. In the concluding scene Katya and her father, Ivan Ilyich, are left alone to contemplate the ruin of their lives:

On a clear evening, when the cicadas had already ceased and pale-lilac shadows were creeping along the receding promontories, and, in the quiet before nightfall, waves were breaking with soft splashes on the warm sand, Ivan Ilyich lay on the terrace and Katya sat beside him crying and saying in a little girl's complaining voice:

'I don't want to go on living! Why should I? Scraping together bits of stick for a fire in this miserable hole, keeping chickens, feeding a pig... I don't want this any more! Why go on wearing ourselves out?'

Ivan Ilyich gazed with clear eyes at the darkening emerald sea. He said slowly:

'It's all right living when one has a firm purpose, but like it is now... It's over now, there's nothing left. The revolution's been turned into filth. One side wins, then the other, and there's no joy in victory and no bitterness in defeat. Dog eat dog, and the devil'll have what's left. And then there'll be an even blacker reaction than before.'

Katya may wish to commit suicide, but such a conventional intelligentsia evasion of life's problems is not permitted to her. Her story ends with the death of her father and her departure into an uncertain future. She has stood – and will continue to stand, we must assume – for a sense of justice and decency and humanity. These are the ideals that she quixotically pursued under both Bolshevik and

White administrations. Though not converted to Bolshevism, she can admire such obviously sincere communists as her cousin Leonid or Voronko and yet remain caught in the cul-de-sac of intelligentsia non-commitment and holier-than-thou idealism. This intelligent, episodic, well-written novel is not so much a lament as a kind of hysterical laughter through tears at the lunatic courses taken by men and events when civil war defeats all judgement and reason.

Bulgakov's *The White Guard*[92] carries the problem of idealism and conscience a stage further than does Veresaev's novel. It is couched in terms both lyrically nostalgic and unsparingly realistic, which invite interpretation of the work on the level of allegory as well as the level of historical reality. The levels of the novel's own reality – the cosmic level on which it opens and closes, the level of the Turbins' apartment (No. 13) on the steep St Andrew's Hill above the level of Vasilisa's, the elevation of the Turbins' ideals above the mundane, opportunist level of the Kievan urban world – suggest the implicit erection of higher and lower levels of moral rectitude in the work's very structure. The cosmic level, given a biblical or religious frame of reference, is supposedly permanent and unchanging, whereas the level of the Turbins' experience is afflicted with all the changes associated with revolution, though it illustrates the survival of precisely those ideals – loyalty to family and country, honour, love, generosity of spirit and honesty – which help to ensure stability in human relations.

The novel opens with the death of the mother and her funeral in May 1918. The personal loss is overshadowed at the outset by the portentous tone of the first lines describing the cosmic events: 'Great and terrible was the year of Our Lord 1918, of the Revolution the second. Its summer abundant with warmth and sun, its winter with snow, highest in its heaven stood two stars: the shepherds' star, eventide Venus; and Mars – quivering, red.'[93] On the level of historical reality the novel describes events in and around Kiev at the end of 1918 and the beginning of 1919 but presented from the point of view of the family of the Turbins and with the family as the vital social organism that gives the novel its centre. Despite this, it is a work of fiction, largely autobiographical in origin, about social and political attitudes of a class dominant before the revolution and threatened with destruction by the coming of Bolshevism.

The crisis facing the Turbin family may be compared to the crisis that faced the Russian intelligentsia. Both are orphaned from their past and oppressed by the lack of a guiding faith. As the author asks, posing the unanswerable question: 'Mother, bright queen, where are you?'[94] Or the youngest of the Turbins, Nikolka, asks of the sad and enigmatic old man, God, who winks at him seemingly from the vaulted ceiling above the altar: 'Why had he inflicted such a wrong on them? Wasn't it unjust? Why did their mother have to be taken away, just when they had all been reunited, just when life seemed to be growing more tolerable?' (p. 7). How can one go on living? is the question, like Katya's, that the eldest Turbin son, Aleksey, poses to the priest, Father Alexander, only to be told that despair is a great sin. The inference of all the questions in the novel's opening chapter is that, for those who are motherless, how can anything be new-born, how can anything live, let alone a faith in the future?

The novel answers such questions through the example of one intelligent, attractive and courageous family that survives the coming of revolution in the shape of the satanic Petlyura. When the Germans retreat, leaving Kiev exposed to the assault of Petlyura's armies, Talberg, the Turbins' brother-in-law, goes with them, abandoning Helen, his wife, and the defence of the city rests entirely upon a handful of monarchist officers and cadets out of whom the Turbin brothers, Aleksey and Nikolka, have a representative role as out-numbered and doomed members of a lone White Guard. From the calm, clock-dominated haven of their apartment, with its stove and Dutch tiles, the red velvet furniture, the Turkish carpets and their rich oriental designs, the 'finest bookshelves in the world full of books that smelled mysteriously of old chocolate' (p. 8), all of which had been bequeathed to the children by their mother – from this civilised, loving haven, the Turbin brothers go out to defend Kiev. Bulgakov emphasises, in some of the finest descriptive prose in any of the novels of the period, the manifold richness of the Turbin heritage. Theirs is a world of beautiful, treasured objects, which matches in its uniqueness the rare beauty of the holy city of St Vladimir, whose guardians they are to be. They are to guard it, moreover, not only from Petlyura's hordes (which are to prove no more than a temporary menace), but also from 'another city, threatening and mysterious Moscow' (p. 51). The opposition between the two cities, the first capital of the Russian lands, Kiev, and Moscow, the seat of Bolshevism, is represented in this novel as one between new and old, sacred and profane and even between Christ and Antichrist. Kiev as the mother of Russian cities is left paradoxically in the hands of its motherless sons to defend it from an encroaching revolutionary barbarism.

The detail of Aleksey's and Nikolka's experiences, under the protective and understanding leadership of the veteran Colonel Nai-Turs (a superb portrayal of a valorous soldier), is fragmentary but extraordinarily vivid. The approaching enemy is largely invisible; the efforts of the officers and cadets in defence are largely ineffectual. The incongruity of Madame Anjou's shop, 'Le chic parisien', turned into a recruitment centre for volunteers, or the glimpse of Myshlaevsky outside the school's assembly hall instructing the bugler how to sound the 'General Alarm' ('"Pa-pa-*pah*-pa-*pah*", shrieked the bugle, reducing the school's rat population to terror' (p. 89)) are quotable instances in a work chiefly composed of such vivid cameo pictures and resonant with a remarkable sense of the sheer sonority of urban disorder and rebellion. Bulgakov's eye particularly lights on the comicality of the incongruous. The actual tragedy, though plain for all to see, leaves its wounds and deaths. Yet it is as though the very incongruity of it somehow defuses its power to shock and so leaves the reader faintly detached, admiring but uninvolved. The real becomes invaded by the surreal in ways perhaps now more familiar to us from Bulgakov's greatest novel *The Master and Margarita*. In this case there is so much surreal matter in the *grotesquerie* of revolution itself that the line between the two supposed levels of reality appears exceedingly fluid.

The situation quickly becomes hopeless for the defenders and they are ordered to tear off their badges of rank. Nai-Turs is killed. Aleksey is badly wounded. The simultaneous arrival in the Turbin apartment of the wounded Aleksey and the newcomer from Zhitomir, Lariosik, well illustrates Bulgakov's interest in the juxtaposition of comic and tragic aspects of life, of elements of the real and the surreal. Such disjuncture of events and experiences, of Lariosik's bizarre arrival carrying a cock-canary and Aleksey Turbin's serious wound, or of Lariosik's comic, unconscious destructiveness (the smashing of the dinner service) and of Nikolka's witnessing of disconnected, scattered events, is symptomatic of a ruptured time in which the 'tonk-tonk' of their father's chiming clock is interrupted by the bird's tweet-tweet, and this disjuncture or rupture exposes the meaning of revolution for the Turbin family more keenly than do all the guns of Petlyura. In Aleksey's own experience the revolution has a deeper meaning, involving more than the pain and delirium associated with his wound. It exposes revolution as a progression from instinctive reaction to violent change towards an appraisal of its meaning in terms of ideals.

The flashback account of Aleksey's wounding (ch. 13) emphasises the initial instinctive reaction to confrontation with the enemy. 'It was an instinct', we read. 'The men were chasing him hard and obstinately, they wouldn't stop, and once they'd caught up with him they'd inevitably kill him. They'd kill him because he'd run' (p. 183).[95] So he runs, the fear going straight through his body and down his legs into the earth, to be replaced by an intense fury that ran up his legs like icy water and came boiling out of his mouth. Dream-like, as if it were part of the delirium to come, he fires at his pursuers and desperately flings himself down the length of the most fantastic street in the world, turns the corner and receives a brief respite. Perhaps improbably, but it is an improbability appropriate to the strangeness of the moment, he is rescued by a woman ('like the heroine in a melodrama' (p. 184)) who sleeps beside him and eventually takes him back to the apartment. The time of his real delirium then begins and it resembles a personal Calvary, a travail through death to rebirth and renewal of life.

The framework for the Turbins' experience of this life crisis is religious. If Nikolka makes a modern descent into hell by going to the Kiev city morgue in search of the body of Nai-Turs (ch. 17), then at the crisis of Aleksey Turbin's typhus Helen prays for her dying brother on a Christmas Eve that is symbolically transposed to the time of the first Gethsemane:

Outside there was complete silence, darkness was setting in with terrible speed and another momentary vision filled the room – the hard glassy light of the sky, unfamiliar yellowish-red sandstone rocks, olive trees, the cold and the dark silence of centuries within the sanctuary of the temple.

'Holy Mother, intercede for us', Helen muttered fervently. 'Pray to Him. He is there beside you. What would it cost you? Have mercy on us. Have mercy. Your day, the festival of the birth of your Son is approaching. If Aleksey lives he will do good for others...' (p. 252).

It is clearly intimated that Aleksey had died, but through his sister's intercession a miracle has occurred, it seems, and he has been permitted to arise from the dead. By February 1919 he has recovered and is able to resume his practice. He is visited by the syphilitic poet Rusakov. In his religious mania this poet–prophet insists that Moscow has become the kingdom of Antichrist and the seat of Satan, of Abaddon, the destroyer, reincarnated in the shape of Trotsky. The crazy, spite-filled words of the syphilitic poet can be dismissed as the babblings of a maniac, but they contain an apocalyptic truth.[96] They tend also to merge into the cosmic vision of last things, of a world no longer dominated by the planet Mars but recreated anew, which serves as the final frame to the novel. For Rusakov, we read (ch. 20):

Illness and suffering now seemed...unimportant, unreal. The sickness had fallen away, like a scab from a withered, fallen branch in a wood. He saw the fathomless blue mist of the centuries, the endless procession of the millennia. He felt no fear, only the wisdom of obedience and reverence. Peace had entered his soul and in that state of peace he read on to the words:

> And God shall wipe away all tears from their eyes; and there shall be no more death, neither sorrow, nor crying, neither shall there be any more pain: for the former things are passed away (pp. 268–9).[97]

A kind of domestic peace falls upon the Turbin family at the novel's end, but the close weave of private and public issues, the magnitude of the cosmic and historical changes and the interaction of comic and tragic in the forming of human lives make the peace which passeth all understanding seem, in Bulgakov's final judgement, as fragmented as the multifarious cameos that comprise his fiction. All that really survives the disintegrating effect of revolution is the human capacity for turning our eyes towards the stars, for seeking the ideal vision. Such ideal vision, religious in its ultimate meaning, is drawn from the Book of Revelation and has spiritual revelation, the vouchsafing of cosmic truths, as its answer to the dark forces of revolution surrounding the Turbins and their private world. Central to this answer in terms of life is the ideal of man as healer, both of body and soul. This is the ideal exemplified by Aleksey Turbin himself, the medical doctor whom revolutionary events force into the contradictory role of killer, but who appears to transcend the conflict, as he transcends death through some providential agency that looks very much like a miracle, and returns to life to 'do good for others' and resume his work as a healer. His Christ-like travail and healing role anticipate similar symbolic associations in the greatest of such idealisations in the Russian revolutionary novel, that of Yury Zhivago.

Bulgakov's *The White Guard* treats revolution as diverse, complex, untidy and – ultimately – inscrutable. The hordes of Petlyura vanish away from Kiev after an occupation of only forty-seven days. In the course of that time the Turbin family has undergone traumatic private experiences that are lent a certain vaguely defined cosmic meaning, but the final image, similarly vague and suggestive, is of the midnight cross of St Vladimir appearing as sharp and menacing as a sword above the bank of the Dnieper. Revolution is similarly composed of double meanings, of cross and sword, Venus and Mars, salvation and destruction, in the novel's projection of it. Such ambiguity must have been the reason for official suppression of the novel (which is of course far more assertive of such ambiguity than the play based on it) and yet the ambiguity exposes the essence of revolution as a fact and a concept more profoundly than does any novel written in the first half of the 1920s.

Dialectics and dualism: *The Rout, Envy, Over the Border, Honey and Blood, Sevastopol'*

By 1927 the Soviet literary response to revolutionary change had matured to the point where the classical tradition of the nineteenth-century Russian novel could reassert itself. Character-creation and its accompanying concern with social–psychological portraiture formed a part – a substantial part, admittedly, but not the exclusive concern – of an emergent novelistic tradition that attempted to examine the complexities of adjustment to revolution on the socio-political, cultural and philosophical levels, as well as on the level of individual emotion and psychology. The Tolstoyan 'dialectics of the soul' (*dialektika dushi*) became re-adapted and refurbished as a suitable method of portraying the interaction between character and setting or social relationships generally, though with an increasing accent on the morally improving aspect of such interaction. Emphasis fell correspondingly on detailed evocation of locale and background, on the relating of character traits to social conditioning, on examination of the ideas motivating human conduct and on the right of a novelist to explore the *pro* and *contra* of particular attitudes in his study of human relationships. Such features were not new even in the experimental revolutionary novel of the 1920s, but they acquired new meaning and wealth of expression in certain novels of the late twenties through the very complexity with which they were combined.

In Fadeyev's *The Rout* (*Razgrom*) and Olesha's *Envy* (*Zavist'*), both of 1927, it is easy to sense a new literary competence characteristic of a new generation of novelists, who drew upon earlier traditions while bringing a freshness and vitality of their own to their work. The literary quality of their two novels is of special importance. They are to be judged by the standards of excellence that are to be anticipated in a tradition of the novel that includes Turgenev, Dostoyevsky and Tolstoy. Small in scale though both novels are, they have about them a neatness of expression in their language and a compactness of incident and character that at once create readily comprehensible worlds of individual experience and social relationship. Moreover, they are novels in which the private life of the characters, involving memory, imagination, sexual impulse and emotional frustration, can be seen to assume a proper importance in defining a character's role. They are also novels that emphasise the contrast or confrontation between essentially *differing* characters, or sets of characters, with the result that they explore the dialectical nature of revolutionary change and reveal the dualism present in human responses to such change. It is difficult, therefore, to speak of a central heroic figure in these novels (unlike, for instance, *Cities and Years* (Andrey Startsov), *The Deadlock* (Katya Sartanov) and *The White Guard* (Aleksey Turbin)); nor are they novels devoted exclusively to the interests and problems of the intelligentsia, although they are as concerned with defining the 'true essence' of revolutionary idealism as any novels of the period.

Because a confrontation between differing attitudes to revolution, rather than differing revolutionary attitudes, is present in these novels, there is no relatively simple juxtaposition of Red and White or Cossack and Bolshevik, but there is in each case a rather schematic grouping of characters and issues intended to highlight and dramatise the *pro* and *contra*. To some extent it is arguable that these novels show the acceleration of a process already discernible in earlier novels (especially the last three examined): the partially autobiographical basis of the fiction is beginning to acquire figurative or symbolic meaning; the novel as recording genre is transforming itself with the passage of time into the novel as interpretive genre, with the accompanying danger of succumbing to a didactic or propaganda role. Put another way, a decade after the October revolution it is not surprising that the novel's response to revolution should be less immediate, more reflective and therefore better able to assess in a dialectical fashion the problems of choice thrown up by revolutionary experience. Simultaneously it can be seen that the 'revolutionary novel' is beginning to acquire some of the features of a historical novel – that is to say, it is related to the past and is conscious of the need to interpret the past to the present.

Fadeyev had no doubt that his role as a Soviet novelist was partly interpretative. Addressing the first All-Union Congress of Proletarian Writers in 1928, a year after his novel was first published, he declared among other things:

To show a living man means in the final estimate to show the entire historical process of social change and development. And since the reflection of social processes in the psychology of each individual man is not direct, not mechanical, but there occurs here an extraordinarily complex dialectical process of interaction between man and his environment... it transpires that to give a consistent and accurate picture of man as a product of a social environment is difficult, and it is difficult because no one has so far shown man in such a way.[98]

Though aware of the difficulty, as his words suggest, Fadeyev did not aspire in his novel to achieve anything as ambitious as showing 'the entire historical process of social change and development' in depicting his characters. On the other hand, he did succeed in suggesting something of the 'extraordinarily complex dialectical process of interaction between man and his environment' in his portrayal of selected members of the partisan detachment. The point, of course, of his novel is that the scale of the social environment, limited in effect to scarcely a dozen separately identifiable characters, is small, but the implication of larger issues, particularly of class as a determining factor, is always present as a reminder of the greater social and historical setting against which the relatively minor incidents of the novel are to be judged.

The Rout[99] is set in the Soviet Far East in the three-month period between July and September 1919.[100] It tells the story of a mounted partisan detachment under the leadership of a Jewish intellectual, Levinson. The detachment has a proletarian backbone drawn mainly from coal miners, though the difference between the coal miners and the peasant members of the detachment is acknowledged rather than stressed.[101] The two characters who represent the central opposition in the novel are the twenty-seven-year-old miner Morozka and the young *intelligent* Mechik whom he saves from certain death (or so we assume) and recruits as a member of the detachment. Morozka's is the more interesting and detailed of the two portraits, but the rivalry that develops between them over Morozka's amiable, sluttish 'wife' Varya serves to emphasise the happy-go-lucky, uncomplicated, honourable nature of the one and the selfish, self-pitying, feckless irresponsibility of the other. If Mechik finds himself unable to adjust to the collective needs of the detachment and finally turns traitor,

Morozka becomes gradually more fully committed to the collective ethos of the partisans and sacrifices himself in the end to warn the detachment of the danger that Mechik's failure of vigilance has caused. In the ensuing ambush the detachment is decimated by the Cossacks and only Levinson and eighteen others survive to fight again. They ride out into a scene of harvesting at the end of the novel and the final two sentences convey both something of the work's literary quality and the sense of muted optimism, of hope born from tragedy, which is the rather too facile concluding note of the work:

Beyond the river, leaning against the sky and growing in spurs into the flaxen-haired banks, shone the blue crests of the mountains, and through their sharp peaks there flowed into the valley a translucent foam of pinkish-white clouds, salt-laden from the sea, foaming and bubbling like fresh milk.

Levinson directed his silent, still moist-eyed gaze at this expansive sky and earth which promised food and rest, at the distant people engaged in the threshing, whom he would soon have to make into people as much his own, as close to him, as were the eighteen who silently rode behind him – and he stopped weeping; for one had to go on living and fulfilling one's responsibilities.

The didactic note is clearly to be heard, whether it be authorial or supposedly Levinson's final thought, in the last words. The whole intent of the novel as Fadeyev's interpretation of revolution and civil war is to be discerned in the emphases that are given to concepts of class solidarity, responsibility, awareness of the collective and an implicit conviction of the ultimate rightness of the partisans' struggle against the Whites and the interventionists. As Fadeyev claimed in defining the primary and basic idea of the novel:

In civil war a selection of human material occurs, everything hostile is swept away by revolution, everything incapable of real revolutionary struggle which accidentally finds its way into the revolutionary camp is sifted out, and everything growing from genuine revolutionary roots, from the millions-strong masses of the people, is forged and grows and evolves in the struggle.[102]

Naturally, such claims for the novel have the benefit or disadvantage of hindsight about them. If we feel inclined to pay less respect to them than to the inherent interest of the novel, it is because it retains an authentic literary freshness that decades of Stalinist and later official adulation have not succeeded in totally mummifying.

Although the characters in the novel may seem no more than

ciphers by virtue of their single denominating titles (Levinson–leader, Morozka–orderly, Mechik–*intelligent*, etc.), they acquire individuality through the twofold and interacting revelation of their private, memoried experience and their relationships within the detachment. Levinson's private world is suggested both through mention of his former life, the image of his boyhood self watching in wide-eyed Jewish wonder for the 'beautiful birdie' that should pop out of the camera lens (ch. 13), the letter from his wife and his reply to it, and, more fully and satisfyingly, through the revelation of his private fears and inner debates while striving outwardly to preserve a calm imperturbability and determination for the sake of the detachment as a whole. His strengths as a leader are not attributable to clearly defined political ideals but to a realistic conviction that revolutionary change is essential. It is his strength, also, that he recognises the need to reject his bourgeois past and the damage that may be done to people who place their trust in the illusion of the 'beautiful birdie':

And when he was really convinced of this, he understood what incalculable damage is done to people by the falsehoods about beautiful birdies, about birdies which should pop out of somewhere and which many waited for all their lives in vain...No, he had no more use for all that! He mercilessly suppressed in himself all the unreal, sweet taste of such yearnings for dreams, for all the inheritance of so many frustrated generations nurtured on falsehoods about beautiful birdies! 'To see everything just as it is, in order to change what is and bring ever nearer what is in process of being born and must be' – it was to that most simple and most difficult wisdom that Levinson had come (ch. 13).

Levinson's conviction that he is assisting at a birth is more than custodial; it is the source of a myth of infallibility surrounding his leadership that is gladly accepted and encouraged by the detachment itself.[103] His role is paternal in several senses. To his assistant Baklanov he appears literally as a father, to be emulated in all things; father-confessor to Mechik, he has a fatherly feeling towards several other members of his detachment and naturally assumes a parental responsibility for the welfare of all under his command. But chiefly he embodies a realistic commitment to revolutionary change, a recognition that, despite human weakness, revolutions demand unsentimental leadership and a purposeful idealism hardened by struggle against the enemy.

The enemy, however, is epitomised not so much by the Cossacks or the Japanese interventionists as by the false idealism of Mechik.

City-bred and city-orientated, Mechik's radicalism – or 'maximalism' – is portrayed as a typical intelligentsia illusion based on a romantic view of the revolutionary struggle. In short, he is a 'bourgeois' revolutionary who fails to understand the realities of the struggle, takes for granted the pleasures of Varya's company and the gossip against Levinson, neglects his wretched horse and ends by slipping back to the city when his carelessness leads to the final disastrous ambush. The whole tone of his portrayal suggests that it is his bourgeois proclivities that contribute to his weakness – so much so that it is a portrait without depth and vitality. By contrast (as ch. 8, 'Enemies', makes clear) the portrait of the former miner, Morozka, has a vital *élan* that permits a discernible development of character. His initially unthinking and spontaneous commitment to the revolution becomes through trial and error a reasoned conviction and a final justification for laying down his life.[104] The conviction is one reached primarily through the influence of another partisan, Goncharenko, who invites Morozka to think seriously about his class allegiance and his mission. Bouts of depression and drunkenness, even a temporary and shaming friendship with Mechik, as well as the stormy relationship with Varya, combine to provide a multi-faceted picture of Morozka's character and behaviour. Not as interesting in terms of psychological portraiture as Levinson's, Morozka's portrait has freshness in its combination of sheer physical vitality and unpretentious sincerity.

Whereas Mechik's relationship to the partisan detachment is always ambivalent in its dualism, Morozka's acceptance of the collective principle becomes morally edifying and transforming. This is probably the best evidence in the novel for the supposed Tolstoyan influence.[105] That Morozka is morally better at the end of the novel than at the beginning cannot be doubted, but to ascribe too much significance to this change, as has frequently occurred in Soviet estimates,[106] tends to highlight the fact that instances of characters morally improved by revolution are rare in Soviet novels, especially those of the first decade after the revolution and civil war. Nevertheless, such change was the simplest index of the success of the revolution as a morally transforming force and the Soviet novel had to face the challenge of illustrating it.

Fadeyev's characters tend to have the appearance of stereotypes, not because one may find countless examples of stout-hearted miners like Morozka prepared to lay down their lives, but because critical adulation has over-exaggerated the importance of the type and, with the exception of the Jewish Levinson, the other characters in his novel have little claim to originality. Also, of course, the thrust of his novel, designed to disregard the tragic in favour of the politically optimistic message, is clearly Socialist Realist and therefore propagandist of officially acceptable Soviet attitudes towards revolutionary change. The idealism that inspires Levinson and Morozka is unaffected by critical heterodoxy and hardly at all by doubt. Not so in the case of Yury Olesha's short novel *Envy*,[107] which poses the issue of revolutionary idealism in more complex ways, though it has to be stressed that Olesha was not writing of an embattled political idealism beset by enemies in a civil-war situation. He writes of peacetime adjustment when the immediate conflict is over, but the relevance of his novel to issues raised by the revolution is no less real for all that. It exhibits, first, a needle-point fineness in the writing that marks it out at once as exceptional among the many forceful but crude literary works of the period. Secondly, it contains a uniquely fresh view of the conventional contrast between new and old in Soviet society. More than half a century after its first publication it has a shining, mint-new quality that gives it the appeal of a bright coin or a lustrous ornament. What it lacks is the sense of having veins and a bloodstream that one can discern instantly. in the pulse of L. N. Tolstoy's prose or the rough-skinned feel of Sholokhov's. Olesha's is a world of patinas and mirroring surfaces. Its brilliance is composed of many seemingly fragile parts that have a steely edge to them. The reader's eye is continually arrested by the sharpness of definition, the keenly accurate photographic exactitude, the nearly surreal, Dali-like arrangement of life as Olesha finds it, the miniaturising and childlike estrangement of the visible world that Olesha's back-to-front view manages to evoke:

I find that a landscape viewed through the wrong end of binoculars gains in brightness and relief. Colours and contours seem more precise. Familiar objects suddenly become new in their unfamiliar smallness. The observer sees them the way he saw them in his childhood. It's like dreaming. The odds are that a man looking through the wrong end of binoculars will at some point dissolve into a blissful smile.

After rain the city acquires brilliance and stereoscopic relief. Anyone can see it; the streetcar is carmine; the pavement stones are far from being all the same colour, some of them are even green; a housepainter who was sheltering from the rain like a pigeon has come out of his niche and is now moving against the background of his brick canvas; in a window, a little boy is catching the sun in a splinter of mirror.[108]

The view that we have of the world here is revolutionary in the sense not only that it is defamiliarised by being seen through the wrong end of binoculars, but also in the sense that it comprises the opposition of a man-made instrument, the binoculars and their lens, to the externally visible, non-human world of nature and surrounding things. Or seen as the opposition of two principal emotions, envy and indifference – envy towards the new Soviet world on the part of those who might wish to participate in it and cannot, indifference towards it by those who have dropped out of it or have become powerless to feel. The most fascinating characteristic of Olesha's short novel is precisely its ambivalence, its statement of the issues as an equation of *pro* and *contra*.

The 'old' and the 'new', meaning the world of the old intelligentsia, of bourgeois egoism and utopian idealism, on the one hand, and the world of new Soviet man, of communism and a new technological society, on the other, are represented by three different types of character paired off by age and sex. The brothers Andrey and Ivan Babichev are a mutually opposed pair belonging to the older generation, whereas Volodya Makarov, a representative 'new man' of the young generation, is opposed to Nikolay Kavalerov, the introspective, self-pitying representative of a younger generation who cannot accept the revolution. Valya, Ivan Babichev's daughter, represents future Soviet woman, whereas Anichka Prokopovich is a middle-aged slut obviously representative of an outdated past. The characters are not related to each other quite as schematically as this brief analysis might suggest, but the general lines of the opposition, and therefore the confrontation between issues, are not seriously distorted by stating them in these terms.

If Andrey Babichev, the inventor of the perfect salami sausage, the 'new' Soviet bureaucrat, is depicted to some extent as a figure of caricature, then his brother Ivan is endowed with eccentricities and mannerisms that at least make him a figure of some human interest. Andrey is always distanced in Olesha's portrayal of him. The impudent, witty, caustic observations that Kavalerov passes on his morning ablutions, the appearance of his groin and his 'correct' behaviour unfairly pillory him as a type, whereas Ivan's continual soliloquising suggests, again unfairly, the ego-tripping of a man given to verbal excess and over-indulgence in alcohol. The two brothers are Gogolian in the stress laid on particular features of their personality. The implication in so exaggerating such features is to urge the need for both types, a union of the zealously practical and the extravagantly visionary. If the bias of the fiction is always towards Nikolay Kavalerov and Ivan Babichev as the principal figures, the very extravagance of their viewpoints, not to mention the eccentricity of their visions, tends to countervail against the bias and lend distinction to the bureaucratic and athletic zeal of their opponents.

The novel is constructed on a mirror principle. This is well illustrated by Kavalerov's sight of Ivan Babichev walking towards him into a street mirror at the end of Part I:

It is impossible to tell which way a pedestrian is going as long as you do not turn your face away from the mirror...I was looking into the mirror chewing the last bite of my French loaf.

Then I turned my head.

A pedestrian was walking toward the mirror, having emerged from somewhere to one side. I prevented him from being reflected. I was the recipient of the smile he had prepared for himself. He was considerably shorter than me and raised his face.

He had been in a hurry to reach the mirror in order to locate and brush off a caterpillar that had crawled over his shoulder. He brushed it off with a flick of his middle finger, having previously twisted his shoulder round like a violinist.

I was still thinking about the optical illusions, about the mirror tricks. So I asked the newcomer, whom I still had not recognised:

'Which side did you come from? Where did you emerge?'

'Where from?' he said. 'Where from?' He looked at me with clear eyes. 'I have invented me myself' (pp. 60–1).[109]

Part I of the novel is the invention of Kavalerov's 'I'; Part II is concerned with Ivan's invention of himself and his own invention called 'Ophelia'. If Part I is concerned with Nikolay Kavalerov, the envious one, who eventually becomes Ivan's sole disciple perhaps despite himself, Part II celebrates both Ivan's 'conspiracy of feelings' and his final indifference, both his fictitious anti-machine 'Ophelia' and the triumph of the 'new' machine-man Volodya Makarov. The visible land that Kavalerov may envy – the land, in other words, of the perfect salami, the new Soviet aeroplane, the creation of Andrey Babichev's giant cheap-food restaurant (the *Chetvertak*) and the perfect Soviet girl, Valya – is opposed by an invisible land that is nevertheless reflected in the visible, or may indeed create the visible. For, as has been suggested in a comparison of Olesha's *Envy* with H. G. Wells's 'invisible man': 'The invisible man in his invisible land is the artist in his world of art. His is the responsibility for the view which posterity will have of his age.'[110] The Ivan Babichev who populates his invisible land with an avenging anti-machine called Ophelia is the true artist of the invisible, the pantocrator-*poshlyak*, the godhead of the vulgarly human who seeks to preserve in mankind the old senses, the non-new, the inwardly visible imagination that can obliterate the purely visible. He asserts the need for an image of himself which can only be seen in a mirror, which can only be reflected in his disciple, Nikolay Kavalerov. In such self-assertion he no doubt seeks also to control and dominate. As Elisabeth Klosty Beaujour puts it:

The ultimate tool for those Olesha heroes who desire to control and appropriate the world and turn it into their personal possession through tricks of vision is the mirror. The mirror first reassures them of their own existence. The mirror also gives one the power to project one's image – *my* reflection. In general, the constant need to seek one's self in other objects, to superimpose one's self on them, and thus to acquire them, is all part of the problem of mirrors – an assertion of the self which takes the form of a need to see one's self reflected, one of the central problems in Olesha's works.[111]

The need to control, superimpose, dominate – functions of any machine and of all state structures – is epitomised in the all-purpose invisible machine invented by Ivan Babichev. It can be said to have a political connotation as a reflection of the sterile urge to exercise power over others, allegedly for their own good, which Ivan's brother Andrey displays towards Soviet housewives or his artificial 'sons', Kavalerov and Makarov. But the fundamentally ironic difference between the two brothers' separate wills to power is that Andrey's urge to create a better visible world involves a sterilising of human impulses, particularly of the most vulgar human emotions,[112] while Ivan's power-seeking presupposes a contradictory fertility, both in his paternal relationship to the goddess of the visibly new, his daughter Valya, and in his invention of 'the mightiest creation of technology', which he had endowed with 'the most vulgar of human feelings'.

Technological progress and a progressive vulgarisation of human feelings can arguably be regarded as the real legacy of all twentieth-century revolutions, and it is in an effort to avenge himself upon his own age that Ivan Babichev, the representative of the pre-revolutionary bourgeois intelligentsia, invents his Ophelia and proclaims his philosophy of 'the best machine' in an age devoted to worship of the machine *per se*. As he asserts:

'My machine is a dazzling flash of the sneering tongue the dying era will stick out at the newborn one. Their mouths will water when they see it. The machine, think of it, their idol, the machine...and suddenly...And suddenly the best machine will turn out to be a liar, a sentimental wretch, full of petty-bourgeois traits. It can do everything. But what will it actually do? It will sing our love songs, the silly love songs of the dying century, and gather the flowers of the past era. It will fall in love, become jealous, cry, dream. I did this. I have insulted the machine – the god of these people, of the future. And I have even given it the name of a girl who went out of her mind with love and despair. I've called it Ophelia, the most human, the most touching name' (p. 92).

Such a vision of the ultimate emotion-flawed machine can be ascribed simply to nineteenth-century envy of the twentieth, or the intellectual's scorn and derision of the technological, but it suggests also that the machine itself will never acquire feelings in advance of its human inventors', that even the technologically progressive future will return to the emotions of the past and undergo a progressive *embourgeoisement*. Ivan Babichev's private revolution therefore takes the form of a counter-revolution by all the old emotions that have been abolished – such emotions, that is, as pity, tenderness, pride, jealousy and love – in the form of what he calls 'a conspiracy of feelings'. To his surprise and dismay, he discovers that such emotions had not in fact been abolished in Soviet society but had, if anything, been strengthened. In the epitaph to his own envy, Ivan Babichev cries out to his own daughter:

'Blind me, Valya. I want to be blind...I don't want to see anything: no lawns, branches, flowers, knights in shining armour, cowards – I've just got to go blind, Valya. I was wrong, Valya...I thought that all the feelings'd perished – love and devotion and tenderness...But everything had remained, Valya...Though not for us, all that had remained for us was envy... envy...O blind me, Valya, I want to be blind...'[113]

Ivan is a latterday Lear of the Moscow backstreets seeking in a kind of *folie de grandeur* an exculpation of his own foolishness. Unlike Lear he is not blinded, he merely becomes indifferent to the triumph of the visible. This triumph is signalled by the heroic success of the machine-man Volodya Makarov in the international football game against the German team – a success crowned by the sexual triumph of Valya's collapse into Volodya's arms. The invisible

Ophelia meanwhile avenges itself upon its creator and reduces him to the final emotional sterility of acknowledging that man's best feeling is indifference. Like its bedmate vulgarity or, in the Russian, *poshlost'*, indifference demotes the grandiose purposes of social engineering in the name of human happiness to the squalid but cosily vulgar proportions of happiness experienced ('Hurrah! Cheers!') in the shared bed of the middle-aged slut, Anichka Prokopovich.

It is no service to Olesha's *Envy* to treat it over-seriously. If it explores the ideal of revolution as 'a new beginning' in ways that border on caricature, it exhibits no malice in exposing either the weaknesses of the old or the pretentiously callow strengths of the new. The failure of the old intelligentsia to adapt to the circumstances of Soviet life may be its principal message, but it is a novel so gently irradiated by good humour and warm irreverence that it invokes smiles rather than sadness. The back-to-front view of life, as if seen through the wrong end of binoculars, is matched by a schematic but delicately balanced opposition of new and old in the representative characters, which reveals above all the human lineaments of the problem of readjustment to revolutionary change.

Of those novels on revolutionary and civil-war themes which appeared in Soviet literature towards the end of the 1920s, only three have been chosen here for study, although many more could be cited.[114] The three novels chosen for study have the distinction of being the best written and among the least known. Each novel poses the problem of revolution and idealism with particular interest and subtlety. In each case, similarly, a dialectical process can be seen at work in the presentation of the characters and the issues.

Over the Border (*Po tu storonu*) by Viktor Kin is a short novel that first appeared in 1928.[115] Entertainingly written, it opens with a description of one of those endless train journeys of the civil war (the time is 1921). Two young Komsomol officials – Matveyev is twenty, Bezais is eighteen – are travelling to Khabarovsk in the Far East. Their conversations, the girls they meet, the general tone of the novel, are initially witty, laconic, even a trifle facetious. No other novel of the period treats the civil war in such a light-hearted manner. In Khabarovsk, however, Matveyev is shot in the leg and it has to be amputated. Though he makes a good recovery, the lightness of heart has gone. He has moments of despair when he contemplates suicide. Finally he is cornered by marauding White troops one night while foolhardily taking a walk on his crutches and, after a bold struggle for life, is murdered.

Bezais is the autobiographical figure; Matveyev is the memorable creation. The novel is memorable for its cumulative and ennobling portrayal of Matveyev's predicament at the end when, for all his skill in using his crutches, he faces the despair of knowing that he cannot be as he was and meets a doubtless inevitable death at the hands of the Whites. The effectiveness of this ending is perhaps marred by an over-emphasis on the heroics, but there is psychological truthfulness in Matveyev's last struggle, as much with himself as with his enemy, and there is a final poignancy in the mannered writing of his poeticised death:

Suddenly he saw a large shadow. In front of him, alone in the empty city, stood his horse, with its white marking on its head in the shape of a heart, and it looked in his face with dark and devoted eyes. The dark mane shone like darkened silver, the finely moulded hooves stood there still and firm.
'Is it you?...'
He took hold of the reins, jumped into the cold saddle and flew off straight along the moonlit road to catch up with his friends.
'Well, you see...I'm not all that bad at it,' he whispered, just as if he were answering a question someone had once asked him.
It was his final vanity.

The work's quality is in the careful, expert writing, which exactly captures an ironic thought, a casual verbal exchange, a momentary glimpse of forest seen through a train window. It is in the warmth of the characterisation of the two heroes. It is in several expert vignettes – the girl Varya who falls in love with Matveyev, the doctor who attends to his wound. It is chiefly in the youthful idealism that pervades the heroes' devotion to their revolutionary tasks and the recognition – unstressed though it may be – that the idealism cannot overcome the 'final vanity' (*posledneye tshcheslaviye*) of death, even in the shape of the much-loved dead horse that comes to carry Matveyev away at the end.

Though this novel, like its author, passed into oblivion under Stalin, it has been revived. Another novel that deserves revival but has been out of print since 1933 is the work of a virtually unknown poet, writer of short stories and novelist, N. I. Kolokolov (1897–1933). The reasons for this neglect are unclear, though a study of his work may shed some light on them.

Nikolay Kolokolov's only novel, *Honey and Blood* (*Myod i krov'*), was published in two editions (1928, 1933).[116] It tells of a small provincial town containing scarcely a dozen brick-built houses, not counting the church. According to legend the town had been founded by a family who arrived on the scene with nothing

apart from axes, spades and the young saplings of fruit trees and cultivated berries. And when the family came upon the place where the town now stands a swarm of wild bees flew out of the forest and settled on them. Like a golden cloud in the sun's rays the bees flowed out towards them and settled on their heads and shoulders and arms, but they did not sting. The unknown family – a father, mother and four sons with their wives – built a house for themselves here and planted round it the young saplings of fruit trees and cultivated berries and set up hives for the bees. From those saplings grew plentiful orchards and kitchen gardens, from those first hives abundant bee-hives, from that family a strong and soft-spoken race of people.

Vigorous and independent, the town flourished on the strong healthy blood of its inhabitants and the honey for which it became famous. A backwater familiar to us from so many literary accounts in Russian literature, it mingled provincial tranquillity and the apathy of *Okurovshchina* in a blend that, to Gorky, seemed depressingly boring on first acquaintance.[117] Kolokolov's picture is a good deal more subtle (as Gorky at once admitted) than the first impression might suggest. He summons into being an interesting and multi-faceted portrait of this small provincial township of vegetable-cultivators and bee-keepers where the unchanging pace of life remains unaffected by outside events until the beginning of the First World War. War news filters through; the wounded arrive; there is talk of building a factory to produce dried vegetables. Then the inhabitants are startled to learn that there is no more Tsar. Although Kerensky's picture takes his place and a Soviet of sorts is formed, local news, such as the death of an eccentric general who had built a house for himself in the town, claims equal importance. Preparations are made for elections to the Constituent Assembly. 'But September brought rain and scare-mongering and the papers, like a forest in a high wind, were filled with a veritable storm of words in which apprehensions, warnings and calls for vigilance in the face of some approaching threat were all jumbled together.' After the October revolution a Bolshevik party committee is hastily formed and a former post-office worker, who has become chief of police, is elected chairman. He harangued the townspeople who maintained a faultless outward calm, displaying neither undue favour nor hostility towards the Soviet government, hoping only in secret for the change which, so it seemed to them, someone at the top and very remote must surely hasten to bring about. And against this general expectation of sudden change from above there repeatedly broke like waves the voices of so many orators, so that the speeches and slogans of the Bolsheviks floated on the surface of the town's life like oil on water.

Attempts to enforce the obligatory surrender of foodstuffs by the peasantry produced increased support for a brigand known as Tishka, who begins attacking local Red Army men. Four of them are killed. Simultaneously a fugitive White officer arrives in the town and attempts to persuade a sixteen-year-old schoolboy, Sobolev, to join the White cause. This boy, doted on by his mother and sister, is a gifted but sickly youth who has more than once been saved from death by the good offices of the local doctor, Dr Dolgov. He is to prove the tragic central figure in what is to become the major ideological confrontation of the novel.

The killing of the Red Army men and the 'bourgeois' state of mind in the town precipitate the arrival on the scene of the Chekist Nakatov. He arrives on a motorbike and proceeds to impose a new style of vigorous anti-bourgeois control. One of his earliest acts is to order the shooting of the five detainees in the town's jail:

And while the Chekists were talking, the pencil of the new chairman of the commission slid over the paper and there appeared on it little faces, houses and trees that only a pre-school infant would have been up to drawing. And it was incredible and fantastic what difference there was between these drawings and what the new arrival said:
'Tomorrow they must all be shot', he said. 'And in such a way that the whole town should hear the shooting.'

The detainees are shot:

The simultaneous shots of the firing squad crashed over the town like the rumbling of an avalanche.
In the wooden streets days of fearful anxiety passed like clouds as heavy as stone. And the heavy days were filled with the sinister and unfamiliar smell of benzine. And the days were shaken by the ghostly gunfire of the motorbike carrying the chairman of the Cheka from one end of the town to the other.

Nakatov, the vengeful and sinister epitome of Soviet power, is depicted as one who menaces not only the tranquillity of the provincial town but also its ethos. Apart from his motorbike and his inscrutability, he appears deliberately alien to the townspeople by installing himself and his Cheka in the house of the lately deceased eccentric general. Opposed to him and representative of the traditional virtues of the town is Dr Dolgov. The sanctity of human life is naturally central to his creed and involves a sacred duty that he also identifies with – or perhaps confuses with – his fondness for his patients. If 'politics smelt of blood' in his estimation and were therefore directly contrary to the 'honey' of his own benevolence, then Nakatov's killing of the detainees aroused in Dr Dolgov's heart an anguished hatred for him, while his concern for Sobolev, stricken with typhus:

grew almost into love, almost into paternal tenderness. The doctor had the feeling that all the human ailments with which he had struggled for so many years were throwing down their challenge to him in the delirium and fever of the sick boy who lay before him.

To Nakatov the town is just a provincial place to which he feels no special attachment. He looks at it one evening:

Only here and there among the houses the windows shone yellow as if the rooms had been filled to the brim with honey. 'Warm hives full of bees', thought Nakatov in a flash. 'This little town of bee-keepers with vegetarian habits...'

But this little town of bee-keepers with vegetarian habits, afflicted by a typhus epidemic and the anti-Soviet counter-revolution of Tishka and his band, is to become the ultimate testing-ground of Nakatov's career. We learn that he has abandoned everything – mother, sister, brother, sweetheart – for his political beliefs and his work in the political underground. Killing has become a necessary part of his political activism and yet he can still insist to himself that 'ubivat' tak tyazhko! Tyazhko!' ('It's so hard to kill, so hard!') Meanwhile, Nakatov's involvement with the doctor is made inevitable by two events. First, it is brought to his notice by the former post-office worker turned police chief that the schoolboy Sobolev, whom the doctor has succeeded in rescuing from typhus, has had associations with a White officer. Moreover, during the boy's delirium he had mentioned the existence of some 'All-Russian army'. On the strength of such hearsay evidence and other incriminating material discovered after his arrest, Sobolev is shot on Nakatov's orders. Secondly, though Nakatov succeeds in capturing the brigand Tishka and executing him by his own hand, he is himself struck down by typhus and the doctor is called to attend him.

The contrast between Nakatov and Dolgov is made explicit initially in Nakatov's own analysis of his political career, which he outlines in a letter to a friend. He explains how he had grown to admire the type of revolutionary leader 'who looks at himself through a thousand strange eyes and carries on his own shoulders the greatest of burdens – a right to the life and death of enemies and friends without any right to his own life and death'. This represents for him the most crushing of arguments that can be used against the cheap and nasty sanctity of mind that steps aside from the pools of blood out of fear of dirtying its own snowy-white garment, clean as a doctor's coat:

The true holy garment is the doctor's coat. I haven't conceived this idea by accident. You must surely know that I almost wore this coat myself. I was a hard-working medical student before I embarked on a revolutionary career. And now I don't want to recall those days. In the 'coat' I now wear you'll not find a single thread that's not stained with blood. But I don't hide from people's eyes the bloodstains on me; I will endure my lot until my heart breaks...And the ataman Tishka has also endured his lot after his fashion – true, not for good, but for ill. Tishka's band suffered with him, just as our Red Army men suffered with us. Both are long in the tooth – two sides, two camps, two wills, two faiths...But on the sidelines are the greynesses, the humanly stagnant, souls stranded within four walls, flightless from birth – and proud of the irreproachable whiteness of their pacifism.

The doctor, confronted by the sick adversary whom fate, it seems, has placed so conveniently in his hands, is overwhelmed by conflicting emotions. Should he avenge the death of Sobolev by administering poison to Nakatov? Should he renounce his oath as a doctor and refuse to treat his new patient? Finally, with anguish, the doctor tells Nakatov that he cannot treat him:

The sick man's eyes opened wide, and now his head actually rose from the pillow. Leaning on an elbow, without taking his eyes off the doctor, he asked almost in a whisper and blinking his eyes, as if trying to make sure he had heard what the doctor had just said or was once more feverishly embroiled in a new hallucination:

'What d'you mean – you can't?'

Again there shone before the doctor's eyes, from floor to ceiling, an iridescent gossamer, at moments seeming smooth and translucent in the mercurial quivering of sunbaked air on some July skyline or frosting over into the finest of pure mica. But there was no such enfeebling gossamer clinging any more to his body; it felt strong and uplifted by an unusual lightness. His heart was filled to the brim with a bitter-sweet sense of solemn selflessness. Instead of some unachieved deed beyond his strength, he now saw his way forward with lightning clarity towards another, more Christian, more selfless and more dangerous exploit. Dolgov leaned his elbows on his knees and began speaking straight into Nakatov's face. It was a homily bubbling up from inside him, a ferocious plea, and a naked confession...

The doctor began speaking in praise of human health and the life of man – the most precious things that medicine was called upon to serve, and in a few minutes he was speaking bluntly, with love and grief and pain, of Sobolev, of how he'd saved him three times from death, of how infinitely dear to him had become the sickly and gentle boy, who would never, of course, do anyone any harm. The doctor, beginning to choke over his words and paying no attention to the tears filling his eyes, told of the vigil beside the boy's bed during the crisis hours, what a mere child Sobolev had seemed in his moments of delirium and how there had grieved for him two women for whom he had been the sole joy in life.

'In my innermost heart I bore the burden of caring for him, with all my doctor's sense of duty and my fatherly love I saved him from death and seized him from the grave, bearing him in my arms...I almost resurrected him!...But you cast him down into the grave, you crucified my love, you nailed my heart to the cross with bullets!...After that – to treat you?...No, you can do what you like with me when you're better, you can shoot me as well, but it isn't medicine I've brought you, it's this...' He took the little bottle of atropine out of his pocket. 'Poison! I, a doctor, wanted to poison you! To poison you!...You were in my hands, but I couldn't. I don't doubt that by this one murder dozens, if not hundreds, of other murders would be prevented. And I didn't stay my hand because I doubted my right to kill you...No, my humanity was revolted by the horror of dying to which I would have condemned you, revolted against the very sight of dying. That's what saved you. But I cannot give you treatment...'

The doctor goes on to condemn Nakatov as an enemy of humanity who must be prevented from taking human life ever again. To this the sick man replies, momentarily surmounting the enfeebling effects of his illness, that he recognises what is meant by 'the horror of dying' and he knows only too well the dilemma facing anyone who tries to weigh one drop of poison against many tons of medicine. It is then that he confesses his own medical training, how he had once been a doctor of sorts himself and had dispensed medicines among the exiles. He proceeds to turn Dolgov's argument round. If the doctor has in so many words just admitted that it may sometimes be necessary to take away someone's life in the interests of other people's lives, then he, Nakatov, had long ago to face this contradiction. He invites the doctor to rethink his ideas:

'...Subject to doubt the value of a humanity that avoids inhumanity by keeping its eyes closed and its hands clean. Once again weigh out on the scales of benefit to humanity the idea...of compassion for compassion's sake. And, finally, take back your homily...the homily by which you wanted to turn me from the path of sin and error to the path of holiness and truth.'

Nakatov's words, formerly calm, flowed now more swiftly. Dolgov listened in astonishment. The most unexpected and shocking thing was that the chairman of the Cheka was answering the doctor's passionate speech, his violent spiritual outpourings, so simply and quietly, as if he had been anticipating this conversation for a long time.

'Of course, doctor, you refused to give me treatment without proper thought...After all, that's indirect murder, and the fact that it's indirect won't save you from later attacks of guilt or from anguish at the horror of my dying: See, you're shaking! That thought hadn't entered your head half an hour ago and now you're astonished by it!...No, you'll stay as you are, you'll give me treatment. The matter's closed. I'll stay as I am. In your case your civic sense prevented you from administering a grain of poison where you thought it necessary. In my case my civic sense made me hurl bombs where I thought they were needed...and shoot bullets like dried peas. My heart and my brain were close to dying not three times, as happened with your patient, but hundreds of times! So by what right do you judge me? First of all, give me poison...Do you hear?...Give me one drop of poison, and then experience what it feels like to kill a man even for the good of all men! One drop of poison. Do you dare? Well, then, if you can't dare that much, just go on dispensing your tons of medicines and let your life flow with milk and honey...let it flow past the rivers of blood...Ha!...flow with milk and honey...past the blood...past me, doctor...past...'

And Nakatov dies despite all the doctor's attempts to save his life. The confrontation between Dolgov's unduly complacent assumption that all human life is precious and Nakatov's anguished conviction that some human lives must be sacrificed for the good of others is offered on a fairly low level of philosophical dispute, but it is nevertheless a confrontation between easily recognisable attitudes of mind, each governed by its own preconceptions. The doctor's abhorrence of politics, quite understandable in a man of his profession and background, gives rise to a semi-religious justification of pacifist attitudes, just as Nakatov's political activism, despite his special pleading for his own oft-repeated martyrdom in the name of political necessity, amounts in the end to little more than an *apologia* for terrorism and the terrorist. But the issues are stated in a cleverly orchestrated metaphorical confrontation of honey versus blood, the provincial stagnation and complacency of the town versus the

ghostly gunfire of Nakatov's motorbike, the doctor's well-meaning
heroism in the name of his single patient (even though it is indirectly
on behalf of all of them) versus Nakatov's blood-stained heroism in
the name of the revolution and a society purged of anti-revolutionary
elements. That Nakatov perhaps has the last word does not by any
means imply authorial approval of his attitude. Each side is duly
allowed its say; the result is noteworthy as a balanced statement of
fundamentally opposed views of justice, just as the novel's treatment
of such concepts as 'humanity', 'compassion' and 'right' is far from
dogmatic in its human appraisal of their meaning. Kolokolov's novel
poses them in an eloquent dialectical framework and sets them in
dramatic relief against a background of epidemic and civil strife.[118]

Such a relatively clear statement of the issues *pro* and *contra* is rare
but by no means unique in the Soviet novel of the first decade after
the revolution. By the end of the 1920s the possibilities for real
candour on the subject of the dualism surrounding intellectual
commitment to revolution were becoming limited. In any case, they
were beginning to be of historical rather than topical interest. It is
therefore possible to discern in a novel like Aleksandr Malyshkin's
Sevastopol' (1931) a final – and unusual – word on the problem of
adjustment to revolutionary change; as distinct, that is to say, from
an increasing number of Soviet novels devoted to conventional
confrontations between youthful heroes and the realities of Soviet
life in the Reconstruction period, at the opening of the Five Year Plan
periods and so on.

Aleksandr Fadeyev remarked about the novel's hero that he was
a representative of what he called 'an intermediate, very lowly and – in
the past – very oppressed layer of the democratic intelligentsia, of
minor officials of the civil service, a kind of demi-intelligentsia which
is numbered *in millions* in our country'. And he went on to pose a
question and then answer it:

Is it necessary to write about *the great difficulty* with which representatives
of this layer rid themselves of their egotistical habits and illusions, rid
themselves of ideals of life designed only for themselves and in their own
name and often enough clothed for them in the most 'beautiful', the most
'learned', the most 'gilded' words? It is only by putting the question *in this
way* that one can see that Malyshkin's novel about one of the representatives
of this layer is necessary and useful and significant.[119]

Aleksandr Malyshkin's *Sevastopol'* opens with a picture of a
school for officer cadets in Petrograd at the time of the February

revolution of 1917. The hero is Sergey Shelekhov, who has entered the naval training college direct from university. He is a dreamer, a romantic and a young man of modest social background who has an ambition to rise in the social hierarchy of bourgeois, pre-revolutionary Russia. At university he had been attracted to early Russian literature and in his dreams he supposes that he has discovered a new copy of the 'Slovo'.[120] Chiefly, though, he dreams of girls and love and glory. The eroticism of his own dreams is counterpointed by a fascinated and wary disgust at the obscene and perverse sexuality of some of his fellow cadets, especially those who belong to the upper class, such as one Yelkhovsky:

In the depths of cadet Yelkhovsky there always seemed to lurk the dregs of something filthy and unimaginable, like, for instance, the secret and shameful traditions of the military schools with the masturbation of under-age cadets and the concealment beneath one's clothes of the running sores of dirty infections...Yelkhovsky belonged to that alien, hostile caste who learned from their youth upwards to look upon civilians and those of lower rank with impassively wooden *hauteur*.

Shelekhov's sense of repugnance, however natural, does not actually extend to rejection of the bourgeois world as well. He is in thrall to a dream 'of a white dress running away from him on to a sunlit hill' – an image, in other words, of fey loveliness and romantic rapture. The incongruity and tenuousness of this image for one such as the innocent Shelekhov are highlighted by the brutal realities of the revolutionary situation. He is shy of women when confronted by them. The exploration of Shelekhov's sexual innocence is done sensitively, without any demeaning parody, and in its candour it makes this novel the most humanly interesting study of the way in which revolutionary change and coming to manhood coincide, interact and finally appear to show the way to maturity. The novel successfully captures the callowness, shyness, gaucheness and evident intelligence of this young man without romanticising or guying his dilemma.

Shortly after the February revolution he is made an officer. This, he believes, is likely to be a passport into a world of fairytale experiences. He dresses in his uniform and looks in the mirror:

Turning as he walked, Shelekhov surveyed a dark-looking naval officer, short in stature, well-built, with a tightly in-drawn girlish waist, glancing over his shoulder with dark youthful perplexed eyes.
He froze in amazement.

This was exactly the sort of inaccessible officer he had seen at the Alexandrovsky Gardens or on the Morskoy Boulevard or somewhere in some busy region full of well-dressed women and automobiles. The women had looked at him with an enticing scorn and there had awaited him a very special, a very beautiful fate.

There follows a vivid picture of Petrograd in the first days of the provisional government. Increasingly, though, the novel assumes a documentary tone as it tells of Shelekhov's trip to the south to join the Black Sea Fleet at Sevastopol'. Such historical figures as Kerensky and Kolchak have their place in the detailed picture of revolutionary changes that gradually affect the fleet, but equally 'documentary', if not historical, is the story of Shelekhov's relationship with a girl called Jackie (*Zheka*) whom he had met on the train trip from Petrograd. She infatuates him in part because she seems to embody that image of 'a white dress running away from him on to a sunlit hill'. She also represents for him the newly attainable high-class erotic pleasure formerly denied him. Similarly accessible to him now are the superior restaurants and hotels of Sevastopol'. But Shelekhov is gradually drawn away from the allure of such bourgeois pleasures, even though he makes speeches that draw on the slogans used by Kerensky. His search for erotic satisfaction is accompanied by an attempt to justify himself intellectually. Speaking to his girl-friend, he claims in an exhibitionist and unconvincing way that Kant was no less a figure for humanity than were Christ and Mahomet. He says: 'Kant used to say that the visible world was no more than the system of our illusions. But Kant worked it all out intellectually, and now life itself has quietly turned into its own kind of nightmare...' Despite which he still seeks for reality and does not deserve the girl's scornful retort that he is no more than a boy inhabiting a world of his own imaginings. When, after seeming to promise him erotic happiness on a trip to Odessa, she in fact refuses him admission to her cabin, this particular erotic dream evaporates for Shelekhov just as surely as does the bourgeois world to which she belongs. An unsuccessful attack on Rostov, the shooting of officers and the ascendancy of Bolshevism in October 1917 finally force Shelekhov into the realisation that he has so far done nothing to further the revolution, apart from play at it. The sailors elect him leader of a volunteer detachment to fight on the Red side at the beginning of the civil war and he thus acquires the feeling of fusion with the people that he had earnestly sought for earlier. The sea imagery underlines the point: 'He was lifted up by the crests of the waves, those very waves which had passed by so unattainably all the while external to him – and now they received him into their bosom, nursed him, dandled him.' When the time comes for him finally to leave for the civil war, the futility of his travelling baggage of bourgeois romanticism is neatly summarised towards the end of the novel:

He recalled a sentence from a book he had read, some novel or other: 'On leaving he took with him his favourite volume of Boethius...' He had no favourite volume of Boethius. He had nothing that he could take with him on his trip to distant places...A sad but alleviating penury! (*Grustnaya, no i oblegchitel'naya nishcheta!*)

The portrayal of Shelekhov lacks real depth or subtlety. It possesses in compensation a degree of candour rare in portraits of the revolutionary hero. Arguably he is not such a hero, but a young man involved in revolutionary events who tends to confuse romantic and revolutionary ideals. That interpretation is less rewarding than the simpler one of regarding the novel as in most essentials autobiographical, but with the emphasis placed on an emotional reaching towards maturity that tends to coincide with a dawning consciousness of the revolution's unromantic, anti-bourgeois meaning. Shelekhov's gradual adjustment to the revolution has little about it to stir the imagination, he is cast in too shallow a mould for that, but he appears young enough, impressionable enough and sufficiently intelligent for the dualism of his romantic and revolutionary ideals to have more than cursory interest. And if in the end he is seen to travel light into the experience of civil war, we are permitted to know enough from his characterisation to suspect that total orthodoxy of political commitment would never come easily to him, as one suspects it never came easily to Aleksandr Malyshkin himself.

4

The revolutionary epic

Introduction

The epic novel in Russian and Soviet literature is a branch of historical fiction. Greatly elaborated and enlarged though it may have been, the epic novel in nineteenth-century Russian literature had as its source the novels of Walter Scott and only emerged as a novelistic genre in its own right when the conventionally 'historical' features of the historical novel were deliberately 'made strange' or defamiliarised by L. Tolstoy and given epic proportions in his famous *War and Peace* (1863–9). In a strict sense, the term 'epic' when applied to a novel meant little more than 'large in scale', but the term has grown implicitly to denote an enlarged historical novel describing heroic events of national significance. The pattern and model for all epic novels in this sense are supplied by *War and Peace*, which has almost automatically been referred to by critics who seek to identify the epic novel in a context of Russian or Soviet literature.

The epic proportions of *War and Peace* – and therefore the work's novelty – can be identified in several ways. The work's temporal range spans approximately seven years (1805–12), to which can be added the time scale of the first epilogue and the further enhancement of the work's temporal significance through the way it mirrors obliquely the ethos and problems of the decade (the 1860s) in which it was written. The range of settings similarly extends geographically from Moscow to St Petersburg, from Borodino to Smolensk, and so on. More significant, though, than such compass in time and space is the multiplication of hero-figures, the creation of social worlds (of family, urban or rural communities, army associations, high-society status and so on) to which the central figures belong and which explain or condition quite as much as supposed biographical background the behaviour of the central heroes and heroines. This process naturally involves an enlargement of the range of social relationships from emperors to peasants, parlour-maids to princesses, from the historical personality represented in public posture to the most private intimacies between mother and daughter or a man and his conscience. Technically, a variety of viewpoints, seemingly cinematic glimpses in scene-by-scene succession, rapidity of movement from one locale to another, all contribute to the kinetic impression of the historical fiction, but neither the range of material treated nor the technical brilliance of the accomplishment would have added up to epic proportions had not *War and Peace* been concerned with demonstrating and defining the causes of the Russian people's heroic defence of their country against the invading Napoleonic armies.[1]

The greatness of Tolstoy's masterpiece is attributable to the power of characterisation above all, and the greatness of all epic novels, no matter how extensive their treatment of a heroic historical event, is always in the end determined by the power of characterisation. In the case of the revolutionary epics that are to be considered in chapter 4, the assimilation of history to the fictional form is also to be adjudged on the same basis, though here in Gorky's *The Life of Klim Samgin* and in Sholokhov's *Quiet Flows the Don*, a central hero-figure either determines the nature of the fiction (in Klim Samgin's case) or dominates it to the virtual exclusion of any equivalent figure (Grigory Melekhov). A multiplication of central heroes and heroines in Aleksey Tolstoy's *The Road To Calvary* perhaps shows closer formal identity with *War and Peace*, but an inherent falsity in the characterisation, the treatment of historical events and personalities as little more than decor features and the tendency of the story element to resemble an adventure narrative seriously impair the value of the work both as historical fiction and as literature. Characterisation as a means of explaining history in the fate of a central figure (something most particularly relevant to Pierre Bezhukhov's role in *War and Peace*) is successfully achieved among the three works under discussion only in Sholokhov's masterpiece.

The revolutionary epic is of course distinguishable from other fictional treatments of historical subjects by its concern with revolutionary events. The assimilation of history to the fictional form is to be adjudged in this case by the extent to which the fictional central figures comprehend and react to revolutionary events. Unless the central figures are direct participants in historical events that have revolution, meaning the overthrow of one form of government by another, as their central purpose and comprehend that purpose from a point of view central to the fiction, the novel will tend to be no more than a chronicle work. The central commitment to an awareness of revolution is essential. But the very size or range suggested by the use of the term 'epic' implies that the revolutionary epic strives to comprehend all – or practically all – the shades of *pro* and *contra* that may be present in a revolutionary situation. It is this enlargement of choice between pro- and anti-revolutionary factors that makes both the central figure and the reader aware of the enormous complexities and paradoxes caused by revolution and civil war. The revolutionary epic is the ultimate and most mature response of the revolutionary novel to the Russian Revolution and it is not surprising that the most grandiose and accomplished heroic portraits are to be encountered in its pages.

The Life of Klim Samgin (Zhizn' Klima Samgina)[2]

Gorky's last unfinished work of fiction has been dismissed as unreadable by more than one critic. It is a four-volume novel, designed to cover the forty years (one of Gorky's original titles for the work) immediately preceding the 1917 revolution. The first volume is divided into lengthy chapters, but the remaining volumes form an uninterrupted torrent of narrative. Central to this epic novel are both Klim Ivanovich Samgin, the intelligentsia hero present throughout its pages, and the revolution of 1905, which is the pivotal point of the narrative, straddling volumes II and III. The novel culminates with the February revolution of 1917. Fragmentary notes at the close of volume IV indicate that the return of Lenin to Russia in April 1917 may have been intended as the finale.

If Gorky's final intentions are obscure, we do at least know that his initial plan for the novel dated from shortly after the 1905 revolution and grew from 'a desire to portray the figure of such a typical *intelligent*'.[3] In the course of the portrayal of such a typical member of the Russian intelligentsia, the novel acquired certain features of both a *Bildungsroman* and an enormous chronicle offering a panoramic overview of the intelligentsia's place in Russian pre-revolutionary history.[4] It also showed up more clearly than any other literary work of the post-revolutionary period the complexities and paradoxes of choice that faced the intelligentsia in pre-1917 Russia. Perhaps of greater importance, it can help to explain and set in context the dilemma of a Dr Zhivago who, despite his intelligentsia commitment to revolution, cannot adjust himself to the kind of change that revolution actually demands of him. Moreover, it has come to be regarded by Soviet critics as an epic twentieth-century novel, having world significance,[5] and as the first socio-philosophical novel in Soviet literature.[6]

Samgin is christened Klim Ivanovich through the whim of a somewhat eccentric father, who wanted to give him an unusual name but finally plumped for the 'peasant' name Klim because it didn't oblige him to be anything. Consequently, Klim Samgin spends a lifetime trying to invent himself. The background to Klim's life is a numerically small intelligentsia like himself who, neither strictly bourgeois (Klim has no capital), nor peasant, strive also to invent themselves, to discover a way of serving the peasant masses, that is to say, while remaining anti-establishment and true to themselves. Simple enough, it may seem, as a morality, but full of pitfalls in practice. Klim, for example, is encouraged by his parents to cultivate the role of an 'unusual', a 'significant' person, meaning on the whole that he tends to accumulate and repeat a large number of received opinions that he passes off as his own. He naturally assumes the pose of a spectator at life's carnival whose view of things is invariably tinged by scepticism. Educated, with a lawyer's training, Klim becomes fully-fledged as an *intelligent*, undergoing the familiar emotional experiences of growing up, the sexual forays, but finding it almost as hard to commit himself emotionally as intellectually. He prides himself on standing aside from the crowd and keeping silent, the only central meaning to his life being his honest attitude towards himself.

After the breakdown of his parents' marriage, his mother eventually marries the wealthy entrepreneur Varavka with whom she had been living. His brother becomes an unsuccessful revolutionary and suffers the inevitable arrests and imprisonments. The true image of the dedicated revolutionary is to be found only in the bearded, loud-mouthed Kutuzov, whose Bolshevik sympathies impress, even if they do not influence and convert, the sceptical Klim Samgin. For Kutuzov the vocation of revolutionary involves 'a lifelong heroism, the heroism of a labourer, of a craftsman of revolution', and this, of course, Samgin and the great majority of the intelligentsia cannot be. Surrounded as he constantly is by a crowd of endlessly talking members of the intelligentsia, of multifarious shades of political and cultural opinion, Samgin is partly a sounding-board, partly a

fulcrum, partly an authorial chorus or commentator for a succession
of different characters and groupings of characters drawn from the
whole spectrum of Russian pre-revolutionary society. Though he is
arrested and interrogated on more than one occasion, he is oppo-
sitional in his own views only as intelligentsia fashion dictates and
through the mask of his scepticism it is hard to discern more than
a generalised habit of mind. He became, we are told, 'accustomed
to thoughts of revolution as one becomes accustomed to the
prolonged rains of autumn or to surrounding talk'. As an accumu-
lator of others' opinions, he is described as being sure that all human
fabrications are suspended in him like dust in a ray of sunlight, but
when he attempts to put his thoughts on paper he recognises with
genuine astonishment that what he writes betrays a man of very
conservative outlook. Recently married to his wife Varvara, he
returns from his honeymoon in the Caucasus to metropolitan life and
aphoristically declares (every character in the novel speaks in a
theatrically aphoristic manner):

'I respect people who can enter disinterestedly into the lives of others. They
are true heroes.'

Samgin very quickly became one of those very conspicuous, even respected
people, who stand at the junction, at the very centre of various cross-roads
of public opinion but, without joining any, know all the groups and circles,
sympathize with all and, on occasion, are even ready to render overt or covert
services of a not too dangerous characer; they always value their own
services very highly. Samgin's well-made figure and dry face, with its small
dark beard, his not too powerful but impressive voice, with which he was
always capable of uttering words that chilled excessive fervour – gave him
the appearance of a man who knew something, who perhaps knew everything.
He spoke little, with restraint, and in a way which made his listeners conclude
that although what he said was not of vast profundity, this was only because
his other words were not for everybody, but reserved for the elect. His
blue-grey eyes glittered coldly behind his spectacles, looking straight into the
face of his interlocutor and assuming an air of mystery. Most people talked
so incessantly that a silent man was made conspicuous. Samgin's capacious
memory established for him the reputation of being a widely informed
person.

As the revolution of 1905 approaches, Samgin seems prepared to
recognise the correctness of Kutuzov's Leninist, Bolshevik interpretation of events. More significantly, it is only Kutuzov, of all the
many radical members of the intelligentsia in the novel, who is
portrayed as sufficient of a human being to feel the private anguish

of his revolutionary vocation. But when Samgin (always conveniently on the spot for the most important historical events) witnesses the massacre of workers on Bloody Sunday, his eyes may view the revolutionary scene with the concern for factuality of a good journalist (he has worked as a journalist over the years), yet his intellectual response obliges him to admit that 'revolution is necessary in order to get rid of revolutionaries'. Indeed, he achieves the greatest social success of his life when he describes to select groups what he witnessed at the time of the 1905 revolution. Later, as the 1905 revolution reaches its climax, his Moscow apartment happens to be situated close by the street barricades and he is once more a witness of the defeat of the workers. The total effect of these events is not only to turn him against revolution but also to cause a disintegration of personality. In the post-revolutionary aftermath he visits a provincial town on a mission connected with Kutuzov and meets there Marina Zotova, a religious fanatic of wealth and energy who supports the Bolsheviks and eventually fascinates Samgin more than any other character in the novel. On the first night of his visit to the town he experiences a nightmare in which he is confronted by his own double in a world without shadows. It is a vision of hell after its fashion and it recurs to Samgin at various stages in his later career. It is of course also a clue to Gorky's vision of Samgin's personality as one that disintegrates, as does the Russian intelligentsia, under the pressures of revolutionary events. Since Samgin is so central and essential a figure for the entire fiction, the disintegration of his personality must also be a clue to the breakdown that gradually overtakes Gorky's epic novel.

Samgin, the personification of scepticism, finds much that is intriguing and sympathetic to him in studying the grotesque world of Hieronymus Bosch, whose pictures he first comes across on a visit to Berlin. Bosch, he concludes, depicts a nightmare (similar, that is, to his own), though one that Samgin discerns now close to the surface of reality. Despite the neutral colour of his personality and the bitterness underlying his scepticism, Samgin becomes transformed in the novel's final volume into a character of greater integrity in his respect for himself than the many other, more colourful and volatile, characters with whom he has been associated. Indeed, practically all his closest associates die or are murdered or simply vanish into the oblivion of Samgin's indifference. More and more frequently he reflects upon the senselessness and insignificance of life not in the manner of a commentator but as a thinker in his own right. On one occasion he contemplates writing a book on the theme of 'Life and Thought' that will show how much violence thought has done to life. Reminding himself that man has a right to live for himself and not only for the future, he blames Chekhov – and Gorky, by the way – for propagating a brand of trivial positivism that has developed into Marxism, 'an even more misshapen extreme' of the same theory.

The idea, therefore, that revolution can change the world is quite as strongly challenged by Samgin's scepticism as is the notion that the intelligentsia must mortgage its present existence for the sake of a remote future happiness. For all the unpleasantness of Samgin's personality, he acquires features that make him appear as an authorial *persona* and suggest the extent to which Gorky's attitude towards the triumph of Bolshevism in 1917 was informed by a kind of double-think. Kutuzov, the Bolshevik, has only a small role to play in the final volume and is absent from the scene in the final phase when Samgin witnesses the beginnings of the February revolution. Who, Samgin asks himself within half-a-dozen pages of the end of the extant text, should be the leader, the Napoleon, of the masses of hungry demonstrators on the streets of Petrograd? The answer, of course, must be Lenin, for historical fiction cannot violate history, but the scepticism of Samgin (and of Gorky, one suspects) should denigrate even Lenin if it is to follow the generalised habit of mind that had dominated all the preceding fiction. The novel disintegrates at this very point. The implication of the final fragments that Samgin is trampled to death and ends up as no more than a bag of bones cannot be ignored; nor can it be substantiated. The profounder implication of Gorky's revolutionary epic, namely that the Russian intelligentsia, principally in the person of Klim Ivanovich Samgin, could not accept the revolution of 1917, is one that also, if only by inference, criticises revolution as such.

For all its clumsiness and tedium Gorky's four-part novel offers a multi-faceted, multi-voiced kaleidoscope of social types always revolving, through Samgin's own involvement, about a succession of intellectual and political crisis-points in Russian pre-revolutionary life. The sheer abundance of the dialogue passages must impress every reader. The effect is to suggest a remarkably full life lived often at great intensity, no matter how faint-hearted or uncommitted a participant the central observer may be. The novel's fictional life flows with the steadiness and majesty of the Volga that runs through so much of Gorky's work as a writer. Samgin himself, despite his arid, complacent priggishness, is endowed through his very scepticism with a similar steadiness of viewpoint and begins to achieve a certain majestic objectivity in his response to war and revolution towards the novel's close. His personal stance is critical of war for its waste, of revolution for its irrelevance (he prefers to believe in the need for reforms). But essential in any estimate of his ambivalent, uncommitted, deeply sceptical view of things is the paradox of the novel as a whole, which, through its ubiquitous hero, represents a nation's life as dominated by identity-seekers who create mirror images of each other, who are duplicates or doubles in a fictional replica of history that seems deliberately to emphasise the ambivalence of all historical processes. As a result, the novel invites scrutiny as an anti-epic, or as an epic of an anti-hero, with the clear implication that revolution itself deserves the same sceptical dethronement in terms of life's values and priorities as does the unrevolutionary hero.

As a revolutionary epic Gorky's *The Life of Klim Samgin* has the dignity of a flawed literary monument, dignified, that is to say, by its assertion of the right of literature to illuminate history and pass judgement on it, flawed of course by its incompleteness and shapelessness. But it is the dignity of the work even in its failure that demands respect, and that dignity is due to the sustaining talkativeness of so many dozens of characters, the very vitality of the polyphony, however tedious on occasion, so that it literally seems to recreate in its cacophonous way a picture of Russian intellectual history before 1917 (so Samgin thinks to himself, recalling someone else's phrase) as 'one continuous dialogue interrupted from time to time by pistol shots and bomb explosions'. At the centre of all the talkativeness is the theme of revolution, but the very futility of the talk increasingly highlights the futility of the theme. If Samgin himself had been cast in a nobler mould, it might have seemed a tragic waste. As it is, his life seems to be an epic of futility.

Quiet Flows the Don (*Tikhiy Don*)

No prose work in Soviet literature has greater majesty than Sholokhov's masterpiece. There is a quality of the miraculous about a young man with little formal education, who starts writing an extended, four-volume work of such power at the age of twenty, completes the greater part of it before he is twenty-five and finishes it, after serious interruptions, before he is half-way through his thirties.[7] The contemplation of these facts has inevitably given rise to accusations of plagiarism and speculations on the likelihood of authorship.[8] For want of strong evidence to the contrary, it has to be assumed that Mikhail Sholokhov (b. 1905) is the author of *Quiet Flows the Don* and that its manifest greatness, as well as those parts of it which seem to fall short of the generally high standard, are attributable to Sholokhov's predilections and background, as well as his genius, as the work's author.

Quiet Flows the Don is an epic of counter-revolution. 'I am describing', Sholokhov is quoted as saying, 'the Whites' struggle with the Reds and not the other way round. This is the big difficulty.'[9] In a sense, it is a difficulty common to all the examples of the revolutionary epic. The central figures in each case display an anti-revolutionary bias which, though discredited, is not flatly condemned. Moreover, Sholokhov's epic of counter-revolution among the Don Cossacks celebrates Vendean attitudes that are given some degree of historical and cultural justification. They have a deep tragic meaning, both because they are misguided and because they highlight an enduring divide in Russian social and political life.

Sholokhov's birthright was unusual. He was born in the steppe village of Kruzhilin on the river Don, the illegitimate child of Anastasiya Danilovna Chernikova, who worked as a maidservant on a large local estate. His father, Aleksandr Mikhaylovich Sholokhov, had several jobs in commerce and finally became manager of a steam flour-mill. He was not of Cossack origin but came from Ryazan in Central Russia. When the couple eventually married in 1912, Sholokhov was officially described as 'the son of a bourgeois (*meshchanin*)'.[10] Poor eyesight necessitated a trip to Moscow for treatment in 1914 (in the same hospital as the one in which Grigory Melekhov receives treatment for an injured eye) and he had some two or three years of formal education in Moscow before returning to the Don region in 1918 and becoming an eyewitness of the counter-revolutionary developments in that area.

Born, therefore, not only out of wedlock but also outside Cossack life, as the son of a Russian rather than a Cossack, Sholokhov had a divided birthright and an ambivalent – half-rural, half-bourgeois – view of Cossack life. The contradictions implicit in such a heritage were compounded by the fact that, during his most formative years, he experienced at first hand the fratricidal violence of civil war. Apart from actively participating in the establishment of Soviet authority in the Don region, he was a schoolteacher for a time, took part in amateur dramatics and had a more militant role as a Red Army soldier engaged in fighting Makhno and other bandits. His return to Moscow in 1922 led to his association with the journal *The Young Guard* (*Molodaya gvardiya*) and to the publication of his first articles. Before he was twenty years of age, then, Mikhail Sholokhov had been formed as a writer and was already taking his first steps, in the shape of his *Tales from the Don*, on the road to becoming the author of *Quiet Flows the Don*.

A page of *Quiet Flows the Don* will convince any reader of two things. First is the astonishing freshness and brilliance of the visual sense that informs the writing.[11] Sholokhov's writer's eye, perhaps through an abnormality in his own eyesight, has extraordinary clarity, unusual receptivity to colour and the natural ability to relate foreground to background, vividness of human action and emotion to an equivalent vividness in the natural scene, and, most particularly, man to the earth, the soil, the place of his birth. The instinctive relationship of man to the earth is the second thing that no reader can fail to notice. Sholokhov celebrates instinct as a basic constituent of human experience. All his central characters – and especially Grigory Melekhov – exist as human beings principally through their sense of belonging to the Don region. Their instinct for survival is linked closely to the Don itself, just as the huge river, so symbolic of the everlasting flow of life, is the ceaseless presence in the background of their lives and fates.

But if these twin elements can be regarded as part of Sholokhov's own birthright, equally a part of it, if one can judge correctly from the sparse detail available on the subject, is the sense of being an outsider in Cossack life, even a rebel in its midst. He knew, as D. H. Stewart has put it (speaking of course of Mishka Koshevoy), 'the humiliation of growing up *in*, but not quite *of*, Cossack society'.[12] This humiliation may well have been at the source of Sholokhov's love–hate attitudes to Cossack tradition and Cossack nationalism. He was part of both but party to neither, and this ambivalence is at the heart of his epic novel. But, as a study of revolutionary events, the novel appears to have had its beginnings in Sholokhov's concern for the first instance of Cossack rebelliousness in 1917 – the Kornilov revolt. The first draft, entitled *Donshchina*, has apparently been lost. The second half of Part IV of the extant novel, which describes the Kornilov revolt, may derive from it. If it does, the novel would initially have been conceived as a kind of historical panorama of Russian and Cossack life – without, that is to say, the presence of Grigory Melekhov. Very possibly his leading role sprang from Sholokhov's meeting with Kharlampy Ermakov, upon whose exploits in the war with the Central Powers and in the civil war some of Grigory Melekhov's experiences may be based.[13] The novel's counter-revolutionary emphasis was there at its inception, we may assume, and as a study of Cossack resistance to Bolshevism it deepened into a very complex examination of the manifold forces at work in both Cossack society and human nature under pressure of revolutionary change.

As an epic novel, Sholokhov's work corresponds to the criterion of 'epic' on the model of *War and Peace* in the sense that its action extends over a considerable period of time – from 1912 to 1922. It is similarly concerned with a heroic, if tragic, national feat, meaning the attempt of Cossack nationalist elements, on the pattern of the Vendée, to oppose the forces of the central revolutionary government. But it differs from *War and Peace* in being an epic of rural life in all essentials. The standards of conduct and morality are non-urban, non-civic and even un-modern. The world of *Quiet Flows the Don* has a timelessness that is literally signalled by the absence of clocks. 'No character wears a watch which he can break when time's passage becomes unendurable', D. H. Stewart perceptively notes.[14] The ethos of Sholokhov's Cossackdom seems medieval in its simplicity, governed by a rigid patriarchalism and an unpoliticised, instinctive awareness of the earth and the natural cycles, so that a folkloristic manner appears entirely apt as a means of suggesting the mythlike or legendary character of the events under scrutiny. The laws that govern the treatment of such events are also devoid, it seems, of a bias towards historical and dialectical materialism. 'Life dictates its own unwritten laws to people' (Part III, xxii) is the aphoristic explanation given, for example, to account for Aksinya's submission to Listnitsky after the death of her daughter. The very traditionalism of Cossackdom and of the basic premises of the fiction consequently highlight the iconoclastic nature of revolutionary change and endow Sholokhov's work with special power as a revolutionary epic.

Although an epic of rural life, *Quiet Flows the Don* is not only about peasant socio-economic relationships. Such relationships are of course important in defining the differences in Cossack society, for peasants, as Lenin pointed out, are 'half labourers and half property-owners'.[15] These contradictions are amply illustrated in the gradations of wealth and privilege that separate the Listnitskys from the Melekhovs and the Melekhovs from the Koshevoys, but they are also there in Grigory's feelings towards his fellow officers and, more profoundly, in his contradictory loyalties, first to Reds, then to Whites. For, over-riding in many respects the socio-economic contradictions, is the special loyalty of all Cossacks to their ethos as a military caste. This instinctive militancy can be seen to govern the lives of the Melekhov menfolk, as it does many others, in ways that approximate to the rules of conduct governing medieval knights or samurai warriors. In short, they fight because it is their nature to fight, as well as their tradition, in defence not only of Tsars, but also of their natural rights.

Grigory Melekhov is at the very centre of the epic, and the real source of its power. He contains in his characterisation all the major contradictions and pressures that affect the political and social scene, but in his case the contradictions are *lived*[16] and he appeals as a character through the riddle posed by his life.[17] His heredity explains part of his enigma. The Melekhov lineage and the Melekhov property are both off-centre, towards the perimeter of Cossack life. The brief history of the family at the opening of the novel tells of the Turkish wife brought to Tatarsky by Grigory's grandfather after the Russo-Turkish War of 1877–8. Her violent death shortly after giving birth to Panteley, Grigory's father, introduces the reader both to the violence so characteristic of Cossack society and to another aspect of the hero's birthright, the half-Cossack, half-Turkish lineage, which endows Grigory with the hook-nose appearance derived from his father, the blue-tinted almonds of fierce eyes in slightly oblique slits and a similar savage smile. If the lineage keeps him at one remove from the true, pure-blood centre of Cossack life, similarly the Melekhov property is on the village limits with a cattleyard opening towards the north, towards the Don. The Don itself, beneath a 60-foot (18-metre) slope of bank, is like the flow of life circumscribing Grigory's experience, from the moment when he goes fishing in the novel's second chapter to the moment when he ascends from the Don at the novel's end to hold his son in his arms. As the famous final words state: 'That was all that remained to him in life, that still linked him to the earth and to the huge expanse of the world glittering under a cold sun.'

Grigory, then, has a mixed birthright and an ambivalent relationship to the Cossack world, but he also, as Roy Medvedev points out, 'appears to combine the best qualities of both the Lower [Don] and Upper [Don] Cossacks, the ardent personality, warlike nature and severe taciturnity of the former and the latter's attachment to the land and to hard work'.[18] His general taciturnity and the infrequency with which readers are permitted to share his thoughts naturally reinforce the impression of a character governed by instinct and passion rather than by reason and ideas. Although little is actually told, we know that he had difficulty in completing his education at a church school and that his poor knowledge gives him only a shaky literacy (Part VII, x). He blows his nose not with a handkerchief but with two fingers, wipes his fingers when eating either on his boots or his hair, either bites his fingernails to trim them or uses his sword. The litany of his uncouth traits could be extended. He is portrayed, in fact, as the product of a crude, peasant society, accustomed as much to sudden birth as to sudden death, and combining in an exotic, extremely sensuous fashion a natural violence of behaviour with a direct, unsophisticated apprehension of the sensuous beauties of the natural scene. His characterisation as a sensual man is inseparable from his total awareness of the surrounding natural world. Take away the natural scene from *Quiet Flows the Don* and Grigory Melekhov is denied his sensual vitality.

Grigory's portrayal is given that added vitality and particular appeal which make him truly heroic through his love for Aksinya Astakhov. Her violent initiation into sex and her maltreatment by her husband Stepan help to explain Grigory's sensuous fascination for her. Their love story is the thread of gold in Grigory's life that links him to humanity and softens and humanises his whole image in the fiction. His feelings for her transform him. They are the revolutionary element in his personality, which parallels his actual revolt against Cossack custom in leaving his own household and wife Natalya in order to live with Aksinya. Yet greater even than his attachment to Aksinya is his attachment to the land and the farm, despite her plea that he should find work in the coalmines (Part I, xii). The whole of Part I of the novel fixes Grigory in his attachment to place, to his village of Tatarsky and the Don, to his Melekhov family and background, but principally in his sensual attachment to the earth.

Part II broadens the social and political framework of the novel

by offering a history of the Mokhovs, the petty-bourgeois representatives of the merchant class in Tatarsky society. At the same time
the first indications of some kind of dissidence are suggested by a
description, if sketchy, of the role of the village intelligentsia. With
the exception of the local schoolteacher, we are told, the inhabitants
of the village had their own houses and lived cut off from the outside world behind bolted shutters. This fierce property-owning
individualism is seriously challenged by the arrival of Shtokman, the
agent of the Singer Sewing Machine Co., who forms a discussion
group for the study of Marx and Social Democracy. By this means
the two main protagonists of Bolshevism in the novel, Mishka
Koshevoy and the engineer Ivan Alekseyevich Kotlyarov, are established as politically articulate representatives of revolutionary
change. Personal friends of Grigory though they may be, it is clearly
intimated that their political convictions will always have priority
over all personal attachments, even those dictated by blood and
marriage. Meanwhile, Grigory finds employment as a coachman at
the Listnitsky estate of Yagodnoye, where he has escaped to live with
Aksinya. The picture of upper-class Cossack life has its eccentricities –
General Listnitsky's habit of masticating his food and then spitting
it onto a silver salver is one such – but on the whole the portrayal
of the landowners is sympathetic. The bucolic, uneventful, provincial
life of pre-revolutionary Cossackdom has its moments of excitement
and horror – the wolf hunt with General Listnitsky, for instance, or
the hideous self-maiming by Natalya, in her attempt to commit
suicide with a scythe – and yet it has a fixed, even flow, it seems,
which, but for the coming of the First World War, would have
changed only gradually and then only in small particulars.

Exiled temporarily from his native Tatarsky and the Don for which
he pines, Grigory is already depicted as a partial outsider to Cossack
life. His experience during the First World War is equally depicted
as that of a loner, partisan for no particular cause, and if, for
example, he feels that there exists between him and the officer class
'an unscalable, invisible wall' (Part III, ii), then he feels himself just
as individualist in his objection to the collective rape of Franya. His
killing of the two Austrian soldiers is the beginning of a process that
slowly deadens his spirit without markedly denting his loyalty to the
Cossack ethos. The source both of his dexterity with a sabre and of
his philosophy of killing is the Mephistophelean Uryupin, who more
than once acts as the evil mentor of Grigory's conscience:

'Kill a man boldly. He's soft, is a man, like dough,' advised 'Tufty' Uryupin, laughing with his eyes. 'You mustn't bother about the how and the what of it. You're a Cossack, it's your job to kill without asking questions. You have a sacred duty to kill your enemy in battle. For every man you kill God'll forgive you a sin, same as if you'd killed a serpent. You mustn't kill an animal without the need for it – a heifer, say, or something like that – but you can always do away with a man! Men are foul things, unclean, they pollute the earth! They live like toadstools!...' (Part III, xii).

This influence remains as deeply engraved in him as any save his instinctive, sensual awareness of the earth. It is the crude, ugly justification of all his Cossack militancy.

Paralleling Grigory's experience is that of the volunteer Bunchuk, the former munitions worker who wants to know war in practice, not only in theory. His advocacy of Lenin's interpretation of the war, although obviously propagandist, provides the kind of counterweight to Grigory's apolitical view of things that may arguably give the whole novel a pro-Bolshevik bias. With impeccable working-class credentials, Bunchuk is the only real proletarian revolutionary in the novel, and yet his influence on Grigory is virtually non-existent and his love affair with the Jewess, Anna Pogudko, has been seriously curtailed during the novel's revisions.[19] The only other major influence on Grigory apart from Uryupin is the Ukrainian Garanzha, whose arguments against the war overturn all Grigory's former ideas about the Tsar, about his fatherland and his Cossack military duty. The influence is vague, despite the claims made for it, and Grigory remains the individualist who will follow his own path of conduct, whether in sternly punishing both the younger Listnitsky and Aksinya when he learns of their misconduct, or conducting himself in war with a scrupulously hard heart:

Grigory held firm to his Cossack honour, took every opportunity to display selfless courage...His heart grew coarse and hard as salt flats in a drought; and as dry salty earth cannot absorb water, so Grigory's heart could not absorb pity. With cold contempt he played with his own and others' lives; so he earned a reputation for bravery and was rewarded with four St. George crosses and four medals (Part IV, iv).

During the revolutionary year of 1917 Grigory is no participant in any of the revolutionary events. Commissioned in January of that year, he is reputed to have been fighting on the side of the Bolsheviks by the late autumn, but the revolutionary events – notably the Kornilov revolt – are witnessed chiefly by such secondary characters as Listnitsky, Kotlyarov and Bunchuk. By this time, even though Grigory's family life may have taken a turn for the better with the birth of twins to Natalya, his own loyalties remain as ever ambivalent. The appeal of Cossack separatism, already implanted by the mischievous Uryupin, is sedulously cultivated in Grigory by the eloquent Izvarin. As if he is a latterday Everyman besieged by advocates of God and the Devil, Grigory compares Izvarin's ideas with Garanzha's, but is simultaneously influenced by the Bolshevik Podtyolkov and, on the eve of civil war, he cannot make up his mind conclusively, as a glimpse of him near the beginning of Part v shows:

Standing before the steamy window, Grigory gazed for a long time at the street, the children playing some made-up game, at the wet roofs of the opposite houses, at the pale-grey branches of a bare poplar in the fence and did not hear what Drozdov and Podtyolkov were arguing about; he was trying hard to make sense of the turmoil of his thoughts, to think something out and reach a decision (Part v, ii).

Part v illustrates the intent of Sholokhov's novel and the dilemma that it poses with extraordinary clarity. Allegiance to a cause may be total in the case of Bunchuk's devotion to communism, surmounting even his love for Anna, but the two-dimensional, contrived flatness of both their characters brings not a teardrop to the reader's eye when Anna is struck down by a Cossack bullet in Rostov and Bunchuk is shot along with other Red guardsmen. The realities of civil war as a problem of divided allegiances are brought home to the reader in the total reversal of Grigory's loyalties, not through any profound change of conviction but through an understandable sense of outrage in the face of Podtyolkov's calculated brutality. Grigory commits himself to Bolshevism so long as the fight is clean. When Podtyolkov orders the massacre of the captured officers, Grigory turns against him (Part v, xii) and abandons the Red cause. The atavistic Cossack hatred of the Russians as foreigners soon obsesses the entire Melekhov household, Grigory included, so that by the end of Part v and the close of the second volume Grigory has participated in the dreadful vengeance meted out to Podtyolkov and his followers. It is for Grigory a point of no return, but it is also the point at which his status as the work's hero is established beyond doubt. That he is mistaken in his convictions, limited by a natural human shortsightedness and hidebound by traditional values, enhances rather than diminishes his stature and appeal. If we are to speak of Grigory Melekhov as tragic, then it is in the dilemma of choice posed by the

events of Part v that his tragedy begins, for, as the best Soviet scholar
of the subject has recognised, the tragedy of Grigory is a symptom
of a tragic epoch, 'the harsh reality of a time which destroyed as well
as created'.[20]

The bloodshed and horrors narrated in the remaining three parts
and two volumes of this epic work recall the similar blood-lettings
and atrocities of Greek tragedy. Gods may not be wreaking vengeance
on human ambition and folly, but the holocaust described is no less
awful and has features that liken it to genocide. The struggle between
the regions of the Northern and Southern Don was historically of
long standing, as is made clear at the opening of Part vi, and yet this
antagonism was now to be exacerbated by the political confrontation
of Bolshevism and Cossack separatism as well as by the historical
north–south conflict between Russian and Cossack, urbanism and
agrarianism, proletariat and peasantry. The full extent of the dilemma
of choice, though illustrated mostly in the contradictory fate of
Grigory, has ramifications that embrace, for instance, Listnitsky's
relations with Olga Gorchakova (Part vi, v), concluding with his
suicide, the vendettas that decimate the Koshevoys and Korshunovs,
the hypocrisy and self-seeking of Panteley Melekhov, the cynicism
of the officer class and the double standards of the interventionists.
In each case it is a story of destruction, unedifying in its detail,
awesome in its cumulative effect.

The touchstone, of course, is Grigory. As his brother reminds him,
he may be against the Reds, but he has still not found himself, and
the paths that had previously united them

had become overgrown with experience and made their hearts inaccessible.
So above a gully there slips down a steep slope a winding path beaten out
by horses' hoofs and then suddenly stops at a turn, cut off, plunging into
nothing – so the path is no more, finishing up in the dead end of a thicket
(Part vi, ii).

It is a graphic and earthy metaphor for the ending of the ways so
far as Grigory and his brother are concerned, but it is not quite the
end of his vacillations. His growing hatred for the Bolsheviks as
invaders of his Cossack homeland is fuelled by the Red Army soldiers
who occupy Tatarsky. If his hatred grows, their hostility to him is
equally obdurate. Taxed by Kotlyarov about which way he will turn,
towards the Bolsheviks or the White generals, Grigory declares he
is his own master, but he is recognised by Kotlyarov and Koshevoy

as an enemy of Soviet authority and he acknowledges to himself that there is no turning back:

Grigory walked away, experiencing the feeling that he had burned his boats and that what had seemed unclear was now suddenly clear as daylight. In effect he had only said out loud in a fit of anger what he had been thinking for a long time, what had accumulated in him and needed to be said. And because he had reached the parting of the ways in the struggle of the two elements, refusing to accept either of them, there was born within him a dumb but unrelenting exasperation (Part VI, xx).

Exasperation is precisely what he nurses in his aggrieved Cossack way, justifying what is basically indifference to the outcome by presuming there is 'no one truth in life', just as there is no one woman in his life. His private revolution is, strictly speaking, the only true justification. As he leaves Tatarsky in the early spring of 1919, abandoning his wife and children, it is of Aksinya that he dreams as he falls asleep:

Shouting lazily from time to time at the oxen, Grigory dozed as he leaned against the ammunition boxes. After a smoke he snuggled down in the hay smelling of dry clover and the sweet fragrance of June days and fell asleep. In his dream he was walking with Aksinya through the tall rustling corn. Aksinya was carefully carrying a child in her arms and looking sideways at Grigory with watchful eyes. And Grigory listened to the beating of his own heart, to the singing rustling of the ears of corn, saw the fairytale embroidery of the grass verges and the aching blue of the sky. A feeling burst and stirred in him – he was in love with Aksinya with his old, exhausting love, he felt it with his whole body, with each beat of his heart, and at the same time he knew none of it was real, that only death stared him in the eyes, that it was all a dream. And he rejoiced at his dream and took it for life. Aksinya was the same as she had been five years before, but very restrained and touched by a certain coldness. With a blinding clarity unlike anything in real life Grigory saw the fluffy ringlets of hair on the nape of her neck (the wind was playing with them) and the ends of her white headscarf... He awoke with a jerk, sobered by the sound of voices (Part VI, xxi).

By such inner knowledge of Grigory, through such lyrically evocative writing, the reader of Sholokhov's masterpiece is drawn irresistibly into a close awareness of the hero's romanticism of spirit, which is the essence of his greatness of character. It is a romanticism composed of the twin instinctive loyalties to Aksinya and his native earth. At the beginning of the Cossack uprising, in what is probably the most consciously decisive act of his life, he commits himself to

the dream of Cossack freedom as completely as he had envisaged
Aksinya in his dream of past happiness:

He felt such a fierce, enormous joy, such an access of strength and
resoluteness that against his will a whistling, croaking explosion of sound
burst from his throat. Within him all the captive, long-secreted feelings were
set free. It seemed that his path was now clear before him as bright as a
moonlit highroad.

Everything had been weighed in the balance and decided during those
exhausting days when he had lurked like a beast among the dung heaps and
had started at every sound and every voice from outside. It was as if they
no longer existed, those days of seeking after truth, those vacillations,
changes of loyalty and difficult inner struggle.

Like cloud-shadows those days had gone by, and now his searchings
seemed futile and empty. What was there to think about? Why had his spirit
dashed about like a wolf beaten from cover in search of a way out, in search
of an end to all the contradictions? Life now seemed absurdly, wisely simple.
It now seemed to him that life had never had a truth under whose wing all
might find warmth and shelter, and, in a final extreme bitterness, he thought:
each man has his own truth, his own furrow in life. For a piece of bread,
for an allotment of earth, for the right to live, men had always fought and
would always fight so long as the sun shone on them and there was warm
blood to run in their veins. You had to fight those who wanted to take away
your life and your right to it; you had to fight hard, without wavering, firm
as a wall, and the fight would steal your hatred and firmness. You mustn't
rein in your feelings, but give them their head in all their ferocity.

The ways of the Cossacks had become entangled with the ways of the
landless peasant Russia, with the ways of the factory workers. Fight them
to the death! Seize from them the rich Don earth, washed with Cossack
blood! Drive them like the Tatars beyond the borders of the Don! Make
Moscow tremble, force on them a shameful peace! (Part VI, xxviii).

In its simplest form, of course, this is a restatement of the case for
Cossack separatism, just as it lays bare the ethos of Cossack
militancy, but in the very assertiveness of its naive heroics it has a
slightly cracked or false ring. Nevertheless, it is upon such false
heroics that the enmities of revolution and civil war usually feed. For
Grigory Melekhov the heroics appear instinctive, as much part of his
instinct for life as for his Cossack heritage. Such a celebration of
instinct gives credence to the harrowing violence of the succeeding
pages – the death of Grigory's brother at the hands of Mishka
Koshevoy, Grigory's slaying of the Red sailors, the killing of
Shtokman, the gruesome death-march of the twenty-five Communist
prisoners, concluding with Darya's murder of Kotlyarov and Kosh-

evoy's killing of Grandfather Korshunov and the burning of the Tatarsky homes in retribution. The collapse of Cossack resistance and the retreat southwards have the awful, slow-motion, cumulative grandeur of unfolding tragedy. Grigory achieves the summit of his military authority as a divisional commander at this time, but the White officers and generals are as indifferent to him as he is indifferent to his fate. Leaving to fight for the last time as a divisional commander, and parting for the last time from his wife Natalya, he wonders whether it matters where an enemy bullet will hurl him to the earth (Part VII, viii); indifference possesses him when he decides not to order his Cossacks to fight for the officers (Part VII, xi); indifference gradually surpasses Cossack wrath as his dominant feeling. When the tragedy of events finally strikes the Melekhov household and Darya, his sister-in-law, contracts syphilis and drowns herself, Natalya kills herself in trying to abort herself of Grigory's child and Panteley dies of typhus during the retreat, it may seem that the fullest possible retribution has been exacted. But the process has such a relentless impetus that Grigory is slowly stripped of all he possesses.

The dispossession is threefold in character. So far as the Melekhov household is concerned, Grigory's natural right to head the household after the death of his brother and father is usurped by his enemy, the Mishka Koshevoy who has claimed the role by his marriage to Grigory's sister. With Il'yinichna, Grigory's mother, dead of a broken heart, and Mishka Koshevoy appointed chairman of the Tatarsky revolutionary committee, Grigory's hereditary place in Cossack society is undermined, and Koshevoy's hostility towards him, though politically motivated, is so unrelenting that even Grigory's change of allegiance in fighting for Budyonny's Red Cavalry in the Russo-Polish War cannot apparently redeem him. When he attempts to justify himself to Koshevoy, it is not hard to see that he is doing no more that restate his indifference ('...I've served my time...I'm fed up with everything, both the revolution and counter-revolution': Part VIII, vi), but such self-justification must mean little to a Koshevoy, for whom indifference is equivalent to political apostasy. In terms of the hero's fate, he is an unforgiving nemesis, though we understand his avowal of total commitment much less profoundly than we do Grigory's vacillation. This is expressed at its most obvious in the recognition that he had been torn between the twin choices posed by Listnitsky, on the one hand,

and Koshevoy, on the other. Speaking to his friend Prokhor, he admits:

Everything was clear to them right from the beginning, but nothing's clear to me even now. For them, for both of them, their roads were straight, they knew where they were going, while I've been going round in circles ever since 1917, stumbling about like a drunkard (Part VIII, vii).

The second stage in the process of dispossession involves the final abandonment of his private revolution. Preferring a life of banditry to the imprisonment that seems to await him, he joins the Fomin band. Cast out of society, manifestly now an enemy of the new world born of the revolution and civil war, his only hope of rehabilitation to humanity lies with Aksinya. Among the greatest pages in the novel are those that describe their brief, final days together, as fugitive a last happiness as is their fugitive condition, and Aksinya's accidental death is the ultimate curtailment of all his hopes: 'And Grigory, mortally stricken with horror, realised that everything was over, that the worst thing which could have happened in his life had happened.' So he buries his Aksinya and, with her, that dream of personal happiness in revolt against Cossack life which had so differentiated him from the other members of his own family and given him such an independence of spirit as the novel's hero. Nature itself wears a funeral garb in an act of mourning for this death and burial:

Now he had no reason for hurrying. Everything was finished.
    In the smoky haze of a dry hot wind the sun rose above the ravine. Its rays silvered the thick grey hair on Grigory's uncovered head and slid over his pale face, terrible in its immobility. Literally as if he had awakened from an oppressive dream, he raised his head and saw above him the black sky and the blindingly dazzling black disk of the sun (Part VIII, xvii).

The third and last stage in the process of dispossession is consciously his own act, one of quite deliberate, almost simultaneous reparation and repatriation. A whole winter spent 'convulsively clinging to the earth' after pitiless death had taken everything from him convinces him that he must abandon his outlaw life. The carving of wooden cups and spoons, not wounding and killing, becomes his occupation. Before the amnesty due on 1 May, in a conscious act of reparation, Grigory throws his rifle, pistol and cartridges into the freezing waters of the Don and thereby repudiates his militant Cossack past. He then crosses the Don by the already thawing March ice and meets up with his small son Mishatka, standing by the gate of his home. The act is one that acknowledges not only Grigory's loyalty to the earth, that instinct for place which had dominated his behaviour throughout the novel, but also the significance of parenthood as the single, final token of continuity and renewal, of the past relating to the future, of the death–birth process that Sholokhov's *Quiet Flows the Don* demonstrates in its total epic effect with such anguish and majesty.

The work has been described as 'a broad panorama of the death of the old world and the painful birth of the new',[21] but the natural processes of change and the trauma associated with them, although evident in the havoc wrought in Tatarsky society and the Melekhov household, are fully demonstrated only in the individual fate of Grigory Melekhov. His tragedy may be minor, small-scale – we are not concerned here with the deaths of kings – but it mirrors the tragic conflicts of the epoch and it has a public as well as a private aspect. The novel illustrates the doom that overtakes counter-revolutionary attitudes as a nemesis on the public level in its picture of the defeat of Cossack separatism, though whether it illustrates the fate of such a counter-revolutionary Vendée as historically inevitable is matter only for speculation. Grigory Melekhov is, however, inevitably caught up in the conflicts of the epoch; to blame him for vacillation is seriously to discount the character of the epoch itself. It would require the wisdom of Solomon to apportion the blame fairly. On the private level, his tragedy is determined by his mixed ancestry, his instinctive loyalties and his individual revolt against convention and custom in his love for Aksinya. All is taken from him save the final right to repudiate his Cossack militancy and to make a deliberate choice (perhaps dooming himself to the imprisonment that he had done so much to avoid) to reassert his organic links with his home, his earth and his son. There are no ideological justifications for such a choice. It is, quite simply, in character, as Sholokhov somewhat defensively admitted in 1929:

Those who know the history of the civil war on the Don, who know the course of it, know that it wasn't only Grigory Melekhov who vacillated, and it wasn't only dozens of Grigory Melekhovs who vacillated, prior to 1920, so long as there was no limit to such vacillations. I take Grigory as he is, and as he was in fact, that's why he vacillates, but I have no wish to go against historical truth.[22]

Historical truth may explain the vacillation of Grigory Melekhov to some extent, but it does not explain the powerful human traits with which his portrait is invested. That is a product of the miraculous power of the epic novel itself and Sholokhov's genius. The tragedy of *Quiet Flows the Don* springs in the last resort from the tragic divide in Russian social and political life. This divide was brought sharply into focus by the counter-revolutionary movements of the civil-war period. As Juergen Ruehle has noted in this very connection:

All the risings grew out of the Revolution and the acceptance of a socialist society. But they demanded an end to terror, to 'shooting and looting', and the recognition of democratic freedom. In that respect they represented the first steps in a post-Bolshevik, democratic revolution.

The risings failed because they were scattered and uncoordinated.

But they also failed because there was a historical divide between the revolutionary forces:

For centuries, two currents ran parallel in the democratic movement in Russia: an intellectual and a plebeian one...The two streams never converged. The first remained remote from the people and the second lacked a creative social theory.

Sholokhov's father was a *raznochinets*, that is, a member of the old revolutionary intelligentsia, whereas his mother was an illiterate Cossack peasant. The two streams combined in him. Though by conviction a Bolshevik, he was able to create the figure of Grigory Melekhov, whose revolutionary ideas are the expression of the basic concerns and longings of the masses and also of the principles of a humanitarian democracy.[23]

The Road to Calvary (*Khozhdeniye po mukam*)

A. N. Tolstoy's three-volume epic novel stands in ambiguous and uneasy opposition to Sholokhov's *Quiet Flows the Don* as a work that aspires to illustrate the role of the intelligentsia in revolution and civil war. It is a conventional historical novel, written by a gifted writer whose antecedents no doubt helped him,[24] but whose gratitude to state and party during the height of Stalin's 'cult of personality' irreparably damaged his literary achievement and reputation. Not that Aleksey Tolstoy could be considered a party hack. His fluency as a stylist, his descriptive powers and his mastery of characterisation lend distinction to the most propagandist of his novels (*Bread* (1937) is the most notorious example in its deliberate disfigurement of Trotsky's role in the civil war). The panoramic sweep of *The Road to Calvary* gives it a consciously epic intent, with scenes and characters introduced to provide examples of what, for Stalinist purposes, would be considered the correct interpretation of history. Such a prescriptive approach naturally tended to distort the organic flow of the fiction and to make contrivance, whether based on coincidence or sheer improbability, essential to the narrative impulse. In this respect alone, A. N. Tolstoy's work suffers very greatly by comparison with Sholokhov's, but it is a symptom of a more profound flaw in the very intent of the fiction.

The Road to Calvary was written between 1919 and 1941.[25] Critical comment is generally agreed that the first volume is better than the last volume, and there is no doubt that the portrayal of the two sisters Dasha and Katya in pre-revolutionary St Petersburg is done with verve and freshness despite the authorial mockery of the literary circles and the self-conscious decadence of the period. The critique of the intelligentsia in the first volume develops into an exposure of the futility of the White cause in the second volume. Here Roshchin, who is to become Katya's husband, fights on the White side, whereas Telegin, who is married to Dasha, is a Bolshevik, but in the final volume, as the civil war progresses, Roshchin becomes converted to the Soviet cause, Katya, who falls into the clutches of the peasant anarchist Makhno, has her own faith in the future of Russia restored and the four of them, after Telegin and Dasha are happily reunited, attend a meeting in the Bolshoy Theatre, Moscow, where plans for the electrification of the U.S.S.R. and the building of communism are announced in the presence of the architect of such plans, V. I. Lenin, and his ever-loyal colleague, J. V. Stalin.

The contrasts in the first volume are chiefly those between pre-1914 metropolitan society, with its frivolous bourgeois pastimes, and the horrors and futilities of the First World War, though on a moral level the most pointed contrast is made between the diligent engineer Telegin and the decadent poet Bessonov. If the characters of the sisters Dasha and Katya have certain points of difference, these facets receive little emphasis. They are portrayed sympathetically as essentially virtuous heroines, misled by the immorality of the period, perhaps, but capable of rising above their bourgeois background. Revolution is signalled by conversational hints. The wartime conditions, leading to military collapse, are obviously a contributory factor. Yet overt political guidance of the revolutionary events receives scant attention, presented as they are largely from the sisters' apolitical viewpoints or through the experience of Roshchin with the White volunteer army. Increasingly, a major contrast becomes

discernible: the sense of the work as historical fiction becomes
founded on a reiterated contrast between present and past experiences, between present disorder and past stability; between the
ephemeral chaos of the present and the wider historical context of
events – a contrast made plain in passages of text-book commentary;
and between the privations of the present and the promise of a
socialist future to replace the capitalist world of the past.

The fiction shows the strains of this imposed intent on many
occasions. It is an epic novel of ideas in which the political ideas tend
in the end to manipulate the characters. Indeed, with the possible
exception of Roshchin, the ideas espoused by the characters appear
to be implanted in them literally by authorial *fiat*. As a critique of
the past and, by implication, of the Russian intelligentsia's flirtation
with Christian ideas in the decade prior to the October revolution,
the novel has at its centre an eloquent attack on the flaws inherent
in Christianity. But the attack is voiced not by one of the novel's
principal characters, nor by a spokesman for the intelligentsia; it is
voiced by a German intellectual in German military uniform whom
Katya meets on a train journey during the civil war in the south. It
is the most important ideological plea for a socialist future in the
whole three-part novel.

The decline of the West anticipated by Oswald Spengler is the
context in which the German states his case. Just as the Roman world
was destroyed by the idea of Christianity, so the ideas of socialism
will destroy Christianity and its influence. At the downfall of the
Roman Empire all Christianity had to offer were the destructive ideas
of 'equality, internationalism and the moral superiority of poverty
over riches', but there was no creative idea in Christianity: it had
no way of organising labour. 'On earth it contented itself with
destruction and it left everything else as a promise in heaven.
Christianity was no more than a sword of destruction and punishment', becoming the religion not of those who sow and reap but of
emperors and conquerors. The speaker then asserts:

'Labour remained unorganised and outside morality. The second coming of
barbarians who will destroy the second Rome will bring a religion of labour
into the world. Have you read Spengler? He's a Roman from head to toe,
who's right only in one thing: it's on *his* Europe that the sun is setting. But
for us it's rising. He won't succeed in dragging down the workers of the world
into the grave with him. Swans sing before dying, they say, and it's the
bourgeoisie that's made Spengler sing his swansong... It's their last idealistic

trump card. Christianity has lost its teeth. Ours are strong as iron...We're opposing it with the Socialist organisation of labour. To think they're trying to make us fight the Bolsheviks! O-ho! Do you think we don't understand who's nudging us forward and against whom? Oh, we understand a lot better than it may seem...Previously we used to despise the Russians. Now we're starting to wonder at them and respect them...' (*Nineteen Eighteen*, chapter 7).

Those in whose name the German speaks, the revolutionary proletariat, have few representatives in the novel. In the final volume the number of characters is multiplied to include such members of Telegin's brigade as Latugin and Sharygin, not to mention the extremely interesting vignette-like portrayal of Anisya, but though such 'ordinary' figures are clearly designed to enhance the political meaning of the novel they are less effective as characters than the representatives of the intelligentsia. Through one of those unlikely coincidences which abound in the final volume the German intellectual who spoke to Katya meets Roshchin in beleaguered Yekaterinoslav and informs him that Katya has very likely fallen into the hands of Makhno. The meeting with Makhno is an occasion for Roshchin to explain briefly his reasons for abandoning his intelligentsia role ('It turned out that the intelligentsia wasn't up to it. In October they took us by the scruff of the neck like so many kittens and flung us on the rubbish heap...'), but it also develops into one of these dialogue set pieces in which Nestor Makhno's anarchism is shown up as a baseless, squalid religion of death and destruction.

The shallowness of the ideas produces an equivalent shallowness in the characterisation. Comrade Stalin is efficiently directing the Red armies in the civil war while Roshchin, for example, does his bit for the Red cause by reconnoitring Yekaterinoslav unobserved and then leading the assault on the city without receiving any injury. In short, all the leading characters have virtue on their side. Mistaken though they may have been at earlier points in the civil war, by 1920 there is no doubt that reason has prevailed and the only opposition to the Soviet state is provided by such renegades as the Ataman Zelyony. All right-thinking characters have succumbed to the vision of a socialist future.

The euphoric intent of the fiction in its final stages naturally minimises all likelihood of misfortune and leaves no room for doubt about ultimate purposes. The happiness of Telegin and Dasha is crowned by true love ('Now their love, in particular for Dasha, was full and palpable like the air of early winter, when the November storms had passed and in soft frost-laden silence the first snow smelled of sliced melon': chapter 13), though other storms disturb their lives before they are finally united in the Bolshoy Theatre. Roshchin's is to be the last word, suitably monumental and resonant, on the purposes to which their generation has dedicated itself:

'Katya, the task's inordinate...We didn't dream we could achieve it...You remember how much we talked, what a lot of tedious nonsense the cycles of history seemed, the collapse of great civilisations, the ideas turned into miserable parodies of themselves...Under the evening dress-shirt was the very same hairy chest belonging to *pithecanthropus* – Rubbish! Now the veil's been torn from our eyes! The whole of our past life was based on crime and falsehood! Russia has given birth to a new man...That man has demanded the right for people to become human beings. It's not a dream, it's an idea, it's at the ends of our bayonets, it's close to realisation! A blinding light has lit up the half-ruined arches of all passed millennia! It's all firmly based, it's all in order! A purpose has been found!' (chapter 20).

The message of the words is in no need of elaboration. It is manifestly propagandist and obvious. What needs stressing is the assumption that the trauma of revolution has not only destroyed the past but has also brought to birth a new man and new purposes. The spurious aggrandisement of these ideas through comparing them with cosmic distances, their significance in relation to eternity and the coming of a new millennium is clearly discernible in parts of the final volume. It is in the nature of historical fiction to romanticise the past and in this case the process of glorifying the Russian Revolution and civil war appears to have reached a peak of false magniloquence. Completed on the eve of the Great Fatherland War, Aleksey Tolstoy's *The Road to Calvary* very likely appealed as much to patriotic as to revolutionary feelings but in the same breath it could hardly avoid both exalting the historical role of the Russian people as the creators of socialism and representing the experience as governed above all by rational purposes in the name of a socialist future.

The work has a spurious air of literary quality about it. The skill in the writing is sustained even through protracted dialogue exchanges and the need to ensure happy dénouements. Lacking from it is the sense of human destiny inexorably linked, by some profound instinct for survival, to earth and home, a sense, in short, of the rootedness of human experience. As an epic of revolutionary ideas, *The Road to Calvary* parades the fictional embodiments of commitment to Bolshevism or White revanchism or anarchism or intelligentsia ideals like counters in an elaborate board-game, which end up not by demonstrating the choices *pro* and *contra*, but by making the pattern of a hammer and sickle.

5

Revolution and resurrection

Introduction

In a general sense the revolutionary epics of Sholokhov and Aleksey
Tolstoy explore revolutionary experience in terms, respectively, of
instinct and ideas. Both epics end on a note of optimism for the future
that subsumes that their heroes, or principal figures, have undergone
some fundamental change in their lives as a consequence of revolution
and civil war. If the political implications of this change seem obscure
in the case of Grigory Melekhov, they are explicit in the case of
Roshchin, Dasha and Katya. Renewal of hope may seem instinctive
in Grigory Melekhov's repudiation of his past, his hereditary
Cossack militancy, and in his reassumption of a parental role. Such
renewal seems to be motivated by ideological *fiat* in Aleksey Tolstoy's
happy ending.

After the adoption of Socialist Realism as the official doctrine for
Soviet literature at the First Congress of Soviet writers in 1934,
optimism about the outcome of the revolutionary process as depicted
in literature became mandatory. Tragedy and revolution became
officially incompatible. A concept of 'optimistic tragedy'[1] can be seen
to absolve Soviet writers of the need to examine the full tragic
implications of human mortality. No work of the 1930s in Soviet
literature accomplishes this task better than *How the Steel was
Tempered* (*Kak zakalyalas' stal'*) (1934) by Nikolay Ostrovsky
(1904–36). Although only the first part of this two-part novel is
concerned, strictly speaking, with the events of the civil war in the
Ukraine, as a whole the novel is designed to show how the revolution
fundamentally changed the life of its youthful hero, Pavel Korchagin,
making him physically its victim while fortifying and guiding his
spirit in a manner admirably suited to the concept of 'optimistic
tragedy'.

Ostrovsky's novel enjoyed all the popularity and acclaim of a
bestseller in its time. Nowadays its shallow characterisation, frag-

mented narrative and moralising tone make it hard to read. Yet in the figure of its hero this novel still has the power to impress the reader with the author's (literally) blind dedication to the cause of communism. Largely autobiographical, the novel tells how Pavel Korchagin is conscripted into the Bolshevik cause by a sailor, Fyodor Zhukrai, fights on the Red side against Petlyura and the Poles in the Ukraine, loses the sight of one eye during the Russo-Polish War of 1920 and eventually, after superhuman efforts on behalf of communism, has his health undermined and goes blind. His story, if tragic in its account of a young life impaired so terribly by polyarthritis, is optimistic in its ideological fortitude.

The literary quality of the novel has been highly praised by Soviet critics, but its manner is frankly uneven and often pedestrian. At certain climactic moments the writing acquires a metaphoric power, as is the case, for example, when Ostrovsky describes Korchagin's first semi-conscious state after being injured in battle. The metaphor of an octopus graphically suggests the effect and extent of his pain:

The octopus has a bulging eye the size of a cat's head, a glazed reddish eye green in the centre with a pulsating phosphorescent glow. The octopus is a loathsome mass of tentacles, which writhe and squirm like a tangled knot of snakes, the scaly skin rustling hideously as they move. The octopus stirs. He sees it next to his very eyes. And now the tentacles creep over his body; they are cold and they sting like nettle. The octopus shoots out its sting, and bites into his head like a leech, and, wriggling convulsively, it sucks at his blood. He feels the blood draining out of his body into the swelling body of the octopus. And the sting goes on sucking and the pain of the sucking is unbearable (Part I, chapter 9).[2]

We are told that after thirteen days of oblivion, consciousness returned to Pavel Korchagin and he was 'born again'. His recovery from this injury sustained at the age of sixteen is never total, but he devotes what remains of his active life to a single-minded and unduly solemn pursuit of communist aims. His association with girls, for example, always governed by a prissy moral tone that puts class considerations before spontaneous affection, has a priggish, self-justifying complacency to it when he solemnly announces to his mother: 'No, Mother, I've given my word to keep away from girls until we've finished with all the bourgeois in the world' (Part II, chapter 3).

The theme of youth transformed by revolution is virtually a

commonplace in Soviet literature. During the 1930s novels on such
a theme naturally emphasised, in conformity with the doctrine of
Socialist Realism, the political significance of such a transformation.
A. S. Yakovlev,[3] for instance, whose *October* (1923) had given an
'objectivist'[4] view of revolutionary events in Moscow, largely abandoned the colourful manner of his early work and employed a
simpler, though effective, narrative style in his novel of 1935, *The
Ways of a Simple Heart* (*Puti prostogo serdtsa*). It is a straightforward
account of a young recruit in a guards' regiment, Starostin, who,
while on duty as one of the palace guards, is spoken to by the Tsar.
The incident arouses in him convictions of deep loyalty to the
autocracy, which are gradually eroded by his experiences during the
revolution of 1905. Arrested for his association with the priest
Gapon, he is exiled to Siberia and when he returns to St Petersburg
he is unable to find work and migrates to Yekaterinburg. Through
an ironic juxtaposition of roles he finds himself in the end one of those
responsible for imprisoning the Romanovs in the Ipat'yev house and
entitled to order the deposed Tsar not to speak to his captors. A
somewhat contrived change of heart must account for the intense
bitterness of Starostin's final attitude, though the description of the
Tsarist family's last days seems to have historical veracity. More
obviously owing its provenance to Ostrovsky's novel is Boris
Solov'yov's *The Education of Character* (*Vospitaniye kharaktera*)
(1940)[5] in its evidently autobiographical story of Kolya Shalyagin's
upbringing in Yekaterinburg, his removal to a factory town,
Sineistochinsk, under the tutelage of an elderly ethnographer and
antiquarian and his adolescent experience there during the civil war.
Themes of love and friendship mingle engagingly with scenes of
violence, but to the young Shalyagin the events of the civil war seem
often to have the spurious, unreal excitements and strangeness of
episodes in adventure novels or the cinema.

It has become quite as much of a commonplace for Soviet novels
to use themes of revolution and civil war to point up differences between generations and classes while simultaneously combining revolutionary events with exotic or unusual regional settings. Regional
historical novels may be one way of describing them. Of dubious
literary value in many cases, usually designed to celebrate not only
the victory of Bolshevism but also the steadfast political commitments
of one or another of the revolutionaries, such novels contribute to
an on-going literary industry in the Soviet Union. Numerous

instances could be quoted, a large number of them having appeared since Stalin's death in 1953.[6] In some cases these novels have used revolutionary settings and themes to point up issues of injustice and the abuse of authority in ways that have an oblique but significant relevance to similar issues in contemporary Soviet society.[7] For the most part they represent a branch of writing in the Soviet novel that employs themes of revolution and civil war to add some relish and historical veracity – or manifest lack of veracity, especially when it involves the role of Trotsky – to what are basically contrived narratives without even the justification of semi-autobiographical content. To this extent, they hardly justify the title of 'revolutionary novels', for they are not concerned with exploring the meaning of revolutionary experience in instinctive or ideological terms or in any terms, for that matter, that raise serious issues of choice.

Three novels from Soviet literature of the 1920s, 1930s and 1940s, from a period, in short, when Stalin's 'cult of personality' was becoming a paramount feature of Soviet life, can be said to have relevance both to the experience of revolution as one involving serious issues of choice and to the further treatment of the problem in literary terms. They demonstrate, in fact, that Soviet Russian literature was anticipating some of the elements employed by Pasternak in his treatment of revolution and civil war in his masterpiece *Doctor Zhivago*. In doing so, they help to show that *Doctor Zhivago* belonged in certain respects to a developing tradition in Russian and Soviet literature and should not be regarded as an isolated phenomenon.

The work of V. Tan-Bogoraz was known well before the revolution of 1917.[8] A polymath, with an expertise of that liberal variety which can easily cross the boundary between science and literature, he had a minor reputation as a poet, travel writer and novelist. His novel of 1928 *The Union of Youth* (*Soyuz molodykh*) has a Siberian setting and a manner reminiscent of Jack London in its depiction of the artless ways of Dyka, remarkable though she is as a hunter, and her brief love affair with a feckless, attractive giant of a man, Vikenty Avilov. He abandons her and their son at the time of 1905, finding the call of revolution stronger than the call of the wild. When, after extensive travels in Europe, North America and Alaska, he returns to the Kolyma region of Siberia during the civil war he becomes the violent and murderous leader of a gang of renegade Whites. His son has meanwhile grown up into a youthful revolutionary who becomes his father's principal adversary and eventually, in a dramatic climax, his executioner.

The moral and psychological issues in the story are not revealed by this brief account of it. Tan-Bogoraz's novel is composed of three stories, which illustrate what he describes in an afterword as 'a tragedy of the north', and, beside the apparently authentic details of the savagery of the civil war in Siberia, there is to be discerned another dimension to this tragedy, as he puts it:

The revolution has shown us that disillusioned sons have punished their bankrupt and criminal fathers.

Such a new twist to an old tale must attract the writer. Babel made use of it in one of his stories, but simply en passant. I used it as the basis of my novel-trilogy.

There is, however, something else to this tragedy of the north. A young man, pure in body and soul, associates in complete freedom with a young girl, as pure and innocent as he is, and creates a family. Later, under the influence of a higher impulse, he destroys what he has made and goes away. He is drawn away by a struggle, the highest and most precious thing in a man's life. But behind him he has left two abandoned lives – and that is unforgivable. One cannot let another person down without incurring consequences, even though one may journey ten thousand miles, for one always carries within oneself the sting of one's own treachery.[9]

This problem, certainly conceived as tragic, though offered in other terms, may be said to anticipate the tragedy that overtakes the relationship between Lara and Pasha Antipov in *Doctor Zhivago*. The assumption that a man can sacrifice wife and family for revolutionary struggle that represents to him the highest and most precious thing in his life is one that obviously determines Antipov's behaviour and turns him, as in the case of Avilov, into Strelnikov, the revolutionary leader, whose aims have become obscured and distorted by the paradoxical circumstances of civil war.

Similarly, the problem of the spectator or bystander (*obyvatel'*) in circumstances of civil war, posed in the form of the dilemmas of choice facing a doctor, is examined in anticipation of Pasternak's masterpiece in the interesting short novel by A. M. Linevsky, *Doctor Podobin* (1937).[10] It is the story of an egotistical, somewhat uncouth doctor and his wife who leave Petrograd during the hungry days of the civil war in search of a simple but well-nourished life. They move to Petrozavodsk. There they are advised to find 'somewhere in the forest'. This turns out to be a small village where the doctor has to face a choice between joining the Bolsheviks, a group of Whites supporting the local priest or a pro-Finnish group. Because he is elected to serve on the local Soviet and makes a speech in favour of Lenin, the doctor finds that he is refused milk and provisions by his landlord on instructions from the priest. These and other trials make the doctor and his wife decide to move to Murmansk. They find a place to live and work there, but on a visit to Arkhangelsk in July 1919 to obtain medical supplies Dr Podobin is forced into acting as the official doctor at the execution of Red Army soldiers. Upon returning to Murmansk he finds himself placed in the invidious position of inspecting the local prisons, only to find among the prisoners his two former friends, Nikita Tyuttiev and Fonvizin, who are being submitted to the grossest maltreatment. Then they are sentenced to be shot. His wife finally deserts him and leaves for England on the liner *Majestic* in the company of her lover, an English sailor.

Dr Podobin's story is unedifying. He tries to remain uninvolved but ends by betraying those who had earlier befriended him. As a Soviet commentator has put it, he is 'a psychologically complex social character, created in the realistic traditions of Russian literature', and his portrait 'with its parasitic psychology and bourgeois individualism...has retained its interest into our days'.[11] Although his personality is not very attractive, his dilemma has features in common with those affecting the intelligentsia in Veresaev's *The Deadlock*. *Doctor Podobin* lacks that novel's literary power, but it has memorable authenticity and clarity in the writing.

The most important, however, of the problems posed by *Doctor Zhivago* is one that few novelists chose to confront. It is the problem of the opposition between the creative artist's right to independent creative expression and the ideological commitment demanded of him by revolutionary circumstances and revolutionary politics. No novelist of the Stalin period toyed with the problem more boldly than did Konstantin Fedin, but it is really not possible to regard his treatment of it as more than a tentative broaching of issues that were of vital concern to all Soviet writers of his generation. He first posed the problem in his second novel *The Brothers* (*Brat'ya*) (1928). Nikita Karev, the composer–hero of the novel, experiences great difficulty in adjusting to the post-revolutionary expectations of art, but is finally persuaded under the rejuvenating guidance of his niece Irina, with whom he falls in love, to complete his symphony. The work is

an instantaneous success. Whether this success is attributable to
Nikita's altered understanding of the revolution or to the inspiration
of his feeling for Irina is unclear, but the complexity of his problem
of choice, though over-complicated by emotional entanglements, is
one that Fedin does not shirk. However, when Nikita finally resolves
his problem, the solution appears to come about with indecent haste.

In his 'dilogy' of novels[12] of the 1940s Fedin poses the issue of
choice only in the case of the fashionable St Petersburg playwright
Pastukhov. *Early Joys*, set in a lovingly and beautifully recreated
Saratov of 1910, introduces most of the characters who are to be
encountered nine years later in *No Ordinary Summer*: the Bolshevik
Ragozin, the young recruit to revolutionary activity Izvekov, the
actor Tsvetukhin, the girl Liza with whom Izvekov falls in love and
Annochka Parabukina, the girl from 'the lower depths' of Saratov
life who becomes his true love in the end. Fedin's portrait of Saratov
is peopled with many characters and given a certain brilliant
coloration in a Stalinist realist manner. Yet the inherently counterfeit
nature of the whole novel, despite its supposed living semblance, is
revealed by the intrusion into the fiction of the single most tragic
event of 1910 in the life of Russia: the death of Tolstoy. Of all the
characters only Pastukhov reflects with any depth of meaning on
Tolstoy's significance for the future:

A sentence took shape in his mind and he did not know whether it belonged
to him or had occurred in one of the articles he had been reading: 'If the
inhabitants of other planets were to ask our world: Who are you? – mankind
might answer with pride, pointing to Tolstoy: We are he!' (ch. 30)[13]

According to Pastukhov, Tolstoy's legacy took the form of a
maxim as plain as the divine words: 'Here is the earth. Here is man
on earth. And here is a task: to build a life worthy of man' (p. 306).
The maxim unfortunately has the kind of simplistic menace that
attached to so many of Stalin's utterances; and if Stalin can hardly
be said to have ruled the world in 1910, then by 1919, the year of
No Ordinary Summer, he appears to have taken charge of the civil
war almost to the point of enjoying sole responsibility for the success
of the Bolshevik cause. At the end of *No Ordinary Summer* Izvekov
is ushered into Stalin's presence and shakes his hand. The familiarity
of his and Voroshilov's 'unexpected informality of address' thrilled
him, we are told, 'and reminded him of the extraordinary feeling that
had pervaded him that day in his youth when on the Saratov uplands

an old worker had called him "comrade" for the first time in his life and he had run into the hills to calm his emotion'.[14] Of such things are cults made!

If Kirill Izvekov experiences such profound change from such slight causes, his revolutionary commitment is nevertheless not in doubt, nor is that of any of the principal characters with the possible exception of Pastukhov. Returning to Saratov on the Volga from revolutionary Petrograd, Pastukhov, in the company of his beautiful wife Asya and his young son Alyosha, finds himself an outcast both physically and ideologically. His attitude of mind is stated candidly as anti-collectivist and therefore anti-revolutionary:

He was bored by analyses of schools and tendencies in art. He was convinced that everything of artistic value was created in spite of artistic tendencies, and that it was more important for a school of art that you call yourself its adherent than that you actually be it. Like political parties, schools of art solicited supporters. Actually he had contempt for them all and did not wish to be hypocritical. Such was his platform... In his heart he had decided once and for all that the times were irrational, as proved by the fact that reason was being applied to things which, like the dance, defied reason. He was convinced that his own tastes and views could never be changed, and this afforded him a proud, though bitter satisfaction (Part I, pp. 322–3).

When Tsvetukhin the actor claims that 'The revolution is youth', Pastukhov grumpily complains that 'unfortunately youth has nothing to do with art...Youth interferes with art' (Part I, p. 326). As the civil war approaches Saratov, the issue of choice assumes a deeper and more compelling significance for a Pastukhov who senses that history, the times, the calendar, the hands of the clock (Part II, p. 47) all sentenced him to death.

What crime had he committed? Of what was he guilty? He was not a Red, so he was counted a White. He was not a White, so he was counted a Red. He was sentenced because he was neither Red nor White. Was it possible that the whole world was either Red or White?...He was lost, he was condemned. That was a fact. And it was impossible to find meaning in that fact. One who has been sentenced to death may find some meaning in his death for others, but he cannot possibly find any meaning in his death for himself: his death may be demanded by history, by the times, by the calendar, by the hands of the clock – but never by himself. For himself – for Pastukhov, who is about to die – his death has not the slightest meaning. And his mind protests against the idea of his death.
But his mind seeks some sort of reconciliation with death, though he himself does not wish to be reconciled...

No, Pastukhov has no friends. Perhaps his whole trouble was that he had
no friends. Perhaps if he had some friends they would help him make up
his mind which side to choose...A choice, a choice, that was what
Pastukhov had to make! The meaning of his whole life, its very essence,
boiled down to one thing – a choice (Part II, pp. 47–50).

The testing time comes for him when he is thrown into a crowded
prison cell by the Whites. Taunted by the inner voice of his
conscience, he is forced to re-examine the self-deluding notion that
he had been born choiceless into a world governed by biological and
social–historical laws. His refusal to accept personal responsibility
for the injustice in his society now appears to him as a contributory
factor in his imprisonment and he resolves to make a choice. After
his release by the Reds, he returns home to his loving wife and son,
only to be faced by the need to reconsider the whole matter in a
discussion of Tolstoy's theory of history. The result, though not hard
to anticipate, comes with unseemly speed. He declares that he has
made his final choice – 'I made it there – in that local branch of
Dante's inferno' (Part II, p. 409) – and he now places himself firmly
on the side of Izvekov and the Bolsheviks. The most daring aspect
of his choice takes the form of a minor disagreement with Tolstoy:

'You actually support Tolstoy's opinion if you consider that the whole
problem resolves itself into a mere submitting to circumstances. I disagree
with him. If the choice lies with me, then of my own free will I contribute
to the development of circumstances. The sum of such free choices is one
of the forces determining history. In other words, to a certain degree history
is created by the free will of man. By *my* free will.'
'That is just what I was going to say,' whispered Asya, hugging his head.
'Of course you are free in all your actions...' (Part II, pp. 412–13).

In celebration of his commitment to the Red cause he agrees to
write a play for the local theatre. Art and revolution are thus
satisfactorily reconciled. Though the crisis of choice in his life seems
to have been resolved, it must be assumed that his subsequent
'freedom' has no more actuality than any self-fulfilling prophecy. As
an intellectual exercise the problem is of some note in a novel of the
Stalin period, but in any other terms it is a travesty of the kind of
heart-rending choice that the revolution and civil war demanded of
the human conscience.

Fedin's treatment of revolution and civil war has a sanitised,
artificial air to it in *No Ordinary Summer*. The novelty of *Cities and*

Years has given way to a ponderous monumentalism designed to eliminate tragedy from the literary appraisal of revolution. In this it has assumed that, unlike the profound and utterly transforming nature of the changes that occur in such Tolstoyan heroes as Pierre Bezukhov and Konstantin Levin, the change resulting from Pastukhov's crisis of choice was inevitable from the beginning. His unreformed state in the past was merely attributable to his self-deluding individualism. A brief spell of imprisonment quickly brought him to his senses.

No legacy of Russian literature has been greater than its readiness to confront issues of life and death and to examine the problems of human conscience in terms of ultimate meaning. Freedom of choice and life as sacrifice have become enshrined as the twin ideals of the Russian world-view. Nowhere have these ideals received fuller or more profound interpretation than in the Russian novel, and nowhere has a writer needed greater courage to express them than in the Russian revolutionary novel. Fedin's compromise with authority and the official demands made of literature has to be set beside Solzhenitsyn's boldness for the full extent of its timidity to be seen. When Solzhenitsyn, speaking directly to Konstantin Fedin in the presence of the Secretariat of the Union of Soviet Writers in 1967, spoke of his own novel *Cancer Ward*, which had been condemned for its 'anti-humanistic' character, he insisted that it was about 'life overcoming death, the future overcoming the past' and he went on to offer a general defence of his position:

But I consider that the tasks of literature both in relation to society and in relation to individual man do not consist in hiding the truth from him and softening it, but in telling truly how it is and what he can expect...In general a writer's tasks are not to be reduced to defending or criticising one or another means of distributing the social product, or to defending or criticising one or another form of the state system. A writer's tasks are concerned with questions of more general and more eternal significance. They concern the secrets of the human heart and conscience, of the conflict between life and death, the overcoming of spiritual sorrow and those laws extending throughout all humanity which were born in the immemorial depths of the millennia and will cease only when the sun is extinguished.[15]

It requires the 'courage of genius', the expression used by Edmund Wilson in his review of Pasternak's *Doctor Zhivago* and chosen by Robert Conquest for his own book,[16] to make a statement of principle of the kind offered by Solzhenitsyn. Though he may not have written about revolution,[17] Solzhenitsyn's *The First Circle*, *Cancer Ward* and *August 1914* comprise their own revolutions against the orthodoxies of Socialist Realism and can be regarded as leading examples of the dissident Soviet literature that arose in the wake of the controversy over *Doctor Zhivago*. Pasternak showed the 'courage of genius' in reinterpreting revolution and civil war both by asserting the right of his poet–hero to make his own choices, no matter how paradoxical, and by questioning the sanctity of revolution as holy writ. The transformation subsumed in revolutionary experience became in Zhivago's case a challenge to death, just as *Doctor Zhivago*, the novel, challenged the dead hand of Soviet official approval. In doing so, it resurrected the independent spirit of Russian literature, just as it offered its own concept of resurrection as a revolutionary ideal.

Doctor Zhivago

The publication of Pasternak's novel in an Italian translation in 1957 and in English a year later, coupled with the decision of the Swedish Academy in October 1958 to award him the Nobel Prize for Literature, led to a controversy that precipitated him into the full glare of Western press publicity, forced him to give up the prize and caused his expulsion from the Union of Soviet Writers.[18] The reasons for his persecution by Soviet officialdom may have been declared to be that his novel had made him 'a tool of bourgeois propaganda', one who 'has joined the struggle against the progressive advance of history...has severed his last links with his country and his people'[19] and so on and so forth in a manner typical of Soviet official invective, but the grounds for rejection of his novel by the journal *Novy mir* in 1956, which were first published in *Literaturnaya gazeta* on 15 October 1958, were less overtly scurrilous. Apart from claiming that the spirit of the novel is 'that of non-acceptance of the socialist revolution', that Pasternak had failed to offer a 'definite appraisal of the social differences between the February and October revolutions' and had regarded 'the story of Zhivago's life and death as a story of the life and death of the Russian intelligentsia', the letter concluded:

It seems to us that your novel is profoundly unjust and historically prejudiced in its description of the revolution, the civil war and the years after the revolution, that it is profoundly anti-democratic and that any conception of the interests of the people is alien to it.[20]

The grounds can therefore be seen to be chiefly political: it is an anti-socialist, anti-revolutionary, anti-democratic novel. From this, of course, it is a short step to the almost irrelevant literary judgement that *Doctor Zhivago* is not as good as Tolstoy's *War and Peace* or that it is 'the weakest book he has ever written. It is a petty travesty of history. Throughout the book there is not one sympathetic portrait of a revolutionary.'[21] On the whole, these are the standards that have prevailed in Soviet estimates of the novel.

In Western criticism it has provoked a voluminous response, ranging from recognition of its greatness as a poetic novel, to extravagant interpretations of its mythophoric or apocalyptic meaning, to treatment of it as dissident literature and criticism of it as a failure.[22] One of the most crucial elements in the more critical approaches to the novel has been the question of its form. Is it in the tradition and of the same pattern as the classical nineteenth-century Russian realistic novel, like Tolstoy's *War and Peace*, for instance, or Dostoyevsky's *Crime and Punishment*? Should it be judged by criteria applicable to such works? In terms of its construction, *Doctor Zhivago* obviously has the chronicle form of Tolstoy's epic but it does not have the multiplicity of central figures, being based clearly on Zhivago himself; yet if it has a single hero-centred construction, like *Crime and Punishment*, it equally clearly does not possess that novel's dramatic form. That it lays claim to be considered as a great work of literature in the tradition of nineteenth-century Russian realism – that is to say, as a social–psychological study of character – cannot be doubted. Where it differs from the nineteenth-century Russian novel while simultaneously complementing it, is in its concern with the experience of revolution. Much confusion has arisen in critical appraisals of the novel through the failure to interpret it in terms appropriate to a revolutionary novel, a novel, that is, which explores the meaning of revolutionary experience with a revolutionary realism appropriate to its subject.

Max Hayward, whose English translation of *Doctor Zhivago* can now be recognised as a masterpiece of sensitivity despite minor omissions and compressions, pondered the text very closely and made observations on the novel that deserve to be respected. 'I believe myself', he wrote in his valuable introduction to Gladkov's memoirs,

that – whether one thinks it for better or worse – ...*Doctor Zhivago* is, within the Russian tradition of prose-writing, *sui generis* – and was consciously intended to be ... it is clear that *Doctor Zhivago* was not the caprice of a poet who late in life decided to try his hand at writing a novel, but that it was something which in form as well as in content had 'matured' over many years ... One of the chief criticisms of *Doctor Zhivago* in the West was that it relies too much on coincidences, but in this, as in other respects, Pasternak was only emphasising the realism of his approach.[23]

A close and sympathetic reading of the novel can hardly fail to bear out these impressions, though whether the final judgement is acceptable – '*Doctor Zhivago* is less a novel in the usual sense than what might be called a lyrical kaleidoscope'[24] – depends on what one considers a 'usual' novel. To Pasternak himself the novel was not 'usual', it was 'novel' in quite specific ways, as he explained (in his own English) in a letter to Stephen Spender:

For this characterisation of reality of the being, as a substratum, as a common background, the nineteenth century applied the incontestable doctrine of causality, the belief that the objectivity was determined and ruled by an iron chain of causes and effects, that all appearances of the moral and material world were subordinate to the law of sequels and retributions...

I also from my earliest years have been struck by the observation that existence was more original, extraordinary and inexplicable than any of its separate astonishing incidents and facts...

...There is an effort in the novel to represent the whole sequence of facts and beings and happenings like some moving entireness, like a developing, passing by, rolling and rushing inspiration, as if reality itself had freedom and choice and was composing itself out of numberless variants and versions.

Hence the not sufficient tracing of characters I was reproached with... hence the frank arbitrariness of the 'coincidences' (through this means I wanted to show the liberty of being, its verisimilitude touching, adjoining improbability).[25]

This testimony is of enormous value in assessing both Pasternak's intentions and his achievement in *Doctor Zhivago*. The idea that Pasternak was no more than a superb lyric poet unable to comprehend the nature of his times contains a partial truth only; he well knew that his times demanded more than lyrical poetry to express them. As he told Olga Carlisle:

I believe it is no longer possible for lyrical poetry to express the immensity of our experience. Life has grown too cumbersome, too complicated. We have acquired values which are best expressed in prose. I have tried to express them through my novel.[26]

The 'immensity of our experience' embraced all the phases of pre-revolutionary and Soviet history through which Pasternak and his generation had lived, but it has to be stressed that, for Pasternak at least, such experience was not identical with history or 'historical experience' as it is commonly understood. In speaking to Olga Carlisle he mentioned that in a lecture he gave in 1910, on the eve of Tolstoy's death, he referred to the idea that 'although the artist will die, the happiness of living which he has experienced is immortal. If it is captured in a personal and yet universal form it can actually be relived by others through his work.'[27] We know from *Doctor Zhivago* how profoundly this idea informed his portrayal of the novel's hero and the whole meaning of the work. Similarly, virtually on the eve of the revolution of 1917, he set out to distinguish between the dissimilar planes of poet and hero, poetry and history, eternity and time. Both, he insisted, 'are equally a priori and absolute' but 'history' is 'of time', as it were, and the poet's concern is 'eternity', which is transcendent, not concerned with 'the preparing of history for tomorrow'. As Max Hayward has interpreted the idea: 'The poet as the temporal representative of "eternity" is thus always the antithesis of those who "make history".'[28] Pasternak may therefore be seen in the context of his time not only as a 'temporal representative of "eternity"' who bore witness to the immensity of the experience of his generation – that this is reflected in the role allotted to Zhivago scarcely requires emphasising – but also as an antithesis to the dominant 'maker of history' in his time. Or, as Olga Ivinskaya has so eloquently and powerfully expressed it:

It is said that the true measure of a country's civilization is the kind of men it produces. The same country, in the same era, gave us Pasternak, and gave us Stalin. Both are the measure of their age: the measure of its humanity, and the measure of its cruelty; the measure of its greatness of mind and spirit, and the measure of its perfidy and baseness... Measures at opposite poles. Principles at the utmost remove from each other, and as contradictory as the age which brought them forth.[29]

As an antithesis to Stalin, Pasternak was not passive. Certainly he was not a political opponent of Stalin in the consciously political sense that Solzhenitsyn was an opponent, and for which he was arrested and sentenced,[30] but Pasternak was not, it seems, politically aware in a Marxist sense, nor did he 'play the political game' as a poet and novelist. His integrity, trustfulness and innocence, as a poet and as a man, were notorious.[31] But, if he was an antithesis to Stalin, it may also be true that Stalin recognised and respected him as a living contradiction of all he stood for and was prepared to spare his life when so many others had to surrender either their lives or their careers to satisfy the levelling and sycophantic orthodoxy of Stalin's 'cult of personality'.[32] Pasternak's sense of duty as a witness, as well as his desire to reach a large audience, a large readership ('I would give a lot', he is reported as saying, 'to be the author of *The Rout* or *Cement*... what I mean is that major works of literature exist only in association with a large readership'[33]), were of equal importance in making him turn from poetry to the form of large prose novel in which he had previously had no experience. The influence of Shakespeare and Goethe, as well as his own original work for the theatre, united in prompting him to seek that large readership which only a major work of literature can procure – yet always, it cannot be over-stressed, provided such a major work was an act of truthful witness to the revolutionary nature of his own time.

Olga Ivinskaya tells us much – some of it invaluable testimony, some of it intriguing speculation – about the way *Doctor Zhivago* emerged from its literary chrysalis. The name Zhivago, for instance, derived from a name on a manhole cover; his personality was partly autobiographical ('The hero will be something intermediate between me, Blok, Yesenin and Mayakovsky, and whenever I write poems nowadays they go into the notebook of this man Yury Zhivago', Pasternak is reported as writing in a letter in 1948), and Lara Guishar was based on Olga Ivinskaya herself, just as Tonya, Zhivago's first wife, was based on Pasternak's first wife Zinaida Nikolayevna.[34] Perhaps one of the most intriguing of Olga Ivinskaya's speculations concerns the possibility that Antipov may originally have been intended to be the hero of the novel, and she quotes Victor Frank's suggestion that certain characteristics of Mayakovsky may be reflected in Antipov-Strelnikov while those of Pasternak himself are reflected in Zhivago.[35] Central to their relationship is the figure of Lara, signifying the ideal for which both men strove in their separate ways, an ideal both of history and of eternity, and just as that ideal stretched throughout their adult lives in the fiction, so the ideal of writing a novel stretched throughout almost the whole of Pasternak's life as a writer, as Marina Tsvetayeva has helped to show.[36] *Doctor Zhivago* 'matured' out of Pasternak's experience as a writer, out of his life and his times and his reflections on them, and it represented for him the summit of his achievement in a lifetime devoted to the poet's craft and the revolutions that made their irreparable divides across it.

The novel clearly has a formal structure that attempts to 'recreate whole segments of life'.[37] In a very loose sense, it can be regarded as 'epic', though not in the way that *War and Peace* can be construed as a national epic, devoted to describing an act of national heroism, nor is it 'epic' in its concern with agencies and causes – the role of gods, for instance – in determining human behaviour or the course of history. It can be called 'epic' only in its formal concern with representing the experience of revolutionary change as one involving a whole life-span. In this it is unique among all the examples of the Russian revolutionary novel. Pasternak insisted that, in his view, there was no 'incontestable doctrine of causality' at work in ordering the moral and material world and that 'There is an effort in the novel to represent the whole sequence of facts and beings and happenings like some moving entireness…as if reality itself had freedom and choice and was composing itself out of numberless variants and versions.' By these means he wanted to show what he called 'the liberty of being, its verisimilitude touching, adjoining improbability', so that the arbitrariness of coincidence and of lives interacting with each other (the most striking instance, although not wholly arbitrary, is that of Zhivago and his half-brother Yevgraf) imposes its own freedom on the form of the fiction.[38] The novel illustrates the scale of the revolution precisely by this intertwining of lives and fates and worlds, and it reinterprets history both through the segments of such lives in their interlocking relations and through the notion that history is, strictly speaking, without causality, invisible, not made by anyone, 'a moving entireness'. Dialectical and historical materialism is here repudiated quite as much as the 'theological' understanding of the world to which Pasternak took such strong exception.[39] The interpretation of the novel must spring out of the novel itself, as a novel about the experience of revolutionary change defined for us chiefly through the life of the doctor–poet Yury Zhivago.

The total chronological span of the fiction encompasses at least fifty years, from 1903 to 1953. It is concerned not only with Zhivago's life and world, but with the adjoining lives and worlds of Lara Guishar, the Tiverzins, the Gromekos, Misha Gordon and Nicky Dudorov and Antipov-Strelnikov, illuminated, nevertheless, and given meaning only through their relationship to Zhivago's. The novel opens with the death of Zhivago's mother when the boy Yura is ten years old; his father commits suicide by throwing himself from a train under the malign influence of his lawyer, Komarovsky. Orphaned, Yura Zhivago is placed in the charge of the professorial Moscow family, the Gromekos. The death of his adoptive mother, buried in the same churchyard as his real mother, inspires in him a recognition of his poetic gift, just as the gift of life seems to be received by him on trust, to be acknowledged in his training as a doctor. Lara Guishar, seduced as a girl by the unscrupulous Komarovsky, had meanwhile married Pasha Antipov; they have lived in Yuryatin in the Urals and Pasha has left her to go to war. Zhivago also marries and has a child, but when he meets Lara during the First World War he realises that she represents for him an ideal in whose name he must make a conscious choice, though he is not forced into that choice until much later. Returning to Moscow after the October revolution, he accepts the privations and exigencies of the period in an affirmative spirit, but he and his family, including the father-in-law, eventually decide to leave Moscow for the haven of the Urals. There, at Varykino, not far from Yuryatin, they live out several seasons of the civil war. One day, in the Yuryatin library, Zhivago encounters Lara again; their love revives. At a crucial moment he chooses a life with her, but in that instant he is ambushed by local partisans and becomes their virtual captive, forced to act as their doctor though growing increasingly appalled at the rigidity of their revolutionary doctrines. He eventually escapes, makes his way back to Lara and for a short interval they are reunited at Varykino. His family and father-in-law, supposing him to be dead, have meanwhile returned to Moscow and are due to be deported from the Soviet Union. In the depth of winter Komarovsky, like a nemesis, discovers Lara and Zhivago at Varykino, offers them some kind of safe conduct to the east and, duped by Zhivago's promise to follow, Lara leaves with her daughter in Komarovsky's company. In the days remaining to him at snow-bound Varykino Zhivago is visited by Lara's former husband, Pasha Antipov, who has become renowned as a local partisan leader under the pseudonym of Strelnikov. Their long conversation ends with Antipov-Strelnikov's suicide. Finally Zhivago returns to Moscow, in a desultory way resumes his career as a doctor, but his life becomes ever more obviously an inner emigration dominated by his poetry. Though he marries again, he cannot endure the 'life of constant, systematic duplicity'[40] to which the majority of people have grown used and dies in August 1929 during a protracted journey by tram along a Moscow street. Lara reappears before his burial and delivers a final epitaph to their love. Much later, in an epilogue, his friends Gordon and Dudorov accidentally come across Zhivago's daughter during the Second World War, and at the novel's end we have a glimpse of his friends thinking about Yury Zhivago and his poetry on a summer evening some while after Stalin's death. A novel in sixteen chapters, or parts,[41] divided into Parts One and Two between chapters 7 and 8, it culminates in a section comprising twenty-five of Zhivago's poems.

Such an account of the novel's 'story' must highlight the supposed improbabilities of coincidence and accident that hold the narrative together. Though they can be viewed as narrative contrivances, they are better seen as functions of a realism that endows reality with a revolutionary freedom. Pasternak's fiction, which obviously evolves through styles reminiscent of his early short stories in the first chapters of his novel to more expansive and leisurely prose in the chapters describing Zhivago's maturity, has as its principal motiva-tion 'a developing, passing by, rolling and rushing inspiration' suggestive of nature itself, of human lives caught up in the very movement of nature and borne along as if by the flow of a huge stream of events, as Lara remarks so touchingly in her farewell to Zhivago, whose life had been a river to her: 'Goodbye, my quick, deep river, how I loved your day-long plashing, how I loved bathing in your cold, deep waves' (p. 448). The seasons dictate by their regularity, but the involvement of human beings in the history of their times is not governed by any regularity of law in Pasternak's fiction; all that seems to be drawn by way of a lesson from such 'history' is a pattern of coincidence, of near-miraculous proportion, in which the glimpse of a girl's face through a glass partition, the glimmer of a candle flame, the vicious killing of a loquacious commissar or the reappearance of a Swiss national, Mademoiselle Fleury, walking along a Moscow street in August have the character of epiphanies or milestones that illumine and possibly explain the 'moving entire-ness' of the fiction. They have meaning in the fiction in much the same way that art has meaning for Zhivago as 'a particle' that 'outweighs all the other ingredients in significance and turns out to be the essence, the heart and soul of the work' (p. 256), much as Yury Zhivago has meaning for his novel and poetry has meaning in his life. These are the signifiers of transformation – of seduction admitted, love confessed, murder acknowledged, life outlived – which

run their natural courses through Pasternak's realism, but outweighing them all in significance is that particle of revolution which
is the novel's essence.

It is a novel both about the Russian intelligentsia and about the
'revolutionism' so pervasive in Russian life. The world to which the
ten-year-old Yura Zhivago is introduced at the opening of the novel
is one where he is motherless and the only comforting voice, so like
his mother's, is that of his Uncle Kolya. The orphaned state of
Zhivago emphasises his inherent separateness and isolation, like the
Russian intelligentsia itself, which was destined to be isolated and
destroyed by the very 'revolutionism' it religiously worshipped as the
only means of transforming Russian society. Zhivago is born to an
inheritance of élitism, but scarcely in a worldly sense. The Zhivago
wealth has been squandered, and what remains of it, if anything, has
been exhausted by dishonest litigation or has been left to the keeping
of Zhivago's half-brother Yevgraf. A surname that was once a
conversational commonplace has 'vanished' and the Zhivagos have
become poor. The transforming power is no longer worldly in their
case, nor is it political in any real sense. Uncle Kolya Vedenyapin,
described as a priest, a former Tolstoyan and revolutionary idealist,
has become the conscience of the Russian intelligentsia, like those
leading thinkers of the intelligentsia who contributed to the symposium *Signposts* (*Vekhi*) (1909).[42] We are told that he 'craved for
an idea, inspired yet concrete, that would show a clear path and
change the world for the better, an idea as unmistakable even to a
child or an ignorant fool as lightning or a roll of thunder. He craved
for something new' (p. 17).

When we first encounter Yura with his uncle in the summer of
1903, during the Feast of the Virgin of Kazan, he is being taken to
Duplyanka to visit Nicky Dudorov, the young epitome of that
'revolutionism' so respected in their intelligentsia world. His father
is a terrorist. He himself, half-Georgian, attractive, charming, given
to testing his extrasensory will-power by making trees freeze into
immobility at his command, entertains a romantic idea of running
away to his father in Siberia and starting a rebellion. The characterisation of Nicky Dudorov, though only sketchily developed, can
be said to offer a counterpoint to Zhivago's, just as Misha Gordon's
simultaneous, though distanced, role as witness at the suicide of
Zhivago's father on the five o'clock express becomes one of witness
to Zhivago's life as a whole and by this means exemplifies a principle

in Pasternak's fiction that Misha's own hypersensitivity at his Jewishness seems momentarily to contradict. The principle evokes a collectivity of feeling, a *sobornost'*, in life, which presupposes some common purpose to human endeavour:

This feeling came from the comforting awareness of the interwovenness of all human lives, the sense of their flowing into one another, the happy assurance that all that happened in the world took place not only on the earth which buried the dead but also on some other level known to some as the Kingdom of God, to others as history and yet to others by some other name (p. 22).

The real transforming power at work in life is conceptualised in Nikolay Nikolayevich Vedenyapin's idea of individual personality. He asserts, for example, that 'the truth is sought only by individuals' (p. 18); belief of the type that demands group loyalty is rejected by him in preference for belief in immortality, 'which is another word for life, a stronger word for it'. For Vedenyapin human history begins with the transfiguring ideal of Christ, whose immortality has initiated, as he puts it, 'centuries of systematic work devoted to the solution of the enigma of death, so that death itself may eventually be overcome' (p. 19).[43] For such a task two things are described as essential:

'Firstly, the love of one's neighbour – the supreme form of living energy. Once it fills the heart of man it has to overflow and spend itself. And secondly, the two concepts which are the main part of the make-up of modern man – without them he is inconceivable – the ideas of free personality and of life regarded as sacrifice.'

The first of these – the love of one's neighbour – involves for Pasternak's fiction the principle of collectivity or interwovenness, which seems in so many ways to be the only real motivation of his novel. The second of them – the ideas of free personality and life as sacrifice – explains the principle from which Pasternak derives his portrayal of character. Zhivago's life in the fiction is governed as much by this principle of individual freedom of choice and life as sacrifice as it is by the assumption that the revolutionary epoch through which he lives has its meaning transfigured in his experience and receives its fullest interpretation in the transformation occurring in his poetry. If much of this may seem, as it seems to Vedenyapin's companion, a species of metaphysics that he finds it hard to stomach, their lives at that moment in the novel become an inadvertent witness to the suicide of Zhivago's father and a clear demonstration of Pasternak's claim to be creating a realistic fiction in which 'reality itself had freedom and choice'. For if reality influences their lives only inadvertently, it similarly influences Zhivago's – remotely, but nevertheless significantly – in chapter 2: 'A Girl from a Different World'. As Vedenyapin is to express it, within the context of his novel interpretation of Christian doctrine: 'The idea which underlies this is that communion between mortals is immortal, and that the whole of life is symbolic because the whole of it has meaning' (p. 48).

As a novel about revolution *Doctor Zhivago* poses the issue of the real nature of revolutionary feeling, as distinct from the 'revolutionism' of the intelligentsia, in ways that are arguably not 'anti-democratic' at all but commendably orthodox in a Soviet sense. The 'Different World' (or 'Circle': 'Devochka iz drugogo kruga') to which Lara Guishar belongs is a world of the socially exploited and deprived, of petit-bourgeois commerce and the working class. In 1905 that 'different world' is depicted as undergoing a revolution both moral and political, in which Lara falls victim to Komarovsky and the political ferment among the railway workers leads to the arrest of Pasha Antipov's father and his own admission to the Tiverzin household where, through old Tiverzina, Olga Demina's grandmother, he is to encounter Lara and fall in love with her and remain committed to her for life. If she is exploited by Komarovsky, the wealthy lawyer, then she in her turn exploits the wealth of Pasha's feeling for her, perhaps less unscrupulously but with a similar transforming effect. She represents for him an ideal of purity that lacks precisely the 'treachery' that was Komarovsky's chief asset in suborning the weak and dependent. Her own submission to her seducer is likened by her to the blessed state of all the downtrodden and poor in spirit, to whom Christ offered His gospel of salvation. Revolution, in the shape of the Presnya rising, is interpreted by her as an innocent pastime, its participants – Nicky Dudorov and Pasha Antipov – are innocent as children, and for her personally it means freedom from Komarovsky and a personal commitment to a freedom of spirit that is the revolutionary ideal: '"How splendid", she thought, listening to the gun shots. "Blessed are the downtrodden. Blessed are the deceived. God speed the bullets. They and I are of one mind"' (p. 57).

Until the conclusion of this chapter Zhivago is absent. He enters Lara's world as a naive adolescent observer of the circumstances surrounding her mother's attempted suicide and becomes inadvertently a *voyeur* of her total sexual enslavement to Komarovsky. The scene is one of startling revelation. It reveals Komarovsky as 'the master of a puppet show' and Lara as 'a puppet obedient to his every gesture' (p. 64). In the process it reveals to Yura the full meaning of his sexual awakening, all its 'vulgarity' and destructiveness, while also providing a glimpse of that other, 'revolutionary' world of which Lara is to become the chief representative and symbol. She is charged, as he admits to her much later, 'with all the femininity in the world' (p. 383) and appears to symbolise in her person the electrical energy of love. This energy, whether described as love for one's neighbour or as a transfiguring ideal, is at the source of the principle of collectivity or interwovenness underlying the fiction.

Zhivago's heritage is threefold, as chapter 3 makes clear. It is formed, first, by Uncle Kolya's neo-Christian view of man's purpose in history and the twin concepts of individual freedom of choice and life as sacrifice that make up modern man. All Zhivago's highest ideals in life are traceable to his uncle's ideas; they are the link with his dead mother, signifying for him both his apartness, his orphaned isolation, and his individuality, his unique transforming role. A central nucleus of Uncle Kolya's thinking, at least as it affects Zhivago, insists on the notion of history as a 'universe built by man with the help of time and memory in answer to the challenge of death' (p. 68). When Zhivago comforts the dying Anna Gromeko, it is this idea in a slightly modified form that he advances as the true gift of consciousness and life. Consciousness is 'a beam of light directed outwards' (p. 70), and in this objectified form it gives human beings an identity in others' awareness of them: 'You in others are yourself, your soul...You have always been in others and you will remain in others.' Such an idea is to become the single most significant legacy of Zhivago's life-affirming philosophy. His name, his reference to St John and the resemblance of his fictional life to a latterday hagiography can naturally tempt commentators into offering theological or mythophoric interpretations of Yury Zhivago's significance.[44] But his own message is simpler and more direct. There is no eschatology, strictly speaking, attaching to it. In speaking to his adoptive mother on her death-bed, he makes clear that resurrection is not a crude matter of literally raising from the dead but ultimately a question of talent or, as he puts it, talent 'in its highest and broadest sense is the gift of life'.[45]

The second component in his heritage mirrors this life-giving talent of his: it is his conviction that man should do something useful in his practical life. Hence, his decision to study medicine and become a doctor. The specifics of his medical training and experience are touched on only lightly in the course of the novel. Presumably the altruism entailed in the Hippocratic oath has an appeal for the literary mind when novelists fix on doctors as their heroes – the tradition is of long standing in the Russian revolutionary novel – but in Zhivago's case the overtones of salvationism ('Muttering incantations, laying on hands...' (p. 71) he thinks scornfully about himself) are deliberately muted. They merge into the third component of his heritage as it is revealed in chapter 3, his poetic vocation. The autobiographical element naturally enters into the portrayal of Zhivago at this point. The hero dreams the author's dream 'of writing a book in prose, a book of impressions of life in which he would conceal, like buried sticks of dynamite, the most striking things he had so far seen and thought about' (p. 68). Being too young for this, he writes poetry instead. But Zhivago's vocation as a poet grows out of a context of death in the novel, as a challenge to it, whether it be the corpses in the basement dissecting-room or the churchyard where both Anna Gromeko and his mother are buried. In acknowledgement of this, at the time of Anna's funeral, we are told:

In answer to the challenge of the desolation brought by death into the life of the small community whose members were slowly pacing after him, he was drawn, as irresistibly as water funnelling downwards, to dream, to think, to work out new forms, to create beauty. He realised, more vividly than ever before, that art has two constant, two unending preoccupations: it is always meditating upon death and it is always thereby creating life. He realised that this was true of all great and genuine art (p. 89).

Poetry as a defiance of death is the revolutionising or transforming dynamite concealed in Zhivago's life as it is concealed in the 'book of impressions of life' that is to comprise his novel.

His own art is to be a revolutionary dynamite, whereas the destructive dynamite of the conventional revolutionary belongs to Pasha Antipov's life. The sanctity of Pasha's vocation as a revolutionary is signalled by the candle flame melting ice on the window at the very moment that Lara is determining on her own revolt against Komarovsky and Yury and Tonya are passing along Kamerger Street on the way to the Sventitskys' Christmas Party. Not only does Yury's poem 'A Winter Night' spring from this moment, but the candle flame also intimates the sanctity of his own final resting-place before burial, where Lara is to confess her love for him as she was unable to confess her sinful state to Pasha. The transforming, perhaps miraculous, qualities that revolutionise lives and relationships form an electric current in Pasternak's novel at this point and grow luminous, so that we recognise the glow of the future in the present, the beam of consciousness reaching forward, and it can be seen that, in addition to Zhivago's threefold heritage, the threefold phases of his future love are clearly foreshadowed here by his betrothal to Tonya, by the Lara who shoots Komarovsky at the Sventitskys and by Markel's little daughter Marinka, who sucks barley sugar at the chapter's opening.

Simultaneously, then, Lara marries Pasha and her confession on their wedding night lights the fuse of his vocation as revolutionary, just as Yury marries Tonya, qualifies as a doctor and becomes a father in the second autumn of the war. The war is to separate them and in so doing to realign their relationships. It lights the fuse of the revolutionary process, but the historical fact of the war, notwithstanding its attendant horrors, acquires meaning for the fiction – and for every participant human being – not through the bland and cynical reportage of the war correspondent but through the transformations resulting from the fact itself, 'because', as Yury claims, to Misha Gordon's emphatic approval, 'facts don't exist until man puts into them something of his own, some measure of his own wilful, human genius – of fairy tale, of myth' (p. 116). The Christian era has already effected the fundamental transformation, creating converted, transformed people, and the whole point, so Misha goes on to make clear, is in the transformation. That the Jews should have permitted themselves to miss the chance of Christianity, as it were, rather than becoming 'the first and best Christians in the world' (p. 118), has left them in Misha Gordon's view with no choice save to be persecuted 'people', whereas the Vedenyapin doctrine of Christianity envisages a Kingdom of God based on love where there are no nations, only persons.

The wounding of Yury coincides with the beginning of the February revolution of 1917 and with his second meeting with Lara. Through Galiullin's concern for her husband she is reminded of 1905, but she is equally aware that 'everything had changed suddenly' (p. 121) and that at such a time 'you felt the need to entrust yourself to something absolute – life or truth or beauty – of being ruled by it now that man-made rules had been discarded'. Her awareness of this need acts as a form of catalyst for Yury. It is to her, as if she were an embodiment of the new freedom brought by the revolution, that he confesses his personal wonderment at the miraculous changes wrought by the revolution, though he is quite as clearly confessing the emotional and spiritual revolution that has occurred in himself through knowing her. The bizarre political changes seem incidental. The short-lived Zabushino republic, the young commissar Gints,[46] in his tight-fitting tunic, 'burning like a candle with the flame of his ideals' (p. 128) and Ustinya speechifying about the deaf–mute leader in the village square are the colourful pyrotechnics of the volcanic eruption of revolution, but the true transformation, in which not only people but stars and trees and flowers converse and talk philosophy,[47] is identified by Yury Zhivago when he tells Lara:

'The revolution broke out willy-nilly, like a breath that's been held too long. Everyone was revived, reborn, changed, transformed. You might say that everyone has been through two revolutions – his own personal revolution as well as the general one. It seems to me that socialism is the sea, and all these separate streams, these private, individual revolutions are flowing into it – the sea of life, of life in its own right. I said life, but I mean life as you see it in a work of art, transformed by genius, creatively enriched. Only now people have decided to experience it not in books and pictures but in themselves, not in theory but in practice' (p. 136).

Lara's meetings with Yury coincide with revolutions and form the axial points in his life. She represents for him life lived at its most intense, the creative enrichment to his own living experience. The encounters when they occur between them involve his discovery of her, for she is of the places to which he is the stranger and their relationship only ends when she leaves, as she leaves Meluzeyevo and is later to leave Varykino. Her need to entrust herself to something absolute – life or truth or beauty – receives its fulfilment in her love for Yury, just as he is fulfilled only in her. Their private, individual revolutions come together and flow into the sea of life. In the revolving of their lives other lives are sucked in, like Mademoiselle Fleury's, which is present at the beginning of their love and at the end of Yury's life, or Gints's, so bizarrely and cruelly ended by Pamphil Palykh, who is eventually to kill his wife and children in a fit of bloody atonement. Most of all, though, Yury's private, individual revolution is to bring into his life along with Lara the opposed and irreconcilable lives of her seducer and her husband.

Until this point in the novel Yury Zhivago had not come face to face with the political implications of revolution. Seated in the train taking him back to Moscow (ch. 4, 15), he recognises two circles of thoughts, one familiar – about his wife and home and revolution on the pattern of 1905 – the other unfamiliar, about the earthquake that had occurred in the life of Russia with 'the soldiers' revolution' and in his own life through his feelings for Lara. These thoughts are a preliminary to his encounter with the strange Pogorevshikh, the deaf–mute revolutionary, who preaches a doctrine of disorder and destruction in a voice rising to a tinny falsetto.[48] The meeting sickens Yury. Significantly it occurs in transit. All Zhivago's confrontations with explicitly political concepts of revolution occur while he is transient, whether on this occasion or while travelling from Moscow to Yuryatin or while he is leading a transient life with the partisans. Politics as such acquire by this means the status of a transient element in his life, as, for example, when he criticises Marxism for its lack of scientific objectivity while talking to Samdevyatov outside Yuryatin (ch. 8, 4) or attacks Liberius Mikulitsin, the partisan leader, for trying to reshape life according to his doctrinaire political ideals (ch. 11, 5). The extremism and rigidity of such political attitudes are essentially impermanent, it would seem, to judge from Zhivago's scorn of them, and moreover the lesson of Zhivago's life is that they do not produce a fundamental transformation in human nature. They are at best pretexts for Zhivago's own interpretations of the nature of the change occurring in Russia, just as the plump duck supplied by Pogorevshikh provides the occasion for his speech on the future of Russia when he is reunited with his family in Moscow.

The occasion (ch. 6, 4) is celebratory, expansive and extremely loquacious, in which revolution is marked quite as much by a flow of words as by 'the sea of blood' (p. 166) that Yury prophesies for all of them. His speech evokes the revolution as a flood, as an event of such titanic proportions that it must appear historically causeless, obliterating the personal lives of those who experience it and making it seem that in a mere five or ten years they have experienced more than most people would experience in a century. The scale of the Russian Revolution is equated with the universe itself, and that is the measure of its greatness. But if Yury can conceive the scale of it, as no other character in the novel seems able to, with the possible exception of Strelnikov, he is also able to recognise the twofold consequences of it, both universal and personal. Russia, in his view, is destined to become 'the first kingdom of socialism in the world'[49]

and, more important, when this happens 'it will stun us for a long
time, and when we come to ourselves we shall still be only half-
conscious and with half our memory gone' (p. 167). The halving of
Yury Zhivago's memory, and the memory of his generation, is
essentially where the tragedy of the novel resides. It involves the issue
of personal choice, but it is more closely concerned with demonstrating how revolution acts traumatically upon human experience,
divides it, separating the past from the present and transforming the
future into a 'monstrous machine' (p. 168) before which Yury feels
he is no more than a pygmy experiencing fear, love and a secret pride.
To his gloomy diary of those days, which he entitles 'Playing at
People' ('Igra v lyudey'), he confides the feeling 'that half the world
had ceased to be itself and was playing goodness only knew what
part' (p. 169). The part he was to assign to himself was that of a
latterday Hamlet but graced by the spiritual ideal of humanity
resurrected and transfigured; and it is precisely such resurrection and
transfiguration that Yury Zhivago discerns in the autumn of 1917,
at a literal moment of transition in history and in nature:

On such days the sky rises to its topmost height and an icy, dark-blue
radiance from the north steals into the transparent air between sky and earth.
Everything in the world becomes more visible and more audible. Every sound
is carried, iced and ringing, into immense distance. The country opens out
as if to show the whole of life for years ahead. This clarity would be
insupportable if it were not so short-lived, coming at the end of the brief
autumn day just before the early dusk (p. 169).

Role-playing can of course have its genuine as well as its artificial
side. The political events of the October revolution were invested with
a surgical role by Yury when he read the first broadsheets issued by
the new administration:

What a splendid surgery! You take a knife and you cut out all the old
stinking sores...This fearlessness, this way of seeing the thing through to
the end, has a familiar national look about it. It has something of Pushkin's
blazing directness and of Tolstoy's bold attachment to facts (p. 177).

In moments of this kind, as the natural scene intimated to Yury so
clearly, the signifying role and the fact itself enter into a total
correspondence. The revolution, 'this new thing, this marvel of
history, this revelation is exploded right into the very thick of daily
life' (p. 178) as he puts it, and it appears to be accompanied by a
coincidence of the providential and accidental in his own life. The

encounter with the wounded political leader at the bewitched intersection of Silver and Silent Streets is one instance of the providential seeming to intervene in his life, as are the two further coincidental meetings with Olya Demina, who revives memories of Lara for him (ch. 6, 13), and with his half-brother Yevgraf who finally brings succour to the whole family after the starving winter (ch. 6, 16). The role of Yevgraf, though too close to that of a *deus ex machina* for proper suspension of disbelief, is related very obviously to Zhivago's role as poet, as his name (Greek *eugraphos*, 'good writing' or 'good writer') seems to suggest.[50] He seems to enact a custodial and resurrecting role in relation to Zhivago the poet, the spirit overseeing his life and identified by Zhivago as his death, but also bringing succour at moments of particular stress and seeming thereby to resurrect Zhivago's inspiration. The imagery accompanying such moments of private revolution in his life is religious and hints very strongly at that identity of the roles of Hamlet and Christ which form the twin poles of his poetic vision. At the close of winter, as Zhivago begins to recover from typhus, the picture conjured up by his thoughts is apocalyptic, though it is equally explicitly representative of the way his life is to become a challenge to death:

Near him, touching him, were hell, corruption, dissolution, death; yet equally near him were the spring and Mary Magdalene and life. – And it was time to awake. Time to awake and to get up. Time to arise, time for the resurrection (p. 188).

The resurrection is of course not only coincidental with the coming of spring, it also coincides with the decision to leave Moscow for Yuryatin and Varykino in the Urals. The journey, while seemingly an escape from revolution, becomes a preliminary to the real revolution in Zhivago's life, when his experience is irrevocably divided between past and future. It is an enactment of the poem 'Turmoil' ('Smyateniye'), which Yury had been writing on recovering from typhus – 'The subject of his poem was neither the entombment nor the resurrection but the days between' (p. 188) – and it is the first occasion in the novel when he finds himself actively involved in the turmoil of the revolutionary process. The crowded wagon, the frequent halts, the inexplicable incidents and, finally, Zhivago's encounter with the ostensible cause of the turmoil, Strelnikov himself, arouse in him a desire both to shout out 'that salvation lay not in loyalty to forms and uniforms, but in throwing them away'

(p. 224) and to wonder whether Strelnikov ('a finished product of the will') might be possessed not so much by the gift of originality as by one of imitation. Perhaps this very play-acting of the role of revolutionary leader in Strelnikov's case highlights the contrast between him and Zhivago. He readily proclaims in a rhetorical fashion what Yury Zhivago has struggled to encompass at a deeper level in his poetry, as he declares: 'These are apocalyptic times, my dear sir, this is the Last Judgment. This is a time for angels with flaming swords and winged beasts from the abyss, not for sympathisers and local doctors' (p. 227). He has already cut himself off from his past, represented by Lara and his daughter Katya, and can be seen to forecast, like some *alter ego*, the similar fate that awaits Zhivago as the turmoil of revolution and civil war takes its toll.

Part II of the novel describes this process with all the seeming irreversibility of tragedy. Yet it is not a tragedy in which the forces of history overwhelm the human will. The tragedy evolves as much from Zhivago's choice, paradoxical though it may seem, as it does from the circumstances in which he finds himself. He *chooses* revolution after his fashion as consciously as Strelnikov had chosen it for his reasons. There is no doubt that Yury Zhivago is faced by temptations. Samdevyatov, the Bolshevik, is one such tempter. Zhivago repudiates the temptation of Marxism both on the grounds of its lack of objectivity and on the grounds that, like its proponents, it is self-justifying ('those who wield power are so anxious to establish the myth of their own infallibility that they turn their back on truth' (p. 235)); and when Samdevyatov argues for radical change by violent means, Yury protests that 'now I think nothing can be gained by violence. People must be drawn to goodness by goodness' (p. 237). Similarly, there are the temptations of Varykino – the temptation to hide from the surrounding turmoil, the temptation to conceal his medical knowledge, the temptation to live vicariously in his diary, the entries for which provide most of our knowledge of the Varykino stay. Tonya's pregnancy in the spring – presumably of 1919 – turns him simultaneously to thoughts of motherhood, in which each mother is glorified, as it were, by the idea that God is her child, and to consideration of the idea that art is not a category but a principle 'which comes into every work of art, a force applied to it and a truth worked out in it...the essence, the heart and soul of the work' (p. 256). And as if it were an infection, like that transforming principle of art working itself out in his own life, he acknowledges to his diary that in a muddled dream he had been haunted by a woman's voice, which we know is Lara's. He also acknowledges to his diary that what his life needs is a diet of the normal, the everyday, just as in his estimate of Pushkin's poetry (as of his own, one might add), what it needed to achieve greatness was 'concrete things' – 'It's as if the air, the light, the noise of life, of real substantial things burst into his poetry from the street as through an open window' (p. 258). What he calls 'the childlike Russian quality of Pushkin and Chekhov, their shy unconcern with such high-sounding matters as the ultimate purpose of mankind or their own salvation' (p. 259) now appeals to him more than the worried searching for a meaning in life to be found in Gogol, Tolstoy and Dostoyevsky. The final acknowledgement in his diary is the most private and revealing. It concerns the second incursion into his life of his half-brother Yevgraf, whom he now identifies as 'a secret, unknown force' (p. 261) in his life equivalent to that transforming principle which he identified as the essence of a work of art and which, as the rest of the chapter makes amply clear, is most fully exemplified in Lara.

As the mature woman with whom Yury Zhivago falls in love, Lara Antipov may frequently give the impression of being a surrogate Zhivago or, as Henry Gifford has put it, 'sometimes the exchanges between Yury and her sound like the colloquy of a mind with itself'.[51] In a technical sense it is true that the speech patterns of Yury and Lara seem barely distinguishable from each other. Theirs is nonetheless a meeting of minds as well as hearts, and if she seems to mirror him in what she says she is also the one in whom Yury encounters himself most clearly. He learns to see himself transfigured in her. Central to their relationship, as it is central to Zhivago's life and to the novel, is that transient period when he is captured by the partisans and forced to participate in the October revolution, as he considers it, against his will. The transfiguring ideal then becomes for him the archetypal Lara, emerging both from a vision of nature and from the very source of his being:

Ever since childhood Yury had been fond of woods seen at evening against the setting sun. At such moments he felt as if he too were being pierced by blades of light. As if the gift of the living spirit were streaming into his breast, piercing his being and coming out by his shoulders like a pair of wings. The archetype, which is formed in every child for life and seems for ever after to be the inward image of his personality, arose in him in its full primordial strength and compelled nature, the forest, the afterglow and everything else visible to be transfigured into a similarly primordial and all-embracing likeness of a girl. 'Lara', closing his eyes, he whispered and thought, addressing the whole of life, all God's earth, all the sunlit space spread out before him.

But the everyday, current reality was still there: Russia was going through the October Revolution and Yury was a prisoner of the partisans (p. 310).

As Lara herself emphasises on several occasions, though especially when she and Yury are together for the first time in her rat-infested apartment opposite the House of Caryatids, the revolution is closer to her than it is to him. Apart from her personal experience of it, which brought her into contact with Galiullin (now transformed into a White General), probably her most profound insight into the revolution derives from her husband Antipov-Strelnikov. When Yury accidentally mentions his meeting with him and judges him as a doomed man, a non-party revolutionary who had gone horrifyingly out of control like a runaway train, he seems to Lara to be much harsher than he had been previously. The point is, as he says, 'that there are limits to everything' (p. 269) and it now turns out that the native element of the revolutionaries is universal turmoil, that for them 'transitional periods, worlds in the making, are an end in themselves'. To this he opposes life itself, the gift of life, which is so much more serious than the childish harlequinade of immature ideas that the revolutionaries strive to impose on it. In his truth he is true to Lara, and the whole novel at this point becomes an acknowledge-ment of such a revolutionary, life-transforming truth, for as Lara says towards the end of their conversation: 'It's only in bad novels that people are divided into two camps and have nothing to do with each other. In real life everything gets mixed up!' (p. 270).

It is precisely at this point in *Doctor Zhivago* that the novel chooses, as it were, to become a revolutionary novel by deliberately repudiating the characteristics of a bad novel. It is here that its realism demonstrates what Pasternak called 'the liberty of being, its verisimilitude touching, adjoining improbability' by its very insis-tence on the primacy of life. This is not to say that, in terms of its vision of man, it is inconsistent with the twofold ideal of free personality and life as sacrifice. The freedom implicit in Pasternak's realism is what recalls the depth and vitality of the major nineteenth-century Russian realistic novels. The assumption that humanity is not segregated by class or social role or money informs the vision of Turgenev, Dostoyevsky and Tolstoy, even though they recognised as clearly as such radical critics as Chernyshevsky and Dobrolyubov the extent to which socio-economic pressures and their accompanying ideologies worked to divide human beings one from another in Russian society. But their assumption was deferential towards the complex abundance of life; it sought to perceive unity, not difference, in the sanctity of human beings; it presupposed a human need for reconciliation while always respecting the implicitly free privacy and separateness of human experience. Such freedom was only demonstrable in terms of choice, but the choice tended almost invariably to highlight the very paradoxicality of the freedom. So it is with Yury Zhivago at this moment in the novel, at the end of chapter 9, when he chooses to return to Lara and in so doing falls into the hands of the partisans.

All that follows sets in relief the paradox of his problem. Equally, it reveals the character of *Doctor Zhivago* as a revolutionary novel. Chapter 10, 'The Highway' ('Na bol'shoy doroge'), marks a central point in the work. It is the only chapter in the novel from which Yury Zhivago is wholly absent. It is the chapter that marks a divide in his life and, more clearly than any other, it demonstrates the supposed divide that characterises revolution. It portrays in serio-comic and near-caricature fashion the two sides in the civil-war conflict. In this sense, it is the 'bad' novel at the heart of Pasternak's novel. It is 'bad' (in Lara's terms) because it shows people divided into two camps, just as the Siberian highway 'cut through the towns like a knife, slicing them in half like a loaf of bread along the line of their main streets' (p. 277). The vital and unifying spirit in the novel is absent, being replaced by the musings and memories of Galuzina, which yield to the scene of the meeting attended by Liberius, Tiverzin, Kostoyed and others, and the scene of the drunken party for the recruits to the White cause. Just as the unifying spirit in the novel is absent, so the unity of chronology is broken. At this point the historical calendar becomes a fictional calendar. If Yury Zhivago was a prisoner of the partisans for 'almost two years' (p. 298) and the partisans were still engaged in fighting Kolchak, then Pasternak appears to have extended the civil war by some two or three years. This violation reflects also on Zhivago, for his life loses its chronological unity. It reflects his own prophecy by literally rendering him half-conscious, with half his memory gone. After this, through his captivity, he is never to see his wife and child again and he is never to be as he was.

The resulting paradox is finely and tragically illustrated by the incident in chapter 10, 4 (to which the editorial board of *Novy mir* took such strong exception) when Yury Zhivago, in violation of the Red Cross International Convention, is forced to participate in an engagement between the partisans and the Whites. In a revolutionary situation Zhivago's hope of remaining uninvolved must always be compromised, yet the very hope itself serves to strengthen his belief in life. Rejecting the partisan leader's enthusiasm for the idea of social betterment, he eloquently asserts that life 'is never a material, a substance to be moulded' (p. 306). It is for Zhivago a principle of self-renewal that throughout his captivity and in the remaining years of his life seems to be projected to him in the image of Lara. His life has continuity only through Lara and it achieves a final purpose only in his love for her. The greatness of *Doctor Zhivago* is that, in its depiction of the love between Yury and Lara, it transcends its revolutionary content; but there is never any doubt that the trans-figuring ideal that their love brings to their lives has its origins in the revolution.

Zhivago's reaction to enforced involvement in the revolutionary conflict could well be summarised as 'a plague on both your houses'. The reminder of *Romeo and Juliet* is apposite for, after his escape from the partisans, he remarks to Lara during their first conversation that her husband, Antipov-Strelnikov, is 'one writ with me in sour misfortune's book'.[52] The revolution has meant a far more terrible rupture in Antipov's life than it has in Zhivago's. In Antipov's case the transfiguring ideal has soured into the colourlessness of the revolutionary Strelnikov and the purity that so attracted Lara in the young Pasha has gone out of him. Lara accounts for it by arguing that he fell victim to the falsehood of the glittering phrase, he tried to live a cliché and he became divorced from history. Her longing for purity is now assuaged in her love for Zhivago, though if Strelnikov should transform himself back into Antipov all her love for him would be rekindled. Meanwhile, her verdict on what has happened to Russia in the revolutionary period reads like a vale-dictory epitaph not only on her relations with Yury Zhivago but on the loneliness of the Russian intelligentsia and the ideals for which it once stood:

'Everything ordinary and everyday has been overturned and destroyed. There has remained only the non-material, immaculate force of a naked spirituality threadbare and in tatters, for which nothing has changed, because it has at all times been cold and shivering and reaching out to its nearest neighbour, just as bare and lonely as itself. You and I are like the two first people, Adam and Eve, who had nothing to cover themselves with in the beginning of the world, and now we are just as unclothed and homeless at its ending. And you and I are a last reminder of all that immeasurable greatness which was created on the earth in the many thousands of years between their time and ours, and in memory of those vanished wonders we breathe and love and weep and hold each other and cling to one another.'[53]

On both a historical and a private level, as representatives of their age and as individuals, Lara and Yury can be seen to have become remnants from an earlier era, spokesmen of that initial vision of a transformed humanity which Uncle Kolya had preached and which is now echoed in the visionary words of Sima Tuntseva. Her recapitulation of the idea that with the birth of Christ 'the basis of life is no longer to be compulsion, it is to be...inspiration instead of compulsion' (p. 370) does not lead her to deny that 'our revolutionary era is a wonderful era of new, lasting, permanent achievements' (p. 371), but what she cannot accept is the rhetoric about leaders and peoples; for they were replaced by the doctrine of personality and freedom and, as she expresses it, 'the story of a human life became the life story of God and filled the universe' (p. 370). Almost echoing Lara's words on Adam and Eve, Sima appears to suggest an identity between Zhivago and Adam when she claims that 'now God was made man so that Adam should be made God' (p. 371). This reference, like the succeeding references to Christ and Mary Magdalene, not only calls to mind the last of Zhivago's poems, but also re-emphasises the Christ-like heritage and purpose ordained for man, the principle of rebirth and renewal in life. Emerging, as it were, from Sima Tuntseva's words, accompanied by the magpies and the snow, comes the news from Tonya of Zhivago's new daughter and their imminent deportation from the Soviet Union; and, as if Sima's thoughts on the supernatural meaning of the virgin birth have a celebratory relevance, at this moment it may be that Yury's love for Lara has led to the conception of their love-child Tanya, who is later to tell her frightening tale to Yevgraf, Gordon and Dudorov.[54] Lara's twofold identification as Sima suggests, with Mary Magdalene and Eve – the Mary Magdalene who is mentioned on the very eve of Easter, at the time of Christ's death and resurrection, who 'begs Christ to accept her tears of repentance...reminding Him that in the rushing waves of her hair

Eve took refuge when she was overcome with fear and shame in
Paradise' (p. 372) – is echoed in Tonya's claim that Lara, unlike her,
was born to complicate life and knock if off course ('sbivat' s
dorogi'). Hers is a legacy as complicating as the revolution, having
its origin in the squalor of her past, whereas Zhivago's past,
represented by his wife, his children and especially Uncle Kolya, is
being swept out of the life of Russia, leaving him only with his
intelligence and his own 'gift of life', his talent.

The sudden reappearance of Komarovsky revives Lara's fear of
her past, makes them leave for Varykino and inspires Yury to
allegorise their relationship in the legend of St George and the
Dragon. After Yury has hoodwinked Lara into leaving with Komarovsky, he acknowledges to himself that she was the storm of
revolution passing through his life and he will celebrate her image
on paper

as the sea, after a fearful storm has churned it up to its foundations, leaves
the traces of the strongest, furthest-reaching wave on the shore...This is how
you were cast up in my life, my love, my pride, this is how I'll write of you
(pp. 404–5).

Inspiration comes to his poetry, transforming him from the doctor
into the poet, 'like a message sent to him by Lara from her
travels...and he rejoiced at this ennobling of his verse' (pp. 405–6).
Simultaneously, among the jottings accompanying his poems, as his
poems accompany and reflect his life, he notes that the revolution
occurring perennially in nature is for him the image of 'the eternally
growing, ceaselessly changing life of society, of history moving as
invisibly in its incessant transformation as the forest in spring'.[55]
Zhivago's repudiation of the course taken by the Russian revolution
since his first experience of it in Melyuzeyevo – and his first love for
Lara – now concludes with a wholesale indictment of the one-sided
fanatics and geniuses of self-limitation ('genii samoogranicheniya')
who 'overturn the old order in a few hours or days; the whole
upheaval takes a few weeks or at most years, but for decades
thereafter, for centuries, the spirit of narrowness which led to the
upheaval is worshipped as holy'. So far as the novel is concerned,
it is Lara's husband who chiefly epitomises this spirit of narrowness;
yet when Yury and Strelnikov meet for the last time, his justification
of his revolutionary fanaticism centres on the differences in background between them. He invokes a vision of two nations – 'the

world of the suburbs, of the railways, of the slums and tenements...
And there was the world of the mothers' darlings, of smart students
and rich merchants' sons' (p. 411) – and out of this conflict between
exploited and exploiters grew his conviction that life resembled a war.
For Lara's sake he harnessed himself to the revolutionary destiny of
Russia. It was to be retribution for the misdeeds of the old world,
a retribution expressed and personified in Lenin; and it was to be
a light of redemption for all the sorrows and misfortunes of mankind.

Strelnikov is the least fully realised of all Pasternak's portraits in
Doctor Zhivago. The intent of the portrayal can be readily discerned,
but it is not fleshed out into a living semblance. A voice having about
it the falsely romantic ring of a melodramatic tale of sacrificial love,
theatrical rhetoric dominates the portrayal, and he seems scarcely
more ample as a character than the County Paris whom Romeo will
bury 'in a triumphant grave', as no doubt Zhivago buries Strelnikov
after his suicide. Yet Zhivago is also stricken by an awareness of the
one-sidedness that the post-revolutionary world imposes on him.
Nature itself, during his return from Siberia with his boy companion
Vassya Brykin, whom he had first met on the outward journey, seems
similarly stricken, as if the fields were sick with a torrid fever and
woods were incandescent with convalescence and God and the Devil
were present in them. When Yury and Vassya arrive in Moscow in
the spring of 1922 (ch. 15, 5), Yury is suffering from heart disease,
forced to suppress his private awareness that his own 'gift of life'
far exceeds that of his friends Gordon and Dudorov ('The only bright
and living thing about you is that you are living at the same time
as myself and are my friends!' (p. 430)) and aware also, like the
doctor he is, of the diagnosis to be given to the universal illness he
shares with his contemporaries:

'Nowadays there are more and more cases of small cardiac haemorrhages.
They are not always fatal. Some people get over them. It's the common
illness of our time. I think its causes are chiefly moral. The great majority
of us are required to live a life of constant, systematic duplicity. Your health
is bound to be affected if, day after day, you say the opposite of what you
feel, if you grovel before what you dislike and rejoice at what brings you
nothing but misfortune. Your nervous system isn't a fiction, it's a part of
your physical body, and your soul exists in space and is inside you, like the
teeth in your head. You can't keep violating it with impunity' (p. 432).

For him, if not for the others, there is the final escape into an inner
emigration. What matters is not that the slow, frequently stopping

tramcar takes him on the final journey of his insupportable life in
August 1929, from which he steps down as if stepping out of history,
but that the journey that he makes in his poetry from Hamlet to
Christ summarises the meaning of his life and illustrates the transfiguring ideal of his time. Zhivago's poems are the warmth in this
book, as Pasternak put it.[56] They give warmth, for example, to that
rather banal identification of the Russian intelligentsia with an
introspective Hamlet which had been used so frequently to explain
the intelligentsia's inability to act. In the poem 'Hamlet' the need
to act is fundamental, despite the paradox of it. Zhivago's interpretation recognises that Hamlet is both no more than an acted role
and an enactment of a duty, both one who listens to what will happen
in his time and the spectacle for his time to watch, both the Christ,
asking that the cup should pass from Him, and the human actor in
history who is faced by the drama of his time, both the one who is
the sole witness to truth in a philistine world and the one who
recognises that living is not acting a role, it is living the life to be lived.
But the single most illuminating facet of this Hamlet-paradox is the
association of Hamlet's duty and destiny with Christ's, for here
the sacrificial life of the seeker after justice receives its apotheosis in
the ideal of humanity resurrected, its life transfigured. That ideal is not
present in the 'Hamlet' poem; it is only intimated. The remaining
twenty-four poems of the Zhivago cycle enact the miracle of the
apotheosis.[57]

The awakening of the earth in 'March' suggests renewal of life,
which is paralleled on a religious level by the overcoming of death
through the power of the resurrection ('In Holy Week'). Personal
themes enter the cycle with 'White Night' and a dream of love,
calling to mind Zhivago's own love for Lara in his captivity (as
'Spring Floods' suggests) and offering a love poem in 'Explanation'
and an occasion of love ('Summer in Town'). 'The Wind', addressed
to a beloved, uses the natural element to evoke the love as a
continuity and lament, a grief and a lullaby, but above all to indicate
its force, like love as an intoxication ('khmel'', in the poem of that
name, referring to the hops encircling the branches of the trees as
love encircles the lovers), and 'Indian Summer' ('Bab'ye leto')
acknowledges that, though summer may be on the wane, laughter
overcomes the sorrowing season. For life (as 'The Wedding Party'
makes clear) is only an instant, a dissolving of ourselves in others
in an act of giving ('Kak by im v daren'ye'). This poetic affirmation

of Zhivago's philosophy of life is followed by one of the most personal poems ('Autumn'). It is the love poem of a man who acknowledges the loneliness of his life but finds its autumn blessed by a woman's love – given boldly, for that is the root of beauty. 'A Fairy-Tale' is also a fable of courage and love, obviously linked to Zhivago's experience, as 'August' similarly celebrates the challenge of their love, even beyond the grave. Though 'Winter Night' refers directly to Lara's meeting with Pasha (ch. 3, 10), it also seems to mark the real divide in Zhivago's life, particularly the sense of loss that he felt on receiving the letter from his wife (ch. 13, 18). 'Parting' continues that theme, as 'Meeting' seems to celebrate the lovers' apartness as much as their meeting; however, in 'Christmas Star' renewal comes out of winter with the birth of Christ, as the new day ('Daybreak') is a recognition of the way the past is divided from us, people from each other, but what 'Daybreak' avows is the need to be part of people, to be dissolved in them, as if there is no other victory over death and oblivion. For out of the temptation in the wilderness comes the miracle, out of direst distress the instantaneously miraculous. The miraculous transformation of the earth in springtime ('The Earth'), which directs us back to the beginning of the cycle, is accompanied by the real transformation, the prevention of lone-liness, whether it be the loneliness of distances or of people; so that the coming together of friends suggests not only Zhivago and his friends but also Christ and His apostles; and the remaining poems of the cycle manifestly celebrate the miracle of the apotheosis in their depiction of Christ as the giver of life, whose greatest gift was the resurrection.

The poems are the epitaph to Zhivago's life and his testament. But the epitaph to the Russian Revolution is given by Misha Gordon after hearing the story of Zhivago's child, Tanya. It is at once terrible and majestic, an indictment of the revolution's failure and an assertion of the miraculous that may spring even from the terrors of such reality:

'This has happened several times in the course of history. A thing which has been conceived in a lofty, ideal manner becomes coarse and material. Thus Rome came out of Greece and the Russian Revolution out of the Russian enlightenment. Take that line of Blok's, "We, the children of Russia's terrible years": you can see the difference of period at once. In his time, when he said it, he meant it figuratively, metaphorically. The children were not children, but the sons, the heirs of the intelligentsia, and the terrors were not terrible but apocalyptic; that's quite different. Now the figurative has become literal, children are children and the terrors are terrible. There you have the difference' (p. 463).

Later, when Gordon and Dudorov hold the book of Yury Zhivago's writings in their hands as they sit by a window overlooking the cityscape of Moscow, they sense that the 'freedom of the spirit' for which the revolution had been made and for which Zhivago had lived 'had become almost tangible in the streets below'. Post-Stalin Moscow in the mid-1950s did miraculously seem to promise such freedom, but the object of their contemplation is as much the book in their hands as the holy city of Moscow. The book in their hands, though it is Zhivago's testimony, testifies also to the resurrecting principle that Zhivago identified in life and to the fact that, as they themselves and their children can bear witness, its truth endures and outlasts, as *Doctor Zhivago* can be seen to outlast the philistinism of its official suppression and the Russian revolutionary novel outlasts the historical facts from which it is derived.

Conclusion

The death-birth of a world

'Behold', cried Thomas Carlyle, in an ecstatic aside while describing the initial stages of the French Revolution, 'the World-Phoenix, in fire-consummation and fire-creation...skyward lashes the funeral flame, enveloping all things: it is the Death–Birth of a World!'[1] It is at such points that history and myth coalesce, but the mythologising process is one that turns history into literature. In the Russian literary response to revolution an imagery of death and birth is paramount and the death–birth concept becomes itself a transfiguring ideal.

Revolution as a fanaticism that would, like some fiery apocalypse, consume the existing world and create a new one, a World-Phoenix, is the legacy that the events of 1789 bequeathed to nineteenth-century history and culture. Many great nineteenth-century minds were influenced by such a vision of revolution giving birth to a new world and a new life and among those most deeply affected by it were the leading minds of the Russian intelligentsia. For if the world needed changing, to put it at its simplest, there seemed no likelihood that God would suddenly alter His creation, any more than would the Tsar. The only phenomenon in recent history that could so alter the known world as to transform it utterly in the name of Liberty, Equality and Fraternity was the French Revolution. De Tocqueville's description of its effect on Europe reveals the essence of its appeal:

...the Revolution pursued its course; the head of the monster was seen to appear; its singular and terrible aspect was uncovered; after having changed the laws, it changed the manners, the habits, and even the language; after it had destroyed the fabric of government, it disturbed the foundations of society, and finally seemed to wish to attack God himself.
   ...That which had at first seemed to the princes and statesmen of Europe an ordinary accident in the life of nations, now appeared so novel, so contrary to everything that had ever occurred in the history of the world, and withal so universal, so monstrous, so incomprehensible, that in view of it the human mind was lost in bewilderment.[2]

Bewilderment of so total a kind, it should be said, that it naturally evoked visions of apocalypse and turned humanity to thoughts of first and last things, to beginnings and ends, towards, that is, a reawakening of interest in the Graeco-Roman origins of European culture and myth and towards the metaphors, if not always the substance, of the one religious source available to all Europeans, the Bible. In short, the bewilderment of the human mind tended to interpret the political cataclysm in religious terms. De Tocqueville stresses that:

The French Revolution was... a political revolution which in its features and characteristics resembled in a way a religious revolution. Notice the features in which it resembled the latter. Not only did it spread like the latter into distant lands, but also like the latter it made its way by preaching and propaganda. A political revolution which inspires proselytism! Preached as ardently to foreigners as it is conducted with passion at home! What a novel spectacle! Of all the hitherto unheard-of things, which the French Revolution revealed to the world, this is surely the most novel.[3]

The novelty of the French Revolution was undoubtedly its principal characteristic. The Russian Revolution was similarly to sanction novelty and a new beginning as its self-justifying attributes, and the literary response to the October revolution of 1917 and its consequences was initially to be a demand for novelty, particularly in the novel. But how was such novelty first expressed in response to the French Revolution, which after all set the tone for the modern idea of revolution? It was expressed not by the idea of revolution as such, but by the idea of regeneration. In June 1789, as Renee Winegarten reminds us,

it seems strangely significant that the word 'revolution' was not used... when the oath was taken at the Tennis Court, this being the essential revolutionary act which led to all the rest. The Assembly spoke of 'national regeneration', and only fifteen months later did 'revolution' appear in a procla-mation...Indeed, it was just this 'air of tending to the regeneration of the human race' that, according to de Tocqueville, gave the revolution of 1789 its unique similarity to the revolution caused by Christianity in the ancient world.[4]

The novelty of the event demanded by its very character that there should be no precedents for it. It had no traditions on which to draw save those deriving from pre-Christian times, since Christianity itself, in its established forms, was not a celebrant of the revolution and its imagery could not be used to promote revolutionary feeling. This is not to say that biblical imagery, in a literary and graphic sense, did not contribute to celebration of the French Revolution, but the idea of 'regeneration' demanded less specific, more universal, symbolism. Probably the most conspicuous symbol of the freedom and regeneration signified by the revolution was the liberty cap. This symbol, 'which appeared almost immediately on official seals and engravings, recalled the cap of Roman times that was worn by freed slaves'.[5] If such pre-Christian symbolism was used to denote the first achievement of the revolution, then the establishment of the Republic led to the adoption of the most famous allegorical representation associated with the French Revolution, that of the goddess of liberty. Although not invented by the Revolution (such a feminine allegory dated in French painting from the 1770s), the universality of such symbolism appears to have been at the heart of its appeal. This goddess figure, always robust, nubile, even matronly, and significant as much of fertility as virginity, betokened that spirit of regeneration for which the revolution and the Republic stood.

The figure of the Republic was compelling for different, even contradictory, reasons. To some she no doubt evoked the Virgin Mary with her innocence and concern for the 'enfants de la Patrie'. To others, the Republic with her antique accoutrements recalled a purer time supposedly free of fanatical superstition and the machinations of an overweening clergy...
...Since she was dressed in the Roman style, the Republic, like her prototype, the Goddess of Liberty, was not identified with any one political faction or group. Like the spoken and written rhetoric of the revolutionaries, the visual image of the Republic represents universalistic values.[6]

In representing universalistic values it was also of course stressing a fact about the French Revolution and revolution in general that may hardly need emphasising, but is most certainly essential in interpreting the phenomenon; that it is anthropocentric. Revolution, for all the supposed laws of economics or society, politics or science, that may explain it, is an iconoclastic phenomenon, and the iconoclasm lays bare the fact that human beings have to resort to the simplest, most elemental, features of their own experience to interpret it. And the most elemental of such features are those associated with birth and death. The two are inseparable. This implies that the birth of the new must be dependent on the death of the old. The two extremes of human experience unite in the death–birth that is to give rise to the new world of the revolution.

In his famous essay 'On Death' Francis Bacon wrote: 'It is as natural to man to die as to be born; and to a little infant, perhaps, the one is as painful as the other.' Carl Sagan used this quotation at the head of his chapter on what he called 'the amniotic universe' of all initial human experience.[7] Perithanatic, or near-death, experiences struck him as having certain common factors that might have their origins in the four stages of the perinatal, or near-birth, experience common to all mankind. 'Every human being, without exception', he writes,

has already shared an experience like that of those travellers who return from the land of death: the sensation of flight; the emergence from darkness into light; an experience in which, at least sometimes, a heroic figure can be dimly perceived, bathed in radiance and glory. There is only one common experience that matches this description. It is called birth.[8]

The four stages of the foetus in the womb and after birth involve the loss of an ideal universe, the enduring of pain and the emergence on another level of experience into another world. Perhaps such an experience, suggests Carl Sagan, 'motivates us powerfully to change the world and improve human circumstance. Perhaps that striving, questing aspect of the human spirit would be absent if it were not for the horrors of birth.'[9]

For an anthropocentric interpretation of revolution this must imply that the desire for such change, inevitably associated with violence and blood, is a universal human heritage. But if we accept the idea that 'every birth is a death – the child leaves the amniotic world',[10] then the birth–death process is similarly universal, finding expression possibly in the fundamental assumptions of religion, of our view of the cosmos and of psychology. Emergence from the womb and loss of the amniotic fluid perhaps arouse in humanity the need to reacquire that primal contentment by symbolic use of water in acts of rebirth, such as total-immersion baptism; or perhaps it invites humanity to leave earth and explore the cosmos.[11] Carl Sagan offers a concluding thought:

It is customary in the world's religions to describe Earth as our mother and the sky as our father. This is true of Uranus and Gaea in Greek mythology, and also among Native Americans, Africans, Polynesians, indeed most of the peoples of the planet Earth. However, the very point of the perinatal experience is that we leave our mothers. We do it first at birth and then again when we set out into the world by ourselves. As painful as these leave-takings are, they are essential for the continuance of the human species.[12]

The idea, then, is simple. Whether expressed in terms of mythology or religion and its accompanying symbolism, humanity has used the idea of birth to suggest fundamental change. It has perhaps no other experience upon which it can draw. In perceiving death, its own final state, it can do no more than recall first things, its primal condition, expressed perhaps in images of paradise and heroic divinity. Literature, the most clearly articulate of the arts, has enshrined this idea throughout centuries of human culture. A literature that consciously endeavours to change the pattern of human life should be supposed to express the essence of the idea more starkly and immediately, even if not in full consciousness of its meaning, than a literature designed to serve the requirements of the *status quo*, the ephemeral and the trivially fashionable. The revolutionary novel, as a phenomenon unique to Russian literature, is to be defined not only by its relevance to Russian circumstances, but also by its seriousness as a genre or tradition of writing that explored the fundamental change revolution entailed for generations of Russians.

The revolutionary situation that gave rise to the Russian revolutionary novel hinged upon the central social and political event in the life of nineteenth-century Russia, the emancipation of the serfs. The younger generation's challenge to an older generation in the name of the natural sciences and nihilism had profound political implications, especially if allied to peasant rebellion, but of greater potential threat to the security of society and the political establishment was the ideal of 'the new man' that sprang into such prominence after the Crimean War. In this connection Russian literature exhibited for the first time its power to respond to social change and influence it in turn. No literature can do more, of course, than act the role of mourner at the death of an old world or be midwife to the birth of a new. Russian literature projected this contrast at once boldly and succinctly, in remarkable and enduring portrayals that gave the Russian novel a place at the head of European writing in the 1860s. This was the beginning of a twofold influence of things Russian on European sensibilities, which gathered momentum in the remaining decades of the century. As Stepniak-Kravchinsky described it,

the principal forces at work in the accomplishment of this decided transformation were undoubtedly the Russian novel on the one hand and the Russian revolutionary movement on the other: the poetry of form and the poetry of action; the fascination of the genius of creation and the genius of self-sacrifice.[13]

It was no accident that in 1860 Turgenev published both his *On the Eve*, the first novel in which he identified the younger generation's aspiration for change, and his final epilogue to *Rudin* in which he revolutionised his hero by representing him as sacrificing his life on the Paris barricades of 1848. It is no accident also that Chernyshevsky, when he came to write his own novel about the younger generation, chose to copy the format of *On the Eve* while paying direct lip service to Turgenev's influence by using the name Kirsanov in his *What is to be Done?* But however keenly aware both writers were of 'the body and pressure of time' in defining the content of their novels, each was similarly conscious of the universal purpose of their fiction. For Turgenev the impulse to change had to be interpreted in the context of a contrast of types, between Hamlet and Don Quixote, the embodiments of 'two rooted, contradictory characteristics of human nature – the two ends of that axis on which it turns'.[14] His exploration of the meaning of the Quixotic type served as the basis for his study of Insarov, his first attempt to portray a revolutionary hero. In the case of Bazarov the Quixotic characteristics – his self-sufficiency, the primacy of science, his repudiation of romanticism and aesthetics – were contained within a tragic vision of man's essential insignificance in the face of nature and eternity. There is no doubt, however, that the power of Turgenev's creation sent shock waves through generations of readers. It still perhaps suggests the true source of liberal *Angst* in that combination of Jacobinism and technocracy which Bazarov seems to personify.[15] The image of man as perfectible through science, or capable of perfecting himself in order to improve society, was new and prophetic of future positive heroes in Russian literature, but it was fundamentally less potent, it seems, than an image of womanhood emancipating itself from a subservient role and attaining freedom and independence. The true potency of the Quixotic ideal is revealed in Turgenev's fiction in Yelena of *On the Eve*, and it is the heroine of Chernyshevsky's novel who achieves the true fundamental change in her life.

That Chernyshevsky aimed to change society and social relationships with his novel cannot be in any doubt. In its political effects, as a fundamental text of Russian socialism, this novel has probably changed the world more than any other. The vision of the socialist future projected by the novel is usually assumed to be the Crystal Palace constructed of aluminium, with conditions of controlled humidity and a surrounding hydraulic civilisation (Part IV, ch. 14:

10). Freedom and equality, based on principles of rational egoism, here reign supreme. But the anthropocentric form of this vision, which appealed more to Chernyshevsky than the institutional or even technological (if we are to judge his novel in terms of characterisation), is epitomised in the deliberate idealism of the heroine, Vera Pavlovna, in her fourth dream. The ideal of emancipated womanhood becomes clearly identified with the creation of myth. The Shining Beauty ('Svetlaya krasavitsa') who appeared first in the third dream now reveals to Vera Pavlovna the progress of womanhood through the ages, from the servile Goddess of Fertility worshipped by the Phoenicians, Astarte, to the Greek Goddess of Love, Aphrodite, and finally the Immaculate Virgin ideal glorified by the Middle Ages. All such divine ideals of womanhood were, of course, representative of one or another form of subjection to male dominance. It is only in the Shining Beauty born of the French Revolution (though originally portrayed in Rousseau's *Nouvelle Héloïse*) that the ideal of womanhood achieves its true status of equality with men and begins to enter into its rightful kingdom of love and equality, the true purpose, in short, of the revolution. The radiance surrounding the Shining Beauty, the Goddess of Equality, is so great that Vera Pavlovna cannot discern her features and asks that the radiance should be reduced.

'Yes,' said the Goddess, 'you wanted to know who I am and you have recognised me. You wanted to know my name, but I have no name other than what I appear to be. My name is her name. You've seen who I am. There is nothing greater than mankind and womankind. I am she who appears before you, who loves and is loved.'

Yes, and Vera Pavlovna saw that it was she herself, she herself but transformed into a goddess. The face of the goddess was her own face, her own living face, whose features were far from perfect, and of which she daily saw more beautiful examples. It was her face illumined with the radiance of love, more beautiful than any of the ideal images created by the sculptors of antiquity and the great masters of the great age of painting, yes, her very own face, but lit by the radiance of love, it was her face, of which there were hundreds of more beautiful examples even in St Petersburg, a city poor in beauty, it was she, more beautiful than the Venus de Milo, more beautiful than all the beauties of the past (Part iv, ch. 14: 5).

For all the false rhetoric of the excerpt, Chernyshevsky's attempt to mythologise the ideal of revolutionary woman must be obvious. As an attempt it implied something of far-reaching importance for the Russian realistic novel. It implied, for example, a clear assumption that the novel had the power to prescribe for the future as well as interpret the present or the past; that the artifices employed in making the fictional seem real were inseparable from the novelists' pretensions to change reality, to proclaim 'what is to be done' under the guise of their fiction; and that to this extent 'realism' as a literary method in the novel had a role in revolutionising both the function of the fiction and the reader's perception of reality. But this is really to say little more than that Chernyshevsky was using the genre of the novel to further utopian political ends and that, in essence, there is little difference between such a purpose and the realistic novel's function from its beginnings in eighteenth-century England as a moral tale designed to show how life may be lived better. How 'revolutionary' was Chernyshevsky's novel? And why should the implications be so far-reaching?

It was revolutionary in the sense that it proclaimed science and reason as the true levers of change, but the fundamental change in humanity was to be achieved by acknowledging the need for 'development' (*razvitiye*) in human beings, by assuming that human beings could liberate themselves from their former subservience to prescribed roles through rational egoism and the co-operative principles of its work ethos, though rigorism and a recasting of their own human images on the mythologising pattern of Vera Pavlovna in her fourth dream. In a socio-political sense, the revolutionism of Chernyshevsky's vision amounted to no more than an assertion that, if you change society (and all that that implies), you change man; but in the psychological, personalist sense, his novel implied that, if literature can project an image of humanity transformed, then the realistic novel invites gods to walk among us, as it were, invites us to see a transcendent humanity developing from the everyday humanity of the real world. Positive heroes, whether Dostoyevskian and Tolstoyan or Soviet, have their literary beginnings in this post-Chernyshevsky concern for a vision of humanity transformed into exemplars, given a pattern of Christian humility to follow in Dostoyevsky, of structured religious doctrine in Tolstoy or of Marx-Engels-Leninism and scientific truth in Soviet literature.

It was also revolutionary in the paradoxical sense that Socialist Realism has been defined as demanding from the writer 'an authentic, historically specific depiction of reality in its revolutionary development. This authenticity and historical specificity in the depiction of reality should be combined with the task of ideologically reshaping and educating the toilers in the spirit of socialism'.[16] Apart from the educative and frankly propagandist elements in this definition offered by Zhdanov in 1934, what clearly stands out is the paradox implicit in the juxtaposition of the two concepts of 'revolution' and 'development'. Chernyshevsky used the term 'development' in a sense that asserted the human potential for change, but in the name of transformation and liberation. 'Revolutionary' as used by Zhdanov implied conformity to the doctrine of Socialist Realism, in the name of the October revolution and leadership by the Communist Party. The evils committed in the name of such ideals have become part of the history of Soviet Russia, but their purpose, it has to be stressed, has always been the elimination of the tragic from life in the name of some higher, collective ideal of future happiness. Referring to Rufus Mathewson's fine study of the positive hero in Russian literature, Geoffrey Hosking has written:

Mathewson has shown how, in the absence of a Marxist tradition of positive heroes, the writers and critics of the twenties and thirties, searching for an officially acceptable aesthetic, found a source for these 'voluntarist' heroes in earlier Russian models: in the criticism of Belinsky, Dobrolyubov and Chernyshevsky, and in the fictional heroes of Chernyshevsky and Gorky. From these prototypes came a hero with his face set towards the future, committed to the destruction of the present fallen world, gripped by his own vision of life as it ought to be, and bound to the closely knit group that shared his vision.[17]

The spirit of collectivism remains the most important attribute of *narodnost'* or *ideynost'* or *partiynost'*, the three pillars upon which the doctrinal edifice of Socialist Realism mainly rests.[18] The emphasis, therefore, in Soviet literature has always fallen on the positive hero's relationship to the collective, his embodiment of its highest aspirations and his dedication to its purpose in ways that absolve him of the taints associated with individualism and purge him usually of all tragic meaning. His 'revolutionary development' has a prescribed, conformist character to it, and he has about him an air of compromise, a sense that his very revolutionism is counterfeit and devalued by the surrogate role attributable to him. He has tended to epitomise the paradox of a literature committed to revolutionary change that is essentially not in control of its destiny.

The Russian revolutionary novel has asserted something more fundamental than this. By definition it is of course concerned with revolution. This means that it has been concerned with describing the way in which human beings and their relationships can be fundamentally changed; it has been concerned with revolutionary politics, with the overthrow of one form of government and its replacement by other forms; it has been concerned with describing revolutionary experience, with the adjustment to new beginnings in social and/or political relationships as a result of revolution; and it has been concerned with endeavouring to match the trauma of revolution by revolutionising itself. As a genre it has been concerned with some or all of these things in varying degrees. Even though there are undeniable historical reasons why such a genre or tradition of writing in the novel should be so prominent in Russian and Soviet literature, the uniquely novelistic problems associated with it have a general bearing on the nature of realism in literature and must in part account for the genre's vitality as the principal literary vehicle of protest and dissent.

Committed as it obviously must be to the social and political realities of life, the revolutionary novel asserts the right of literature to make an independent, unorthodox, free judgement of social and political reality in the name of revolutionary change. To this extent it has become exceedingly vulnerable to censorship and repression. Being about fundamental change, the revolutionary novel in its Russian and Soviet context has been as little concerned with justifying the existing state of things as it has been concerned with emphasising the ephemeral. In its finest examples, its realism has been anticipatory, that is to say, it has anticipated a revolutionised human reality and subsumed by its realism a transforming role. The transformation may have religious parallels and draw on religious imagery, but it is irreligious and anthropocentric in its essentials. It is about the experience of death–birth. In this, it strives to encompass and explore the first and last things of human experience, the most fundamental of the changes to which humanity is heir.

A list of the most prominent authors in the history of the Russian revolutionary novel will contain such a diversity of names, of such different social and political attitudes and origins, that a concern with revolution would seem to be all they have in common. At a conservative estimate the list would comprise Turgenev, Cherny-shevsky, Stepniak-Kravchinsky, Gorky, Savinkov, Bely, Zazubrin, Pilnyak, Libedinsky, Vsevolod Ivanov, Malyshkin, Lavrenyov, Sera-fimovich, Leonov, Furmanov, Zamyatin, Fedin, Veresaev, Bulgakov, Olesha, Fadeyev, Sholokhov, Aleksey Tolstoy and Pasternak. If it be assumed that all these authors wrote novels about revolution or revolutionary manifestations in their time because they not only observed but also hoped, because they recognised the need for change, because revolution as a new beginning seemed to them the only real promise for the future, then what we appear to confront here is a tradition of writing in the novel governed by common assumptions of purposefulness and by a vision of life as essentially amenable to change. Theirs were novels seriously concerned about the purpose of life and the way revolution affected it. They offered in each case secular visions of life in which the revolutionary experience or revolutionary aspiration is represented, at its ultimate point, as challenging death or being the equivalent of regeneration and rebirth.

Chernyshevsky's utopian vision of the socialist future and his idealisation of Vera Pavlovna as a modern goddess of equality suggest a process of mythologising that owes much to religious precedent. The religious connection is plainly apparent in Stepniak-Kravchinsky's picture of Russian revolutionaries in *The Career of a Nihilist*. 'I wanted to show', he declared in the preface to his novel, 'in the full light of fiction the inmost heart and soul of those humanitarian enthusiasts, with whom devotion to a cause has attained to the fervour of a religion.' The revolutionary word was declared to have, in the case of the novel's hero, Andrey Kojukhov, 'the force to overturn and remould the human soul'. Such religious imagery is repeated and greatly extended in its relevance and significance in the most important instance of the revolutionary novel in pre-revolutionary Russian literature, Gorky's famous novel *Mother*.

The principal emphasis in Gorky's novel, as in Chernyshevsky's, falls on the image of womanhood remade through the discovery of a new revolutionary idea. Nilovna's commitment to socialism was presented as a species of God-building in which the gospel of socialism developed, like Old Testament into New Testament, into a form of salvationism designed to save the soul of mankind. Pavel Vlasov may exhort mankind to follow socialism, but the fundamental change is seen to occur in Nilovna herself. She declares: 'It's just as if a new God had been born for mankind!' Socialism is the new truth that the mother finally embraces, and she embraces it in terms of religious salvation when she announces to the people at the railway station in the novel's conclusion:

'In order to change this life, in order to free all the people, to raise them from the dead, as I have been raised, some persons have already come who have in secret seen the truth in life...'[19]

The injunctions that follow are manifestly biblical in the references to Pavel Vlasov's revolutionary word:

'It is fearless, and if necessary it goes even against itself to meet the truth. It goes to you, working people, incorruptible, wise, fearless. Receive it with an open heart, feed on it; it will give you the power to understand everything, to fight against everything for the truth, for the freedom of mankind. Receive it, believe it, go with it towards the happiness of all people, to a new life with great joy!...'

Motherhood in this interpretation is representative of the potency of the revolutionary ideal as a fundamentally transforming, even resurrecting, force in life. The propagandist, extraliterary purpose of Gorky's novel no doubt made it, as he admitted, 'long, boring and carelessly written',[20] but the focus of realism in the Russian novel had always been towards such purposefulness, and central to it in this case is the explicit equation of revolution with the mother's role. In Bely's *Petersburg* the revolutionising process deliberately fragments the realism of the novel, explodes it, incorporating into its complex symbolism the fissionable contraries of Russian historical experience, of East versus West, Turanian atavism versus Kantian rationalism, the symmetrical statehood of the city versus the anarchic fragmentation of the islands, generation versus generation, the Bronze Horseman versus the insidiously ticking bomb. Revolution as such has no symbolic regenerative power ascribed to it in Bely's novel. Arguably a class-based fear of political upheaval dictated in his case that revolution should be symbolically equated with sterility, for the fundamental change, anthroposophically speaking, must occur in the spirit of man.

Gorky's *Mother* and Bely's *Petersburg* establish a pattern of opposites in the Russian revolutionary novel, which can be seen to emerge through the otherwise apparently formless and disparate examples of the novel in early Soviet literature. The pattern is at best faint, but its presence is the thread of Ariadne by which the pre-revolutionary novel and the post-revolutionary novel are joined and which, in the final estimate, reveals both the vitality of the genre, of the novel as a literary form, and its significance as a continuing tradition of writing in Russian and Soviet literature. For the earliest revolutionary novels of the Soviet period display all the fragmentation, experimentalism and novelty of Bely's work, but to such an advanced degree that it is frequently hard to describe this or that work as a novel. The experience of revolution so revolutionised the genre that it literally fragmented it into the chiaroscuro of Pilnyak's *The Naked Year*, the patchworks of Vsevolod Ivanov's *Coloured Winds* and *Sky-blue Sands*, the quasi-medieval monumentalism of Malyshkin's *Fall of Dair* and the raciness of Lavrenyov's *The Wind*, not to mention such obviously fragmentary forms as those created by Nikitin, Budantsev, Vesyoly and Babel (though his *Red Cavalry* cannot be described as a novel). Revolution as instinctive, biological and bloody in human terms is matched by metaphors of natural disaster, violent winds and ferocious cold or heat, in which all individual judgement is suspended. The novelty of the first revolutionary novels expressed itself most clearly in a dehumanising, even reifying, portrayal of humanity, on a pattern already evident from Gorky's and Bely's works, but motivated not so much by capitalist society as by the emergence of primitive instinct in man himself. Revolution was consequently violent, anarchic, liberating in its elementalism, and if, in such early novels as Zazubrin's *Two Worlds* or Libedinsky's *One Week*, it appeared to have political significance, the sheer violence of the events described tended to dwarf and diminish the political issues.

The pattern of opposites is not distinguishable in these early works, but with the start of the mythmaking process the notion of revolution as the death–birth of a world assumed a special meaning. Serafimovich's *The Iron Flood* and Furmanov's *Chapayev*, both obvious instances of mythmaking, whether of the hero-mass or the revolutionary civil-war commander, emphasised revolution as regeneration, the forging, in the first case, of the iron flood into 'a single, inhumanly enormous heart' under Kozhukh's guidance and, in the second case, of Furmanov-Klichkov's identity as a human being, while simultaneously creating the myth of Chapayev. If these novels emphasise through their central figures the regenerative force of revolution, then novels that explore the dilemma of the post-revolutionary intelligentsia – Fedin's *Cities and Years*, Veresaev's *The Deadlock* and Bulgakov's *The White Guard* – clearly expose in their central characters the sterility of the intelligentsia's revolutionism. The same may be said of Leonov's exploration of the heroic myth in *The Badgers*. In these cases, the revolution as a fundamental change implied death rather than rebirth, the separation from the parent or the precipitation into an alien world and a consequent doomed surrender to the womb-like retreat of the badger-hole (of Leonov's novel), the 'solid ring' (as Fedin called it) that metaphorically enclosed Andrey Startsov of *Cities and Years*, the trap that closes on Katya in *The Deadlock*. Only in Bulgakov's *The White Guard* does the miracle apparently occur that literally raises Aleksey Turbin from the dead and invokes the idea of revolution as spiritual renewal.

The pattern of opposites emerges more clearly in the most mature of the revolutionary novels of the early Soviet period, in Fadeyev's *The Rout*, Olesha's *Envy* and, among others, in Kolokolov's *Honey and Blood*. The issues are presented in these novels as dialectical, as contrasts, say, between Mechik and Morozka in Fadeyev's novel, which are resolved at a higher level in Levinson, or as a contrast between the two brothers in *Envy*, resolved in the implication that the revolution needs a union of the zealously practical and the extravagantly visionary. The statement of the issues receives clear expression in the opposed attitudes of Dr Dolgov and the Chekist Nakatov in Kolokolov's *Honey and Blood*. In each case the fundamentally regenerating principle of the revolution is symbolised by the assumption of a parent–child relationship that subsumes salvation, reconciliation, healing as its purpose; whereas the death of the old is signalled by egoism, sterility, indifference and pleas for an outworn 'humanity'. But in none of these works is the dilemma of revolution as a fundamental change explored as fully or exhaustively as it is in the revolutionary epic novel, particularly in Sholokhov's *Quiet Flows the Don*.

Gorky's portrayal of Klim Samgin demonstrates the sterile and ultimately futile character of intelligentsia revolutionism, just as Aleksey Tolstoy's *The Road to Calvary*, while grandiosely proclaiming the ideal of the revolution as the birth of a new man, so romanticises its characters and its subject that it seems to turn the Russian intelligentsia into so many counters on the board-game of history. The profound and agonising interaction of public and private, historical and subjective factors in the characterising of Grigory Melekhov sets in relief the real personal dilemma posed by revolution and civil war. It emphasises both the tragedy of Cossack separatism and the tragedy of Grigory's own separateness, both the tragedy of his isolation from the Cossack world and his tragic love for Aksinya.

For Grigory the death of the past involves his deliberate renunciation of the Cossack militancy to which he was heir, his repudiation of his past rootless life and a return at springtime to his native Tatarsky where he is reunited with his small son. His renewal of his parental role is symbolic of his possible rebirth, but of course the open-ended form of conclusion invites suggestions of 'optimistic tragedy' or of authorial refusal to submit to official Stalinist pressures to make his hero end up as a communist. However inadvertently, Sholokhov here underscores the right of historical fiction to establish its own priorities in interpreting the past. His hero survives and in that survival he is witness to his own independence as a human being.

Such independence of character becomes a rare and dissident feature in Soviet literature after 1934. The revolutionary who has not been transformed for the better by revolution becomes an impossible paradox in Soviet fiction, just as the revolutionary epic has become a branch of historical fiction in Soviet literature that paradoxically enjoys the self-sustaining pseudo-contemporary appeal of any literature that celebrates the existence of the Soviet state. Ostrovsky's *How the Steel was Tempered* established an orthodox Soviet vision of a younger generation ready to devote itself totally to the cause of building communism and thereby achieve a form of rebirth. Other novelists explored aspects of the dilemma of commitment, but Konstantin Fedin's 'dilogy' of *Early Joys* and *No Ordinary Summer* was the only major literary work of the 1940s to attempt to deal with the complex issues of choice thrown up by revolution and did so in a whitewashing Stalinist fashion. No novels of the Stalin period contributed to that enlargement of understanding which Sholokhov's epic novel achieved so majestically in the portrayal of Grigory Melekhov. But certain works of the Stalin period can be seen to have paved the way for that masterly and courageous reappraisal of the October revolution and its consequences which Pasternak was to offer in his masterpiece.

The scope of the revolutionary epic novel as a judgement on Russian and Soviet life in the first half of this century has only been fully demonstrated in *Doctor Zhivago*. As a novel it does, in Pasternak's own words, 'recreate whole segments of life' or call to mind 'some moving entireness' in several senses.[21] It is a revolutionary novel, for instance, in its unique striving, as no other writer before Pasternak had done, to describe the experience of revolutionary change as one involving a whole life-span. Its elaborate plotting illustrates the scale of the revolution; and it reinterprets history both through Zhivago's own ponderings on the meaning of his experiences and through the notion that history is, strictly speaking, without causality, invisible, not made by anyone, 'a moving entireness'. Moreover, it offers a treatment of revolution as purposefully centred in man himself, in Zhivago and Lara and Antipov-Strelnikov, and representative in their fates not only of Pasternak's affirmation, as Henry Gifford has put it, 'that poetry and life, art and history, mean most in their interplay'[22] but also of an ideal, obviously Christian in its example, though universal in its meaning, which has its source in Zhivago's belief that life is a principle of self-renewal and that art, in its turn, 'is always meditating on death and...thereby creating life'.

Choice is the central problem in Zhivago's attitude to revolution. Until he is faced by the likelihood, in historical as well as personal terms, that Russia is destined to become the first kingdom of socialism, he is not made to confront the necessity of choice, but once that likelihood is acknowledged he predicts the shock of it and the outcome: that his life will be cut in half. The novel, though divided into two parts, expresses this division in Zhivago's life through chapter 10, from which he is wholly absent. It marks the break in the chronological unity of Zhivago's experience, as it also marks a break in the historical chronology of the fiction. It sets in relief the tragedy and the paradox of Zhivago's issue of choice, but it also illuminates the whole meaning of the novel. It demonstrates that the purpose of Zhivago's life, as of the novel that is his memorial, is exactly to bear witness, as Pasternak insisted, or to be 'the living memory of a nation',[23] as Solzhenitsyn described the purpose of literature in his Nobel speech. In this respect *Doctor Zhivago* has assumed the noblest purposes of a dissident literature.

Choice, though, is of the essence in defining what for Zhivago, as for his Uncle Kolya (Vedenyapin), are the twin components of modern man – 'without them he is inconceivable – the ideas of free personality and of life regarded as sacrifice' (ch. 1, 5). In countless ways Zhivago epitomises these twin ideas in his life. They are most aptly symbolised in that identity between Hamlet and Christ which forms the origin and end of his life's journey in poetry. In one sense, orphaned as he is in childhood, Zhivago's choices may be said to be dictated by the 'moving entireness' of the revolutionary period; for him the revolution may seem to be alienating and destructive. But in another sense, through the providential alignment of his fate with that other world to which Lara belongs, he is privileged to experience in his own life her transforming love and inspiration – a process, incidentally, that is directly associated with the revolutionary events of his time. He chooses Lara's love and in that demonstrates his own free personality. Just as art, in his own definition, is a particle outweighing all other ingredients in a work, so the freedom he enjoys in Lara's love outweighs all else in his life and becomes the poetry that, like some alchemical agency, transforms his vision of himself and Pasternak's vision of man. The metaphor of death–birth as one that ultimately defines the fundamental change implied by revolution is made explicit in the last Zhivago poem. Christ's words on the resemblance of the procession of the ages to a parable appear to receive their fullest endorsement in the story of Zhivago's life, and that parable may, as one feels it did not only in Judea but in Russia also, burst into flame. In the name of its awful majesty the Son of God will go down willingly into the grave, will die and will rise again on the third day. And from that day forth He will judge the procession of the ages as they appear successively out of the darkness like river barges to receive the illumination of His word:

> Ты видишь, ход веков подобен притче
> И может загореться на ходу.
> Во имя страшного ее величия
> Я в добровольных муках в гроб сойду.
>
> Я в гроб сойду и в третий день восстану,
> И, как сплавляют по реке плоты,
> Ко мне на суд, как баржи каравана,
> Столетья поплывут из темноты.

Similarly, Zhivago's word, ignited by the revolution in his own times, will be a parable surmounting his own death and the death of his world.

The Christian ideal of a mankind new-born in the image of its creator certainly found a place in the vision of man that we receive from nineteenth-century Russian literature. It is central to the image of man that we find in Tolstoy and Dostoyevsky. Tolstoy's concern, for instance, for a reconciliation between all men, whether deriving from the little green stick of his boyhood dreams, his Rousseauism or his growing religious convictions, found its first real fictional embodiment in Pierre Bezukhov's realisation that 'life is God' and

the conviction ensuing from it that Russian society must be based
on a principle of 'active good'. Dostoyevsky similarly assumed that
God's presence was immanent, if not actual, in Russian life and in
repeated characterisations offered us representatives of the divine in
human semblance. His novels were concerned not with the 'development' of human beings but with the ferocity of their conflicts, both
internal and in confrontation. Raskolnikov confronted by the choice
of Sonya and Svidrigaylov, a nineteenth-century Everyman challenged by the demon of scientific free will and the archangel of
Christian love, has his demonic arrogance hugely magnified and
tested in the dramatic psychological exploration of his crime.
Myshkin's confrontation with a capitalist St Petersburg may rely on
an appeal to the transfiguring power of beauty and the ideal of a
Russian Christ, but it cannot finally overcome the forces of sectarian
darkness and nihilism threatening Russian life. No more than the
quasi-Populist idealism of Stepan Trofimovich Verkhovensky can
compensate for the nihilist ideas that have taken possession of the
Russian intelligentsia through Nikolay Stravrogin, his disciples
Kirillov and Shatov, or the most vividly created of all Dostoyevsky's
nihilist figures, Pyotr Verkhovensky. No Christian ideal can save
Anna Karenina in Tolstoy's judgement of her, though the Christian
bases of salvation are clearly posited as first principles in his
portrayal of Konstantin Levin's discovery of God. Christian ideals
similarly guide Alyosha Karamazov in his challenge to Ivan's
assertion of mankind's total liberation from the constraints of
morality in the name of free will. The Christian model was always
the ideal that Dostoyevsky and Tolstoy opposed to the revolutionism
and materialism of their times, though it was a model adapted to suit
their particular purposes. The Dostoyevskian 'new man', like the
Tolstoyan, may have been conceived as a denial of Chernyshevsky's
vision of man, but it was a vision deriving quite as much from the
idea that humanity *could* change. In their view, the potential for
development in mankind may have been anti-revolutionary and
essentially non-political, but it challenged social norms while attri-
buting prior importance to ethical standards; it presupposed divine
guidance of human endeavour and the hope of ultimate salvation.

   Their deep commitment to a vision of humanity regenerated by
Christian example led Dostoyevsky and Tolstoy to portray humanity's
regeneration in terms of a challenge to death, but in ways that
suggested that the force of divine love or religious faith were the only

guarantees of eternal life. Andrey Bolkonsky's death in *War and Peace* was accompanied by a vision of God as an eternal source of love. The breath of corruption so scandalously surrounding the death of Zosima in *The Brothers Karamazov* evaporated quickly in the re-enactment of the faith of the first miracle at Cana in Galilee. These instances of death in Dostoyevsky and Tolstoy admit of a redemptive principle, but the faithless, godless deaths by suicide of Svidrigaylov, Stavrogin, Anna Karenina and Smerdyakov are challenging reminders that mankind has a duty to exercise the gift of choice. The Dostoyevskian and Tolstoyan visions of man enforce the notion that biblical injunctions have to be accepted. If they are not, the human condition is at the mercy of the world's evil.

In the Russian revolutionary novel the Christian ideal is present from beginning to end, but secularised and so altered from its biblical model as to seem quite unlike it. Though the ideal of 'the new man' in the context of the Russian revolutionary novel must be regarded as secular, essentially non-religious and even anti-religious in its impulse, the anthropocentric – or scientific – image of modern man that it projects owes something to Christian example. The twin ideas of free personality and life as sacrifice acknowledge the precedent. On the other hand, it is the nature of the revolutionary novel to dispense with precedents, to pass free and independently objective judgements on those phenomena which it identifies as revolutionary. In this sense, the Russian revolutionary novel, from its beginning to its end, has sought to project its own objectified, independent image of a liberated, revolutionised humanity. The masterpieces at the beginning and the conclusion of its evolution exemplify the genre's distinction as a 'judgment', in Fielding's sense, on the revolutionary image of man.

Turgenev's portrait of Bazarov was conceived and executed in this spirit. His was the free personality representative of a mankind liberated by science, just as his destiny was to be that of a life sacrificed in the name of a vision of human perfectibility. What sustains this secular literary vision of 'the new man', or of modern man, from Turgenev's Bazarov through to Pasternak's Zhivago and to our own age, is that it is posed in each case in basically the same terms, as a vision of mankind's transformed and transforming role as healer. The vision of man as miracle-worker, as divinely ordained to be lord of creation, is secularised in the ideal of the doctor trained to put his gift of life at the service of a sick world. More than this, each is seen to diagnose his own mortality, to know the inevitable consequences of typhus infection or to predict what will happen to a nervous system violated by 'a life of constant, systematic duplicity'. Each cherishes his own freedom while acknowledging his superfluity in life, each recognises the Hamlet in himself while proclaiming his independence of establishments and institutions. Each by his very independence of spirit repudiates collectivism as an ideal and is in revolt against the norms of his time. Despite the contrast between Bazarov's materialism and anti-aestheticism, on the one hand, and Zhivago's spirituality and poetic vocation, on the other, despite Bazarov's pugnacity and Zhivago's readiness to accept, each in his death poses a challenge to the future and has as memorial an ideal of eternal reconciliation and life everlasting. Within the chronological limits defined by *Fathers and Children* and *Doctor Zhivago* many types of revolutionary hero are to be encountered in the Russian novel, but none poses a secular challenge to death so powerfully as do Bazarov and Zhivago, none exhibits as fully as they do the tragedy of life as sacrifice to secular ideals of radical or revolutionary change, and none epitomises as well as they do the attempt of literature to pass its own independent judgement on the revolutionary image of man. In this respect, *Fathers and Children* and *Doctor Zhivago* can be regarded as offering first and last words on a phenomenon unique to Russian literature and vital to the history of the Russian novel between 1860 and 1960, that of the Russian revolutionary novel.

Notes

1. *Egoistic nihilism and revolutionary nihilism*

1 The expression – *Zamechatel'noye desyatiletiye* – was coined by P. V. Annenkov, whose recollections of the decade 1838–48 provide one of the most vivid and expressive sources for our understanding of its ideas and personalities. See P. V. Annenkov, *Literaturniye vospominaniya* (Goslitizdat, 1960), pp. 135–374.

2 Alexander Herzen, *From the Other Shore*, translated from the Russian by Moura Budberg, with an introduction by Isaiah Berlin (O.U.P., 1979), p. 11.

3 Details of the characters and an outline of the three parts of the projected novel have survived, but Turgenev apparently destroyed his first draft of the first part after receiving adverse criticism from some of his friends. See I. S. Turgenev, *Polnoye sobraniye sochineniy*, vol. VI (M.–L., 1963), pp. 379, 594.

4 For an enlightening discussion of the many issues involved in the emergence of the 'positive' hero at this stage in the evolution of Russian literature, see Part I of Rufus W. Mathewson, Jr, *The Positive Hero in Russian Literature*, 2nd ed. (Stanford U.P., 1975).

5 N. A. Dobrolyubov, *Russkiye klassiki* (M., 1970), p. 211.

6 The influence of *On the Eve* on Chernyshevsky's *What is to be Done?* is probably greater than *Fathers and Children* (despite Chernyshevsky's use of the surname Kirsanov). Yelena Stakhova was obviously a model for Vera Pavlovna, in part as a type, in part as a heroine enjoying a central role, while the two suitors Shubin and Bersenev are matched by the two 'husbands' Lopukhov and Kirsanov and the revolutionary hero Insarov is matched by the Russian revolutionary hero Rakhmetov.

7 H. T. Buckle, *History of Civilization in England*, 2nd ed., vol. I (London, 1858), p. 840.

8 *Ibid.* p. 836.

9 A. I. Gertsen (A. I. Herzen), *Sobraniye sochineniy v 30 tomakh* (M., 1954–66), vol. XVII, 1, p. 80.

10 I. S. Turgenev, *Pis'ma*, vol. IV (M.–L., 1962), p. 116.

11 Turgenev, *Poln. sobr. soch.*, vol. XIV (M.–L., 1967), p. 97. All other quotations from his *Reminiscences* are taken from this source.

12 Turgenev refers to him as 'D.', which has been taken to mean Dmitriyev. For a description of this and other possible prototypes (none

of them, however, at any time resident in the Isle of Wight), see
P. G. Pustovoyt, *Roman I. S. Turgeneva 'Ottsy i deti' i ideynaya bor'ba
60-ykh godov XIX veka* (M., 1964), pp. 80–110.

13 The reference may be to N. Ya. Rostovtsev (1831–97), or it may well
have been to his close friend Pavel Annenkov, whose recollections are
a principal source of our knowledge of Turgenev's Ventnor holiday.

14 The review was of Nathaniel Hawthorne's *A Wonder Book*.

15 One source for this assumption is Turgenev's alleged statement: 'I was
once out for a walk and thinking about death...Immediately there rose
before me the picture of a dying man. This was Bazarov. The scene
produced a strong impression on me and as a consequence the other
characters and the action itself began to take form in my mind'
(Hjalmar Boyesen, 'A visit to Tourguéneff', *The Galaxy*, 17 (1874),
456–66). Quoted from the Russian in 'K biografii I. S. Turgeneva',
Minuvshiye gody (1908), no. 8, p. 70. See also Richard Freeborn,
Turgenev, The Novelist's Novelist (Greenwood Press, 1978), p. 69.

16 See in particular E. L. Rudnitskaya, *N. P. Ogaryov v russkom revolyu-
tsionnom dvizhenii* (M., 1969). No doubt originating in the ideas of
Babeuf, Ogaryov's organisational ideas may have influenced Lenin, as
S. V. Utechin has suggested. See in particular his edition of Lenin's
What is to be Done? (O.U.P., 1963).

17 The suggestion was made by M. Nechkina when the Prague materials
of Herzen and Ogaryov were first published in 1953. See her 'Novyye
materialy o revolyutsionnoy situatsii v Rossii (1859–61 gg.)', *Literaturnoye nasledstvo*, vol. LXI (M., 1953), pp. 459–522.

18 This is the term used by Ya. I. Linkov to describe the principal
revolutionary object of Ogaryov's planning. See his *Revolyutsionnaya
bor'ba A. I. Gertsena i N. P. Ogaryova i taynoye obshchestvo 'Zemlya
i volya' 1860-kh godov* (M., 1964), p. 57.

19 See Herzen's corrections to his *Letters to an Old Comrade* in which
'apostoly nam nuzhny, a ne...sapery razrusheniya' is changed to
'apostoly nam nuzhny prezhde...saperov razrusheniya' (Gertsen
(Herzen), *Sobr. soch.* vol. XX, pp. 719, 513; quoted from *Voprosy
literatury*, 3 (1977), 274).

20 N. P. Ogaryov, 'Pis'ma k sootchestvenniku', *Kolokol* (1 August 1860).
See my article 'Turgenev at Ventnor', *The Slavonic and East European
Review*, 51 (July 1973), for a fuller discussion of these and other
issues.

21 Turgenev, *Poln. sobr. soch.*, vol. XV (M.–L., 1968), pp. 245–52.

22 *Ibid.* p. 247.

23 Patrick Waddington suggests as further reasons for Turgenev's interest
in education at this time his concern for his daughter's education and
the possibility that while in Ventnor he may have encountered Elizabeth
Missing Sewell, 'one of the best English educationalists of the nineteenth
century' (*Turgenev and England* (London, 1980), p. 120; chs. 6 and 7

of Professor Waddington's book contain an unsurpassed account of Turgenev's stay in Ventnor).

24 Turgenev, *Pis'ma*, vol. IV, p. 380.

25 For a fuller discussion of the formal and other aspects of the novel, see my *Turgenev, The Novelist's Novelist*. A reading that emphasises the 'family' aspect of the novel is to be found in Victor Ripp, *Turgenev's Russia* (Cornell U.P., 1980).

26 Turgenev asserted as much in his letter to Sluchevsky (*Pis'ma*, vol. IV, p. 381).

27 Turgenev, *Poln. sobr. soch.*, vol. XIV, pp. 100–2.

28 *Pis'ma*, vol. IV, p. 380.

29 Bazarov's insistence on his insignificance echoes Pascal almost word for word. The soliloquy beginning: 'The little space I occupy...' (ch. 26) appears to have its – unacknowledged – source in *Pensées* 68: 'When I consider the brief span of my life...' (Pascal, *Pensées*, trans. A. J. Krailsheimer (Penguin Classics, 1972), p. 48). For a comprehensive examination of the philosophical problems and sources in the novel, see A. Batyuto, *Turgenev-romanist* (L., 1972), pp. 38–165.

30 To Isaiah Berlin, for instance, Bazarov in the end exemplifies a new Jacobinism: 'Turgenev may have loved Bazarov; he certainly trembled before him. He understood, and to a degree sympathized with, the case presented by the new Jacobins, but he could not bear to think what their feet would trample' (Isaiah Berlin, *Fathers and children* (O.U.P., 1972), p. 58). Soviet scholarship on Bazarov is inclined to be more cautious. Since the discovery of Annenkov's letter to Turgenev (see V. Arkhipov, 'K tvorcheskoy istorii romana I. S. Turgeneva "Ottsy i deti"', *Russkaya literatura*, 1 (1958)) and the publication of the Paris manuscript of the novel (see A. I. Batyuto, 'Parizhskaya rukopis' romana "Ottsi i deti"', *Russkaya literatura*, 4 (1961)) Soviet criticism has tended to play down the more extreme revolutionary aspects of Bazarov. For a sober, informed assessment, see Pustovoyt, *Roman I. S. Turgeneva*.

31 'Bazarov needs no one, fears no one, loves no one and, consequently, spares no one' (D. I. Pisarev, 'Bazarov' in *Bazarov. Realisty* (M., 1974), p. 13).

32 *Pis'ma*, vol. IV, p. 381.

33 *Pis'ma*, vol. II (1961), pp. 300–1. Chernyshevsky later modified his ideas somewhat.

34 The novel was published in nos. 3, 4 and 5 of *The Contemporary* for 1863. The journal had been banned for eight months from June of the previous year.

35 *Voprosy literatury*, 7 (1957), 132. V. I. Lenin (1870–1924) would have been seventeen in 1887 when his elder brother was executed for being implicated in an attempt to assassinate Alexander III.

36 *Chto delat'?* (M., 1957), Part II, ch. 8; Part III, ch. 2.

37 Her 'underground' is not a *podpol'ye*, as is Dostoyevsky's, but a *podval*

('cellar'), but no doubt Dostoyevsky read as far as her first dream (Part II, ch. 12) and created his own 'underground man' (*Notes from the Underground* (*Zapiski iz podpol'ya*) (1864)) at least in part as a consequence.

38 '...the absence of movement is the absence of work, because work is to be regarded in its anthropological analysis as the fundamental form of movement, providing a basis and a content for all other forms' (Part III, ch. 3).

39 As a sceptical pre-revolutionary commentator put it: 'Chernyshevsky's heroes jump over moral contradiction and social incongruities like circus riders clearing hurdles' (K. F. Golovin-Orlovsky, *Russkiy roman i russkoye obshchestvo*, 3rd ed. (Spb., n.d.), p. 191).

40 *Chto delat'?*, Part III, ch. 31. Chernyshevsky's claim, made here and elsewhere in his novel, that he had personally known the people he describes, has led to a search for possible prototypes. The most likely candidate for Rakhmetov was a certain Pavel Alexandrovich Bakhmetev who sold his Saratov estate to his uncle and in 1857 emigrated. Before leaving Russia he had a meeting with Chernyshevsky, whom he had known earlier in Saratov, Chernyshevsky's birthplace. In London Bakhmetev met Herzen and transferred to him 20,000 francs for use on revolutionary propaganda. This money formed the basic capital of a 'common fund' that Herzen announced on 15 May 1862 in *The Bell*. There is some hearsay evidence to support the view that Bakhmetev was a model for Rakhmetov, but as one commentator has put it: 'Bakhmetev...served as a model for Rakhmetov only in part. Creating in Rakhmetov the image of a revolutionary activist, Chernyshevsky combined in him different elements of revolutionary feeling which had manifested themselves variously in different people' (A. P. Skaftymov, *Stat'i o russkoy literature* (Saratov, 1958), p. 173). The assumption that Rakhmetov is a composite figure simply emphasises the artificiality of his portrait.

41 For a succinct account, excellently annotated, of the oft-told tale of Russian revolutionary manifestations in the period, see James H. Billington, *Fire in the Minds of Men* (London, 1980), ch. 14.

42 Many novels followed in the wake of Turgenev's *Virgin Soil* in offering multi-faceted studies of Populism. For example, N. N. Zlatovratsky's *Hearts of Gold* (*Zolotyye serdtsa*) (1877–8) and *The Foundations* (*Ustoi*) (1878–82), N. A. Arnol'di's *Vasilisa* (1879), K. M. Stanyukovich's *Two Brothers* (*Dva Brata*) (1880) and other novels by Kovalevskaya, Zasodimsky, Ertel' and Dmitriyeva. For an assessment of Zlatovratsky's work, see R. Wortman, *The Crisis of Russian Populism* (C.U.P., 1967), ch. 4. For a discussion of Turgenev's influence on these novelists, see L. N. Nazarova, *Turgenev i russkaya literatura kontsa XIX – nachala XXv* (L., 1979), pp. 151–92.

43 Alexander Solzhenitsyn, *Sobraniye sochineniy v 6 tomakh*, 2nd ed., vol. VI (Frankfurt, 1973), p. 359.

44 These novels are expertly examined in Charles A. Moser, *Antinihilism in the Russian Novel of the 1860s* (The Hague, 1964).

45 V. A. Sleptsov (1836–78), of noble family, earned a reputation for himself as the author of sketches and stories drawn from peasant life, several of which, especially 'The Foster-Child' ('Pitomka'), are works of considerable power. Closely associated with *The Contemporary*, and responsible for organising one of the communes that sprang up in the wake of Chernyshevsky's novel, he was arrested in 1866 after Karakozov's attempt to assassinate the Tsar and imprisoned – an experience that gravely impaired his health. For a sympathetic appraisal of his hero Ryazanov, see William C. Brumfield, 'Bazarov and Rjazanov: The Romantic Archetype in Russian Nihilism', *Slavic and East European Journal*, 21, 4 (1977), 495–505.

46 I. V. Omulevsky (1836–83), born in Petropavlovsk-on-Kamchatka; he was brought up and educated in Irkutsk but went to St Petersburg for his higher education, where he soon began to associate with radicals of the younger generation and started publishing poetry on civic themes in *The Contemporary*. Arrested in 1873 after publishing part of a second novel, he began to experience great difficulty in finding work and eventually died in St Petersburg penniless and alone. ·

47 S. M. Kravchinsky, who took the pseudonym Stepniak for his published work as a mark of his own origins in the steppelands, was born in Poltava in 1851, became associated with the Populists, participated in the 'going to the people' (*khozhdeniye v narod*) of 1874, later in the 1870s became associated with the underground and terrorist activity of 'Land and Freedom' and was then forced to emigrate to England where he actively promoted an interest in the Russian struggle for freedom through his published works (*Underground Russia, The Russian Peasantry*, etc.) and through such organisations as the English Society of Friends of Russian Freedom. His accidental death late in 1895 was oddly consonant with his bizarre reputation as a terrorist revolutionary. He achieved spectacular notoriety in 1878 when he stabbed the Chief of Gendarmes Adjutant-General Mesentsev to death while the latter was out walking in the centre of St Petersburg. The assassination was undertaken as an act of revenge for the shooting of I. M. Kovalsky, an Odessa student, who had offered armed resistance to police arrest. In his pamphlet 'A Death for a Death' Stepniak claimed that he was not acting against the government as such but only against government interference in the rightful struggle of the people (*narod*) against the hated bourgeoisie. For a detailed study of his life and work, see Evgeniya Taratuta, *S. M. Stepnyak-Kravchinsky, revolyutsioner i pisatel'* (M., 1973). For other studies of Stepniak, see T. P. Maevskaya, *Slovo i podvig: zhizn' i tvorchestvo S. M. Stepnyaka-Kravchinskogo* (Kiev, 1968); N. I. Prutskov, *Russkaya literatura XIX veka i revolyutsionnaya Rossiya* (L., 1971), pp. 135–44.

48 As Stepniak pointed out in a letter of 14 April 1890 to Robert Spence

Watson (in the very same month that the English Society of Friends of Russian Freedom was founded), he considered that his novel 'could do more for our cause' than serious scientific works. For a survey history of the English society, see Barry Hollingsworth, 'The Society of Friends of Russian Freedom', *Oxford Slavonic Papers*, 3 (1970), 45–64.

49 *The Star* (Friday, 6 December 1889). George Bernard Shaw, music critic of the newspaper and personal friend of Stepniak, had wanted to review the novel, but the review was in fact the work of Massingham, assistant editor of *The Star*. Several reviews appeared in other parts of the British press – none, however, as enthusiastic as the review in *The Star* – and in some cases fears were expressed that the novel might encourage revolutionary nihilism in its English readers.

50 Taratuta, *S. M. Stepnyak-Kravchinsky*, p. 505. *Andrey Kozhukhov* was the title given to the Russian translation of the novel.

51 *The Star* review concluded by declaring:
'No words that were ever written in print are too bad to describe the loathsome cancer in European life which calls itself the Russian government...The Tsar has been impeached before Europe; and there is and can be no answer to the impeachment. The afflicting part of the business is – and Stepniak's novel entirely confirms the impression – that popular Russian politics seem now to have got into the mere savage brutal state of blind retaliation, the excuse for which, perhaps, is that Russian reformers do not know really where to begin. It all seems a hopeless business.'

52 A friend, Zina Vengerova, writing from Paris in May 1890, congratulated Stepniak on the excellence of his English: 'I had the chance of talking about your style with some Englishmen, who were astounded that the book was written not *by a genuine Englishman (sic)*' (Taratuta, *S. M. Stepnyak-Kravchinsky*, p. 400).

53 Fanny, Stepniak's wife, admitted to a correspondent in 1923 that it had been 'a big mistake' to write the novel in English (*ibid.* p. 393).

54 The passage echoes – whether intentionally or not, it is hard to say – Herzen's words to Turgenev in his letter of 1863 justifying the activity of the London exiles: 'We have saved the honour of the name of Russia – and for this we have suffered from the servile majority' (Gertsen (Herzen), *Sobr. soch.*, vol. XXVII, 2, p. 455).

55 Evgeniya Taratuta would not agree. Her enthusiasm for Andrey appears to have begun as a child and to have become a lifelong influence. 'Most likely', she writes, 'even now, behind some of my convictions and hard and fast rules of life, it would be possible to find, if you scratched me, the figure of Andrey Kozhukhov' (*S. M. Stepnyak-Kravchinsky*, p. 405). This suggests that for some readers the character must have had the appeal of a successfully realised hero, though for a Soviet writer such as D. Granin the character has less appeal: 'In essence Andrey Kozhukhov is a pretty schematic, flat character', he

writes, but in attempting to define the powerful effect of such heroes as Rakhmetov, Bazarov and Kozhukhov he adds: 'What was it about them that attracted such attention? What was their real strength? It was that they provided examples of *active morality* (*deyatel'naya nravst-vennost'*). It was that their lives contained a clear revolutionary idea' ('Roman i geroy', *Voprosy literatury*, 5 (1976), 110).

56 Tsar Alexander II in fact ran in zigzags from the assassin Solovyov's bullets in 1879.

57 In 1878 Vera Zasulich attempted to assassinate the Governor-General of St Petersburg. Her trial became an event of national importance and her acquittal a cause of rejoicing in the ranks of the Populist revolutionaries. Her pistol shot helped to initiate the terrorism of the 'The People's Will' ('Narodnaya volya'), which culminated in the assassination of Alexander II in March 1881. Significantly, in her review of Stepniak's novel published in *Sotsial-demokrat* in 1892 she attributed the action of the novel to late 1878, early 1879.

58 V. I. Zasulich, *Stat'i o russkoy literature* (M., 1960), p. 114.

59 Bernard Shaw, 'A Word about Stepniak', *To-Morrow*, 1 (1896), 105.

60 His close friend and admirer, Prince P. Kropotkin, said of Stepniak at his funeral: 'He could not live in the narrow feeling of party worship – he stood much above that' (G. Woodcock and I. Avakumović, *The Anarchist Prince* (London, 1950), p. 255).

61 *Rudin*, A Novel by Ivan Turgenev. Translated from the Russian by Constance Garnett (London, 1894), p. xi.

62 S. Stepniak, *Nihilism as it is* (London, n.d.), pp. 65–6. Taratuta dates it 1892 (*S. M. Stepnyak-Kravchinsky*, p. 428).

63 G. V. Plekhanov, *Selected Philosophical Works*, vol. 1 (M., 1974), p. 399.

2. *Proletarian heroism and intelligentsia militancy*

1 See James B. Woodward, *Leonid Andreyev: a study* (O.U.P., 1969), for the most comprehensive study in English of Andreyev as writer and thinker.

2 M. Gorki, *Comrades* (London, 1907), p. 7.

3 A. Bely, *Petersburg*. Translated, annotated and introduced by Robert A. Maguire and John E. Malmstadt (London, 1978), pp. 10–11. This translation is based on the shortened version of the novel.

4 M. Gorky, *Polnoye sobraniye sochineniy*, vol. VII (M., 1970) provides the source for the information in this section.

5 V. I. Lenin, 'New Events and Old Questions', *Collected Works*, vol. VI (M., 1964), pp. 282–3.

6 The novel underwent six reworkings of various degrees of importance in the following principal editions: Appleton, N.Y., 1907; Ladyzhnikov, Berlin, 1907; Znaniye (Gorky's own publishing house), Books XVI, XVII, XVIII, XIX (1907) and XX, XXI (1908) containing serious censorship cuts;

Ladyzhnikov, Berlin, 1908; Zhizn'i znaniye, 1917; Kniga: Berlin, 1923.

7 The translator was a Russian émigré, Thomas Zeltzer (or Zel'tser), who apparently made a good deal of money from his work.

8 *The Mother* by Maxim Gorki, with eight illustrations by Sigmund de Ivanovsky (D. Appleton and Co.: New York, 1906, 1907); *Comrades* by Maxim Gorki (Hodder and Stoughton: London, 1907). The London edition was altered to conform to English spelling and, apart from the change of title, had chapter headings but no illustrations.

9 The point is well made in Richard Hare, *Maxim Gorky: Romantic Realist and Conservative Revolutionary* (O.U.P., 1962), pp. 74–5.

10 *Comrades*, p. 426. [A:...] in this and subsequent quotes indicates that words in square brackets were used in the American edition (Appleton, N.Y., 1907).

11 Echoes of the Satin speech were undoubtedly there in the English version. Andrey Nakhodka was then given the following speech:

'Because, mark you, mother dear, a new heart is coming into existence, a new heart is growing up in life. All hearts are smitten in the conflict of interests, all are consumed with a blind greed, eaten up with envy, stricken, wounded, and dripping with filth, falsehood and cowardice...But lo, and behold! Here is a Man coming and illuminating life with the light of reason, and he shouts: "Oh, ho! you straying roaches! It's time, high time, for you to understand that all your interests are one, that every one has the need to live, every one has the desire to grow!"' (*Comrades*, pp. 172–3).

One may be grateful to Gorky that this was omitted from later versions, though it expresses very well the heady mix of political propaganda and salvationism that was so important an element of his socialism at the time.

12 This equation of Christ and socialism has elements of God-building in it. It stresses (as do other statements by Nilovna) the collectivist religious character (*sobornost'*) of socialism as it was to be defined, for example, by Lunacharsky (*Religiya i sotsializm*, vol. I (Spb., 1908); vol. II (Spb., 1911)). For a discussion of this aspect of Gorky's work, especially in relation to *Confession* (*Ispoved'*) (1908), see Christopher Read, *Religion, Revolution and the Russian Intelligentsia 1900–1912* (London, 1979), pp. 85–94.

13 Quoted from M. Gorky, *Polnoye sobraniye sochineniy*, vol. VIII (M., 1970), p. 478. The letter dates from July 1907.

14 *Ibid.* pp. 447–8.

15 To set the question of the intelligentsia's role in perspective, it is important to bear in mind Christopher Read's point: 'As a rough estimate it seems likely that the intelligentsia comprised no more than 50,000 people' (*Religion, Revolution and the Intelligentsia*, p. 7).

16 N. A. Berdyayev (1874–1948), though Marxist in his youth, acquired world-wide fame as a philosopher and exponent of his own brand of

Personalism; S. N. Bulgakov (1871–1944) became well known as a theologian; P. B. Struve (1870–1944), early advocate of legal Marxism, drafted the manifesto of the Russian Social-Democratic Workers Party (1898), subsequently moved to more right-wing views as an economist and sociologist; S. L. Frank (1877–1950) turned from Marxism to Christianity, acquiring renown as a leading émigré religious thinker.

17 *Vekhi: sbornik statey o russkoy intelligentsii*, 2nd ed. (M., 1909), p. 20. The title has also been translated as *Landmarks*. See *Landmarks: a collection of essays on the Russian Intelligentsia*, ed. B. Shragin and A. Todd, trans. M. Schwartz (N.Y., 1977).

18 Precocious sexual stimulation and early masturbation were among the ills arguably attributable to such lack of family influence. Rather charmingly, the author contrasted Russian and English student youth of the time and declared (it is unclear on what evidence): 'In English universities you will not find, as you will among Russian revolutionary youth, that 75% of them are onanists. In the vast majority of cases the English student has no knowledge of brothels. You cannot say the same about progressive Russian students' (*ibid.* p. 108).

19 *Ibid.* pp. 194–5. The German reads: 'The urge to destroy is also a creative urge.'

20 V. Ropshin (1879–1925), pseudonym of Boris Savinkov, an active terrorist, who eventually became an opponent of the Soviet régime and is supposed to have taken his own life in prison after being sentenced to ten years' jail for illegally crossing the Soviet border. For a discussion of Ropshin's novels and other novels of the period devoted to the first Russian revolution, see M. G. Petrova, 'Pervaya russkaya revolyutsiya v romanakh predoktyabr'skogo desyatiletiya', *Revolyutsiya 1905–1907 godov i literatura* (M., 1978), pp. 194–216.

21 Tsushima, the decisive naval battle of the Russo-Japanese War, in May 1905, when the Russian Baltic fleet was almost totally destroyed.

22 First mentioned by Bely in July 1911 and intended as a continuation of his *The Silver Dove* (*Serebryanaya golub'*) (1909), it had an erratic publishing history. Published initially in 1913–14 in almanacs of the Sirin publishing house after having been rejected for publication in P. B. Struve's *Russkaya mysl'*, it was first published as a separate volume in 1916. Bely shortened the novel by as much as a third for his Russian-language version of 1922, published in Berlin; and this edition, with some further changes, was published again in 1935.

23 As Johannes Holthusen, a leading German student of Bely, has put it: 'Die Stadt Petersburg, der eigentliche "Held" des gleichnamigen Romans, ist vor allem zwei im Verborgenen wirkenden Kraeften verfallen, die beide von dem im Roman vielfach genannten "mongolischen Chaos" ausgehen: den Kraft des "revolutionaeren Schauers" und den Kraft des "Eises"' (*Studien zur Aesthetik und Poetik des russischen Symbolismus* (Goettingen, 1957), p. 126).

('The city of St Petersburg, the real "hero" of the eponymous novel, is principally at the mercy of two secretly active forces, which both derive from what is frequently called "Mongolian chaos" in the novel: the force of "revolutionary terror" and the force of "ice".')

24 Bely himself described the origin of his novel in the following terms: 'I, for example, know of the origin of the content of *Petersburg* from "l-k-l-pp-pp-ll" where "k" is a sound of stuffiness, suffocation from "pp-pp" – the pressure of the walls of Ableukhov's yellow house, and "ll" is the gleaming reflection of the "lacquers", "glosses" and "lustres" within "pp-pp" – the walls or the covering of the "bomb" (Pepp Peppovich Pepp). And "pl" is the bearer of this glittering prison – A*poll*on A*poll*onovich Ab*l*eukhov; and the person experiencing the suffocation "k" in "p" on "l" "lustres" is Ni*k*olai Apo*ll*onovich, the son of the senator' (Konstantin Mochulsky, *Andrei Bely: His Life and Works*, trans. Nora Szalavitz (Ann Arbor, 1977), p. 156).

25 G. V. Plekhanov, *Iskusstvo i literatura* (M., 1948), p. 774.

26 *Petersburg*, trans. Maguire and Malmstadt, p. 152.

27 The significance of Dudkin's thoughts on the Bronze Horseman and Russia's future is commented on interestingly in the introduction by A. Myasnikov to A. Bely, *Peterburg* (M., 1978), pp. 7–9.

28 *Petersburg*, trans. Maguire and Malmstadt, p. xx. The 'Translators' Introduction' is of great value for a fuller appreciation of this complex novel.

29 *Ibid.* p. xxi.

30 *Ibid.* p. xiii.

31 The items mentioned here are taken from the first, and fullest, 1916 edition of the novel.

32 L. Dolgopolov, *Na rubezhe vekov. O russkoy literature kontsa XIX-nachala XX veka* (L., 1977), p. 212. Chs. 5 and 6 of this study contain one of the most important Soviet treatments of the literary context and historical significance of Bely's *Petersburg*.

33 Mochulsky, *Andrei Bely*, p. 150.

3. *The revolutionary novel*

1 T. Carlyle, *The French Revolution* (C.U.P., 1930), p. 61.

2 *Ibid.* p. 62.

3 V. I. Lenin, 'Prophetic Words', *Collected Works*, vol. XXVII (M., 1965), p. 498.

4 Raymond Williams, *Modern Tragedy* (London, 1979), p. 71.

5 L. Trotsky, *Literatura i revolyutsiya*, 2nd ed. (M., 1924), p. 11.

6 'It is quite true that it has never been possible to judge, reject or accept a work of art by the principles of Marxism alone. The products of

artistic creation must, in the first instance, be judged according to their own laws, i.e. according to the laws of art' (*ibid.* p. 135).

7 Williams, *Modern Tragedy*, p. 77.

8 W. H. Chamberlin, *The Russian Revolution, 1917–1921* (N.Y., 1965), vol. II, p. 460.

9 A. Voronsky, 'Literaturniye otkliki', *Krasnaya nov'*, 2 (1922), 271.

10 Trotsky, *Literatura i revolyutsiya*, p. 59.

11 'About 2,000 Soviet writers were inspired by the theme of the October Revolution...No less than 20,000 works from poems to epics, from novellas to five-act tragedies, were devoted to the October Revolution and the civil war' (Yu. A. Andreyev, *Revolyutsiya i literatura* (L., 1969), p. 418).

12 At the most elementary level a 'novel' has been considered to be a prose work that displays some degree of fictionalisation; it has usually, but not always, been regarded as exceeding 100 pages in length.

13 Robert A. Maguire, *Red Virgin Soil: Soviet Literature in the 1920s* (Princeton U.P., 1966). His opinion is worth fuller quotation, though it refers to the first period of Soviet literature only (pp. 91–2):

'Out of the turmoil, a new style was born – of hard surfaces that reflected brilliantly and refracted feebly. It moves between understatement and hyperbole, deceiving our expectations at every turn. High lyricism drenches what is ordinary, if not sordid; a matter-of-factness verging on boredom conveys what is extraordinary, if not heroic...

Since this new literature does shun the obvious, we are tempted to call it sophisticated. In fact, it is not. Considering the magnitude of its theme, it is strangely small literature – small in reach, small in emotion. There are violence and death, but no tragedy; action, but no heroics; confrontation, but no exploration. Perhaps this is so because it lacks a firm ethical and moral center, and is therefore unable to raise, except by implication, the large human questions that superior fiction must raise.'

14 Ralph Fox, *The Novel and the People* (London, 1944), p. 112). This judgement belongs in fact to the 1930s, when Ralph Fox's work first appeared.

15 For a valuable examination of this problem in the context of European literature, see Renee Winegarten, *Writers and Revolution: the fatal lure of action* (N.Y., 1974).

16 A. Bely, *Revolyutsiya i kul'tura* (M., 1917), p. 3.

17 *Ibid.* p. 10.

18 The comment was made in the journal *Pechat' i revolyutsiya*, 8 (1926), 204. The trilogy of novels on revolutionary themes, published under the general title *Moscow*, were *A Moscow Crank* (*Moskovskiy chudak*) (1926), *Moscow Exposed* (*Moskva pod udarom*) (1926) and *Masks* (*Maski*) (1932).

19 From the introduction by Pavel Medvedev to N. Nikitin, *Rvotnyy fort* (M., 1928), p. 13.

20 The title of the work was later changed to *The Army Commander* in order not to conflict with the title of Furmanov's last work.

21 For instance: '...ona rasplakala vse glaza...'; words 'vyburkivayut' from lips; 'shli' is used as an imperative.

22 'Yelena' refers to Kalabukhov's wife.

23 M. Charny, *Artyom Vesyoly* (M., 1960), p. 43.

24 *Ibid*. p. 67.

25 Andreyev, *Revolyutsiya i literatura*, p. 138.

26 He suffered 'repression' in 1939.

27 The only exception, though he was principally a poet, was Osip Mandelstam. Izaak Babel (1894–1941) was arrested in 1939. No charges were ever divulged. He died in captivity in 1941, probably in March. The 1926 edition of *Konarmiya* contained thirty-four stories; 'Argamak' was added in 1932.

28 Babel's *Red Cavalry* was based on his participation in the Russo-Polish War of 1920 as a front correspondent of YUG-Rosta and assistant quartermaster of the Sixth Division of the First Soviet Cavalry Army. As a historian of the subject has stated:
   'Babel's experience of the Polish-Soviet War was much narrower than is usually supposed. He served for only ten weeks of the twenty-month war. He saw only one front, the less important of the two, and knew only one of the eight Soviet armies. What is more important, he does not seem to have had much close acquaintance with the fighting' (Norman Davies, 'Izaak Babel''s "Konarmiya" stories and the Polish–Soviet War', *Modern Languages Review* (October 1972), 847).

29 The extracts from *Red Cavalry* are taken from the translation by Walter Morison in Isaac Babel, *Collected Stories* (Penguin Books, 1974), pp, 64, 92–3, 163, 60–1.

30 Babel has received a great deal of attention from critics in the West, particularly in England and America. Lionel Trilling's famous article, which serves as the introduction to the Penguin volume of *Collected Stories*, is one example. Also of note are the following monographs: R. W. Hallett, *Isaac Babel* (Letchworth, 1972); P. Carden, *The Art of Isaac Babel* (Cornell U.P., 1972); James E. Falen, *Isaac Babel: Russian Master of the Short Story* (Tennessee U.P., 1974).

31 For a detailed and interesting study of the place of women in Soviet literature, see Xenia Gasiorowska, *Women in Soviet Fiction 1917–1964* (Wisconsin U.P., 1968).

32 Seyfullina's extended short story 'Humus' ('Peregnoy') of 1922 is a valuable 'introductory' study for *Virineya* in its depiction of the instinctive mass response of the peasantry to revolution. Most of her literary work in later life was devoted to the stage, among her successes being the staging of a play based on her *Virineya*.

33 Quoted from *Istoriya russkogo sovetskogo romana* (M.–L., 1965),

vol. I, p. 86. V. Zazubrin (pseud.; real name Zubtsov, 1895–1938) was an active participant in the civil war in Siberia, first with the Whites, then with the Fifth Red Army during its campaign in the Urals and as editor of the daily army newspaper *The Red Sharp-Shooter*. He later fell into disfavour with the Party and never repeated the success of his first novel. He was 'illegally repressed' during the purges.

34 Boris Pilnyak (pseud.; real name Vogau, 1894–1941) had several brushes with the Soviet authorities during his literary career (for details, see Vera T. Reck, *Boris Pil'niak: A Soviet Writer in Conflict with the State* (McGill U.P., 1975)). He was arrested during the purges and probably died in 1937, though the official date of his death has been given as 9 September 1941.

35 Quoted from 'Afterword' by Alexander R. Tulloch to his excellent translation of *The Naked Year* (Ann Arbor, 1975), p. 197. All page numbers in brackets after quotes refer to this translation, with slight changes. For Patricia Carden, writing of Pilnyak, 'the vices of ornamentalism are multiplied while the virtues of the style are weakened or absent', though she adds that 'the tie between the ornamental style and primitivism of psychology seems to be the key to the readiness with which it was seized upon' ('Ornamentalism and Modernism', *Russian Modernism*, ed. G. Gibian and H. W. Tjalsman (Cornell U.P., 1976), p. 62).

36 Quoted from G. N. Medvedeva, *Yury Libedinsky i yego povest' 'Nedelya'* (Dushanbe, 1963), p. 134.

37 V. Novikov, 'Tvorcheskiy put' Borisa Pil'nyaka', B. Pil'nyak, *Izbrannyye proizvedeniya* (M., 1976), p. 7.

38 Yu. N. Libedinsky (1898–1959) was born in Odessa, the son of a doctor, and was brought up in Chelyabinsk in the southern Urals. He was influenced initially in his writing by Tolstoy, Gorky and Bunin; he particularly admired Bely's *Petersburg*. *One Week* was begun in 1921 in Yekaterinburg (now Sverdlovsk) and completed in the spring of 1922. This appraisal of the novel is based on the first edition (Yekaterinburg, 1923) and the second edition (Moscow, 1926). The reworked edition, now the 'official' version, was first published in 1949. Libedinsky suffered persecution and neglect during the purges and for some years after 1937 his works of the 1920s were not republished.

39 '...his attempt to write rhythmical prose, with constant syntactical inversions, in the manner of Bely and Sologub, produces ludicrous results, quite out of keeping with the subject matter and the general realistic manner of the narrative' (Gleb Struve, *Russian Literature under Lenin and Stalin 1917–1953* (London, 1972), p. 130). This censure is valid for some of the passages in the first version of the novel, but does not apply to the reworked edition. The lack of stylistic distinction in his later novel *The Commissars* contributed to its mediocre literary appeal, although as a picture of Communist Party activities in the immediate post-civil war period it possessed documentary interest.

40 Medvedeva, *Yury Libedinsky*, p. 128.

41 The two heroines in the novel, Anyuta Simkova and Liza, were based on Libedinsky's childhood girl-friend, Marianna Gerasimova, who was to become his wife. The novel was dedicated to her. See Medvedeva, *ibid.* pp. 64–5. The bizarre and tragic story of their relationship is intimated in Harry T. Moore and Albert Parry, *Twentieth-Century Russian Literature* (London, 1976), pp. 55–6.

42 'Cheka' refers to the Extraordinary Commission, active between 1917 and 1922, which was empowered to eradicate all counter-revolutionary tendencies in Soviet Russia. A Chekist is one belonging to the Cheka.

43 V. V. Ivanov (1895–1963), born in Siberia, early left home to work in a circus. Befriended by Gorky, who published his work, he fought in the civil war on the side of the Whites, then on the side of the Reds, particularly among the partisans.

44 V. Shklovsky, *Zhili-byli* (M., 1966), p. 427.

45 *Istoriya russkogo sovetskogo romana*, vol. I, p. 124.

46 As Zamyatin remarked, 'No other Russian writer has written so much with his nostrils as he does. Ivanov sniffs everything indiscriminately...Ivanov's sense of smell is like an animal's – magnificent' (Yev. Zamyatin, *A Soviet Heretic: Essays by Yev. Zamyatin* (Chicago U.P., 1970), p. 95).

47 *Skaz* is a first-person narration in which the style usually helps to illuminate and characterise, in general and specific terms, the social and cultural level of the narrator.

48 Aleksandr Malyshkin (1892–1938) was born in the village of Bogorodsky, in what was formerly Penza province. His father was a peasant who became an overseer. Malyshkin became a student in the Historical–Philological Faculty of St Petersburg University, where he studied medieval Russian literature and hoped to specialise in 'The Lay of Igor's Raid' ('Slovo o polku Igoreve'). Something of this period of his life, and the ensuing experience during the February and October revolutions, is reflected in the experience of Shelekhov, the autobiographical hero of his first novel. He participated in the storming of the Isthmus of Perekop. *Fall of Dair* was originally written in the Crimea in 1921 and first published at the beginning of 1923.

49 V. Ermilov, *O traditsiyakh sovetskoy literatury. Tvorchestvo A. Malyshkina, A. Makarenko, Yu. Krymova* (M., 1955), p. 8.

50 Boris Lavrenyov (1891–1959). Born in Kherson, by training a lawyer, from a bourgeois background. His early writing was coloured by such influences as Lermontov and Futurism, the prose of Bely and the poetry of A. Blok. He was a man of broad culture, with considerable knowledge of French and English literature, who became well known as a playwright in his later career. He first had experience of war in 1915. His early story 'Gala-Peter' tells of a young officer who was both fascinated and tormented by a Swedish chocolate of that name. His life became a succession of different activities: organisation of the Red Cross in the Ukraine, commandant of an armoured train, participant

in the battles in the Crimea, in operations against ataman Zelyony, on the Turkestan front, editor of military newspapers, artilleryman, commandant of Tashkent and friend of Dmitry Furmanov. When he was demobilised in 1923, he went to live in Leningrad where in 1924 he published *Wind*. He is probably best known for his short story 'The Forty-First' (1924), which became a famous film. Another novella-type work of his, *The Seventh Satellite* (*Sed'moy sputnik* (1928)), about a Tsarist general who eventually comes to terms with Soviet rule, is of interest, though less striking in terms of style and treatment than *Wind*. Lavrenyov's reputation suffered during the Stalin period and his prose work has only begun to receive the understanding criticism it deserves since the appearance of Inna Vishnevskaya's study in 1962 (see n. 51).

51 I. L. Vishnevskaya, *Boris Lavrenyov* (M., 1962), p. 23.

52 V. A. Ruzhina, *Veter revolyutsii* (Kishinyov, 1971), p. 211.

53 A. S. Serafimovich (pseud.; real name Popov, 1863–1949) made his reputation many years before the revolution. He was a member of Gorky's *Znaniye* writers, who contributed to the Social-Democratic almanacs published by the non-profit-making co-operative. The *Znaniye* (*Knowledge*) publications began in 1904 and favoured realism and social commitment. Serafimovich's most famous pre-revolutionary work was the novel *City in the Steppe* (1912). His Cossack lineage was later to be of crucial importance in Sholokhov's early career, for it was Serafimovich who first realised the potential value of the disordered manuscript about Cossack life that was to grow into the epic novel *Quiet Flows the Don*.

54 A. S. Serafimovich, *Sobraniye sochineniy v 7 tomakh*, vol. VII (M., 1960), p. 305.

55 *Ibid.* p. 315.

56 Kovtyukh told his own story in E. I. Kovtyukh, *Ot Kubani do Volgi i obratno* (M., 1926). He was arrested in 1937 and is thought to have perished as a victim of the purges.

57 See L. A. Gladkovskaya, *Rozhdeniye epopei: Zhelezhyy potok A. S. Serafimovicha* (M.–L., 1963), p. 87.

58 Serafimovich, *Sobr. soch.*, vol. VII, p. 338.

59 'In essence, the characters of *The Iron Flood* are developed very little. Only the most striking aspects are given prominence. If I had worked on a large canvas, developed the mundane features, shown a man from all sides, it would have turned out to be something like a *War and Peace* of the Soviet period' (*ibid.* p. 319).

60 'I preferred to set in relief only a single most important aspect of character, and if I had depicted a hero from all sides, then this most important characterizing aspect would have been significantly weakened. Take, for instance, Granny Gorpina: in her I concentrated the basic idea of the rebirth of the impoverished peasant mass under the influence of revolution' (*ibid.* p. 315).

61 Zamyatin, *A Soviet Heretic*, p. 115.
62 Serafimovich, *Sobr. soch.*, vol. VII, p. 333.
63 *Istoriya russkogo sovetskogo romana*, vol. I, p. 112.
64 The name obviously has echoes not only of the historical Kovtyukh, but also of the first 'revolutionary' hero in Russian fiction, Andrey Kozhukhov of Stepniak's novel.
65 One Soviet commentator has hinted that the basic idea was less original than it may seem by comparing *The Iron Flood* with a similar story of an epic trek in V. Tamarin's 'The Desert' ('Pustynya'), published in *Red Virgin Soil (Krasnaya nov')* in 1921. See Andreyev, *Revolyutsiya i literatura*, p. 258.
66 In the first edition of the novel the reference to Tolstoy was more obvious and the emphasis on 'scoundrels' ('zhuliki') much sharper. For an indication of the consequences of such changes, see Struve, *Russian Literature 1917–1953*, pp. 99–102.
67 L. M. Leonov, born 1899 in Moscow, though of peasant background, began with stories cast in romantic, Hoffmannesque style, part realistic, part fantastic, and graduated, after *The Badgers*, to write the most original novel of the NEP period, *The Thief (Vor)* (1927); he has since completed such major novels as *Sot'*, *Skutarevsky* and *The Russian Forest (Russkiy les)* in addition to writing several plays.
68 From the jacket to the Progress Publishers translation of the novel (Moscow, 1974), referred to in further references as *Chapayev*.
69 This passage and previous passages are quoted from G. P. Vladimirov, *Soldat revolyutsii. Stranitsy zhizni i tvorchestva Dm. Furmanova* (Tashkent, 1967), pp. 42, 46, 50. The references to 'liquidators' and 're-callers' are to those Social Democrats who demanded, during the period of the third Duma (1907–12), that the conspiratorial form of the Party should be liquidated or the Bolshevik delegates withdrawn. Lenin was opposed to both measures.
70 On 4 January 1923 Furmanov jotted down:
'I have just completed the last lines of *Chapayev*. I've been doing the finishing work. And I've remained, as it were, without my best, my favourite friend. I feel orphaned. It's night-time. I'm sitting by myself at the table – and I can't think of a thing, can't write, can't read. I sit and I remember how I spent night after night writing page by page this first months-long work of mine. I put a lot into this work, spent many sleepless nights over it, thought much and often, thought continuously about it – travelling, sitting down, even at work, my beloved *Chapayev* was never out of my mind. But now I've no mind for anyone or anything' (quoted from Vladimirov, *Soldat revolyutsii*, p. 226).
71 From A. Serafimovich's Preface to D. Furmanov, *Myatezh*, 2nd ed. (M.–L., 1925), p. 3.
72 Zamyatin, *A Soviet Heretic*, p. 107.

73 *Ibid.* p. 109.

74 *Ibid.*

75 *We* (*My*) was written in 1920 and 1921. It was never published in the Soviet Union. It was translated into English in 1924 and first published in Russian by the Chekhov Publishing House, New York, in 1952.

Yevgeny Ivanovich Zamyatin (1884–1937) early joined the Bolshevik Party while studying to be an engineer in St Petersburg. He first enjoyed literary fame in 1913. During the First World War he spent eighteen months in England supervising the building of icebreakers. He returned to Russia in 1917 and soon became a leading writer of the post-revolutionary period. His many important administrative roles in writers' organisations and his influence exercised through lectures on literary themes encouraged the development of an innovative prose literature similar in many ways to his own. He and Pilnyak were regarded as leading members of the new generation of Soviet writers. In the course of the 1920s he came under attack from orthodox Party critics and his persecution had all the character of a witch-hunt. He petitioned Stalin to be allowed to leave the Soviet Union and was eventually permitted to do so in November 1931. He and his wife resided in Paris until his death and refused to associate actively with the émigré organisations.

76 George Orwell, 'Freedom and Happiness', *Tribune* (4 January, 1946). For a most interesting discussion of Zamyatin's novel, see D. J. Richards, *Zamyatin, A Soviet Heretic* (London, 1962), pp. 54–69. A more extensive study of Zamyatin's work may be found in the scholarly and illuminating work by Alex M. Shane, *The Life and Works of Evgenij Zamjatin* (California U.P., 1968).

77 Robert Russell, 'Literature and Revolution in Zamyatin's *My*', *The Slavonic and East European Review*, 51 (1973), 46.

78 The intellectual barrenness of the Soviet novel in the first half of the 1920s is well borne out by the very useful review of prose literature in the period to be found in Vyacheslav Zavalishin's *Early Soviet Writers* (N.Y., 1958). This is by far the most detailed work on the period available in English. It rightly singles out Yakovlev's *October* as 'a gallery of mass scenes and episodes, in the foreground of which are presented the experiences and actions of single persons' (p. 218) and Yakovlev as a writer whose 'description of the revolution is scrupulously veracious' (p. 220).

79 A. S. Yakovlev (1886–1953) should also be mentioned for his second novella-type work *Povol'niki* (1922), which, unlike *October*, is a colourful, racily written, semi-allegorical account of revolution in the Volga region. See the introduction to chapter 5 for a brief discussion of his novel of 1935, *The Ways of a Simple Heart*.

80 'It was obvious that in writing his novel Fedin had been inspired by models of nineteenth-century Russian and English narrative art: his

vast canvas was definitely traditional, and even the motto of the book was borrowed from *A Tale of Two Cities*' (Marc Slonim, *Modern Russian Literature* (N.Y., 1953), p. 308). 'It is a work of considerable originality and undoubted literary merits' (Struve, *Russian Literature 1917–1953*, p. 97).

81 Julius M. Blum, *Konstantin Fedin: A Descriptive and Analytic Study* (The Hague–Paris, 1967), p. 6.

82 Quoted from A. N. Starikov, *Geroi i gody. Roman Konstantina Fedina* (M., 1972), p. 42.

83 In the manuscript version of the novel the chapters were arranged chronologically. See F. F. Eroshcheva, *Romany Konstantina Fedina o revolyutsii* (Krasnodar, 1967), p. 79.

84 K. A. Fedin, 'K romanu "Goroda i gody"', *Goroda i gody* (M., 1957), p. 371.

85 Ernest J. Simmons, *Russian Fiction and Soviet Ideology* (Columbia U.P., 1958), p. 26.

86 Miroslav Zagradka, *O khudozhestvennom stile romanov Konstantina Fedina* (Praga, 1962), pp. 7–8.

87 Fedin, 'K romanu "Goroda i gody"', p. 369.

88 'Kurt – tol'ko ispolnitel'' (quoted from Z. I. Levinson, *Obraz vremeni. Partiya i revolyutsionnyy narod v tvorchestve K. A. Fedina* (Tula, 1964), p. 59).

89 For additional details, see G. A. Brovman, *V. V. Veresaev. Zhizn' i tvorchestvo* (M., 1959), pp. 236ff.

90 *V tupike* was translated into English as *The Deadlock* in 1927 (*The Deadlock*, by V. V. Vieressaev, trans. by Nina Wissotzky and Camilla Coventry (London, 1927)). I have retained the title but I have preferred to translate passages from the novel myself rather than use what is on the whole an inadequate and old-fashioned translation. My source has been V. V. Veresaev, *V tupike*, 4th ed. (M., 1926).

V. V. Veresaev. (pseud.; real name Smidovich, 1867–1945) was born into a doctor's family. He also qualified as a doctor in 1894 but simultaneously began a writing career. His first outstanding success was *A Doctor's Notes* (*Zapiski vracha*) (1901), a semi-autobiographical work critical of medical education and practice, but he had also written novels and long short stories on the problems facing the intelligentsia at the turn of the century (*Bez dorogi* (1894); *Povetriye* (1897); *Na povorote* (1902)). His standing as an author was greatly enhanced by his expert reportage on the Russo-Japanese War of 1904–5 and his criticism of the gross inadequacies in the military conduct of the campaign. He also made a very important reputation for himself as a critic, especially in his pro-Tolstoy study of Tolstoy and Dostoyevsky (*Zhivaya zhizn'* (1910)) and his later books on Pushkin and Gogol. His career as a writer spanned both the pre-revolutionary and Soviet periods (he did not exile himself from Russia) and demonstrated a consistency of attitude and standards without parallel in the writers of his generation.

91 A wretched Russian émigré, so used to the exigencies of life in the Russian Federation (RSFSR), travels to Berlin in the train toilet and when he reaches Berlin asks to be accommodated in the rubbish area under the hotel stairs. He is finally exhibited in a cage with the heading RSFSR, standing for Rare Specimen of Frightful Stupidity of Race.

92 M. A. Bulgakov's *The White Guard* (*Belaya gvardiya*) was written in 1922 after the death of the author's mother and was based on the author's own experiences in the winter of 1918–19. Though some sections appeared in print in 1924, it first appeared as a novel in the journal *Rossiya* in 1925. After two instalments the journal was closed down and the whole novel did not appear until the editions of Bulgakov's works published in the USSR in 1966 and 1973. Meanwhile, the author used it as the basis for his famous play *Dni Turbinykh* (*The Days of the Turbins*). For more details, see A. Colin Wright, *Mikhail Bulgakov: life and interpretations* (Toronto U.P., 1978), pp. 65–8.

93 Mikhail Bulgakov, *The White Guard*, trans. by Michael Glenny (London, 1973), p. 7. Page numbers from this translation are given after quotations.

94 M. A. Bulgakov, *Romany* (L., 1978), p. 13 (not contained in the Glenny translation).

95 Altered slightly from the Glenny translation to bring it closer to the text in *Romany*, p. 186.

96 His spite is directed at the poet Shpolyansky, whose mistress (or so we may assume her to be) is the woman who rescues Aleksey Turbin after his wounding.

97 The quotation is from Revelation 21: 4.

98 A. Fadeyev, *Za tridtsat' let* (M., 1957), pp. 17–18.

99 Also translated as *The Nineteen*, the novel was conceived in 1921 and work began on it in 1925. Fadeyev wrote it in Rostov-on-Don in 1925–6.

100 A. Bushmin, *Roman A. Fadeyeva 'Razgrom'* (L., 1954), p. 44.

101 See, for example, the discussion of the issue between Morozka and Goncharenko at the beginning of ch. 13.

102 A. Fadeyev, *Literatura i zhizn'* (M., 1933), p. 152.

103 As Rufus W. Mathewson, Jr, has put it: 'The parental responsibilities Levinson assumes have a sanction, Fadeev tells us, in the needs of "the children", who collaborate willingly in the manufacture of the myth of Levinson's infallibility' (*The Positive Hero*, p. 194).

104 As a Soviet commentator claims: 'From a man of blind instincts, acting only in response to the immediate circumstances, Morozka is transformed in the course of the revolution into a thinking man' (Bushmin, *Roman A. Fadeyeva 'Razgrom'*, p. 70).

105 For a discussion of the Tolstoyan influence, in general terms, see L. F. Ershov, *Russkiy sove skiy roman: natsional'nyye traditsii i novatorstvo* (L., 1967), pp. 104–6.

106 A good example is the discussion of Morozka in *Istoriya russkoy sovetskoy literatury*, vol. III (M., 1961), pp. 164–70, where his portrayal

is compared with Babel's portrait of Afon'ka. See also *Istoriya russkogo sovetskogo romana*, vol. I, pp. 174–8.

107 *Envy*, published in 1927, was the only novel by Yury K. Olesha (1899–1960). He was a Moscow journalist of bourgeois background whose first language was Polish (his mother's nationality). Neglected under Stalin, his popularity revived in the 1950s and there have been several reprintings of his work in large editions. Apart from *Envy* he wrote a 'novel for children', *Three Fat Men* (*Tri tolstyaka*), a score and more of short stories, film scenarios and a posthumously published volume of sketch-type memoirs.

108 Yurii Olesha, *The Wayward Comrade and the Commissars*, trans. by Andrew R. MacAndrew (N.Y., 1960), p. 58. The 'pavement stones' should more appropriately be 'cobble-stones'.

109 Slightly altered in this version. The final sentence is clearer in the Russian: 'Ya sam sebya vydumal.'

110 D. G. B. Piper, 'Yuriy Olesha's *Zavist'*: an Interpretation', *The Slavonic and East European Review*, 48 (1970), 34.

111 Elisabeth Klosty Beaujour, *The Invisible Land: A Study of the Artistic Imagination of Iurii Olesha* (Columbia U.P., 1970), pp. 53–4.

112 For a discussion of this issue, see William Harkins, 'The theme of sterility in Olesha's *Envy*', *Slavic Review*, 3 (1966), 443–57.

113 The translation is my own.

114 Stimulating discussions of certain novels of the period can be found in Yu. A. Andreyev, *Revolyutsiya i literatura* (L., 1969), pp. 283–364. This, the first edition of Andreyev's work, is useful for its index, but the second edition (M., 1975) has an enlarged section devoted to the novels of the period, though no index. Also, V. Gura, *Roman i revolyutsiya. Puti sovetskogo romana 1917–1929* (M., 1973).

115 Viktor Kin (pseud.; real name Surovikin, 1903–37) joined the Bolshevik Party at the age of seventeen and fought in the civil war, on the Polish front and in the Far East. He became a correspondent of TASS in Rome and Paris. A man of remarkable talent and evidently great personal charm, he liked jokingly to remark of himself that he was a man of average ability. He was arrested in the autumn of 1937 during the purges. The memorial to him is this novel and a volume of reminiscences, edited by his wife, a specialist in Italian art and culture, published in 1966. See *Vsegda po etu storonu: vospominaniya o Viktore Kine* (M., 1966). The novel was first translated into English by Natalie Duddington (*Over the Border* (London, 1932)).

116 The first edition (M., 1928) had a printing of 5,000 copies and was dedicated to Yelena Mikhaylovna Kolokolova; the second edition (Moskovskoye tovarishchestvo pisateley, 1933) had a printing of 5,200 copies. For other details, see my article 'Nikolay Kolokolov', *The Slavonic and East European Review*, 56, 1 (1978), 13–31.

117 *Literaturnoye nasledstvo*, vol. LXX (M., 1963), p. 223. Gorky was very

impressed by *Honey and Blood* and enthusiastic about Kolokolov's talent.

118 N. I. Kolokolov (1897–1933) was the son of a priest and educated in a theological seminary, from which he was expelled for participating in a strike. He worked on a newspaper *Rabochiy kray* in Ivanovo-Voznesensk; later he became a member of the literary group *Pereval*. With Gorky's help he obtained a post on the journal *Nashi dostizheniya*. In addition to *Myod i krov'*, he published two books of poems, *Stikhotvoreniya* (M., 1920) and *Zemlya i telo: Stikhi* (M.–Petrograd, 1923), several children's stories and two collections of short stories, *Shkura laskovaya: Rasskazy* (M., 1929) and *Povelitel': Povesti i rasskazy* (M., 1931). His writing had stylistic distinction, poetic sensitivity and psychological honesty. The reasons for his disfavour, like the cause of his early death, remain obscure.

119 A. Fadeyev, 'O *Sevastopole* Malyshkina', *Na literaturnom postu*, 6 (1929), 13–14. The italic emphases are Fadeyev's.

120 'Slovo' refers to 'Slovo o polku Igoreve' ('The Lay of Igor's Raid'). See note 48 above.

4. *The revolutionary epic*

1 For a discussion of the historical novel, see George Lukacs, *The Historical Novel*, trans. H. and S. Mitchell (London, 1962); on *War and Peace*, see, for example, R. F. Christian, *Tolstoy's 'War and Peace': A Study* (O.U.P., 1962); J. Bayley, *Tolstoy and the Novel* (London, 1966); my own chapter on the novel in *The Rise of the Russian Novel* (C.U.P., 1973); Edward Wasiolek, *Tolstoy's Major Fiction* (Chicago U.P., 1978).

2 Begun in 1925, vol. I appeared in 1927, vol. II in 1928, vol. III in 1931 and vol. IV after Gorky's death in 1936.

3 M. Gorky, *Sobraniye sochineniy*, vol. XXVI (M., 1953), p. 93.

4 Points made by Lunacharsky. See his *Sobraniye sochineniy*, vol. II (M., 1964), pp. 176–7.

5 N. Zhegalov, *Roman M. Gor'kogo 'Zhizn' Klima Samgina'* (M., 1965), p. 287.

6 A. Ovcharenko, *Roman-epopeya M. Gor'kogo 'Zhizn' Klima Samgina'* (M., 1965), p. 8.

7 He is believed to have begun writing it in 1925. Vol. I first appeared in the journal *Oktyabr'*, 1–4, vol. II in 5–10 (1928). Vol. III appeared at intervals in *Oktyabr'* in 1929 and 1932. Vol IV first appeared in *Novy mir* between 1937 and 1940. See V. Gura, *Kak sozdavalsya 'Tikhiy Don'* (M., 1980).

8 The most recent and scholarly investigation of the problem of the authorship of *Quiet Flows the Don* is R. A. Medvedev, *Problems in the Literary Biography of Mikhail Sholokhov*, trans. A. D. P. Briggs (C.U.P., 1977).

9 Quoted from L. Yakimenko, *Sholokhov: a critical appreciation* (M., 1973), p. 116.
10 Originally in M. Sholokhov, *Lazorevaya step'* (M., 1931), p. 13. Quoted from Gura, *Kak sozdavalsya 'Tikhiy Don'*, p. 17.
11 D. H. Stewart, who has written the best study of Sholokhov available in English, refers to Sholokhov's 'innocent eye'. 'Innocence here means mainly the lack of formal education and experience with the city' (D. H. Stewart, *Mikhail Sholokhov: A Critical Introduction* (Ann Arbor, 1967), p. 68).
12 *Ibid.* p. 99.
13 He is supposed to have met Ermakov in 1926. See Gura, *Kak sozdavalsya 'Tikhiy Don'*, p. 98.
14 Stewart, *Mikhail Sholokhov*, p. 89.
15 Quoted from Yakimenko, *Sholokhov*, p. 62.
16 As D. H. Stewart remarks: 'Grigory *lives* the contradictions of his world' (*Mikhail Sholokhov*, p. 93).
17 M. Klimenko makes this point in his *The World of the Young Sholokhov* (North Quincy, Mass., 1972), p. 220.
18 Medvedev, *Problems*, p. 45.
19 The post-1956 editions, upon which this interpretation is based, differ in several important respects from the first edition on which the Stephen Garry English translation was based. As one scholar has put it, the changes involved 'are of great interest since they show the artistic development of a major novelist over a long period, and also throw considerable light on fluctuations in literary politics in the Soviet Union' (A. B. Murphy, 'The Changing Face of "Tikhiy Don"', *Journal of Russian Studies*, 34 (1977), 3). This article provides an excellent summary of these changes and their significance.
20 L. Yakimenko, 'Opyt vremeni – opyt iskusstva', *Voprosy literatury*, 11 (1976), 108.
21 Yakimenko, *Sholokhov*, p. 116.
22 Gura, *Kak sozdavalsya 'Tikhiy Don'*, p. 391. The detail that V. Gura supplies in his excellent study, especially pp. 385–98, shows how closely Sholokhov followed the 'civil war' biography of Ermakov in portraying Grigory Melekhov.
23 Juergen Ruehle, *Literature and Revolution: A Critical Study of the Writer and Communism in the Twentieth Century*, trans. J. Steinberg (London, 1969), pp. 76–7.
24 A. N. Tolstoy (1883–1945) was related to his famous namesake, L. N Tolstoy, through his great-great-grandfather, who was a brother by blood of the great-grandfather of L. N. Tolstoy. Born in Nikolaevsk, Samara province, to a landowning family, Tolstoy was brought up in the home of his mother's lover, A. A. Bostrom. On the death of his father in 1900, Tolstoy came into a legacy, which paid for his higher education. A writing career brought him a modest popularity prior to 1917, but in 1919 he emigrated to France, later moving to Germany,

and in 1923 he decided to return to the Soviet Union. Through prolific writing, including autobiographical works (*Detstvo Nikity* (1921)), science fiction (*Aelita* (1922); *Giperboloid inzhenera Garina* (1925)) and his famous historical novel, *Pyotr pervyy* (1929–45) (unfinished at the time of his death), he became the most privileged writer in the Soviet Union.

25 *Sisters* (*Syostry*) (1919–21); *Nineteen Eighteen* (*Vosemnadtsatyy god*) (1927–9); *The Gloomy Morning* (*Khmuroye utro*) (1939–41).

5. Revolution and resurrection

1 It has been claimed that the concept 'optimistic tragedy' first made its appearance in Russian literature with Chernyshevsky's *What is to be Done?* As a concept it derives from the belief, whether based on Chernyshevsky's 'cyclic' theory of historical progress or on historical and dialectical materialism, that the victory of communism is inevitable. See N. Naumova, *Roman N. G. Chernyshevskogo 'Chto delat'?'* (L., 1978), pp. 109–10.

2 Nikolai Ostrovsky, *How the Steel was Tempered*, trans. R. Prokofieva (M., n.d.), p. 195. The second quote is from p. 272.

3 A. S. Yakovlev (1886–1953) was the son of an illiterate housepainter. He worked as a post-office employee until he succeeded, in 1907, in gaining admittance to St Petersburg university. His political sympathies as an SR maximalist led to his arrest and imprisonment, but after his release he worked for a time as a journalist in Rostov-on-Don and Moscow and later participated in the First World War, where he witnessed, and was a victim of, German gas warfare. Apart from *October* (1923), much of his reputation in later life was based on his work as a journalist.

4 See A. Ovcharenko, 'Aleksandr Yakovlev i yego tvorchestvo' in A. Yakovlev, *Oktyabr'* (M., 1965), pp. 373–82.

5 B. Solov'yov (b. 1904) is best known for his literary-critical studies of A. Blok, particularly *Poet i yego podvig*, but he began his career as a poet and as a novelist. Another novel of his about the civil war in the Urals appeared in 1939, *Stronger than Stone* (*Krepche kamnya*).

6 See, for example, V. Oskotsky, *Negasimoye plamya kostra* (M., 1977), which lists more than fifty works, mostly novels.

7 Deming Brown mentions Pavel Nilin's *Zhestokost'* (1958) and Sergey Zalygin's *Solyonaya pad'. Na Irtyshe* (1968) as examples. See his *Soviet Russian Literature since Stalin* (C.U.P., 1979), pp. 259–60. The same might be said of V. Shukshin's *Lyubaviny* (M., 1965); see Geoffrey Hosking, *Beyond Socialist Realism: Soviet Fiction since Ivan Denisovich* (London, 1980), pp. 168–70.

8 V. Tan-Bogoraz (1865–1936), exiled to Kolyma for membership of the terrorist organisation 'The People's Will' ('Narodnaya volya'), became expert as a linguist and ethnographer through his studies in the

languages, cultures and folklores of tribes of north-eastern Asia. In 1921 he became a professor of ethnography and was instrumental in establishing the Academy of Science's museum of religions, of which he became director in 1932. Among other novels and stories of considerable interest is his *The Resurrected Tribe* (*Voskressheye plemya* (1935)).

9 V. Tan-Bogoraz, *Soyuz molodykh* (M.–L., 1928), p. 367. The reference to Babel presumably refers to his story 'A Letter' ('Pis'mo') from the collection *Red Cavalry* (*Konarmiya*).

10 A. M. Linevsky (b. 1902) began his career as a writer in 1925 and acquired a reputation as a historical novelist on themes relating to the revolutionary and civil-war period in his native Karelia. As a local historian and ethnographer he made an important contribution to a broader understanding of the area. He has written several large historical novels, e.g. *The White Sea* (*Belomor'ye*) (1954), and in the 1960s he returned to the theme of *Doctor Podobin* and developed the character of the Bolshevik, Nikita Tyuttiev, in the short novel *During 1918* (*Shyol vosem'nadtsatyy god*).

11 A. Levitina, *A. M. Linevsky, Kritiko-biograficheskiy ocherk* (Petrozavodsk, 1973), p. 124.

12 The 'dilogy' ('dilogiya' – Fedin's own term) comprised *Pervyye radosti* (*Early Joys*) (1945) and *Neobyknovennoye leto* (*No Ordinary Summer*) (1948).

13 Konstantin Fedin, *Early Joys: A Novel*, trans. G. Filippovsky (M., 1973), p. 310.

14 Konstantin Fedin, *No Ordinary Summer, A Novel in Two Parts*, trans. Margaret Wettlin (2 vols., M., 1950), Part II, pp. 729–30. Page numbers after quotes refer to this edition.

15 Solzhenitsyn, *Sobr. soch.*, vol. VI, pp. 85–6.

16 Robert Conquest, *Courage of Genius* (London, 1961), p. 14.

17 Solzhenitsyn's long-awaited continuation of *August 1914* may indeed prove to be his own contribution to the on-going history of the Russian revolutionary novel.

18 For fuller descriptions, see Conquest, *Courage of Genius*; A. Gladkov, *Meetings with Pasternak*, translated and introduced by M. Hayward (London, 1977), pp. 200–1; Olga Ivinskaya, *A Captive of Time: My Years with Pasternak*, translated and introduced by M. Hayward (London, 1979), especially Part III: 'A Novel about a Novel'.

19 Ivinskaya, *ibid.*, p. 246.

20 Conquest, *Courage of Genius*, pp. 138, 141, 163.

21 *Ibid.* p. 69. The words belong to A. Surkov, quoted in the *News Chronicle* (19 January 1959).

22 Apart from articles that appeared in the immediate wake of the novel's publication in the West (several are collected in *Pasternak: Modern Judgements*, ed. Donald Davie and Angela Livingstone (London, 1969); *Pasternak: A Collection of Critical Essays*, ed. Victor Erlich (Englewood

Cliffs, N.J., 1978)), major critical appraisals are to be found in Helen Muchnic, *From Gorky to Pasternak* (London, 1963) ('*Doctor Zhivago* is not about the Revolution: it is about how and why poetry is written': p. 387); in Mary F. Rowland and Paul Rowland, *Pasternak's Doctor Zhivago* (London and Amsterdam, 1968); in J. W. Dyck, *Boris Pasternak* (N.Y., 1972); in Mathewson, Jr, *The Positive Hero in Russian Literature*; in Henry Gifford, *Pasternak, A Critical Study* (C.U.P., 1977); and in Paul N. Siegel, *Revolution and the 20th-Century Novel* (N.Y., 1979).

23 Gladkov, *Meetings with Pasternak*, pp. 25, 26, 29.

24 *Ibid.* p. 30. On pp. 20–3 Max Hayward gives a remarkable first-hand account of an 'Evening of Poetry' in January or February 1948 at which Pasternak was given a specially appreciative reception by an audience only too ready to acknowledge the poet's independence of spirit at one of the worst periods of Stalinist conformism in the arts.

25 *Encounter* (August 1960), 4–5, quoted from Conquest, *Courage of Genius*, p. 26.

26 O. A. Carlisle, *Voices in the Snow* (London, 1962), p. 200.

27 *Ibid.* p. 210. The lecture may not in fact have been given until 1913; so Henry Gifford has informed me.

28 Gladkov, *Meetings with Pasternak*, p. 11. The reference is to Pasternak's article of 1916 'The Black Goblet' ('Chyornyy bokal') referred to in A. D. Sinyavsky's introduction to Boris Pasternak, *Stikhotvoreniya i poemy* (M.–L., 1965), p. 35.

29 Ivinskaya, *A Captive of Time*, p. 155.

30 Disparagement of Stalin in private correspondence led to Solzhenitsyn's arrest in February 1945 while he was an artillery officer taking part in the battle of Koenigsberg, for which he was sentenced to eight years' imprisonment.

31 Born in Moscow in 1890, into the family of the famous painter Leonid Pasternak, Boris Pasternak, as his autobiographical accounts *Safe Conduct* and *An Essay in Autobiography* show, remained throughout his life true to the aesthetic tenets imbued by his upbringing. When he died in 1960, his funeral at Peredelkino was the occasion of spontaneous and heartfelt grief for one who had epitomised 'an honourable and liberal independence of spirit' (Gladkov, *Meetings with Pasternak*, p. 183).

32 It has been suggested that the apparent protection extended to Pasternak in Stalin's lifetime may have been due to the sincerity of his expression of grief in 1932 at the time of the death of N. S. Alliluyeva, Stalin's wife. See Max Hayward's introduction in Gladkov, *ibid.* pp. 14–15.

33 *Ibid.* p. 87. *Cement* refers to the 'reconstruction' novel of 1925 by F. V. Gladkov (1883–1958).

34 Ivinskaya, *A Captive of Time*, pp. 196, 197, 198, 199.

35 *Ibid.* p. 202.

36 'In a letter written to him from Berlin (June 29, 1922) Marina

Tsvetayeva recalled how: "Once in the spring of 1918, you and I were sitting next to each other at supper with the Tsetlins. You said: "I want to write a big novel – with a love story and a heroine, like Balzac." And I thought: "How good. How exact. How beyond vanity. A poet"' (*ibid.* p. 201).
It is significant that this testimony should refer to a time immediately following the October revolution, suggesting that *Doctor Zhivago* enjoyed a gestation of more than thirty years. Henry Gifford offers a very succinct and rewarding digest of the novel's genesis in chapter 12 of his book, *Pasternak, A Critical Study*, pp. 176–8.

37　Carlisle, *Voices in the Snow*, p. 198.

38　The passages quoted are from Pasternak's letter to Stephen Spender.

39　Carlisle, *ibid.* p. 192.

40　Boris Pasternak, *Doctor Zhivago*, translated from the Russian by Max Hayward and Manya Harari (London, 1958), p. 432. Page numbers placed after quotations refer to this edition. Where a number is omitted, the quotation refers to the previous page number.

41　The English edition of the novel divides into chapters what in the Russian edition (*Doktor Zhivago* (Feltrinelli: Milano, 1957)) were described as 'parts' ('chasti').

42　Also influential was the collection of essays published in 1902, *Problemy idealizma*, edited by P. N. Novgorodtsev. For a discussion of religious belief among the intelligentsia, see Read, *Religion, Revolution and the Intelligentsia*.

43　The 'overcoming' of death, as many commentators have pointed out, reflects the likely influence of N. F. Fyodorov (1828–1903), whose 'Philosophy of the Common Cause' ('Filosofiya obshchego dela'), although unpublished, appears to have been known to Dostoyevsky and may be implicit in Alyosha Karamazov's response to his brother Ivan when asked what his other task in life was: 'To resurrect your dead, who have perhaps never died' (F. M. Dostoyevsky, *Polnoye sobraniye sochineniy v 30 tomakh: khodozhestvenniye proizvedeniya*, vol. XIV (L., 1976), p. 210). For commentators' suggestions on Fyodorov's influence on Pasternak, see Robert Payne, *The Three Worlds of Boris Pasternak* (London, 1962), p. 140; the Rowlands, *Pasternak's Doctor Zhivago*, pp. 22–6; Dyck, *Boris Pasternak*, pp. 149–50.

44　The most conspicuous instance of such interpretation is that offered by Mary F. Rowland and Paul Rowland in *Pasternak's Doctor Zhivago*, where, for instance, we read: 'Zhivago is the Church Slavonic genitive and accusative of the adjective *zhivoi*... *Yuri* is an abbreviated form of *Georgi*... Yuri's patron saint is therefore St George, who in history was martyred by Emperor Diocletian, and who in legend slew the dragon (Paganism) and rescued the maiden (Christianity)' (p. 10); or: 'In view of the preponderance of the mythic element in *Zhivago*, we might call Pasternak's method *mythophoric* (myth-bearing). This mythophoric element in a modern work performs a dual function: it carries us back to ancient myths and, in turn, brings those myths down to the present day' (p. 13); or: 'For the parallels between *Zhivago* and the New Testament Apocalypse constitute one of those "organising centres" around which, Pasternak stated, his book was constructed' (p. 16). The Rowlands' book is of great value for its exploration of the meanings attaching to names and places in *Doctor Zhivago*, but it carries exploration beyond common-sense and seems on occasion to be quite unaware of the sheer fatuousness of its interpretations.

45 The translation is my own.

46 Gints and his death were based on the facts of the biography of F. F. Linde, a military commissar of the provisional government. See Nadezhda Mandelstam, *Hope against Hope* (London, 1971), pp. 153–4, 408.

47 Olga Ivinskaya mentions that among the parts of the novel that Pasternak discarded was a chapter on flowers. 'It was conceived as an attempt to define the place of flowers in a person's life and death' (Ivinskaya, *A Captive of Time*, p. 206).

48 The illustration of Pogorevshikh's comic speech defect given in the Russian text (and not translated in the English edition) is: 'Yeshchyo tol'ko vchera ütrom ya okhotilsya na ütok', which might be rendered in English as: 'Only yesterday morning I went out to chute dukes.'

49 The translation is my own.

50 The Rowlands, *Pasternak's Doctor Zhivago*, p. 107.

51 Gifford, *Pasternak, A Critical Study*, p. 197.

52 *Romeo and Juliet*, V.iii. Pasternak translated this line as 'My v knige bedstviy na odnoy stroke' (V. Shekspir, *Romeo i Dzhul'etta*, trans. from the English by B. Pasternak (M., 1973), p. 175), though in the original Russian of the novel the line reads: 'My v knige roka na odnoy stroke' (Pasternak, *Doctor Zhivago*, p. 411).

53 The translation is my own. See my *The Rise of the Russian Novel*, pp. 278–9.

54 Since Yury and Lara are not to meet again after their brief final sojourn in Yuryatin and Varykino, which even in the fictional calendar of the novel cannot occur much later than 1923, by the time their love-child Tanya tells her story during World War Two she must presumably be twenty years of age and hardly a child at all.

55 The English translation here slightly compresses and rearranges the original Russian.

56 Carlisle, *Voices in the Snow*, p. 192.

57 As Henry Gifford has so sensitively remarked: 'Miracle is the element in which the poems of Yury Zhivago move naturally' (*Pasternak, A Critical Study*, p. 204). The commentaries by Dimitri Obolensky (reprinted in Erlich (ed.), *Pasternak: Critical Essays*, pp. 151–65) and George Katkov (Boris Pasternak, *In the Interlude: Poems 1945–1960*, translated into English Verse by Henry Kamen (London, 1962), pp. 117–43) are informative and illuminating. The commentaries in *The*

Poems of Dr. Zhivago, translated with a commentary by Donald Davie (Manchester U.P., 1965), strive too hard to relate the poems to the text of the novel and the occasional perception does not outweigh either the generally disappointing results of the investigation or the eccentricities and awkwardnesses of the translation.

Conclusion. *The death–birth of a world*

1 Carlyle, *The French Revolution*, p. 62. Carlyle placed the statement in quotation-marks, though he indicated no source.
2 *De Tocqueville's L'ancien régime*, trans. M. W. Patterson (O.U.P., 1933), p. 5.
3 *Ibid.* p. 14.
4 Winegarten, *Writers and Revolution*, p. xxxi; for a definitive discussion of these and other issues relating to the French Revolution, see Billington, *Fire in the Minds of Men*, Book I.
5 Lynn Hunt, 'Engraving the Republic: Prints and Propaganda in the French Revolution', *History Today*, 30 (October 1980), 12.
6 *Ibid.* p. 17.
7 Carl Sagan, *Broca's Brain: The Romance of Science* (Coronet Books: London, 1980), p. 372.
8 *Ibid.* p. 375.
9 *Ibid.* p. 380. The four stages are based on the research of Stanislav Grof.
10 *Ibid.* p. 380.
11 Carl Sagan quotes in this connection an assertion attributed to Konstantin Tsiolkovsky that: 'The earth is the cradle of mankind. But one does not live in the cradle forever.'
12 *Ibid.* p. 387.
13 Stepniak, *Nihilism as it is*, pp. 65–6.
14 I. S. Turgenev, *Poln. sobr. soch.*, vol. VIII (M.–L., 1964), p. 172.
15 See Berlin, *Fathers and Children*, for a very perceptive examination of the threat posed by Bazarov to the liberal conscience.
16 Quoted from Hosking, *Beyond Socialist Realism*, p. 3.
17 *Ibid.* p. 11.
18 For a valuable discussion of Socialist Realism, see C. Vaughan James, *Soviet Socialist Realism: Origins and Theory* (London, 1973), esp. pp. 84–102.
19 Parts of this quotation and the one following are from the English edition of the novel.
20 Gorky, *Poln. sobr. soch.*, vol. VIII, p. 478.
21 From Pasternak's letter (in English) to Stephen Spender. Quoted from Conquest, *Courage of Genius*, p. 26.
22 Henry Gifford, *The Novel in Russia: From Pushkin to Pasternak* (London, 1964), p. 187.
23 Solzhenitsyn, *Sobr. soch.*, vol. VI, p. 359.

Bibliography

This bibliography includes all the sources mentioned in the text and notes and other selected titles that have been consulted in the writing of this study. The dates of publication given here, especially of novels, belong to the sources used for this study and do not always correspond with dates of first publication given in the text.

Alexandrova, V., *A History of Soviet Literature: 1917–1964. From Gorky to Solzhenitsyn*, London, 1964.

Andreyev, Yu. A., *Revolyutsiya i literatura*, L., 1969; 2nd ed., M., 1975. *V poiskakh zakonomernostey*, L., 1978.

Annenkov, P. V., *Literaturniye vospominaniya*, Goslitizdat, 1960.

Anninsky, L. A., '*Kak zakalyalas' stal'' N. Ostrovskogo*, M., 1971.

Arendt, H., *On Revolution*, Penguin Books, 1973.

Arkhipov, V., 'K tvorcheskoy istorii romana I. S. Turgeneva "Ottsy i deti"', *Russkaya literatura*, 1 (1958).

Arnol'di, N. A., *Vasilisa*, Spb., 1879.

Babel, I., *Konarmiya*, M., 1926.

Bakhmet'yev, V. M., *Prestupleniye Martyna*, M.–L., 1928.

Baranov, V., *Revolyutsiya i sud'ba khudozhnika*, M., 1967 (about A. K. Tolstoy).

Batyuto, A. I., 'Parizhskaya rukopis' romana I. S. Turgeneva "Ottsy i deti"', *Russkaya literatura*, 4 (1961). *Turgenev-romanist*, L., 1972.

Bayley, J., *Tolstoy and the Novel*, London, 1966.

Beaujour, Elisabeth Klosty, *The Invisible Land: A Study of the Artistic Imagination of Iurii Olesha*, Columbia U.P., 1970.

Belaya, G. A., *Zakonomernosti stilevogo razvitiya sovetskoy prozy dvadtsatykh godov*, M., 1977.

Bely, A., *Peterburg*, Letchworth, 1967. *Revolyutsiya i kul'tura*, M., 1917.

Berezhnoy, A. F., '*Chapayev' Dm. Furmanova*, M.–L., 1965.

Berlin, Isaiah, *Fathers and Children*, O.U.P., 1972.

Billington, James H., *Fire in the Minds of Men*, London, 1980. *Mikhailovsky and Russian Populism*, O.U.P., 1958. *The Icon and the Axe*, London, 1966.

Blok, A., *Sobraniye sochineniy v 6 tomakh*, vol. v, M., 1971.

Blum, Julius M., *Konstantin Fedin: A Descriptive and Analytic Study*, The Hague–Paris, 1967.

Boyesen, Hjalmar, 'A visit to Tourguéneff', *The Galaxy*, 17 (1874).

Braynina, B. Ya., *Konstantin Fedin. Ocherk zhizni i tvorchestva*, M., 1962.

Brazhnev, E., *Stuchit rabochaya krov'*, M.–L., 1928.

V dymu kostrov, Krug, 1926.

Britikov, A. F., *Masterstvo M. Sholokhova*, M.–L., 1964.

Brovman, G. A., *V. V. Veresaev. Zhizn' i tvorchestvo*, M., 1959.

Brown, Deming, *Soviet Russian Literature since Stalin*, C.U.P., 1979.

Brown, E. J., *Russian Literature since the Revolution*, N.Y., 1963.

Brumfield, William C., 'Bazarov and Rjazanov: The Romantic Archetype in Russian Nihilism', *Slavic and East European Journal*, 21, 4 (1977).

Buckle, H. T., *History of Civilization in England*, 2nd ed., London, 1858.

Budantsev, S. F., *Myatezh*, L., 1925.

Bulgakov, M. A., *Romany*, L., 1978.

Bushmin, A., *Roman A. Fadeyeva 'Razgrom'*, L., 1954.

Buznik, V. V., *Russkaya sovetskaya proza dvadtsatykh godov*, L., 1975.

Byalik, B. A. (ed.), *Revolyutsiya 1905–1907 godov i literatura*, M., 1978.

Carden, P., 'Ornamentalism and Modernism', *Russian Modernism*, ed. G. Gibian and H. W. Tjalsman, Cornell U.P., 1976.

The Art of Isaac Babel, Cornell U.P., 1972.

Carlisle, O. A., *Voices in the Snow*, London, 1962.

Carlyle, T., *The French Revolution*, C.U.P., 1930.

Chamberlin, W. H., *The Russian Revolution 1917–1921*, 2 vols., N.Y., 1965.

Charny, M., *Artyom Vesyoly*, M., 1960.

Put' Alekseya Tolstogo: ocherk tvorchestva, M., 1961.

Chernyshevsky, N. G., *Chto delat'?*, M., 1957.

Christian, R. F., *Tolstoy's 'War and Peace': A Study*, O.U.P., 1962.

Conquest, Robert, *Courage of Genius*, London, 1961.

The Great Terror, London, 1968.

Cornwell, N., 'The Principle of Distortion in Olesha's "Envy"', *Essays in Poetics*, 1 (1980).

Davie, Donald, *The Poems of Dr. Zhivago*, Manchester U.P., 1965.

and Livingstone, Angela (eds.), *Pasternak: Modern Judgements*, London, 1969.

Davies, Norman, 'Izaak Babel''s "Konarmiya" stories and the Polish–Soviet War', *Modern Languages Review* (October 1972).

De Tocqueville's l'ancien régime, trans. M. W. Patterson, O.U.P., 1933.

Dobrolyubov, N. A., *Russkiye klassiki*, M., 1970.

Dolgopolov, L., *Na rubezhe vekov. O russkoy literature kontsa XIX-nachala XX veka*, L., 1977.

Dostoyevsky, F. M., *Polnoye sobraniye sochineniy v 30 tomakh: khudozhestvenniye proizvedeniya*, vols. I–XVII, L., 1972–6.

Dryagin, E. P., *Sholokhov i sovetskiy roman*, Rostov, 1966.

Dyck, J. W., *Boris Pasternak*, N.Y., 1972.

Erlich, Victor (ed.), *Pasternak: A Collection of Critical Essays*, Englewood Cliffs, N.J., 1978.
Ermilov, V., *O traditsiyakh sovetskoy literatury. Tvorchestvo A. Malyshkina, A. Makarenko, Yu. Krymova*, M., 1955.
Eroshcheva, F. F., *Romany Konstantina Fedina o revolyutsii*, Krasnodar, 1967.
Ershov, L. F., *Russkiy sovetskiy roman: natsional'nyye traditsii i novatorstvo*, L., 1967.
Nikulina, E. A., and Filippov, G. V., *Russkaya sovetskaya literatura 30-kh godov*, M., 1978.
Fadeyev, A., *Literatura i zhizn'*, M., 1933.
'O Sevastopole Malyshkina', *Na literaturnom postu*, 6 (1929).
Razgrom, M., 1927.
Za tridtsat' let, M., 1957.
Falen, James E., *Isaac Babel: Russian Master of the Short Story*, Tennessee U.P., 1974.
Fedin, K. A., *Brat'ya*, M., 1928.
Goroda i gody, M., 1924.
'K romanu "Goroda i gody"', *Goroda i gody*, M., 1957.
Neobyknovennoye leto, M., 1948. (*No Ordinary Summer, A Novel in Two Parts*, trans. Margaret Wettlin, 2 vols., M., 1950).
Pervyye radosti, M., 1945. (*Early Joys: A Novel*, trans. G. Filippovsky, M., 1973).
Fox, Ralph, *The Novel and the People*, London, 1944.
Freeborn, Richard, *A Short History of Modern Russia*, London; N.Y., 1966.
'Nikolay Kolokolov', *The Slavonic and East European Review*, 56, 1 (1978).
The Rise of the Russian Novel, C.U.P., 1973.
'Turgenev at Ventnor', *The Slavonic and East European Review*, 51 (July 1973).
Turgenev, The Novelist's Novelist, O.U.P., 1960; repr. Greenwood Press, 1978.
Furmanov, D. A., *Chapayev*, M., 1923. (*Chapayev*, Progress Publishers, M., 1974).
Myatezh, 2nd ed., M.-L., 1925.
Gasiorowska, Xenia, *Women in Soviet Fiction 1917–1964*, Wisconsin U.P., 1968.
Gertsen, A. I., *see* Herzen, Alexander.
Gifford, Henry, *Pasternak, A Critical Study*, C.U.P., 1977.
The Novel in Russia: From Pushkin to Pasternak, London, 1964.
Gladkov, A., *Meetings with Pasternak*, trans. and intro. M. Hayward, London, 1977.
Gladkov, F. V., *Tsement*, M., 1925.
Gladkovskaya, L. A., *Rozhdeniye epopei: Zheleznyy potok A. S. Serafimovicha*, M.-L., 1963.
Vsevolod Ivanov. Ocherk zhizni i tvorchestva, M., 1972.

Golovin-Orlovsky, K. F., *Russkiy roman i russkoye obshchestvo*, 3rd ed., Spb., n.d.

Goncharov, I. A., *Oblomov*, Spb., 1859.

Gorky, M., *Mat'*, Berlin, 1907. (*Comrades*, London, 1907).

Polnoye sobraniye sochineniy v 25 tomakh, M., 1968–76.

Sobraniye sochineniy v 30 tomakh, M., 1949–55.

Zhizn' Klima Samgina, 4 vols., M., 1927–36.

Granin, D., 'Roman i geroy', *Voprosy literatury*, 5 (1976).

Groznova, N. A., *Rannyaya sovetskaya proza, 1917–1925*, L., 1976.

Gura, V., *Kak sozdavalsya 'Tikhiy Don'*, M., 1980.

Roman i revolyutsiya. Puti sovetskogo romana 1917–1929, M., 1973.

Gurenkov, M. N., *Bez Rossii zhit' nel'zya. Put' A. N. Tolstogo k revolyutsii*, L., 1967.

Hallett, R. W., *Isaac Babel*, Letchworth, 1972.

Hare, Richard, *Maxim Gorky: Romantic Realist and Conservative Revolutionary*, O.U.P., 1962.

Harkins, William, 'The theme of sterility in Olesha's *Envy*', *Slavic Review*, 3 (1966).

Herzen, Alexander, *From the Other Shore*, O.U.P., 1979.

(Gertsen, A. I.), *Sobraniye sochineniy v 30 tomakh*, M., 1954–66.

Hollingsworth, Barry, 'The Society of Friends of Russian Freedom', *Oxford Slavonic Papers*, 3 (1970).

Holthusen, Johannes, *Studien zur Aesthetik und Poetik des russischen Symbolismus*, Goettingen, 1957.

Hosking, Geoffrey, *Beyond Socialist Realism: Soviet Fiction since Ivan Denisovich*, London, 1980.

Hunt, Lynn, 'Engraving the Republic: Prints and Propaganda in the French Revolution', *History Today*, 30 (October 1980).

Istoriya russkogo sovetskogo romana, vols. I–II, M.–L., 1965.

Istoriya russkoy sovetskoy literatury, vols. I–III, M., 1958–61.

Istoriya russkoy sovetskoy literatury (1917–1940), ed. A. I. Metchenko and S. M. Petrov, M., 1975.

Ivanov, G. V., 'Roman S. M. Stepnyaka-Kravchinskogo "Andrey Kozhukhov" i russkoye revolyutsionnoye narodnichestvo 1870-kh godov', *Russkaya literatura i narodnichestvo*, L., 1971.

Ivanov, V. V., *Bronepoyezd 14–69*, M., 1922.

Golubyye peski, M.–L., 1923.

Tsvetnyye vetra, Spb., 1922.

Ivinskaya, Olga, *A Captive of Time: My Years with Pasternak*, trans. and intro. M. Hayward, London, 1979.

Iz istorii sovetskoy esteticheskoy mysli 1917–1932: sbornik materialov, compiled by G. A. Belaya, M., 1980.

'Iz knigi N. Valentinova "Vstrechi s V. I. Leninym"', *Voprosy literatury*, 8 (1957).

Izotov, I. I., *Vyacheslav Shishkov. Kritiko-biograficheskiy ocherk*, M., 1956.

James, C. Vaughan, *Soviet Socialist Realism: Origins and Theory*, London, 1973.

Karavaeva, A. A., *Kniga, kotoraya oboshla ves' mir*, M., 1970 (about N. Ostrovsky).

Kastorsky, S., '*Mat''* M. *Gor'kogo: tvorcheskaya istoriya povesti*, L., 1940.

Katkov, G., commentaries on Boris Pasternak, *In the Interlude: Poems 1945–1960*, trans. Henry Kamen, London, 1962.

Keldysh, V. A., *Russkiy realizm nachala XX veka*, M., 1975.

Kin, Ts., *Vsegda po etu storonu: vospominaniya o Viktore Kine*, M., 1966.

Kin, V. P., *Po tu storonu*, M., 1928.

Klimenko, M., *The World of the Young Sholokhov*, North Quincy, Mass., 1972.

Knipovich, E. F., *Romany A. Fadeyeva 'Rasgrom' i 'Molodaya gvardiya'*, M., 1973.

Kogan, P. S., *Literatura velikogo desyatiletiya*, M., 1927.

Kolokolov, N. I., *Myod i krov'*, M., 1928.

Kovalevskaya, S. V., *Nigilistka*, Spb., 1884.

Kovtyukh, E. I., *Ot Kubani do Volgi i obratno*, M., 1926.

Kozlov, N. P., *O romane V. Zazubrina 'Dva mira'*, Uzhgorod, 1963.

Krasnoshchyokova, E. A., *Khudozhestvennyy mir Vsevoloda Ivanova*, M., 1980.

Krestinsky, Yu. A., *A. N. Tolstoy. Zhizn' i tvorchestvo*, M., 1960.

Krutikov, D. I., *Chyornaya polovina*, M., 1928.

Kupryanovsky, P. V., *Gorky, Furmanov, Serafimovich, A. Tolstoy*, Ivanovo, 1960.

Khudozhnik revolyutsii. O D. Furmanove, M., 1967.

Kuznetsov, M. M., *Romany K. Fedina*, M., 1973.

Landmarks: a collection of essays on the Russian Intelligentsia, ed. B. Shragin and A. Todd, trans. M. Schwartz, N.Y., 1977.

Lavrenyov, Boris A., *Veter*, L., 1924.

Lenin, V. I., 'New Events and Old Questions', *Collected Works*, vol. VI, M., 1964.

'Prophetic Words', *Collected Works*, vol. XXVII, M., 1965.

Leonov, L. M., *Barsuki*, M., 1924.

Levinson, Z. I., *Obraz vremeni. Partiya i revolyutsionnyy narod v tvorchestve K. A. Fedina*, Tula, 1964.

Levitina, A., *A. M. Linevsky. Kritiko-biograficheskiy ocherk*, Petrozavodsk, 1973.

Libedinsky, Yu. N., *Nedelya*, Yekaterinburg, 1923.

Linevsky, A. M., *Doktor Podobin*, Petrozavodsk, 1937.

Linkov, Ya. I., *Revolyutsionnaya bor'ba A. I. Gertsena i N. P. Ogaryova i taynoye obshchestvo 'Zemlya i volya' 1860-kh godov*, M., 1964.

Literaturnoye nasledstvo, vol. LXX, M., 1963.

Lukacs, George, *The Historical Novel*, trans. H. and S. Mitchell, London, 1962.

Lunacharsky, A. V., *Religiya i sotsializm*, vol. I, Spb., 1908; vol. II, Spb., 1911.

Sobraniye sochineniy, vol. II, M., 1964.

Lur'ye, A. N., *Poeticheskiy epos revolyutsii*, L., 1975.

Maevskaya, T. P., *Slovo i podvig: zhizn' i tvorchestvo S. M. Stepnyaka-Kravchinskogo*, Kiev, 1968.

Maguire, Robert A., *Red Virgin Soil: Soviet Literature in the 1920s*, Princeton U.P., 1966.

and Malmstadt, J. E., 'Translators' Introduction', to A. Bely, *Petersburg*, London, 1978.

Malyshkin, Aleksandr, *Padeniye Daira*, Krug, 1923.

Sevastopol', M., 1931.

Mandelstam, Nadezhda, *Hope against Hope*, London, 1971.

Mathewson, Rufus W., Jr, *The Positive Hero in Russian Literature*, 2nd ed., Stanford U.P., 1975.

Medvedev, Pavel, Introduction to N. Nikitin, *Rvotnyy fort*, M., 1928.

Medvedev, R. A., *Problems in the Literary Biography of Mikhail Sholokhov*, trans. A. D. P. Briggs, C.U.P., 1977.

Medvedeva, G. N., *Yury Libedinsky i yego povest' 'Nedelya'*, Dushanbe, 1963.

Mochulsky, Konstantin, *Andrei Bely: His Life and Works*, trans. Nora Szalavitz, Ann Arbor, 1977.

Moore, Harry T. and Parry, Albert, *Twentieth-Century Russian Literature*, London, 1976.

Moser, Charles A., *Antinihilism in the Russian Novel of the 1860s*, The Hague, 1964.

Mstislavsky, S. D., *Bez sebya*, M.–L., 1930.

Soyuz tyazhyoloy kavalerii, M.–L., 1929.

Muchnic, Helen, *From Gorky to Pasternak*, London, 1963.

Murphy, A. B., 'The Changing Face of "Tikhiy Don"', *Journal of Russian Studies*, 34 (1977).

Myasnikov, A., 'Vstupleniye', A. Bely, *Peterburg*, M., 1978.

Naldeyev, A. P., *Revolyutsiya i rodina v tvorchestve A. N. Tolstogo*, M., 1968.

Naumova, N., *Roman N. G. Chernyshevskogo 'Chto delat'?'*, L., 1978.

Nazarova, L. N., *Turgenev i russkaya literatura kontsa XIX-nachala XXv*, L., 1979.

Nechkina, M., 'Novyye materialy o revolyutsionnoy situatsii v Rossii (1859–61 gg.)', *Literaturnoye nasledstvo*, vol. LXI, M., 1953.

Neverov, A., *Tashkent, gorod khlebnyy*, M., 1923.

Nikitin, N. N., *Rvotnyy fort*, M., 1922.

Novikov, V., 'Tvorcheskiy put' Borisa Pil'nyaka', B. Pil'nyak, *Izbrannyye proizvedeniya*, M., 1976.

Obolensky, D., 'The Poems of Doctor Zhivago', *Pasternak: a collection of critical essays*, ed. V. Erlich, Englewood Cliffs, N.J., 1978.

Ogaryov, N. P., 'Pis'ma k sootchestvenniku', *Kolokol* (1 August 1860).

Olesha, Yury K., *Zavist'*, M., 1927.

Omulevsky, I. V., *Shag za shagom*, Spb., 1870.

Orwell, George, 'Freedom and Happiness', *Tribune* (4 January, 1946).

Oskotsky, V., *Negasimoye plamya kostra*, M., 1977.

Ostrovsky, N., *Kak zakalyalas' stal'*, Petrozavodsk, 1961. (*How the Steel was Tempered*, trans. R. Prokofieva, M., n.d.).

Osykov, B. I., *Serdtse boytsa*. (*O pisatele D. I. Krutikove*), Voronezh, 1966.

Ovcharenko, A., 'Aleksandr Yakovlev i yego tvorchestvo', A. Yakovlev, *Oktyabr'*, M., 1965.

Roman-epopeya M. Gor'kogo 'Zhizn' Klima Samgina', M., 1965.

Pascal, *Pensées*, trans. A. J. Krailsheimer, Penguin Classics, 1972.

Pasternak, Boris L., *Doctor Zhivago*, trans. Max Hayward and Manya Harari, London, 1958.

Doktor Zhivago, Milano, 1957.

(trans. from the English) V. Shekspir, *Romeo i Dzhul'etta*, M., 1973.

Payne, Robert, *The Three Worlds of Boris Pasternak*, London, 1962.

Pertsov, V. O., *Pisatel' i novaya deistvitel'nost'*, M., 1961.

Petrova, M. G., 'Pervaya russkaya revolyutsiya v romanakh predoktyabr'skogo desyatiletiya', *Revolyutsiya 1905–1907 godov i literatura*, M., 1978.

Pilnyak, Boris, *Golyy god*, M., 1922.

Piper, D. G. B., 'Yury Olesha's *Zavist'*: an Interpretation', *The Slavonic and East European Review*, 48 (1970).

Pisarev, D. I., *Bazarov. Realisty*, M., 1974.

Piskunov, V., *Sovetskiy roman-epopeya*, M., 1976.

Plekhanov, G. V., *Iskusstvo i literatura*, M., 1948.

Selected Philosophical Works, vol. I, M., 1974.

Polyak, L. I., *Aleksey Tolstoy – khudozhnik. Proza*, M., 1964.

Problemy idealizma: sbornik statey, ed. P. N. Novgorodtsev, M., 1902.

Prutskov, N. I., *Russkaya literatura XIX veka i revolyutsionnaya Rossiya*, L., 1971.

Pustovoyt, P. G., *Roman I. S. Turgeneva 'Ottsy i deti' i ideynaya bor'ba 60-ykh godov XIX veka*, M., 1964.

Read, Christopher, *Religion, Revolution and the Russian Intelligentsia, 1900–1912*, London, 1979.

Reck, Vera T., *Boris Pil'niak: A Soviet Writer in Conflict with the State*, McGill U.P., 1975.

Richards, D. J., *Zamyatin. A Soviet Heretic*, London, 1962.

Ripp, Victor, *Turgenev's Russia*, Cornell U.P., 1980.

Ropshin, V., *Kon' blednyy*, Spb., 1909.

To, chego ne bylo, Spb., 1912.

Rowland, Mary, and Rowland, Paul, *Pasternak's Doctor Zhivago*, London and Amsterdam, 1968.

Rudnitskaya, E. L., *N. P. Ogaryov v russkom revolyutsionnom dvizhenii*, M., 1969.

Ruehle, Juergen, *Literature and Revolution: A Critical Study of the Writer and Communism in the Twentieth Century*, trans. J. Steinberg, London, 1969.

Russell, Robert, 'Literature and Revolution in Zamyatin's *My*', *The Slavonic and East European Review*, 51 (1973).

Russkaya sovetskaya povest' 20–30kh godov, ed. V. A. Kovalyov, L., 1976.

Ruzhina, V. A., *Veter revolyutsii*, Kishinyov, 1971 (about B. Lavrenyov).

Sagan, Carl, *Broca's Brain: The Romance of Science*, London, 1980.

Serafimovich, Aleksandr S., *Zheleznyy potok*, M., 1924.

    Preface to D. Furmanov, *Myatezh*, 2nd ed., M.–L., 1925.

    Sobraniye sochineniy v 7 tomakh, M., 1959–60.

Seyfullina, Lydia N., *Virineya*, M.–L., 1924.

Shaginyan, M., *Peremena*, L., 1924.

Shane, Alex M., *The Life and Works of Evgenij Zamjatin*, California U.P., 1968.

Shaw, Bernard, 'A Word about Stepniak', *To-Morrow*, 1 (1896).

Shiryayev, P., *Gul'ba*, M.–L., 1929.

Shklovsky, V., *Zhili-byli*, M., 1966.

Sholokhov, M., *Tikhiy Don*, 2 vols., M., 1959.

Siegel, Paul N., *Revolution and the 20th-Century Novel*, N.Y., 1979.

Simmons, Ernest J., *Russian Fiction and Soviet Ideology*, Columbia U.P., 1958.

Sinyavsky, A. D., 'Vstupitel'naya stat'ya', Boris Pasternak, *Stikhotvoreniya i poemy*, M.–L., 1965.

Skaftymov, A. P., *Stat'i o russkoy literature*, Saratov, 1958.

Sleptsov, A. V., *Trudnoye vremya*, Spb., 1865.

Slonim, Marc, *Modern Russian Literature*, N.Y., 1953.

    Soviet Russian Literature: Writers and Problems 1917–1977, 2nd ed., O.U.P., 1977.

Solov'yov, B., *Vospitaniye kharaktera*, L., 1940.

Solzhenitsyn, Alexander, *Sobraniye sochineniy v 6 tomakh*, Frankfurt, 1970–3.

Sovetskiy roman. Novatorstvo. Poetika, Tipologiya, ed. E. V. Belova, V. Ch. Vorovskaya, and L. M. Nechiporenko, M., 1978.

Stanyukovich, K. M., *Dva Brata*, Spb., 1880.

Starikov, A. N., *Geroi i gody. Romany Konstantina Fedina*, M., 1972.

Steinberg, A., *Word and Music in the Novels of Andrey Bely*, C.U.P., 1982.

Stepniak, S., *Nihilism as it is*, London, n.d.

    The Career of a Nihilist, London, 1889.

    Introduction to Ivan Turgenev, *Rudin, A Novel*, trans. Constance Garnett, London, 1894.

Stewart, D. H., *Mikhail Sholokhov: A Critical Introduction*, Ann Arbor, 1967.

Struve, Gleb, *Russian Literature under Lenin and Stalin 1917–1953*, London, 1972.

Bibliography 295

Tan-Bogoraz, V., *Soyuz molodykh*, M.–L., 1928.
Taratuta, Evgeniya, *S. M. Stepnyak-Kravchinsky, revolyutsioner i pisatel'*, M., 1973.
Thomson, B., *Lot's Wife and the Venus of Milo*, C.U.P., 1978.
  The Premature Revolution: Russian Literature and Society 1917–1946, London, 1972.
Tolstoy, A. N., *Khozhdeniye po mukam*, Minsk, 1958.
Tolstoy, L. N., *Yubileynoye izdaniye*, 90 vols., M., 1928–59.
Tregub, S. A., *Zhizn' i tvorchestvo N. Ostrovskogo*, M., 1964.
Trotsky, L., *Literatura i revolyutsiya*, 2nd ed., M., 1924.
Trusov, V. S., *Rozhdyonnyy burey*, M., 1973.
Tulloch, Alexander R., 'Afterword' to Boris Pilnyak, *The Naked Year*, Ann Arbor, 1975.
Turgenev, I. S., *Pis'ma*, 13 vols., M.–L., 1961–8.
  Polnoye sobraniye sochineniy, 15 vols., M.–L., 1960–8.
Utechin, S. V., *Lenin's 'What is to be Done?'*, O.U.P., 1963.
Vatslavik, A., *Iskusstvo psikhologicheskogo analiza v tvorchestve M. Sholokhova*, Praga, 1962.
  and Zagradka, M., *Stat'i o tvorchestve M. Sholokhova*, Praga, 1966.
Vekhi: sbornik statey o russkoy intelligentsii, M., 1909.
Velikaya, N., *Formirovaniye khudozhestvennogo soznaniya v sovetskoy proze 20-kh godov*, Vladivostok, 1975.
Veresaev, V. V., *V tupike*, 4th ed., M., 1926.
Vesyoly, A., *Rossiya, krov'yu umytaya*, M., 1929–32.
Vishnevskaya, I. L., *Boris Lavrenyov*, M., 1962.
Vladimirov, G. P., *Soldat revolyutsii. Stranitsy zhizni i tvorchestva Dm. Furmanova*, Tashkent, 1967.
Voronsky, A., 'Literaturniye otkliki', *Krasnaya nov'*, 2 (1922).
Waddington, Patrick, *Turgenev and England*, London, 1980.
  Turgenev and George Sand: an improbable entente, Victoria U.P., 1981.
Wasiolek, Edward, *Tolstoy's Major Fiction*, Chicago U.P., 1978.
Williams, Raymond, *Modern Tragedy*, London, 1979.
Winegarten, Renee, *Writers and Revolution: the fatal lure of action*, N.Y., 1974.
Woodcock, G., and Avakumović, I., *The Anarchist Prince*, London, 1950.
Woodward, James B., *Leonid Andreyev: a study*, O.U.P., 1969.
Wortman, R., *The Crisis of Russian Populism*, C.U.P., 1967.
Wright, A. Colin, *Mikhail Bulgakov: life and interpretations*, Toronto U.P., 1978.
Yakimenko, L., 'Opyt vremeni – opyt iskusstva', *Voprosy literatury*, 11 (1976).
  Sholokhov: a critical appreciation, M., 1973.
  Tvorchestvo M. A. Sholokhova, M., 1970.
Yakovlev, A. S., *Oktyabr'*, M., 1923.
  Puti prostogo serdtsa, M., 1935.

Yanovsky, N., *Lidiya Seyfullina. Kritiko-biograficheskiy ocherk*, M., 1972.

Zagradka, Miroslav, *O khudozhestvennom stile romanov Konstantina Fedina*, Praga, 1962.

Zalygin, Sergey, *Solyonaya pad'. Na Irtyshe*, M., 1970.

Zamyatin, Yev., *A Soviet Heretic: Essays by Yev. Zamyatin*, Chicago U.P., 1970.

My, N.Y., 1952.

Zasulich, V. I., *Stat'i o russkoy literature*, M., 1960.

Zavalishin, Vyacheslav, *Early Soviet Writers*, N.Y., 1958.

Zazubrin, V., *Dva mira*, M., 1922.

Zeller, A., *Konstantin Fedin. Aus seinem Leben und Schaffen*, Berlin, 1966.

Zhegalov, N., *Roman M. Gor'kogo 'Zhizn' Klima Samgina'*, M., 1965.

Zilbershteyn, I. S. (ed.), *Tvorchestvo Konstantina Fedina. Stat'i*, M., 1966.

Zlatovratsky, N. N., *Ustoi*, Spb., 1878–82.

Zolotyye serdtsa, Spb., 1877–8.

Index

This index does not contain fictional names. Titles of works mentioned in the text are given under the authors' names but are not repeated in the references to notes.

Alekseyev, M. V. (General), 68
Alexander II, 6, 265 nn. 56–7
Alexander III, 261 n. 35
Alliluyeva, N. S., 283 n. 32
Andreyev, L., 39, 265 n. 1
Andreyev, Yu. A., 269 n. 11, 270 n. 25, 274 n. 65, 278 n. 114
Annenkov, P. V., 259 n. 1, 260 n. 13, 261 n. 30
Appleton, D., and Co., 45, 265 n. 6, 266 nn. 8, 10
Appleton's Magazine, 45
Arkhipov, V., 261 n. 30
Arnol'di, N. A., 262 n. 42
Artsybashev, M. P., 77; *Sanin*, 77
Avakumović, I., 265 n. 60

Babel, I., 81–4, 87, 128, 204, 251, 270 nn. 27–30, 278 n. 106, 282 n. 9; *Red Cavalry*, 81–3, 251
Babeuf, F. N., 124, 260 n. 16
Bacon, Francis, 241
Bakhmetev, P. A., 262 n. 40
Bakhmet'yev, V. M., vii, 129–30; *Martin's Crime*, 129–30
Bakunin, M. A., 19, 54
Batyuto, A., 261 nn. 29–30
Bayley, J., 279 n. 1
Beaujour, E. K., 158, 278 n. 111
Belinsky, V. G., 5, 6, 19, 247
Bell, The, 9, 15
Bely, A., 39, 40–1, 57–64, 77, 87, 92, 248, 250–1, 265, n. 3, 267 nn. 22–3, 268 nn. 24, 27, 32–3, 269 n. 16, 271 nn. 38–9, 272 n. 50; *Petersburg*, 40–1, 57–63, 74, 77, 92, 250; *Silver Dove, The*, 57
Berdyayev, N. A., 52, 266 n. 16
Berlin, I., 259 n. 2, 261 n. 30, 286 n. 15
Billington, J. H., 262 n. 41, 286 n. 4

Bismarck, O. von, 33
Blok, A. A., 88, 214, 237, 272 n. 50, 281 n. 5; *Twelve, The*, 88
Blum, J. M., 276 n. 81
Bolshevism, Bolsheviks, 44, 67, 78–9, 84–5, 88–93, 98–100, 103, 116, 121, 129, 134, 139–45, 150, 162–3, 170, 176–8, 182, 185–94, 199, 201–2, 205, 228
Bosch, Hieronymus, 177
Bostrom, A. A., 280 n. 24
bosyaki ('bare-foot' migrant workers), 41
Botkin, V. P., 18
Boyesen, H., 260 n. 15
Brest-Litovsk, Treaty of, 68
Briggs, A. D. P., 279 n. 8
Brovman, G. A., 276 n. 89
Brown, D., 281 n. 7
Brumfield, W. C., 263 n. 45
Buckle, H. T., 11–12, 259 n. 7
Budantsev, S. F., 78–9, 251; *Revolt*, 78–9
Budberg, M., 259 n. 2
Budyonny, S. M. (Marshal), 69, 191
Bulgakov, M. A., 144–9, 248, 251–2, 277 nn. 92–4; *Master and Margarita, The*, 146; *White Guard, The*, 133, 144–50, 251–2
Bulgakov, S. N., 53–4, 267 n. 16
Bunin, I. A., 39, 271 n. 38
Bushmin, A., 277 nn. 100, 104

Carden, P., 270 n. 30, 271 n. 35
Carlisle, O., 212–13, 283 n. 26, 284 nn. 37, 39, 285 n. 56
Carlyle, Thomas, 69–70, 239, 268 n. 1, 286 n.1
Chamberlin, W. H., 269 n. 8
Charny, M., 80, 270 n. 23